Implementation Techniques

Neural Network Systems Techniques and Applications

Edited by **Cornelius T. Leondes**

Implementation Techniques

Edited by

Cornelius T. Leondes
Professor Emeritus
University of California
Los Angeles, California

VOLUME **3** OF

Neural Network Systems
Techniques and Applications

ACADEMIC PRESS
San Diego London Boston New York Sydney Tokyo Toronto

Academic Press
a division of Harcourt Brace & Company
525 B Street, Suite 1900, San Diego, California 92101-4495, USA
http://www.apnet.com

Academic Press Limited
24-28 Oval Road, London NW1 7DX, UK
http://www.hbuk.co.uk/ap/

Library of Congress Card Catalog Number: 97-80441

International Standard Book Number: 0-12-443863-6

Printed and bound in the United Kingdom
Transferred to Digital Printing, 2011

Contents

Recurrent Neural Networks: Identification and Other System Theoretic Properties

Francesca Albertini and Paolo Dai Pra

Chilukuri K. Mohan (147), Department of Electrical Engineering and Computer Science, Center for Science and Technology, Syracuse University, Syracuse, New York 13244-4100

Raymond M. Sova (259), Applied Physics Laboratory, The Johns Hopkins University, Laurel, Maryland 20723-6099

D. M. Titterington (51), Department of Statistics, University of Glasgow, Glasgow G12 8QQ, Scotland

Meng Wang (371), Department of Computer Science, University of Regina, Regina, Saskatchewan S4S 0A2, Canada

Zong-Ben Xu (183), Institute for Information and System Sciences and Research Center for Applied Mathematics, Xi'an Jiaotong University, Xi'an, China

Chang N. Zhang (371), Department of Computer Science, University of Regina, Regina, Saskatchewan S4S 0A2, Canada

Preface

Inspired by the structure of the human brain, artificial neural networks have been widely applied to fields such as pattern recognition, optimization, coding, control, etc., because of their ability to solve cumbersome or intractable problems by learning directly from data. An artificial neural network usually consists of a large number of simple processing units, i.e., neurons, via mutual interconnection. It learns to solve problems by adequately adjusting the strength of the interconnections according to input data. Moreover, the neural network adapts easily to new environments by learning, and can deal with information that is noisy, inconsistent, vague, or probabilistic. These features have motivated extensive research and developments in artificial neural networks. This volume is probably the first rather comprehensive treatment devoted to the broad area of practical and effective implementation algorithms and techniques architectures for the realization of neural network systems. Techniques and diverse methods in numerous areas of this broad subject are presented. In addition, various major neural network structures for achieving effective systems are presented and illustrated by examples in all cases. Numerous other techniques and subjects related to this broadly significant area are treated.

The remarkable breadth and depth of the advances in neural network systems with their many substantive applications, both realized and yet to be realized, make it quite evident that adequate treatment of this broad area requires a number of distinctly titled but well integrated volumes. This is the second of seven volumes on the subject of neural network systems and it is entitled *Optimization Techniques*. The entire set of seven volumes contains

Volume 1: *Algorithms and Architectures*
Volume 2: *Optimization Techniques*
Volume 3: *Implementation Techniques*

The first contribution to Volume 3 is "Recurrent Neural Networks: Identification and Other System Theoretic Properties," by Francesca Albertini and Paolo Dai Pra. Recurrent neural networks may be characterized as networks in which the neurons arranged in layers have feedforward, feedback, and possible lateral connections. In the terminology of multi-input–multi-output of nonlinear dynamic control systems, in general, such systems can be represented by nonlinear state space system equations and, depending on the application, the time variable may be treated as either continuous or discrete. Such neural network systems models occur in many important applications such as signal processing, diverse control system applications, etc. This contribution treats such broad areas of fundamental importance as observability, controllability, and identifiability. The major issue of minimal recurrent neural networks is also examined in depth. Many results of fundamental importance to the broadly significant area of recurrent neural network systems are presented.

The next contribution is "Boltzmann Machines: Statistical Associations and Algorithms for Training," by N. H. Anderson and D. M. Titterington. Boltzmann machines are a class of recurrent stochastic neural network systems that are normally associated with binary outputs. In the case where the nodes are all visible, they can be regarded as stochastic versions of Hopfield networks, but in practice they often include hidden units. In principle, Boltzmann machines represent a flexible class of exponential family models for multivariate binary data; the flexibility is enhanced by the inclusion of hidden units (or latent variables in statistical terms). They are being applied to numerous practical problems, particularly in the neural network literature, and they are also being used as the foundations of more complicated networks. Methods for efficient training of Boltzmann machines are under active development. Boltzmann machines continue to be an area for strong development, in particularly at the interface between neural network systems and modern statistics. This contribution is an in-depth and rather comprehensive treatment of the issues and techniques involved in Boltzmann machines, and it includes numerous illustrative examples.

The next contribution is "Constructive Learning Techniques for Designing Neural Network Systems," by Colin Campbell. Constructive algorithms determine both the architecture of a suitable neural network system and the neural network system parameters (weights, thresholds, etc.) necessary for learning the data. Constructive algorithms have the inherent advantages of rapid training in addition to finding both the architecture and weights. This contribution is a rather comprehensive treatment of constructive learning techniques for designing neural network systems. It includes numerous methods for treating the various significant aspects of this broad technique.

The next contribution is "Modular Neural Networks," by Kishan Mehrota and K. Mohan. Many problems are best solved using neural networks whose architecture consists of several modules with sparse interconnections between them. Modularity allows the neural network developer to solve smaller tasks separately using small neural network modules and then to combine these modules in a logical manner. In this contribution, various modular neural network architectures are surveyed. Input modularity, output modularity, hierarchical organization, and combinations of expert networks are examined in detail, followed by discussion of four adaptive modular network construction algorithms. These networks have the potential to reduce the total time required for training networks by orders of magnitude while yielding better quality results. Illustrative examples are presented which clearly manifest the significance of the results presented in this contribution.

The next contribution is "Associative Memories," by Zong-Ben Xu and Chung-Ping Kwong. Associative memories are one of the most active research areas in neural network systems. They have emerged as efficient models of biological memory and have produced powerful techniques in various applications of substantive significance including pattern recognition, expert systems, optimization problems, and intelligent control. This contribution is a rather comprehensive and in-depth treatment of associative memory system techniques and their application. It is perhaps worthy of mention that all existing neural network system models can function as associative memories in one way or another. Numerous illustrative examples are included in this contribution which clearly manifest the substantive significance of associative memory systems.

The next contribution is "A Logical Basis for Neural Network Design," by Robert L. Fry and Raymond M. Sova. This contribution presents the characterization of a logical basis for the design of neural network systems. A methodology is developed for the design, synthesis, analysis, testing, and, above all, the understanding of a new type of computational element called the inductive logic unit (ILU). The ILU, as a physical device, may be thought of as being analogous to other physical devices utilized in electronic systems such as a transistor, operational amplifier, or logical gate. Such a characterization facilitates application-oriented designs. The ILU is shown to be a very powerful computational device, and it is also treated as part of a larger system which is called an inductive logic computer (ILC). This contribution focuses on the ILU, but ultimately the ILU will typically be but one of many similar components comprising an ILC that can be configured to treat a wide variety of rather important applications.

The next contribution is "Neural Networks Applied to Data Analysis," by Aarnoud Hoekstra, Robert P. W. Duin, and Martin A. Kraaijveld. This contribution is an in-depth treatment of nonlinear data analysis techniques utilizing neural network systems, primarily of the class of feedforward neural system classifiers. Techniques are presented for the analysis of the data themselves, as well as for the selection, analysis, and stability of classifiers. The nonlinear characteristics of neural network systems are thereby emphasized in the effective process of data analysis. Numerous illustrative examples are presented which clearly manifest the substantive effectiveness of the techniques presented.

The final contribution to this volume is "Multimode Single-Neuron Arithmetics," by Chang N. Zhang and Meng Wang. Interest in modeling single neuron computation has been constantly shaped by two types of considerations: computational ability and biophysical plausibility. This contribution is a presentation of the potential and limitations of single neuron arithmetics. Driven by suitably patterned input signals, passive membranes can effectively perform multimode arithmetic operations on the input conductances. Based on this, an abstract model of a neuronal arithmetic unit is presented. By taking active membrane mechanisms into account, an integrated neuron model can be constructed that may function as a programmable rational approximator. Numerous illustrative examples are presented.

This volume on implementation techniques in neural network systems clearly reveals their effectiveness and significance, and with further development, the essential role they will play in the future. The authors are all to be highly commended for their splendid contributions to this volume which will provide a significant and unique reference source for students, research workers, practitioners, computer scientists, and others on the international scene for years to come.

Cornelius T. Leondes

Recurrent Neural Networks: Identification and Other System Theoretic Properties

Francesca Albertini*
Dipartimento di Matematica
Pura e Applicata
Università di Padova
35131 Padova, Italy

Paolo Dai Pra
Dipartimento di Matematica
Pura e Applicata
Università di Padova
35131 Padova, Italy

I. INTRODUCTION

Neural networks have become a widely used tool for both modeling and computational purposes. From plasma control to image or sound processing, from associative memories to digital control, neural network techniques have been appreciated for their effectiveness and their relatively simple implementability. We refer the reader to Hertz et al. [1] and Hunt et al. [2] (and references therein) for seminal works, and to Sontag [3], Bengio [4], and Zbikowski and Hunt [5] for more recent reviews on the subject.

The rigorous analysis of neural network models has attracted less interest than their applications, and so it has developed at a slower pace. There are, of course, some exceptions. In the context of associative memories, for instance, a rather sophisticated study can be found in Talagrand [6] and Bovier and Gayrard [7].

The purpose of this work is to present up-to-date results on a dynamical version of neural networks, particularly *recurrent neural networks*. Recurrent neural networks are control dynamical systems that, in continuous time, are described

---

*Also: Istituto di Ingegneria Gestionale, Viale X Giugno 22, 36100, Vicenza, Italy.

Implementation Techniques

vertible linear transformations. It turns out that minimal recurrent neural networks have a finite symmetry group, whereas mixed networks have an infinite symmetry group, but much smaller than $GL(n_1 + n_2)$. This reduction of the symmetry group is not surprising, since the nonlinearity of σ prevents linear symmetries. What is remarkable is that the knowledge of linear symmetries is enough to understand observability and identifiability.

Section IV presents some open problems related to the properties of recurrent neural networks and mixed networks discussed in this work.

II. RECURRENT NEURAL NETWORKS

A. THE MODEL

In this section we consider recurrent neural networks evolving in either discrete or continuous time. We use the superscript $+$ to denote time shift (discrete time) or time derivative (continuous time). The basic models we deal with are those in which the dynamics are assigned by the following difference or differential equation:

$$x^+ = \vec{\sigma}(Ax + Bu)$$
$$y = Cx,$$

$$(3)$$

with $x \in \mathbb{R}^n$, $u \in \mathbb{R}^m$, $y \in \mathbb{R}^p$, $A \in \mathbb{R}^{n \times n}$, $B \in \mathbb{R}^{n \times m}$, and $C \in \mathbb{R}^{p \times n}$. Moreover, $\vec{\sigma}(x) = [\sigma(x_1), \ldots, \sigma(x_n)]$, where σ is a given *odd* function from $\mathbb{R}$ to itself. Clearly, if σ is the identity, the model in (3) is just a standard linear system. If σ is a nonlinear function, then systems of type (3) are called (single layer) *recurrent neural networks* (RNNs), and the function σ is referred to as the *activation function*. For continuous time models, we always assume that the activation function σ is, at least, locally Lipschitz, and the control map $u(\cdot)$ is locally essentially bounded, so the differential equation in (3) has a unique local solution.

The system theoretic analysis of RNNs will be carried on under two basic conditions, involving the activation function σ and the *control matrix B*. The first condition is a nonlinearity requirement on σ.

DEFINITION 1.   A function $\sigma : \mathbb{R} \rightarrow \mathbb{R}$ is an *admissible* activation function if, for all $N \in \mathbb{N}$ and all pairs $(a_1, b_1), \ldots, (a_N, b_N) \in \mathbb{R}^2$, such that $b_i \neq 0$ and $(a_i, b_i) \neq \pm(a_j, b_j)$ for all $i \neq j$, the functions $\xi \rightarrow \sigma(a_i + b_i \xi)$, $i = 1, \ldots, N$, and the constant 1 are linearly independent.

Note that no polynomial is an admissible activation function. Sufficient conditions and examples of admissible activation functions will be given in Section II.B.

The next condition is a controllability-type requirement on the matrix B.

DEFINITION 2. A matrix $B \in \mathbb{R}^{n \times m}$ is an *admissible* control matrix if it has no zero row, and there are no two rows that are equal or opposite.

The above assumption is equivalent to saying that, whatever the matrix A is, and provided σ is an admissible activation function, the orbit of the control system

$$x^+ = \vec{\sigma}(Ax + Bu) \tag{4}$$

is not confined to any subspace of positive codimension. In fact, the following statement is easy to prove.

PROPOSITION 3. *If σ is an admissible activation function, then B is an admissible control matrix if and only if* $\text{span}\{\vec{\sigma}(Bu): u \in \mathbb{R}^m\} = \mathbb{R}^n$ *or, equivalently, for all $x \in \mathbb{R}^n$,* $\text{span}\{\vec{\sigma}(x + Bu): u \in \mathbb{R}^m\} = \mathbb{R}^n$.

The relation between the admissibility of B and the controllability of the system (3) will be the subject of Section II.E.

DEFINITION 4. A system of type (3) is said to be an *admissible* RNN if both the activation function σ and the control matrix B are admissible.

B. EXAMPLES OF ADMISSIBLE ACTIVATION FUNCTIONS

In this section we state and prove two criteria for verifying admissibility of an activation function. For the first one see also Albertini *et al.* [25].

PROPOSITION 5. *Suppose σ is a real analytic function that can be extended to a complex analytic function on a strip $\{z \in \mathbb{C}: |Im(z)| \leq c\} \setminus \{z_0, \bar{z}_0\}$, where $|z_0| = c$ and $z_0, \bar{z}_0$ are singularities (poles or essential singularities). Then σ is admissible.*

Proof. Let $(a_1, b_1), \ldots, (a_N, b_N)$ be such that $b_i \neq 0$ and $(a_i, b_i) \neq \pm(a_j, b_j)$ for all $i \neq j$. Suppose $|b_1| \geq |b_2| \geq \cdots \geq |b_N|$, and let $c_1, \ldots, c_N \in \mathbb{R}$ be such that

$$\sum_{i=1}^{N} c_i \sigma(a_i + b_i \xi) = 0 \tag{5}$$

for all $\xi \in \mathbb{R}$. Because σ is odd, we can assume without loss of generality that $b_i > 0$ for all i. Note that the identity (5) extends to $\{\xi \in \mathbb{C}: |Im(\xi)| \leq c/b_1\} \setminus$

$\{(z_0 - a_i)/b_i, (\bar{z}_0 - a_i)/b_i : i = 1, \ldots, k\}$ where $k \leq n$ and $b_1 = \cdots = b_k$. Now let $\xi_n \in \mathbb{C}$ be a sequence with $|Im(\xi_n)| < c/b_1$, such that $\xi_n \to (z_0 - a_1)/b_1$ and $|\sigma(a_1 + b_1\xi_n)| \to +\infty$ as $n \to \infty$. Note that, for every $i > 1$,

$$\lim_{n \to \infty} \sigma(a_i + b_i\xi_n) = \sigma\left(a_i + b_i\left(\frac{z_0 - a_1}{b_1}\right)\right) \in \mathbb{C}. \tag{6}$$

Thus, dividing expression (5) by $\sigma(a_1 + b_1\xi)$ and evaluating at $\xi = \xi_n$, we get

$$c_1 + \sum_{i=2}^{N} c_i \frac{\sigma(a_i + b_i\xi_n)}{\sigma(a_1 + b_1\xi_n)} = 0.$$

Letting $n \to \infty$, we conclude that $c_1 = 0$. By repeating the the same argument, we get $c_i = 0$ for all i, which completes the proof. ∎

It is very easy to show that two standard examples of activation functions, namely $\sigma(x) = \tanh(x)$ and $\sigma(x) = \arctan(x)$, satisfy the assumptions of Proposition 5, and so are admissible.

The above criterion is based on the behavior of the activation function near a complex singularity. There are natural candidates for activation function that are either nonanalytic or entire, so Proposition 5 does not apply. We give here a further criterion that requires a suitable behavior of the activation function at infinity.

PROPOSITION 6. *Let σ be an odd, bounded function such that, for M large enough, its restriction to $[M, +\infty)$ is strictly increasing and has a decreasing derivative. Define*

$$f(x) = \lim_{\xi \to \infty} \sigma(\xi) - \sigma(x), \tag{7}$$

and assume

$$\lim_{x \to \infty} \frac{f(x)}{f'(x)} = 0. \tag{8}$$

Then σ is an admissible activation function.

Proof. Suppose

$$\sum_{i=1}^{N} c_i\sigma(a_i + b_i\xi) \equiv 0, \tag{9}$$

with $b_i \neq 0$ and $(a_i, b_i) \neq \pm(a_j, b_j)$ for all $i \neq j$. As before, we may assume that $b_i > 0$ for all i. We order increasingly the pairs (a_i, b_i) according to the order relation

$$(a, b) > (a', b') \quad \text{if} \quad (b > b') \quad \text{or} \quad (b = b' \text{ and } a > a'). \tag{10}$$

So we assume $(a_1, b_1) < \cdots < (a_N, b_N)$. Letting $\xi \to \infty$ in (9), we get $\sum_i c_i = 0$. This implies

$$\sum_{i=1}^{N} c_i f(a_i + b_i \xi) \equiv 0. \tag{11}$$

We now divide the expression in (11) by $f(a_1 + b_1 \xi)$, and let $\xi \to \infty$. In this way, if we can show that

$$\lim_{\xi \to \infty} \frac{f(a_i + b_i \xi)}{f(a_1 + b_1 \xi)} = 0 \tag{12}$$

for every $i \geq 2$, we then get $c_1 = 0$ and, by iterating the argument, $c_i = 0$ for all i.

Notice that $a_i + b_i \xi = a_1 + b_1 \xi + (a_i - a_1) + (b_i - b_1)\xi$, so for some $c > 0$, and for ξ sufficiently large, we have $a_i + b_i \xi > a_1 + b_1 \xi + c$. Thus, to prove (12), it is enough to show that, for all $c > 0$,

$$\lim_{x \to \infty} \frac{f(x + c)}{f(x)} = 0. \tag{13}$$

By assumption, f' is increasing for x large, and so

$$f(x + c) \leq f(x) + f'(x + c)c \tag{14}$$

for x sufficiently large. Thus

$$\lim_{x \to \infty} \frac{f(x)}{f(x + c)} \geq \lim_{x \to \infty} \left(1 - \frac{f'(x + c)}{f(x + c)} c\right) = +\infty, \tag{15}$$

which completes the proof. ∎

Examples of functions satisfying the criterion in Proposition 6 are

$$\sigma(x) = \text{sgn}(x)\left[1 - e^{-x^2}\right] \tag{16}$$

and

$$\sigma(x) = \int_0^x e^{-t^2} \, dt. \tag{17}$$

C. STATE OBSERVABILITY

In general, let Σ be a given system, with dynamics

$$x^+ = f(x, u)$$
$$y = h(x) \tag{18}$$

where $x \in \mathbb{R}^n$, $u \in \mathbb{R}^m$, $y \in \mathbb{R}^p$; again, the superscript $+$ denotes a time shift (discrete time) or time derivative (continuous time). Assume, for continuous time models, that the map f is, at least, locally Lipschitz. Moreover, let $x_0 \in \mathbb{R}^n$ be a fixed initial state. Then to the pair (Σ, x_0) we associate an input/output map λ_{Σ, x_0} as follows.

- For discrete time models, with any input sequence $u_1, \ldots, u_k \in \mathbb{R}^m$, λ_{Σ, x_0} associates the output sequence $y_0 = h(x_0)$, $y_1, \ldots, y_k \in \mathbb{R}^p$, generated by solving (18), with controls u_i $(i = 1, \ldots, k)$ and initial condition x_0.
- For continuous time models, to any input map $u : [0, T] \to \mathbb{R}^m$, which is, at least, locally essentially bounded, we first let $x(t)$ be the solution of the differential equation in (18), with control $u(\cdot)$ and initial condition x_0, and we denote by $[0, \epsilon_u)$ the maximum interval on which this solution is defined. Then, to the input map $u(\cdot)$, λ_{Σ, x_0} associates the output function $y(t) = h(x(t))$, $t \in [0, \epsilon_u)$.

DEFINITION 7.   We say that two states x_0, $x_0' \in \mathbb{R}^n$ are *indistinguishable* for the system Σ if $\lambda_{\Sigma, x_0} = \lambda_{\Sigma, x_0'}$. The system Σ is said to be *observable* if no two different states are indistinguishable.

The above notion is quite standard in system theory. In the case of linear systems, observability is well understood, and the following theorem holds.

THEOREM 8.   *Suppose $\sigma(x) = x$ in (3). Denote by V the largest subspace of $\mathbb{R}^n$ that is A-invariant (i.e., $AV \subset V$) and contained in $\ker C$. Then two states x, z are indistinguishable if and only if $x - z \in V$. In particular, the system is observable if and only if $V = \{0\}$.*

Among the various equivalent observability conditions for linear systems, the one above is the most suitable for comparison with the result we will obtain for recurrent neural networks. It should be remarked that, for general nonlinear systems, rather weak observability results are known [see, e.g., [26–28]].

Before stating the main result of this section, we introduce a simple notion that plays a significant role in this work.

DEFINITION 9.   A subspace $V \subset \mathbb{R}^n$ is called a *coordinate subspace* if it is generated by elements of the canonical basis $\{e_1, \ldots, e_n\}$.

The relevance of coordinate subspaces in the theory of RNNs comes essentially from the fact that they are the only subspaces satisfying the following property, for σ and B admissible:

$$x, z \in \mathbb{R}^n, \; x - z \in V \Rightarrow \vec{\sigma}(x + Bu) - \vec{\sigma}(z + Bu) \in V \qquad \forall u \in \mathbb{R}^m. \quad (19)$$

This "invariance" property of coordinate subspaces is responsible for the survival of some of the linear theory.

THEOREM 10.   *Consider an admissible system of type* (3). *Let* $V \subset \mathbb{R}^n$ *be the largest subspace such that*

  (i) $AV \subset V$ *and* $V \subset \ker C$;
  (ii) AV *is a coordinate subspace.*

Then $x, z \in \mathbb{R}^n$ *are indistinguishable if and only if* $x - z \in V$. *In particular, the system is observable if and only if* $V = \{0\}$.

Theorem 10 is a special case of Theorem 34, the proof of which is given in Section III.C [see also [14]]. We devote the rest of this section to comments and examples.

First of all, note that the *largest* subspace satisfying i) and ii) is well defined. Indeed, if V_1, V_2 satisfy i) and ii), so does $V_1 + V_2$. Moreover, if $\widehat{V}$ is the largest subspace for which i) holds, then $x - z \in V$ if and only if x, z are indistinguishable for the linear system (A, C). It follows that observability of the linear system (A, C) implies observability of the RNN (3).

We now show that the observability condition in Theorem 10 can be efficiently checked by a simple algorithm. For a given matrix D, let I_D denote the set of those indexes i such that the ith column of D is zero. Define, recursively, the following sequence of subsets of $\{1, 2, \ldots, n\}$:

$$J_0 = \{1, 2, \ldots, n\} \setminus I_C$$
$$J_{d+1} = J_0 \cup \{i: \exists j \in J_d \text{ such that } A_{ij} \neq 0\}. \tag{20}$$

Note that the sequence J_d is increasing, and stabilizes after at most n steps. Now let

$$O_c(A, C) = \text{span}\{e_j: j \notin J_\infty\} \tag{21}$$

with $J_\infty = \bigcup_d J_d$.

PROPOSITION 11.   *The subspace* V *in Theorem 10 is given by*

$$V = \ker C \cap A^{-1}(O_c(A, C)). \tag{22}$$

In particular, the system is observable if and only if

$$\ker A \cap \ker C = O_c(A, C) = \{0\}. \tag{23}$$

Proof.   It is not hard to see that $O_c(A, C)$ is the largest coordinate subspace contained in $\ker C$ and A-stable. Thus, the r.h.s. of (22) satisfies conditions i) and ii) of Theorem 10, and thus it is contained in V. For the opposite inclusion, just observe that, by definition, $AV \subset O_c(A, C)$.   ∎

It is worth noting, and quite easy to prove, that $x - z \in V$ *implies* indistinguishability of x and z, for *any* system of type (3). Admissibility of the system

every admissible initialized RNN $(\Sigma'_{n'} = (\sigma, A', B', C'), x'_0)$ such that (Σ_n, x_0) and $(\Sigma'_{n'}, x'_0)$ are i/o equivalent, $n' > n$ or (Σ_n, x_0) and $(\Sigma'_{n'}, x'_0)$ are equivalent.

Note that the notions in Definitions 15 and 16 can be given for linear systems $(\sigma = \text{identity})$ by replacing G_n with $GL(n) = \{n \times n \text{ invertible matrices}\}$ (and cutting the admissibility assumption). We recall the following well-known result.

THEOREM 17. *A linear system (A, B, C) is identifiable if and only if it is observable and controllable.*

We do not insist here on the notion of controllability; that will be discussed in the next section. Remarkably enough, a formally similar result holds for both continuous time and discrete time RNNs.

THEOREM 18. *An admissible RNN is identifiable if and only if it is observable.*

Theorem 18 is a special case of Theorem 51, so we do not give its proof here. The "only if" part is not difficult to see. In fact, if a RNN Σ_n is not observable, then there exist two different states x_1, x_2 that are indistinguishable, and thus $(\Sigma_n, x_1) \sim (\Sigma_n, x_2)$. Moreover, because the matrix B is admissible, the only matrix $S \in G_n$ such that $B = SB$ is the identity; thus the two initialized RNNs (Σ_n, x_1), (Σ_n, x_2) cannot be equivalent.

In comparing Theorems 17 and 18, it is seen that no controllability assumption is required in Theorem 18. In a certain sense, the role of controllability is played by admissibility. Actual connections between admissibility and controllability will be studied in Section II.E.

We have seen in Section II.C that observability of an admissible RNN is equivalent to

$$\ker A \cap \ker C = O_c(A, C) = \{0\}. \tag{29}$$

Suppose $O_c(A, C) \neq \{0\}$, and let $n_1 = \dim O_c(A, C)$. Then, up to a permutation of the elements of the canonical basis, the system (3) can be rewritten in the form

$$
\begin{aligned}
x_1^+ &= \vec{\sigma}(A_1 x_1 + A_2 x_2 + B_1 u) \\
x_2^+ &= \vec{\sigma}(A_3 x_2 + B_2 u) \\
y &= C_2 x_2,
\end{aligned}
\tag{30}
$$

with $x_1 \in \mathbb{R}^{n_1}$, $x_2 \in \mathbb{R}^{n-n_1}$. It follows that the system $(\Sigma_n = (\sigma, A, B, C))$, with initial state $(x_1, x_2) \in \mathbb{R}^n$, is i/o equivalent to $(\Sigma_{n-n_1} = (\sigma, A_3, B_2, C_2))$ with initial state $x_2 \in \mathbb{R}^{n-n_1}$. Thus we have performed a reduction in the dimension of the state space. On the other hand, if $O_c(A, C) = \{0\}$, then it will follow from the proof of Theorem 18 that for $(\Sigma'_{n'} = (\sigma, A', B', C'), x'_0)$ to be i/o equivalent to (Σ_n, x_0), it must be that $n' \geq n$. Moreover, $n = n'$ if and only if there exists

$S \in G_n$ such that $A' = SAS^{-1}$, $B' = SB$, $C' = CS^{-1}$, and x_0, $S^{-1}x'_0$ are indistinguishable for Σ_n. We summarize these remarks as follows.

DEFINITION 19. An admissible RNN Σ_n is said to be *minimal* if for all $x_0 \in \mathbb{R}^n$, and for any admissible initialized RNN $(\Sigma'_{n'}, x'_0)$ such that (Σ_n, x_0) and $(\Sigma'_{n'}, x'_0)$ are i/o equivalent, it must be that $n' \geq n$.

PROPOSITION 20. *An admissible RNN is minimal if and only if $O_c(A, C) = \{0\}$.*

Notice that, clearly, if an admissible RNN is identifiable, then it is also minimal, whereas the converse implication may be false, as shown in the next example.

EXAMPLE 21. Let $n = 2$, and $m = p = 1$. Consider any RNN $\Sigma_2 = (\sigma, A, B, C)$, where σ is any admissible activation function, and $B = (b_1, b_2)^T$ is any admissible control matrix (i.e., $0 \neq |b_1| \neq |b_2| \neq 0$). Moreover, let $C = (c_1, c_2)$, with $c_i \neq 0$, $i = 1, 2$, and A be the zero matrix. Then, for this model, $O_c(A, C) = \{0\}$, because C has all nonzero columns, thus by Proposition 20, it is minimal. On the other hand, this model is not identifiable, because $\ker A \cap \ker C \neq 0$, and so it is not observable.

E. CONTROLLABILITY AND FORWARD ACCESSIBILITY

A RNN Σ is said to be *controllable* if, for every two states $x_1, x_2 \in \mathbb{R}^n$, there exists a sequence of controls $u_1, \ldots, u_k \in \mathbb{R}^m$, for discrete time models, or a control map $u(\cdot) : [0, T] \to \mathbb{R}^m$, for continuous time models, which steers x_1 to x_2. In general, for nonlinear models, the notion of controllability is very difficult to characterize; thus the weaker notion of forward accessibility is often studied. Let $x_0 \in \mathbb{R}^n$ be a state; Σ is said to be *forward accessible* from x_0 if the set of points that can be reached from x_0, using arbitrary controls, contains an open subset of the state space. A model is said to be forward accessible if it is forward accessible from any state. Even if much weaker than controllability, forward accessibility is an important property. In particular, it implies that from any state, the forward orbit does not lay in a submanifold of the state space with positive codimension.

Unlike the other properties that we have discussed before (observability, identifiability, and minimality), the characterization of which was the same for both dynamics, discrete and continuous time, the characterization of controllability and forward accessibility is quite different for the two dynamics.

1. Controllability and Forward Accessibility for Continuous Time RNNs

Let Σ be a continuous time RNN, that is, the dynamics are given by the differential equation

$$\dot{x}(t) = \vec{\sigma}\big(Ax(t) + Bu(t)\big), \qquad t \in \mathbb{R}. \tag{31}$$

Let X_u be the vector field defined by

$$X_u(x) = \vec{\sigma}(Ax + Bu).$$

Given the vector fields X_u, let Lie$\{X_u | u \in \mathbb{R}^m\}$ be the Lie algebra generated by these vector fields. It is known that if Lie $\{X_u | u \in \mathbb{R}^m\}$ has full rank at x, then the system is forward accessible from x [29]. This result, together with Proposition 3 (which says that the span$\{X_u\}_{u \in \mathbb{R}^m}$ has already full dimension at each $x \in \mathbb{R}^n$), gives the following.

THEOREM 22. *Let Σ be an admissible RNN evolving in continuous time, then Σ is forward accessible.*

REMARK 23. In a recent paper [30], E. Sontag and H. Sussmann proved that if Σ is an admissible RNN, and the activation function σ satisfies some extra assumptions, then Σ is indeed controllable. The extra requirement on σ is fulfilled, for example, when $\sigma = $ tanh. It is quite surprising that these RNNs are controllable for any matrix A.

2. Controllability and Forward Accessibility for Discrete Time RNNs

Let Σ be a discrete time RNN, that is, the dynamics are given by the difference equation

$$x(t + 1) = \vec{\sigma}\big(Ax(t) + Bu(t)\big), \qquad t \in \mathbb{Z}. \tag{32}$$

Unlike in continuous time, characterizing the controllability of discrete time models is quite difficult. We will not give the proofs of the results presented in this section, because they are very long and technical; we refer the reader to Albertini and Dai Pra [15].

It is not difficult to see that, in this case, the admissibility assumption is not enough to guarantee forward accessibility. In fact, let $p = \text{rank}[A, B]$, and $V = [A, B](\mathbb{R}^{n+m})$. Then, except possibly for the initial condition, the reachable set from any point is contained in $\vec{\sigma}(V)$. If $p < n$ then, clearly, $\vec{\sigma}(V)$ does not contain any open set. So a necessary condition for forward accessibility is $p = n$.

The result stated below proves the sufficiency of this condition, provided that the control matrix B and the activation function σ satisfy a new condition that is, in some sense, stronger than admissibility.

DEFINITION 24. We say that the activation function σ and the control matrix B are *n-admissible* if they satisfy the following conditions.

1. σ is differentiable and $\sigma'(x) \neq 0$ for all $x \in \mathbb{R}$.
2. Denote by b_i, $i = 1, \ldots, n$, the rows of the matrix B; then $b_i \neq 0$ for all i.
3. For $1 \leq k \leq n$ let O_k be the set of all the subsets of $\{1, \ldots, n\}$ of cardinality k, and let $a_1, \ldots, a_n$ be arbitrary real numbers. Then the functions $\{f_I: I \in O_k\}$, $f_I: \mathbb{R}^m \to \mathbb{R}$, given by

$$f_I(u) = \prod_{i \in I} \sigma'(a_i + b_i u),$$

 are linearly independent.

A RNN Σ is *n-admissible* if its activation function σ and its control matrix B are *n*-admissible.

REMARK 25. Notice that, in the *n*-admissibility property, we do not require that no two rows of the matrix B be equal or opposite. Moreover, the linear independence on the functions f_I is asked only for a fixed n. On the other hand, because the functions f_I involve products of the functions $\sigma'(a_i + b_i u)$, this third requirement is, indeed, quite strong. Notice that the special case $k = 1$ is equivalent to asking that the functions $\sigma(a_i + b_i u)$ and the constant 1 are linearly independent.

THEOREM 26. *Let Σ be an n-admissible RNN evolving in discrete time. Then Σ is forward accessible if and only if*

$$\text{rank}\,[A, B] = n. \tag{33}$$

REMARK 27. The *n*-admissibility property, as stated in Definition 24, is given as a joint property of $\sigma(\cdot)$ and B. This is not, indeed, what is desirable in applications, because usually σ is a given elementary function. However, it is possible to prove that when $\sigma = \tanh$, σ and B are *n*-admissible for all matrices B in a "generic" subset of $\mathbb{R}^{n \times m}$, that is, for B in the complement of an analytic subset of $\mathbb{R}^{n \times m}$ (in particular, B may vary in an open dense subset of $\mathbb{R}^{n \times m}$). For more discussion and precise statements on this subject, see Albertini and Dai Pra [15, Sect. C].

The next theorem states another sufficient condition for forward accessibility, using a weaker condition on the map σ, but adding a new condition on the pair A, B.

DEFINITION 28.   We say that the activation function σ and the control matrix B are *weakly n-admissible* if they satisfy the following conditions:

1. σ is differentiable and $\sigma'(x) \neq 0$ for all $x \in \mathbb{R}$.
2. Denote by b_i, $i = 1, \ldots, n$, the rows of the matrix B; then $b_i \neq 0$ for all i.
3. Let $a_1, \ldots, a_n$ be arbitrary real numbers, then the functions from $\mathbb{R}^m$ to $\mathbb{R}$ $(\sigma'(a_i + b_i u))^{-1}$, for $i = 1, \ldots, n$, are linearly independent.

A RNN Σ is *weakly n-admissible* if its activation function σ and its control matrix B are weakly n-admissible.

REMARK 29.   Notice that this condition is weaker than the one given in Definition 24; in fact, the third requirement of Definition 28 is exactly the third requirement of Definition 24 for the case $k = n - 1$. It is not hard to show that if B is an admissible control matrix, the activation function tanh, together with the matrix B, is weakly n-admissible. However, the same would be false for the activation function arctan for $n \geq 4$.

THEOREM 30.   *Let Σ be a weakly n-admissible RNN evolving in discrete time. If there exists a matrix $H \in \mathbb{R}^{m \times n}$ such that*

(a) *the matrix $(A + BH)$ is invertible,*
(b) *the rows of the matrix $[(A + BH)^{-1}B]$ are all nonzero,*

then Σ is forward accessible.

It is easy to see that condition (a) of the previous theorem is equivalent to rank$[A, B] = n$; thus (a) is also a necessary condition for forward accessibility. So Theorem 30 adds a new condition on A, B [condition (b)] and guarantees forward accessibility with weaker assumption on σ.

REMARK 31.   It is interesting to note that for the single-input case, condition (b) is independent on H. In fact, the following fact holds. Let $h, k \in \mathbb{R}^{n \times 1}$ be such that $A + bh^t$ and $A + bk^t$ are invertible. Then

$$\left((A + bk^t)^{-1} b\right)_i \neq 0 \ \forall i \Leftrightarrow \left((A + bh^t)^{-1} b\right)_i \neq 0 \ \forall i.$$

It is not restrictive to assume that $k = 0$. Let $w = A^{-1} b$ and $v = (A + bh^t)^{-1} b$. To get the claim it is sufficient to show that there exists $\lambda \neq 0$, such that $v = \lambda w$. Because $A + bh^t$ is invertible, we have that $h^t w \neq -1$, otherwise $(A + bh^t) w = b - b = 0$. Thus we may let

$$\lambda = \frac{1}{1 + h^t w}.$$

Let $v' = \lambda w$; then $(A + bh^t) v' = \lambda (Aw + bh^t w) = \lambda b(1 + h^t w) = b$. So we may conclude that $v' = v$, as desired.

III. MIXED NETWORKS

A. THE MODEL

In this section we consider models obtained by "coupling" a recurrent neural network with a linear system; we called this type of system *mixed network*. Furthermore, for these systems we consider both models to be evolving in discrete and continuous time. Again, the superscript + will denote a time shift (discrete time) or time derivative (continuous time). A mixed network (MN) is a system whose dynamics are described by equations of the form

$$
\begin{aligned}
x_1^+ &= \vec{\sigma}\left(A^{11}x_1 + A^{12}x_2 + B^1 u\right) \\
x_2^+ &= A^{21}x_1 + A^{22}x_2 + B^2 u \\
y &= C^1 x_1 + C^2 x_2,
\end{aligned}
\tag{34}
$$

with $x_1 \in \mathbb{R}^{n_1}$, $x_2 \in \mathbb{R}^{n_2}$, $u \in \mathbb{R}^m$, $y \in \mathbb{R}^p$, and A^{11}, A^{12}, A^{21}, A^{22}, B^1, B^2, C^1, and C^2 are matrices of appropriate dimensions. We let $n = n_1 + n_2$, and

$$
A = \begin{bmatrix} A^{11} & A^{12} \\ A^{21} & A^{22} \end{bmatrix}, \qquad B = \begin{bmatrix} B^1 \\ B^2 \end{bmatrix}, \qquad C = \begin{bmatrix} C^1, C^2 \end{bmatrix}.
$$

As for RNNs, we assume that the activation function $\sigma : \mathbb{R} \to \mathbb{R}$ is an odd map. For continuous time models, we always assume that the activation function is, at least, locally Lipschitz, and the control maps are locally essentially bounded; thus the local existence and uniqueness of the solutions of the differential equation in (34) are guaranteed.

As for RNNs, the system theoretic analysis for MNs will be carried on for a suitable subclass.

DEFINITION 32. A system of type (34) is said to be an *admissible* MN if both the activation function σ and the control matrix B^1 are admissible.

For the definitions of an admissible activation function and an admissible matrix, see Section II.A. Notice that the admissibility conditions involve only the first block of equations in (34), which evolves nonlinearly.

B. STATE OBSERVABILITY

In this section we present the state observability result for MNs. For the definitions of state observability and coordinate subspace, see the corresponding Section II.C.

DEFINITION 33.   Consider an admissible MN of type (34). Let $W \subseteq \mathbb{R}^n$ be the maximum subspace (maximum with respect to set inclusion) such that

(i) $AW \subseteq W$, and $W \subseteq \ker C$;
(ii) $AW = V_1 \oplus V_2$, where $V_1 \subseteq \mathbb{R}^{n_1}$, $V_2 \subseteq \mathbb{R}^{n_2}$, and V_1 is a coordinate subspace.

We call W the *unobservable subspace*.

It is clear that the unobservable subspace is well defined, because if W_1 and W_2 are subspaces, both satisfying i) and ii), then $W_1 + W_2$ also does.

THEOREM 34.   *Let Σ be an admissible MN of type (34), and $W \subseteq \mathbb{R}^n$ be its unobservable subspace. Then $x, z \in \mathbb{R}^n$ are indistinguishable if and only if $x - z \in W$. In particular, Σ is observable if and only if $W = \{0\}$.*

Theorem 34 will be restated in a different form in Theorem 37, the proof of which is postponed to Section III.C.

REMARK 35.   Notice that if Σ is a RNN (i.e., $n_2 = 0$), then the previous theorem yields the observability result given in Theorem 10. On the other hand, if Σ is a linear model (i.e., $n_1 = 0$), then Theorem 34 gives the usual linear observability result stated in Theorem 8.

As done for RNNs, we present a simple algorithm to efficiently check the observability condition given by Theorem 34. First we give a useful characterization of the unobservable subspace W.

PROPOSITION 36.   *Consider an admissible MN of type (34). Let $V_1 \subseteq \mathbb{R}^{n_1}$ and $V_2 \subseteq \mathbb{R}^{n_2}$ be the maximum pair of subspaces (maximum with respect to set inclusion), such that*

P1. *V_1 is a coordinate subspace, $V_1 \subset \ker C_1$, $A_{11}V_1 \subseteq V_1$;*
P2. *$V_2 \subset \ker C_2$, $A_{22}V_2 \subseteq V_2$;*
P3. *$A_{21}V_1 \subseteq V_2$;*
P4. *$A_{12}V_2 \subseteq V_1$.*

Then the unobservable subspace W is given by

$$W = A^{-1}(V_1 \oplus V_2) \cap \ker C.$$

Proof.   First we prove that if $V_1 \subseteq \mathbb{R}^{n_1}$ and $V_2 \subseteq \mathbb{R}^{n_2}$ is any pair of subspaces satisfying properties P1–P4, then $W = A^{-1}(V_1 \oplus V_2) \cap \ker C$ satisfies properties (i) and (ii) of Definition 33.

(i) Clearly, $W \subseteq \ker C$. To see that $AW \subseteq W$, we argue as follows. $AW \subseteq V_1 \oplus V_2 \subseteq \ker C$, because $V_1 \subseteq \ker C_1$, and $V_2 \subseteq \ker C_2$. On the other hand, because $A_{11}V_1 \subseteq V_1$, $A_{22}V_2 \subseteq V_2$, and properties P3, P4 hold, one gets that $A(V_1 \oplus V_2) \subseteq V_1 \oplus V_2$. Thus, if $x \in W \subseteq A^{-1}(V_1 \oplus V_2)$, then $Ax \in V_1 \oplus V_2$, which implies that $A(Ax) \in A(V_1 \oplus V_2) \subseteq V_1 \oplus V_2$. So $Ax \in A^{-1}(V_1 \oplus V_2) \cap \ker C$, as desired.

(ii) We will prove that $AW = V_1 \oplus V_2$. We need only establish that $V_1 \oplus V_2 \subseteq AW$, the other inclusion being obvious. Notice that $V_1 \oplus V_2 \subseteq \ker C$ and, because $A(V_1 \oplus V_2) \subseteq V_1 \oplus V_2$, we get also $V_1 \oplus V_2 \subseteq A^{-1}(V_1 \oplus V_2)$, and so $V_1 \oplus V_2 \subseteq AW$.

It is not difficult to see that if $W \subseteq \mathbb{R}^n$ is any subspace that satisfies properties (i) and (ii) of Definition 33, the two subspaces $V_1 \subseteq \mathbb{R}^{n_1}$ and $V_2 \subseteq \mathbb{R}^{n_2}$, such that $AW = V_1 \oplus V_2$, satisfy properties $P1$–$P4$.

Now, by maximality of both the unobservable subspace W and the pair V_1, V_2, the conclusion follows. ∎

If $V_1 \subseteq \mathbb{R}^{n_1}$ and $V_2 \subseteq \mathbb{R}^{n_2}$ are the two subspaces defined in Proposition 36, then one has

$$W = 0 \Leftrightarrow \ker A \cap \ker C = 0, \qquad V_1 = 0, \qquad V_2 = 0. \qquad (35)$$

In fact, $W = A^{-1}(V_1 \oplus V_2) \cap \ker C$, thus if $W = 0$, then $\ker A \cap \ker C \subseteq W = 0$. Moreover, because $V_1 \oplus V_2 \subseteq A^{-1}(V_1 \oplus V_2) \cap \ker C$, we also have that $V_1 = 0$ and $V_2 = 0$. On the other hand, if $V_1 = 0$ and $V_2 = 0$, then $W = A^{-1}(V_1 \oplus V_2) \cap \ker C = \ker A \cap \ker C = 0$.

Using (35), Theorem 34 can be rewritten as follows.

THEOREM 37. *Let Σ be an admissible MN of type (34), and $V_1 \subseteq \mathbb{R}^{n_1}$, $V_2 \subseteq \mathbb{R}^{n_2}$ be the two subspaces defined in Proposition 36. Then $x, z \in \mathbb{R}^n$ are indistinguishable if and only if $x - z \in \ker C$ and $A(x-z) \in V_1 \oplus V_2$. In particular, Σ is observable if and only if*

$$\ker A \cap \ker C = 0, \qquad and \qquad V_1 = 0, \ V_2 = 0. \qquad (36)$$

Before proving this result, we present an algorithm to compute the subspaces V_1 and V_2, which consists of solving a finite number of linear algebraic equations.

Inductively, we define an increasing sequence of indexes J_d, and two decreasing sequences of subspaces $V_1^d \subseteq \mathbb{R}^{n_1}$, $V_2^d \subseteq \mathbb{R}^{n_2}$, for $d \geq 1$, where V_1^d is a coordinate subspace. Recall that for a given matrix D, we denote by I_D the set of indexes i such that the ith column of D is zero. Let

$$J_1 = \{1, \ldots, k\} \setminus I_{C_1};$$
$$V_1^1 = \text{span}\{e_j | j \notin J_1\};$$
$$V_2^1 = \ker C_2;$$

and, for $d > 1$, let

$$J_{d+1} = J_1 \cup \left\{i | \exists j \in J_d \text{ such that } A_{ji}^{11} \neq 0\right\}$$

$$\cup \left\{i | \exists j, \exists 0 \leq l \leq d - 1 \text{ such that } \left(C^2 \left(A^{22}\right)^l A^{21}\right)_{ji} \neq 0\right\}$$

$$\cup \bigcup_{s=1}^{d-1} \left\{i | \exists j \in J_s \text{ such that } \left(A^{12} \left(A^{22}\right)^{d-s-1} A^{21}\right)_{ji} \neq 0\right\}$$

$$V_1^{d+1} = \text{span}\{e_j | j \notin J_{d+1}\}$$

$$V_2^{d+1} = \left\{w | \left(A^{22}\right)^l w \in \ker C^2 \text{ for } 0 \leq l \leq d,\right.$$

$$\left. A^{12} \left(A^{22}\right)^{d-s} w \in V_1^s \text{ for } 1 \leq s \leq d\right\}.$$

REMARK 38.   It is easy to show that the two sequences V_1^d and V_2^d for $d \geq 1$ are both decreasing; thus they must become stationary after a finite number of steps. One can find conditions that guarantee the termination of the previous algorithm. Assume that a stationary string $V_1^s = V_1^{s+1} = \cdots = V_1^{s+n_1}$ of length $n_1 + 1$ is obtained. Then, using both the definitions of V_1^d and V_2^d, and applying the Hamilton–Cayley theorem, one proves that $V_1^d = V_1^s$ for all $d \geq s$ and that $V_2^d = V_2^{s+n_2}$ for all $d \geq s + n_2$. Thus the two sequences V_1^d and V_2^d become stationary after at most $(n_2 + 1)n_1$ steps, for $n_1 \geq 1$, or n steps, for $n_1 = 0$.

The two sequences V_1^d and V_2^d stabilize exactly at V_1 and V_2, as stated in Proposition 40. Moreover, for MN which evolves in discrete time, the previous subspaces V_1^d and V_2^d have a precise meaning, as stated next. For discrete time models, given any x, $z \in \mathbb{R}^n$ and any $0 < d \in \mathbb{N}$, we say that x and z are indistinguishable in d-steps if any output sequence from x or z is the same up to time d.

PROPOSITION 39.   *Let Σ be a discrete time admissible MN. Then the following properties are equivalent:*

   (i) *x and z are indistinguishable in d-steps,*
   (ii) *$x - z \in \ker C$; $A(x - z) \in (V_1^d \oplus V_2^d)$.*

For the proof of this Proposition we refer to Albertini and Dai Pra [23].

PROPOSITION 40.   *Let $V_1 \subseteq \mathbb{R}^{n_1}$, and $V_2 \subseteq \mathbb{R}^{n_2}$ be the two subspaces defined in Proposition 36 and V_1^d and V_2^d be the two sequences of subspaces determined by the algorithm described above. Then the following identities hold:*

$$V_1 = \bigcap_{d \geq 1} V_1^d, \qquad V_2 = \bigcap_{d \geq 1} V_2^d. \tag{37}$$

Proof. Let

$$J_\infty = \bigcup_{d \geq 1} J_d; \qquad V_1^\infty = \bigcap_{d \geq 1} V_1^d; \qquad V_2^\infty = \bigcap_{d \geq 1} V_2^d.$$

Thus $V_1^\infty = \text{span}\{e_j | j \notin J_\infty\}$. The following four properties can easily be proved by using the recursive definition of J_d, V_1^d, and V_2^d and the fact that, for some $\bar{d}$, it holds that $V_1^d = V_1^\infty$, $V_2^d = V_2^\infty$ for $d \geq \bar{d}$.

$$\{i | \exists j \in J_\infty \text{ so that } A_{ji}^{11} \neq 0\} \subseteq J_\infty. \tag{38}$$

$$\{i | \exists j, \exists l \geq 0 \text{ so that } \left(C^2 \left(A^{22}\right)^l A^{21}\right)_{ji} \neq 0\} \subseteq J_\infty. \tag{39}$$

$$\{i | \exists j \in J_\infty, \exists l \geq 0 \text{ so that } \left(A^{12} \left(A^{22}\right)^l A^{21}\right)_{ji} \neq 0\} \subseteq J_\infty. \tag{40}$$

$$V_2^\infty \subset \{w | \left(A^{22}\right)^l w \in \ker C^2 \text{ for } l \geq 0, \ A^{12} \left(A^{22}\right)^l w \in V_1^\infty \text{ for } l \geq 0\}. \tag{41}$$

We first prove that the pair V_1^∞ and V_2^∞ satisfies properties P1–P4 of Proposition 36.

P1. The only nontrivial fact is the A^{11} invariance of V_1^∞. Let $v \in V_1^\infty$. From (38), we get that $v_i = 0$ for all i such that $\exists j \in J_\infty$ with $A_{ji}^{11} \neq 0$. So, for $j \in J_\infty$,

$$\left(A^{11} v\right)_j = \sum_{i=1}^{n_1} A_{ji}^{11} v_i = 0,$$

and, therefore, $A^{11} v \in V_1^\infty$.

P2. Let $w \in V_2^\infty$. We show that $A^{22} w \in V_2^d$ for every $d \geq 1$. From (41), we first see that $\left(A^{22}\right)^l \left(A^{22} w\right) \in \ker C^2$ for $0 \leq l \leq d$. Moreover, for $1 \leq s \leq d$, again from (41), we have that

$$A^{12} \left(A^{22}\right)^{d-s} \left(A^{22} w\right) \in V_1^\infty \subseteq V_1^s.$$

P3. Let $v \in V_1^\infty$. We need to prove that $A^{21} v \in V_2^d$ for all $d \geq 1$. Using arguments similar to those used to derive P1, one can see that (39) yields

$$C^2 \left(A^{22}\right)^l A^{21} v = 0 \qquad \forall l \geq 0,$$

and (40) yields

$$A^{12} \left(A^{22}\right)^l A^{21} v \in V_1^\infty \subseteq V_1^s \qquad \forall s \geq 1.$$

This implies that $A^{21} v \in V_2^d$ for all d, as desired.

P4. This is an immediate consequence of (41).

Thus we have that $V_1^\infty \subseteq V_1$, and $V_2^\infty \subseteq V_2$. To conclude, we need to show that the converse inclusions also hold. We will prove, by induction, that $V_1 \subseteq V_1^d$, and $V_2 \subseteq V_2^d$ for all $d \geq 1$. The case $d = 1$ is obvious. Now let $e_i \in V_1$. We show that $e_i \in V_1^{d+1}$, that is, $i \notin J_{d+1}$.

- Suppose i is such that there exists $j \in J_d$ with $A_{ji}^{11} \neq 0$. Then we have

$$\left(A^{11}e_i\right)_j = A_{ji}^{11} \neq 0 \Rightarrow A_{11}e_i \notin V_1^d.$$

  This is impossible because $A^{11}V_1 \subset V_1$ and, by inductive assumption, $V_1 \subset V_1^d$.
- Suppose i is such that there exist j and $0 \leq l \leq d - 1$ with $(C^2(A^{22})^l A^{21})_{ji} \neq 0$. As before, this implies

$$C^2\left(A^{22}\right)^l A^{21} e_i \neq 0,$$

  which is impossible, because $A^{21}V_1 \subseteq V_2$ and $V_2 \subseteq \ker(C^2(A^{22})^l)$ for every $l \geq 0$.
- Suppose i is such that there exist $0 \leq s \leq d - 1$ and $j \in J_s$ with $(A^{12}(A^{22})^{d-s}A^{21})_{ji} \neq 0$. This implies

$$A^{12}\left(A^{22}\right)^{d-s} A^{21} e_i \notin V_1^s.$$

  This is impossible because $(A^{22})^{d-s}A^{21}V_1 \subseteq V_1$, $A^{12}V_2 \subseteq V_2$, and, by inductive assumption, $V_1 \subseteq V_1^s$.

Thus we have shown that $e_i \in V_1^{d+1}$.

Now let $w \in V_2$. We need to prove that $w \in V_2^{d+1}$.

- Because $V_2 \subseteq \ker C^2$, and $A^{22}V_2 \subseteq V_2$, it holds that $(A^{22})^l w \in \ker C^2$ for $0 \leq l \leq d$.
- Because $A^{22}V_2 \subseteq V_2$, $A^{12}V_2 \subseteq V_1$, and, by inductive assumption, $V_1 \subseteq V_1^s$ for all $1 \leq s \leq d$, it holds that $A^{12}(A^{22})^{d-s}w \subset V_1^s$, again for $1 \leq s \leq d$. ∎

We conclude with two examples.

EXAMPLE 41.   Assume $A_{12} = 0$ and $A_{21} = 0$. Thus the linear and the non-linear dynamics are decoupled (as in [31, Chap. 6]). By what was observed in Remark 35, we determine that the observability of the whole system is equivalent to the observability of the RNN characterized by the matrices A_{11}, B_1, and C_1 and of the linear models given by the matrices A_{22}, B_2, and C_2. The separate observability is clearly necessary for observability of the combined system, but the sufficiency is not an obvious fact. For instance, if the two components were both linear, then such a "separation property" would generally be false.

EXAMPLE 42. Assume that C_1 has no zero columns. Then there is no nonzero coordinate subspace contained in $\ker C_1$; so $V_1 = 0$. Therefore, V_2 is the largest A_{22}-invariant subspace contained in $\ker C_2$ and $\ker A_{12}$. It follows that the MN is observable if and only $\ker C \cap \ker A = 0$, and the two linear systems with matrices (A_{22}, C_2) and (A_{22}, A_{12}) are observable.

C. PROOFS ON OBSERVABILITY

Throughout this section, even if not specifically stated, all of the models of MNs we will be dealing with are assumed to be admissible.

A basic ingredient in the proof of the observability result is the following technical fact, which also explains how the admissibility assumptions on the activation map σ and the control matrix B^1 are used (see also [14]). Recall that, for a given matrix D, I_D denotes the set of index i such that the ith column of D is zero.

LEMMA 43. *Assume that σ is an admissible activation function, $B^1 \in \mathbb{R}^{l \times m}$ is an admissible control matrix, and $D \in \mathbb{R}^{q \times l}$ is any matrix. Then the following two properties are equivalent for each ξ, η, $\in \mathbb{R}^l$, and each α, $\beta \in \mathbb{R}^q$:*

1. $\xi_i = \eta_i$ *for all $i \notin I_D$,* $\alpha = \beta$,
2. $D\vec{\sigma}(\xi + B^1 u) + \alpha = D\vec{\sigma}(\eta + B^1 u) + \beta$ *for all $u \in \mathbb{R}^m$.*

Proof. We need only prove that property 2 implies property 1, the other implication being obvious. Because B^1 is admissible, there exists $\bar{v} \in \mathbb{R}^m$ such that $b_i = (B^1 \bar{v})_i \neq 0$ for all $i = 1, \ldots, n$ and $|b_i| \neq |b_j|$ if $i \neq j$. To see this, it is enough to notice that the equations $(B^1 u)_i = 0$ and $(B^1 u)_i = \pm(B^1 u)_j$ define a finite number of hyperplanes in $\mathbb{R}^m$; thus to get $\bar{v}$, we only have to avoid their union.

Now, for any $t \in \mathbb{R}$, we consider $t\bar{v} \in \mathbb{R}^m$, and we rewrite (2) as

$$\sum_{i=1}^n D_{li}\sigma(\xi_i + b_i t) - \sum_{i=1}^n D_{li}\sigma(\eta_i + b_i t) + (\alpha_l - \beta_l) = 0,$$

$$l = 1, \ldots, q, \text{ and } t \in \mathbb{R}. \quad (42)$$

Assume that property 1 is false. If $\xi_i = \eta_i$ for all $i \notin I_D$, then the first difference in (42) is always zero. Thus if there exists $\bar{l}$ such that $\alpha_{\bar{l}} \neq \beta_{\bar{l}}$, (42) does not hold for this $\bar{l}$, contradicting property 2. On the other hand, if there exists $\bar{i} \notin I_D$ such that $\xi_{\bar{i}} \neq \eta_{\bar{i}}$, then by definition of I_D, there exists $\bar{l}$ such that $D_{\bar{l}\bar{i}} \neq 0$. Because in (42) all of the pairs for which $\xi_i = \eta_i$ cancel out, we may assume without loss of generality that $\xi_i \neq \eta_i$ for all i (notice that $\xi_{\bar{i}} \neq \eta_{\bar{i}}$; thus not all of the pairs cancel). Consider now equation (42) for $l = \bar{l}$. The pairs (ξ_i, b_i) and (η_i, b_i) are all different; thus admissibility of σ implies that (42) cannot hold for all $t \in \mathbb{R}$, contradicting property 2. ∎

First, we introduce some useful notations. Given $x \in \mathbb{R}^n$ and $u \in \mathbb{R}^m$, for discrete time MNs we denote by $x^+(u)$ the state reached from x by using the control value u. For continuous time MNs, if $v(t)$ is the control function constantly equal to u, we denote by $x_u(t)$ the corresponding trajectory; notice that $x_u(t)$ is certainly defined on an interval of the form $[0, \epsilon_u)$, and it is differentiable on this interval. When dealing with two trajectories of this type starting at two different initial states, by $[0, \epsilon_u)$ we mean the interval in which both trajectories are defined.

Given two pairs of states (x, z), $(x', z') \in \mathbb{R}^n \times \mathbb{R}^n$, we write

$$(x, z) \rightsquigarrow (x', z'),$$

if, for discrete time, we can find an input sequence $u_1, \ldots, u_p$, for some $p \geq 0$, which steers the state x (resp., z) to x' (resp., z'). For continuous time, we require that there exists some control function $u(t) : [0, T] \to \mathbb{R}^m$, such that it is possible to solve the differential equation (34) starting at x (resp., z), for the entire interval $[0, T]$, and at time T the state x' (resp., z') is reached. Using this terminology, two states $(x, z) \in \mathbb{R}^n \times \mathbb{R}^n$ are distinguishable if and only if there is some pair $(x', z') \in \mathbb{R}^n$ such that $(x, z) \rightsquigarrow (x', z')$ and $Cx' \neq Cz'$.

In what follows, proofs in discrete time will be similar to proofs in continuous time, so they will only be sketched. To simplify notations, we write

$$A^1 = \left(A^{11}, A^{12}\right), \qquad A^2 = \left(A^{21}, A^{22}\right).$$

LEMMA 44. *Let $H^1 \in \mathbb{R}^{q \times n_1}$, $H^2 \in \mathbb{R}^{q \times n_2}$, with $q \geq 1$, $1 \leq i \leq q$, and $x, z \in \mathbb{R}^n$.*

(a) *For continuous time MNs, if $(H^1 A^1 x_u(t))_i = (H^1 A^1 z_u(t))_i$ for all $u \in \mathbb{R}^m$ and all $t \in [0, \epsilon_u)$, then we have*

$$\begin{aligned}
\left(H^1 A^{12} A^2 x\right)_i &= \left(H^1 A^{12} A^2 z\right)_i, \\
\left(H^1 A^{11}\right)_{ij} &= 0 \quad \text{for all } j \text{ such that } \left(A^1 x\right)_j \neq \left(A^1 z\right)_j.
\end{aligned} \tag{43}$$

For discrete time MNs, if $(H^1 A^1 x^+(u))_i = (H^1 A^1 z^+(u))_i$ for all $u \in \mathbb{R}^m$, then the same conclusions hold.

(b) *For continuous time MNs, if $(H^2 A^2 x_u(t))_i = (H^2 A^2 z_u(t))_i$ for all $u \in \mathbb{R}^m$ and all $t \in [0, \epsilon_u)$, then we have*

$$\begin{aligned}
\left(H^2 A^{22} A^2 x\right)_i &= \left(H^2 A^{22} A^2 z\right)_i, \\
\left(H^2 A^{21}\right)_{ij} &= 0 \quad \text{for all } j \text{ such that } \left(A^1 x\right)_j \neq \left(A^1 z\right)_j.
\end{aligned} \tag{44}$$

For discrete time MNs, if $(H^2 A^2 x^+(u))_i = (H^2 A^2 z^+(u))_i$ for all $u \in \mathbb{R}^m$, then the same conclusions hold.

Proof. (a) Suppose we are in the continuous time case, and fix $u \in \mathbb{R}^m$. If $(H^1 A^1 x_u(t))_i = (H^1 A^1 z_u(t))_i$ for all $t \in [0, \epsilon_u)$, then $(H^1 A^1 \dot{x}_u(t))_i|_{t=0} = (H^1 A^1 \dot{z}_u(t))_i|_{t=0}$. This equation reads

$$\sum_{j=1}^{p} \left(H^1 A^{11} \right)_{ij} \sigma\left((A^1 x)_j + (B^1 u)_j \right) + \left(H^1 A^{12} A^2 x \right)_i$$

$$= \sum_{j=1}^{p} \left(H^1 A^{11} \right)_{ij} \sigma\left((A^1 z)_j + (B^1 u)_j \right) + \left(H^1 A^{12} A^2 z \right)_i. \qquad (45)$$

Because (45) holds for all $u \in \mathbb{R}^m$, both equalities in (43) follow directly by applying Lemma 43.

The proof for the discrete time case is the same, because the assumption $(H^1 A^1 x^+(u))_i = (H^1 A^1 z^+(u))_i$, for all $u \in \mathbb{R}^m$, implies directly equations (45).

(b) This statement is proved similarly. In fact, by the same arguments as in (a), one easily sees that, for both continuous and discrete time dynamics,

$$\sum_{j=1}^{p} \left(H^2 A^{21} \right)_{ij} \sigma\left((A^1 x)_j + (B^1 u)_j \right) + \left(H^2 A^{22} A^2 x \right)_i$$

$$= \sum_{j=1}^{p} \left(H^2 A^{21} \right)_{ij} \sigma\left((A^1 z)_j + (B^1 u)_j \right) + \left(H^2 A^{22} A^2 z \right)_i,$$

for all $u \in \mathbb{R}^m$. So, again, to conclude, it is sufficient to use Lemma 43. ∎

LEMMA 45. *If $x, z \in \mathbb{R}^n$ are indistinguishable, then $C^2 A^2 x = C^2 A^2 z$ and $(A^1 x)_i = (A^1 z)_i$ for all $i \notin I_{C^1}$.*

Proof. If x, z are indistinguishable, then, for all $u \in \mathbb{R}^m$, we get, for discrete time, $Cx^+(u) = Cz^+(u)$, or, for continuous time, $Cx_u(t) = Cz_u(t)$, for $t \in [0, \epsilon_u)$. This implies, in both cases,

$$C^1 \vec{\sigma}\left(A^1 x + B^1 u \right) + C^2 A^2 x + C^2 B^2 u = C^1 \vec{\sigma}\left(A^1 z + B^1 u \right) + C^2 A^2 z + C^2 B^2 u$$

for all $u \in \mathbb{R}^m$. From Lemma 43 our conclusions follow. ∎

LEMMA 46. *If $x, z \in \mathbb{R}^n$ are indistinguishable, then for all $q \geq 0$, we have*

1. $C^2 (A^{22})^q A^2 x = C^2 (A^{22})^q A^2 z$
2. $(C^2 (A^{22})^q A^{21})_{ij} = 0$ *for all i and all j such that $(A^1 x)_j \neq (A^1 z)_j$.*

Proof. 1. We prove this statement by induction on $q \geq 0$. The case $q = 0$ is the first conclusion of Lemma 45. Assume that part 1 holds for q and for all

in continuous and discrete time, respectively. Now by applying Lemma
44(a) with $H^1 = I$, we get

$$A^{11}_{iq} = 0 \; \forall q, \qquad \text{such that } \left(A^1 \xi\right)_q \neq \left(A^1 \varsigma\right)_q.$$

In particular, $A^{11}_{ij} = 0$, as desired.

- $\widehat{V}_1 \subset \ker C^1$

  If the pair x, z is indistinguishable, then so is any pair x', z' such that
  $(x, z) \rightsquigarrow (x', z')$. Thus the conclusion follows by observing that
  Lemma 45 implies $J \subset I_{C^1}$.

- $A^{21}\widehat{V}_1 \subset \widehat{V}_2$

  It is sufficient to prove

$$\begin{cases} C^2 (A^{22})^q A^{21} e_j = 0 \\ A^{12} (A^{22})^q A^{21} e_j \in \widehat{V}_1 \end{cases}$$

for all $j \in J, q \geq 0$ or, equivalently,

$$\begin{cases} (C^2 (A^{22})^q A^{21})_{ij} = 0 & \forall i, \; \forall j \in J, \\ (A^{12} (A^{22})^q A^{21})_{ij} = 0 & \forall i \notin J, \; \forall j \in J. \end{cases} \tag{49}$$

The first equality in (49) is easily obtained by applying part (b) of
Lemma 46. The second one follows from part (b) of Lemma 47 after
having observed that

(I) if $i \notin J$, then $(A^1 x')_i = (A^1 z')_i$ for all (x', z') such that
$(x, z) \rightsquigarrow (x', z')$,

(II) if $j \in J$, then there exists (x', z') such that $(x, z) \rightsquigarrow (x', z')$ and
$(A^1 x')_j \neq (A^1 z')_j$.

(ii) $\widetilde{V}_2$ is by definition A^{22}-invariant. Thus to prove that $\widetilde{V}_2 \subset \widehat{V}_2$, we need to
show that $\widetilde{V}_2 \subset \ker C^2$ and $A^{12}\widetilde{V}_2 \subset \widehat{V}_1$. This amounts to establish the
following identities:

$$C^2 (A^{22})^q A^2 x' = C^2 (A^{22})^q A^2 z' \quad \forall (x', z')$$
$$\text{such that } (x, z) \rightsquigarrow (x', z') \tag{50}$$

$$A^{12} (A^{22})^q A^2 (x' - z') \in \widehat{V}_1 \quad \forall (x', z')$$
$$\text{such that } (x, z) \rightsquigarrow (x', z'). \tag{51}$$

Because $(x, z) \rightsquigarrow (x', z')$ implies that the pair x', z' is also
indistinguishable, (50) is just part 1 of Lemma 46. Moreover, (51) is
equivalent to

$$\left(A^{12} (A^{22})^q A^2 x'\right)_i = \left(A^{12} (A^{22})^q A^2 z'\right)_i \qquad \forall i \notin J,$$

which follows from part (a) of Lemma 47. ∎

Now we prove Theorem 37.

Proof. Necessity is proved in Proposition 48, thus we need only prove sufficiency.

Assume first that we are dealing with discrete time MN. We will prove that if $x, z \in \mathbb{R}^n$ satisfy the indistinguishability conditions of Theorem (37), then, for all $u \in \mathbb{R}^m$, $x^+(u)$, $z^+(u)$ also satisfy the same conditions. This fact will clearly imply that x, z are indistinguishable.

First notice that the following implications hold:

$$\begin{aligned} A^1(x - z) \in V_1 &\Rightarrow x_1^+(u) - z_1^+(u) \in V_1 \\ A^2(x - z) \in V_2 &\Rightarrow x_2^+(u) - z_2^+(u) \in V_2. \end{aligned} \tag{52}$$

Both implications are easily proved by using the properties of V_1 and V_2, and the fact that V_1 is a coordinate subspace, and so if $\alpha \in V_1$, then $\vec{\sigma}(\alpha) \in V_1$. Because $V_1 \subseteq \ker C^1$, and $V_2 \subseteq \ker C^2$, (52) yields $x^+(u) - z^+(u) \in \ker C$. Moreover, A^{11}-invariance of V_1 and the fact that $A^{12}V_2 \subseteq V_1$, implies

$$A^1\big(x^+(u) - z^+(u)\big) = A^{11}\big(x_1^+(u) - z_1^+(u)\big) + A^{12}\big(x_2^+(u) - z_2^+(u)\big) \in V_1,$$

whereas, A^{22}-invariance of V_2 and the fact that $A^{21}V_1 \subseteq V_2$ give

$$A^2\big(x^+(u) - z^+(u)\big) = A^{12}\big(x_1^+(u) - z_1^+(u)\big) + A^{22}\big(x_2^+(u) - z_2^+(u)\big) \in V_2.$$

Thus $A(x^+(u) - z^+(u)) \in V_1 \oplus V_2$, as desired.

Now we deal with continuous time MN. For a fixed but arbitrary input signal $(u(t))_{t \geq 0}$, let $x(t), z(t)$ denote the corresponding solutions of (34), associated with initial conditions $x(0), z(0)$. The pair $(x(t), z(t))$ solves the differential equation in $\mathbb{R}^{2n}$,

$$\begin{pmatrix} \dot{x} \\ \dot{z} \end{pmatrix} = F(x, z), \tag{53}$$

where

$$F(x, z) = \begin{pmatrix} \vec{\sigma}(A^1 x + B^1 u) \\ A^2 x + B^2 u \\ \vec{\sigma}(A^1 z + B^1 u) \\ A^2 z + B^2 u \end{pmatrix}.$$

Let $Z = \{(x, z) \in \mathbb{R}^{2n}: x - z \in \ker C, A^1(x - z) \in V_1, A^2(x - z) \in V_2\}$. In the proof for the discrete time case, we showed that if $(x, z) \in Z$, then $F(x, z) \in Z$. Thus Z is stable for the flow of (53), that is, if $(x(0), z(0)) \in Z$, then $(x(t), z(t)) \in Z$. Because $(u(t))_{t \geq 0}$ is arbitrary and $(x, z) \in Z \Rightarrow x - z \in \ker C$, the proof is easily completed. ∎

REMARK 56.   Proposition 55 will be proved later; however, the necessity of the conditions in (54) is not difficult to establish, as shown next.

(a) Assume that $V_1 \oplus V_2 \neq 0$, and let $r_1 = \dim V_1$, $r_2 = \dim V_2$, and $q_i = n_i - r_i$ $(i = 1, 2)$. Without loss of generality, we may assume that that $V_1 = \text{span}\{e_1, \ldots, e_{r_1}\}$, where $e_j \in \mathbb{R}^{n_1}$ are the elements of the canonical basis. Thus we must have (in what follows, we specify only the dimensions of some particular matrices, meaning that all of the others have the appropriate dimensions)

$$A^{11}V_1 \subseteq V_1 \Rightarrow A^{11} = \begin{pmatrix} H^{11} & H^{12} \\ 0 & H^{22} \end{pmatrix}, \qquad \text{with } H^{22} \in \mathbb{R}^{q_1 \times q_1},$$

$$V_1 \subseteq \ker C^1 \Rightarrow C^1 = (0, D^1), \qquad \text{with } D^1 \in \mathbb{R}^{p \times q_1}.$$

Using the linear theory, we also know that there exists a matrix $T_2 \in GL(n_2)$ such that

$$T_2^{-1} A^{22} T_2 = \begin{pmatrix} L^{11} & 0 \\ L^{21} & L^{22} \end{pmatrix}, \qquad C^2 T_2 = (D^2, 0),$$

where $L^{11} \in \mathbb{R}^{q_2 \times q_2}$, and $D^2 \in \mathbb{R}^{p \times q_2}$. Moreover, we have

$$A^{21}V_1 \subseteq V_2 \Rightarrow T_2^{-1} A^{21} = \begin{pmatrix} 0 & K^{12} \\ K^{21} & K^{22} \end{pmatrix}, \qquad \text{with } K^{22} \in \mathbb{R}^{q_2 \times q_1},$$

$$A^{12}V_2 \subseteq V_1 \Rightarrow A^{12} T_2 = \begin{pmatrix} M^{11} & 0 \\ M^{21} & M^{22} \end{pmatrix}, \qquad \text{with } M^{22} \in \mathbb{R}^{q_1 \times q_2}.$$

Now, if we denote, for $i = 1, 2$, $B^i = (B^{i1}, B^{i2})^T$, with $B^{12} \in \mathbb{R}^{q_1 \times m}$ and $B^{21} \in \mathbb{R}^{q_2 \times m}$, we may rewrite the dynamics of Σ_{n_1,n_2} as

$$\begin{cases} z_1^+ = \vec{\sigma}(H^{11}z_1 + H^{12}z_2 + M^{11}w_1 + M^{12}w_2 + B^{11}u) \\ z_2^+ = \vec{\sigma}(H^{22}z_2 + M^{11}w_1 + B^{12}u) \\ w_1^+ = K^{12}z_2 + L^{11}w_1 + B^{21}u \\ w_2^+ = K^{21}z_1 + K^{22}z_2 + L^{21}w_1 + L^{22}w_2 + B^{22}u \\ y = D^1 z_2 + D^2 w_1 \end{cases},$$

where $z_2 \in \mathbb{R}^{q_1}$ and $w_1 \in \mathbb{R}^{q_2}$. Thus because the two blocks of variables z_1 and w_2 do not affect the other two blocks and the output, it is clear that $(\Sigma_{n_1,n_2}, (z_1, z_2, w_1, w_2))$ is i/o equivalent to

$$\left(\Sigma_{q_1+q_2} = \left(\sigma, \begin{pmatrix} H^{22} & M^{11} \\ K^{22} & L^{11} \end{pmatrix}, \begin{pmatrix} B^{12} \\ B^{21} \end{pmatrix} (D^1, D^2) \right), (z_2, w_1) \right).$$

Thus we have performed a reduction in the dimension of the state space, because $q_1 + q_2 < n$, and so Σ_{n_1,n_2} cannot be minimal.

(b) Now assume that the pair $(A^{22}, [B^2, A^{21}])$ is not controllable. Let p_1 be the rank of

$$\left((B^2, A^{21}), A^{22}(B^2, A^{21}), \ldots, (A^{22})^{n_2-1}(B^2, A^{21}) \right),$$

and $p_2 = n_2 - p_1$. Then, by the linear theory, there exists an invertible matrix $T^2 \in GL(n_2)$ such that

$$(T^2)^{-1}A^{22}T^2 = \begin{pmatrix} H^1 & H^2 \\ 0 & H^3 \end{pmatrix}, \qquad (T^2)^{-1}A^{21} = \begin{pmatrix} K \\ 0 \end{pmatrix},$$

$$(T^2)^{-1}B^2 = \begin{pmatrix} M \\ 0 \end{pmatrix},$$

where $H^1 \in \mathbb{R}^{p_1 \times p_1}$, $H^2 \in \mathbb{R}^{p_1 \times p_2}$, $H^3 \in \mathbb{R}^{p_2 \times p_2}$, $K \in \mathbb{R}^{p_1 \times n_2}$, $M \in \mathbb{R}^{p_1 \times m}$. Now let $A^{12} = (N^1, N^2)$ and $C^2 = (L^1, L^2)$, where the matrices N^1 and L^1 represent the first p_1 columns. Consider the MN $\widetilde{\Sigma}_{n_1+p_1}$ given by the matrices:

$$\widetilde{A} = \begin{pmatrix} A^{11} & N^1 \\ K & H^1 \end{pmatrix}, \qquad \widetilde{B} = \begin{pmatrix} B^1 \\ M \end{pmatrix}, \qquad \widetilde{C} = (C^1, L^1).$$

It is easy to see that $(\Sigma_{n_1,n_2}, 0) \sim (\widetilde{\Sigma}_{n_1+p_1}, 0)$. Because $n_1 + p_1 < n$, again, Σ_{n_1,n_2} is not minimal.

E. PROOFS ON IDENTIFIABILITY AND MINIMALITY

Now we introduce some useful notations. In what follows, we assume that two initialized admissible MNs, (Σ_{n_1,n_2}, x_0) and $(\widetilde{\Sigma}_{\tilde{n}_1,\tilde{n}_2}, \tilde{x}_0)$, both evolving in either continuous or discrete time, are given. We let $A^1 = (A^{11}, A^{12})$ and $A^2 = (A^{21}, A^{22})$, and similarly for $\widetilde{A}^1$ and $\widetilde{A}^2$.

For discrete time models, for any $k \geq 1$ and any $u_1, \ldots, u_k \in \mathbb{R}^m$, we denote by $x_k[u_1, \ldots, u_k]$ (resp. $\tilde{x}_k[u_1, \ldots, u_k]$) the state we reach from x_0 (resp. $\tilde{x}_0$) using the control sequence $u_1, \ldots, u_k$. Moreover, we let

$$y_k[u_1, \ldots, u_k] = Cx_k[u_1, \ldots, u_k] \quad \text{and} \quad \tilde{y}_k[u_1, \ldots, u_k] = \widetilde{C}\tilde{x}_k[u_1, \ldots, u_k].$$

For the continuous time model, for any $w(\cdot) : [0, T_w] \to \mathbb{R}^m$, we let $x_w(t)$ and $\tilde{x}_w(t)$, for $t \in [0, \epsilon_w)$, be the two trajectories of Σ_{n_1,n_2} and $\widetilde{\Sigma}_n$ starting at x_0 and $\tilde{x}_0$, respectively. Here, with $\epsilon_w > 0$, we denote the maximum constant such that both trajectories $x_w(t)$ and $\tilde{x}_w(t)$ are defined on the interval $[0, \epsilon_w)$. Again, by $y_w(t)$ and $\tilde{y}_w(t)$, for $t \in [0, \epsilon_w)$, we denote the two corresponding output signals (i.e., $y_w(t) = Cx_w(t)$, and $\tilde{y}_w(t) = \widetilde{C}\tilde{x}_w(t)$).

For any vector $v \in \mathbb{R}^n$ with the superscript 1 (resp. 2), we denote the first n_1 (resp. the second n_2) block of coordinates (similarly, for $\tilde{v} \in \mathbb{R}^{\tilde{n}}$).

We will denote by $W \subseteq \mathbb{R}^n$ (resp. $\tilde{W} \subseteq \mathbb{R}^{\tilde{n}}$) the unobservable subspace of Σ_{n_1,n_2} (resp. $\tilde{\Sigma}_{\tilde{n}_1,\tilde{n}_2}$). Moreover, with $V_1 \subseteq \mathbb{R}^{n_1}$ and $V_2 \subseteq \mathbb{R}^{n_2}$ (resp. $\tilde{V}_1 \subseteq \mathbb{R}^{\tilde{n}_1}$ and $\tilde{V}_2 \subseteq \mathbb{R}^{\tilde{n}_2}$), we will denote the two subspaces defined in Proposition 36 for Σ_{n_1,n_2} (resp. $\tilde{\Sigma}_{\tilde{n}_1,\tilde{n}_2}$). Recall that it holds $W = A^{-1}(V_1 \oplus V_2) \cap \ker C$.

Now we establish some preliminary results. First we state a technical fact, which gives the idea on how the admissibility assumption is going to be used in the proof of the identifiability result. For a given matrix D, I_D denotes the set of indexes i such that the ith column of D is zero, and I_D^c is its complement.

LEMMA 57.   *Assume that the following matrices and vectors are given: $B \in \mathbb{R}^{n \times m}$, $\tilde{B} \in \mathbb{R}^{\tilde{n} \times m}$, $C \in \mathbb{R}^{p \times n}$, $\tilde{C} \in \mathbb{R}^{p \times \tilde{n}}$, $D, \tilde{D} \in \mathbb{R}^{p \times m}$, $a \in \mathbb{R}^n$, $\tilde{a} \in \mathbb{R}^{\tilde{n}}$, and $e, \tilde{e} \in \mathbb{R}^p$. Moreover, assume that σ is any admissible activation function, that both B and $\tilde{B}$ are admissible control matrices, and that for all $u \in \mathbb{R}^m$, the following equality holds:*

$$C\vec{\sigma}(a + Bu) + Du + e = \tilde{C}\vec{\sigma}(\tilde{a} + \tilde{B}u) + \tilde{D}u + \tilde{e}. \tag{55}$$

Then we have

(a) $e = \tilde{e}$.
(b) $D = \tilde{D}$.
(c) $|I_C^c| = |I_{\tilde{C}}^c|$, *and for any $l \in I_C^c$ there exists $\pi(l) \in I_{\tilde{C}}^c$ and $\beta(l) = \pm 1$, such that*

  (c.1) $B_{li} = \beta(l)\tilde{B}_{\pi(l)i}$ *for all $i \in \{1, \ldots, m\}$;*
  (c.2) $a_l = \beta(l)\tilde{a}_{\pi(l)}$.
  (c.3) $C_{il} = \beta(l)\tilde{C}_{i\pi(l)}$ *for all $i \in \{1, \ldots, p\}$.*

  Moreover, the map π is injective.

Proof.   Because B and $\tilde{B}$ are admissible control matrices, there exists $\bar{v} \in R^m$ such that

$$
\begin{aligned}
b_i = (B\bar{v})_i \neq 0 \,\forall i = 1, \ldots, n, \quad |b_i| \neq |b_j| &\qquad \text{for all } i \neq j; \\
\tilde{b}_i = (\tilde{B}\bar{v})_i \neq 0 \,\forall i = 1, \ldots, \tilde{n}, \quad |\tilde{b}_i| \neq |\tilde{b}_j| &\qquad \text{for all } i \neq j.
\end{aligned} \tag{56}
$$

Letting $Z \subset \mathbb{R}^m$ be the set of all vectors $v \in \mathbb{R}^m$ for which (56) holds, we have that Z is a dense subset of $\mathbb{R}^m$. Fix any $\bar{v} \in Z$; then by rewriting Eq. (55) for $u = x\bar{v}$, with $x \in \mathbb{R}$, and using the notations in (56), we get

$$\sum_{j=1}^n C_{ij}\sigma(a_j + b_j x) + (D\bar{v})_i x + e_i = \sum_{j=1}^{\tilde{n}} \tilde{C}_{ij}\sigma(\tilde{a}_j + \tilde{b}_j x) + (\tilde{D}\bar{v})_i x + \tilde{e}_i, \tag{57}$$

for all $x \in \mathbb{R}$, and all $i \in 1, \ldots, p$. Fix any $i \in \{1, \ldots, p\}$. After possibly some cancellation, Eq. 57 is of the type

$$\sum_{j=1}^{r} \gamma_{ij} \sigma(\alpha_j + \beta_j x) + ((D\bar{v})_i - (\widetilde{D}\bar{v})_i)x + (e_i - \tilde{e}_i) = 0, \qquad \forall x \in \mathbb{R}.$$

Because σ is admissible, we immediately get

$$e_i - \tilde{e}_i = 0,$$

$$(D\bar{v})_i - (\widetilde{D}\bar{v})_i = 0.$$

The first of these equations implies (a), the second implies (b), because it holds for every $\bar{v} \in Z$, and Z is dense.

Now, because (a) and (b) have been proved, we may rewrite (57) as

$$\sum_{j=1}^{n} C_{ij} \sigma(a_j + b_j x) = \sum_{j=1}^{\tilde{n}} \widetilde{C}_{ij} \sigma(\tilde{a}_j + \tilde{b}_j x). \tag{58}$$

Fix any $\bar{l} \in I_C^c$; then there exists $\bar{i} \in \{1, \dots, p\}$, such that $C_{\bar{i}\bar{l}} \neq 0$. Consider Eq. (58) for this particular $\bar{i}$. The terms for which $C_{\bar{i}j} = 0$ or $\widetilde{C}_{\bar{i}j} = 0$ will cancel (however, not all of them will cancel, because $C_{\bar{i}\bar{l}} \neq 0$); thus we are left with an equation of the type

$$\sum_{p=1}^{r} C_{\bar{i}j_p} \sigma(a_{j_p} + b_{j_p} x) - \sum_{p=1}^{\tilde{r}} \widetilde{C}_{\bar{i}j_p} \sigma(\tilde{a}_{j_p} + \tilde{b}_{j_p} x) = 0, \qquad \forall x \in \mathbb{R}, \tag{59}$$

for some $r \leq n$, and some $\tilde{r} \leq \tilde{n}$. Because σ is admissible, and the b_{j_p} (resp. $\tilde{b}_{j_p}$) have different absolute values, there must exist two indexes j_{p_1}, $j_{\pi(p_1)}$, and $\beta(p_1) = \pm 1$, such that

$$\left(a_{j_{p_1}}, b_{j_{p_1}}\right) = \beta(p_1)\left(\tilde{a}_{j_{\pi(p_1)}}, \tilde{b}_{j_{\pi(p_1)}}\right).$$

So we have

$$\left(C_{\bar{i}j_{p_1}} - \beta(p_1)\widetilde{C}_{\bar{i}j_{\pi(p_1)}}\right)\sigma(a_{j_{p_1}} + b_{j_{p_1}} x) + \sum_{p=1, p \neq p_1}^{r} C_{\bar{i}j_p} \sigma(a_{j_p} + b_{j_p} x)$$

$$- \sum_{p=1, p \neq \pi(p_1)}^{\tilde{r}} \widetilde{C}_{\bar{i}j_p} \sigma(\tilde{a}_{j_p} + \tilde{b}_{j_p} x) = 0.$$

Now, by repeating the same arguments, we will find another index j_{p_2}, a corresponding index $j_{\pi(p_2)}$ with $\pi(p_2) \neq \pi(p_1)$, and $\beta(p_2) = \pm 1$. Notice that necessarily $p_2 \neq p_1$, because, otherwise, $|\tilde{b}_{j_{\pi(p_1)}}| = |\tilde{b}_{j_{\pi(p_2)}}|$ would contradict

(56). Thus we will collect two more terms. Going on with the same arguments, we must have that $r = \tilde{r}$, and after r steps, we end up with an equation of the type

$$\sum_{p=1}^{r} \left(C_{\bar{i}j_p} - \beta(p)\widetilde{C}_{\bar{i}j_{\pi(p)}} \right) \sigma\left(a_{j_p} + b_{j_p}x \right) = 0 \qquad \forall x \in \mathbb{R}.$$

Again, by the admissibility of σ, we also have $(C_{\bar{i}j_p} - \beta(p)\widetilde{C}_{\bar{i}j_{\pi(p)}}) = 0$.

Thus, in particular, because $C_{\bar{i}\bar{l}} \neq 0$, we have shown that there exist $\pi(\bar{l})$ and $\beta(\bar{l})$ such that

$$\begin{aligned} (a_{\bar{l}}, b_{\bar{l}}) &= \beta(\bar{l})\left(\tilde{a}_{\pi(\bar{l})}, \tilde{b}_{\pi(\bar{l})} \right) \\ C_{\bar{i}\bar{l}} &= \beta(\bar{l})\widetilde{C}_{\bar{i}\pi(\bar{l})}. \end{aligned} \tag{60}$$

Notice that, if given this $\bar{l} \in I_C^c$, we would have chosen a different index $\hat{i}$ such that $C_{\hat{i}\bar{l}} \neq 0$; then we would have ended up with corresponding $\hat{\pi}(\bar{l})$ and $\hat{\beta}(\bar{l})$. However, because the $(\tilde{b}_j)$ all have different absolute values, it must be that $\pi(\bar{l}) = \hat{\pi}(\bar{l})$, and $\beta(\bar{l}) = \hat{\beta}(\bar{l})$ (see (60)). Thus we have shown that

$$\forall l \in I_C^c, \qquad \exists \pi(l) \in I_{\widetilde{C}}^c, \ \beta(l) = \pm 1,$$

$$\text{such that} \begin{cases} \text{(i)} & (a_l, b_l) = \beta(l)(\tilde{a}_{\pi(l)}, \tilde{b}_{\pi(l)}), \\ \text{(ii)} & C_{il} = \beta(l)C_{i\pi(l)} \qquad \text{if } C_{il} \neq 0. \end{cases} \tag{61}$$

This implies $|I_C^c| \leq |I_{\widetilde{C}}^c|$. By symmetry, we conclude that $|I_C^c| = |I_{\widetilde{C}}^c|$. From (61) (i), we get directly that (c.2) holds. Again from (61) (i), we also have

$$(B\bar{v})_l = \beta(l)(\widetilde{B}\bar{v})_{\pi(l)},$$

for all $\bar{v} \in Z$. Because Z is dense, this implies (c.1). Moreover, (61) (ii) proves (c.3) for those C_{il} different from zero. On the other hand, if $C_{il} = 0$, then, necessarily, $\widetilde{C}_{i\pi(l)}$ must also be zero. Otherwise, one repeats the argument above, exchanging C with $\widetilde{C}$, and finds an index $\lambda(\pi(l))$ such that

$$\left| \widetilde{C}_{i\pi(l)} \right| = \left| C_{i\lambda(\pi(l))} \right|, \qquad \left| \tilde{b}_{\pi(l)} \right| = \left| b_{\lambda(\pi(l))} \right|.$$

In particular, $\lambda(\pi(l)) \neq l$, because $C_{il} = 0$ and $C_{i\lambda(\pi(l))} \neq 0$. But then $|b_{\lambda(\pi(l))}| = |\tilde{b}_{\pi(l)}| = |b_l|$, which is impossible, because the b_i have all different absolute values.

The injectivity of the map π is also a consequence of $|b_i| \neq |b_j|$ for all $i \neq j$. ∎

LEMMA 58. *Let* (Σ_{n_1, n_2}, x_0) *and* $(\widetilde{\Sigma}_{\tilde{n}_1, \tilde{n}_2}, \tilde{x}_0)$ *be two initialized MNs,* $H_1 \in \mathbb{R}^{q \times n_1}$, $H_2 \in \mathbb{R}^{q \times n_2}$, $\widetilde{H}_1 \in \mathbb{R}^{q \times \tilde{n}_1}$, *and* $\widetilde{H}_2 \in \mathbb{R}^{q \times \tilde{n}_2}$.

- *For continuous time models, if for all $w : [0, T_w] \to \mathbb{R}^m$, and for all $t \in [0, \epsilon_w)$, we have*

$$H_1 x_w^1(t) + H_2 x_w^2(t) = \widetilde{H}_1 \tilde{x}_w^1(t) + \widetilde{H}_2 \tilde{x}_w^2(t), \tag{62}$$

then, for all $u \in \mathbb{R}^m$,

$$H_1 \vec{\sigma} \left(A^1 x_w(t) + B^1 u \right) + H_2 A^2 x_w(t) + H_2 B^2 u$$
$$= \widetilde{H}_1 \vec{\sigma} \left(\widetilde{A}^1 \tilde{x}_w(t) + \widetilde{B}^1 u \right) + \widetilde{H}_2 \widetilde{A}^2 \tilde{x}_w(t) + \widetilde{H}_2 \widetilde{B}^2 u. \tag{63}$$

- *For discrete time models, if for all $r \geq 0$, and for all $u_1, \ldots, u_r \in \mathbb{R}^m$, we have*

$$H_1 x^1[u_1, \ldots, u_r] + H_2 x^2[u_1, \ldots, u_r]$$
$$= \widetilde{H}_1 \tilde{x}^1[u_1, \ldots, u_r] + \widetilde{H}_2 \tilde{x}^2[u_1, \ldots, u_r], \tag{64}$$

(when $r = 0$, it is meant that the previous equality holds for the two initial states) then, for all $u \in \mathbb{R}^m$,

$$H_1 \vec{\sigma} \left(A^1 x[u_1, \ldots, u_r] + B^1 u \right) + H_2 A^2 x[u_1, \ldots, u_r] + H_2 B^2 u$$
$$= \widetilde{H}_1 \vec{\sigma} \left(\widetilde{A}^1 \tilde{x}[u_1, \ldots, u_r] + \widetilde{B}^1 u \right) + \widetilde{H}_2 \widetilde{A}^2 \tilde{x}[u_1, \ldots, u_r]$$
$$+ \widetilde{H}_2 \widetilde{B}^2 u. \tag{65}$$

Proof. Because the discrete time case is obvious, we prove only the continuous time statement. Fix any $\bar{t} \in [0, \epsilon_w)$. For any $u \in \mathbb{R}^m$, let $w_u : [0, \bar{t}+1] \to \mathbb{R}^m$ be the control map defined by $w_u(t) = w(t)$ if $t \in [0, \bar{t}]$, and $w_u = u$ if $t \in (\bar{t}, \bar{t} + 1]$. Then the two trajectories $x_{w_u}(t)$ and $\tilde{x}_{w_u}(t)$ are defined on an interval of the type $[0, \bar{t} + \epsilon)$ and are differentiable for any $t \in (\bar{t}, \bar{t} + \epsilon)$. Because Eq. (62) holds for all $t \in (0, \bar{t} + \epsilon)$, we have, for all $t \in (\bar{t}, \bar{t} + \epsilon)$,

$$H_1 \dot{x}_w^1(t) + H_2 \dot{x}_w^2(t) = \widetilde{H}_1 \dot{\tilde{x}}_w^1(t) + \widetilde{H}_2 \dot{\tilde{x}}_w^2(t).$$

Now, by taking the limit as $t \to \bar{t}^+$, we get (63), as desired. ■

LEMMA 59. *If $(\Sigma_{n_1, n_2}, x_0) \sim (\widetilde{\Sigma}_{\tilde{n}_1, \tilde{n}_2}, \tilde{x}_0)$, then, for all $l \geq 0$, we have*

(a) $C^2 (A^{22})^l B^2 = \widetilde{C}^2 (\widetilde{A}^{22})^l \widetilde{B}^2$;

(b) $|I_{C^2(A^{22})^l A^{21}}^c| = |I_{\widetilde{C}^2(\widetilde{A}^{22})^l \widetilde{A}^{21}}^c|$, *and for all $i \in I_{C^2(A^{22})^l A^{21}}^c$ there exists $\pi(i) \in I_{\widetilde{C}^2(\widetilde{A}^{22})^l \widetilde{A}^{21}}^c$ and $\beta(i) = \pm 1$, such that*

$$\left(C^2 (A^{22})^l A^{21} \right)_{ji} = \beta(i) \left(\widetilde{C}^2 (\widetilde{A}^{22})^l \widetilde{A}^{21} \right)_{j \pi(i)},$$

for all $j \in \{1, \ldots, p\}$;

LEMMA 61.   *If* $(\Sigma_{n_1,n_2}, x_0) \sim (\widetilde{\Sigma}_{\tilde{n}_1,\tilde{n}_2}, \tilde{x}_0)$ *and* $V_1 = 0$, *then* $n_1 \leq \tilde{n}_1$, *and for all* $i \in \{1, \ldots, n_1\}$ *there exists* $\pi(i) \in \{1, \ldots, \tilde{n}_1\}$ *and* $\beta(i) = \pm 1$, *such that*

(a) $B_{ij}^1 = \beta(i)\widetilde{B}_{\pi(i)j}^1$ *for all* $j \in 1, \ldots, m$;

(b) $C_{ji}^1 = \beta(i)\widetilde{C}_{j\pi(i)}^1$ *for all* $j \in 1, \ldots, p$;

(c1) *for continuous time dynamics, for all* $w(\cdot) \in [0, T_w] \to \mathbb{R}^m$, *for all* $t \in [0, \epsilon_w)$, *the following holds:*

$$\left[A^{11}x_w^1(t) + A^{12}x_w^2(t)\right]_i = \beta(i)\left[\widetilde{A}^{11}\tilde{x}_w^1(t) + \widetilde{A}^{12}\tilde{x}_w^2(t)\right]_{\pi(i)};$$

(c2) *for discrete time dynamics, for all* $r \geq 1$, *for all* $u_1, \ldots, u_r \in \mathbb{R}^m$, *the following holds:*

$$\left[A^{11}x^1[u_1, \ldots, u_r] + A^{12}x^2[u_1, \ldots, u_r]\right]_i$$
$$= \beta(i)\left[\widetilde{A}^{11}\tilde{x}^1[u_1, \ldots, u_r] + \widetilde{A}^{12}\tilde{x}^2[u_1, \ldots, u_r]\right]_{\pi(i)}.$$

Moreover, the map π *is injective.*

Proof.   Assume that we are dealing with continuous time MNs (the proof for the discrete time case is very similar and thus is omitted). Because $V_1 = 0$, then, letting J_d denote the set of indexes defined in Section III.B, we have that for any $i \in \{1, \ldots, n_1\}$, there exists $d \geq 1$, such that $i \in J_d$. We first prove (a) and (c1) by induction on the first index $d \geq 1$, such that $i \in J_d$.

Assume that $d = 1$, that is, $i \in J_1$. Thus, by definition, there exists $1 \leq l \leq p$ such that $C_{li}^1 \neq 0$. Because $(\Sigma_{n_1,n_2}, x_0) \sim (\widetilde{\Sigma}_{\tilde{n}_1,\tilde{n}_2}, \tilde{x}_0)$, then for all $w : [0, T_w] \to \mathbb{R}^m$, and for all $t \in [0, \epsilon_w)$, we have

$$C^1x_w^1(t) + C^2x_w^2(t) = y_{w_u}(t) = \tilde{y}_{w_u}(t) = \widetilde{C}^1\tilde{x}_w^1(t) + \widetilde{C}^2\tilde{x}_w^2(t).$$

From Lemma 58 this implies

$$C^1\bar{\sigma}\left(A^1x_w(t) + B^1u\right) + C^2A^2x_w(t) + C^2B^2u$$
$$= \widetilde{C}^1\bar{\sigma}\left(\widetilde{A}^1\tilde{x}_w(t) + \widetilde{B}^1u\right) + \widetilde{C}^2\widetilde{A}^2\tilde{x}_w(t) + \widetilde{C}^2\widetilde{B}^2u. \tag{67}$$

Because $C_{li}^1 \neq 0$, we have $i \in I_{C^1}^c$; thus, by Lemma 57, we know that there exist $\pi(i) \in \{1, \ldots, \tilde{n}_1\}$, and $\beta(i) = \pm 1$, such that

$$B_{ij}^1 = \beta(i)\widetilde{B}_{\pi(i)j}^1,$$

for all $j \in 1, \ldots, m$, and, for all $w(\cdot) \in [0, T_w] \to \mathbb{R}^m$, for all $t \in [0, \epsilon_w)$,

$$\left[A^{11}x_w^1(t) + A^{12}x_w^2(t)\right]_i = \beta(i)\left[\widetilde{A}^{11}\tilde{x}_w^1(t) + \widetilde{A}^{12}\tilde{x}_w^2(t)\right]_{\pi(i)}.$$

Now suppose that $i \in J_{d+1}$, for $d > 0$. If $i \in J_1$, then there is nothing to prove; otherwise we are in one of the following three cases:

1. there exists $j \in J_d$, and $A_{ji}^{11} \neq 0$;

2. there exists $1 \leq j \leq p$ and $0 \leq l \leq d-1$, such that $(C^2(A^{22})^l A^{21})_{ji} \neq 0$;
3. there exists $j \in J_s$, for $1 \leq s \leq d-1$, such that
$(A^{12}(A^{22})^{d-s-1}A^{21})_{ji} \neq 0$.

We will prove the three cases separately.

1. Because $j \in J_d$, then, in particular, (c1) holds for this j. Thus we have, for all $w(\cdot) \in [0, T_w] \to \mathbb{R}^m$, for all $t \in [0, \epsilon_w)$,

$$\left[A^{11}x_w^1(t) + A^{12}x_w^2(t)\right]_j = \beta(j)\left[\widetilde{A}^{11}\tilde{x}_w^1(t) + \widetilde{A}^{12}\tilde{x}_w^2(t)\right]_{\pi(j)}.$$

Now, by applying Lemma 58 to this equation, we get, for all $u \in \mathbb{R}^m$,

$$\left[A^{11}\vec{\sigma}\left(A^1 x_w(t) + B^1 u\right) + A^{12}A^2 x_w(t) + A^{12}B^2 u\right]_j$$
$$= \beta(j)\left[\widetilde{A}^{11}\vec{\sigma}\left(\widetilde{A}^1 \tilde{x}_w(t) + \widetilde{B}^1 u\right) + \widetilde{A}^{12}\widetilde{A}^2 \tilde{x}_w(t) + \widetilde{A}^{12}\widetilde{B}^2 u\right]_{\pi(j)}.$$

Now, because $A_{ji}^{11} \neq 0$, we have $i \in I_{A^{11}}^c$; by applying Lemma 57 to the previous equation, we conclude that there exists $\pi(i) \in \{1, \ldots, \tilde{n}_1\}$, and $\beta(i) = \pm 1$, such that (a) and (c1) hold for this index i.

2. From Lemma 59 (c1), we have that for all $w : [0, T_w] \to \mathbb{R}^m$, and for all $t \in [0, \epsilon_w)$, the following equality holds:

$$C^2(A^{22})^l A^{21} x_w^1(t) + C^2(A^{22})^{l+1} x_w^2(t)$$
$$= \widetilde{C}^2(\widetilde{A}^{22})^l \widetilde{A}^{21} \tilde{x}_w^1(t) + \widetilde{C}^2(\widetilde{A}^{22})^{l+1} \tilde{x}_w^2(t).$$

By applying Lemma 58 to the previous equation, we get

$$C^2(A^{22})^l A^{21}\vec{\sigma}\left(A^1 x_w(t) + B^1 u\right) + C^2(A^{22})^{l+1}\left(A^2 x_w(t) + B^2 u\right)$$
$$= \widetilde{C}^2(\widetilde{A}^{22})^l \widetilde{A}^{21}\vec{\sigma}\left(\widetilde{A}^1 \tilde{x}_w(t) + \widetilde{B}^1 u\right) + \widetilde{C}^2(\widetilde{A}^{22})^{l+1}\left(\widetilde{A}^2 \tilde{x}_w(t) + \widetilde{B}^2 u\right). \quad (68)$$

Because $(C^2(A^{22})^l A^{21})_{ji} \neq 0$, again by applying Lemma 57, we conclude that there exist $\pi(i) \in \{1, \ldots, \tilde{n}_1\}$, and $\beta(i) = \pm 1$, such that (a) and (c1) hold for this index i.

3. Because $j \in J_s$, then, in particular, (c1) holds for this j. Thus we have, for all $w(\cdot) \in [0, T_w] \to \mathbb{R}^m$, for all $t \in [0, \epsilon_w)$,

$$\left[A^{11}x_w^1(t) + A^{12}x_w^2(t)\right]_j = \beta(j)\left[\widetilde{A}^{11}\tilde{x}_w^1(t) + \widetilde{A}^{12}\tilde{x}_w^2(t)\right]_{\pi(j)}.$$

Thus Lemma 60 applies, and from conclusion (b1) of this lemma, we get, for all $l \geq 0$,

$$\left[A^{12}(A^{22})^l A^{21} x_w^1(t) + A^{12}(A^{22})^{l+1} x_w^2(t)\right]_j$$
$$= \beta(j)\left[\widetilde{A}^{12}(\widetilde{A}^{22})^l \widetilde{A}^{21} \tilde{x}_w^1(t) + \widetilde{A}^{12}(\widetilde{A}^{22})^{l+1} \tilde{x}_w^2(t)\right]_{\pi(j)}.$$

and

$$\left(A^{12}(A^{22})^l A^{21} x_w^1(t) + A^{12}(A^{22})^{l+1} x_w^2(t)\right)_i$$
$$= \left(T_1 \widetilde{A}^{12}(\widetilde{A}^{22})^l \widetilde{A}^{21} \tilde{x}_w^1(t) + T_1 \widetilde{A}^{12}(\widetilde{A}^{22})^{l+1} \tilde{x}_w^2(t)\right)_i \qquad (73)$$

By applying Lemma 58, from Eq. (73) we get

$$\left[A^{12}(A^{22})^l A^{21} \vec{\sigma}(A^1 x_w(t) + B^1 u) + A^{12}(A^{22})^{l+1}(A^2 x_w(t) + B^2 u)\right]_i$$
$$= \left[T_1 \widetilde{A}^{12}(\widetilde{A}^{22})^l \widetilde{A}^{21} \vec{\sigma}(\widetilde{A}^1 x_w(t) + \widetilde{B}^1 u)\right.$$
$$\left. + T_1 \widetilde{A}^{12}(\widetilde{A}^{22})^{l+1}(\widetilde{A}^2 \tilde{x}_w(t) + \widetilde{B}^2 u)\right]_i$$
$$= \left[T_1 \widetilde{A}^{12}(\widetilde{A}^{22})^l \widetilde{A}^{21} T_1^{-1} \vec{\sigma}(A^1 x_w(t) + (B^1, \widetilde{B}^{11})^T u)\right.$$
$$\left. + T_1 \widetilde{A}^{12}(\widetilde{A}^{22})^{l+1}(\widetilde{A}^2 \tilde{x}_w(t) + \widetilde{B}^2 u)\right]_i,$$

where, to get this last equality, we have used Eqs. (71) and (69). Now, because the function σ and the matrix B^1 are both admissible, by Lemma 57, we conclude:

$$\left(A^{12}(A^{22})^l A^{21}\right)_{ij} = \left(T_1 \widetilde{A}^{12}(\widetilde{A}^{22})^l \widetilde{A}^{21} T_1^{-1}\right)_{ij}, \qquad \forall i, j \in \{1, \ldots, n_1\}. \quad (74)$$

By Lemma 59, we also get, for all $l \geq 0$

$$C^2(A^{22})^l B^2 = \widetilde{C}^2(\widetilde{A}^{22})^l \widetilde{B}^2 \qquad (75)$$

and

$$\left(C^2(A^{22})^l A^{21}\right)_{ij} = \left(\widetilde{C}^2(\widetilde{A}^{22})^l \widetilde{A}^{21} T_1^{-1}\right)_{ij}$$
$$\forall i \in \{1, \ldots, p\}, \ \forall j \in \{1, \ldots, n_1\}. \quad (76)$$

Let

$$\widetilde{A}^{21} T_1^{-1} = (\widetilde{M}^{21}, \widetilde{N}^{21}),$$

where $\widetilde{M}^{21} \in \mathbb{R}^{\tilde{n}_2 \times n_1}$, and

$$T_1 \widetilde{A}^{12} = \begin{pmatrix} \widetilde{H}^{12} \\ \tilde{K}^{12} \end{pmatrix},$$

where $\widetilde{H}^{12} \in \mathbb{R}^{n_1 \times \tilde{n}_2}$. Then Eqs. (72), (74), (75), and (76) say that the two linear models,

$$\left(\begin{pmatrix} C^2 \\ A^{12} \end{pmatrix}, A^{22}, (B^2, A^{21})\right), \quad \left(\begin{pmatrix} \widetilde{C}^2 \\ \widetilde{H}^{12} \end{pmatrix}, \widetilde{A}^{22}, (\widetilde{B}^2, \widetilde{M}^{21})\right), \qquad (77)$$

are i/o equivalent. Because Σ_{n_1,n_2} is observable, we have $V_2 = 0$. So, by Lemma 62, the pair

$$\left(\begin{pmatrix} C^2 \\ A^{12} \end{pmatrix}, A^{22} \right)$$

is observable. Moreover, the pair $(A^{22}, (B^2, A^{21}))$ is controllable, by assumption, and thus, by the linear theory (see Theorem 17), we get $n_2 \leq \tilde{n}_2$.

So, in conclusion, $n = n_1 + n_2 \leq \tilde{n}_1 + \tilde{n}_2 = \tilde{n}$.

REMARK 63. Notice that, up to this point, we have only used the i/o equivalence of the two MNs together with the facts that $V_1 = 0$, $V_2 = 0$, and the pair $(A^{22}, (B^2, A^{21}))$ is controllable.

Now we must show that, if $n = \tilde{n}$, then (Σ_{n_1,n_2}, x_0) is equivalent to $(\tilde{\Sigma}_{\tilde{n}_1,\tilde{n}_2}, \tilde{x}_0)$. Note that, from what we have seen before, necessarily, $n_1 = \tilde{n}_1$ and $n_2 = \tilde{n}_2$. Moreover, we must have

$$\begin{aligned}
\tilde{B}^1 &= T_1^{-1} B^1 & \tilde{A}^{21} T_1^{-1} &= \tilde{M}^{21} \\
\tilde{C}^1 &= C^1 T_1 & T_1 \tilde{A}^{12} &= \tilde{H}^{12}.
\end{aligned} \tag{78}$$

On the other hand, by the linear theory (again Theorem 17), there must exists $T_2 \in GL(n_2)$, such that

$$\begin{pmatrix} \tilde{C}^2 \\ \tilde{H}^{12} \end{pmatrix} = \begin{pmatrix} C^2 \\ A^{12} \end{pmatrix} T_2, \qquad \tilde{A}^{22} = T_2^{-1} A^{22} T_2, \qquad (\tilde{B}^2 \tilde{M}^{21}) = T_2^{-1}(B^2 A^{21}). \tag{79}$$

By applying Lemma 58 to Eq. (71), we also have

$$\begin{aligned}
&\left[A^{11} \vec{\sigma} \left(A^1 x_w(t) + B^1 u \right) + A^{12} \left(A^2 x_w(t) + B^2 u \right) \right]_i \\
&= \left[T_1 \tilde{A}^{11} T_1^{-1} \vec{\sigma} \left(A^1 x_w(t) + B^1 u \right) + T_1 \tilde{A}^{12} \left(\tilde{A}^2 \tilde{x}_w(t) + \tilde{B}^2 u \right) \right]_i.
\end{aligned}$$

Clearly, this equality implies

$$A^{11} = T_1 \tilde{A}^{11} T_1^{-1}. \tag{80}$$

Now let

$$T = \begin{pmatrix} T_1 & 0 \\ 0 & T_2 \end{pmatrix}.$$

Clearly, $T \in \mathcal{G}_n$, and by (78), (79), and (80), we have

$$\tilde{C} = CT, \qquad \tilde{A} = T^{-1} A T, \qquad \tilde{B} = T^{-1} B. \tag{81}$$

So, to complete the proof, we need only show that $\tilde{x}_0 = T^{-1} x_0$. Let $x_1 = T \tilde{x}_0$. Because $(\Sigma_{n_1,n_2}, x_0) \sim (\tilde{\Sigma}_{\tilde{n}_1,\tilde{n}_2}, \tilde{x}_0)$, and (81) holds, we conclude that x_0 is in-

[6] M. Talagrand. Resultats rigoureux pour le model de Hopfield. *C. R. Acad. Sci. Paris Sér. I Math.* 321:109–112, 1995.

[7] A. Bovier and V. Gayrard. Lower bounds on the memory capacity of the dilute Hopfield model. In *Cellular Automata and Cooperative Systems*, pp. 55–66. Les Houches, Paris, 1992 (reprinted in *NATO Adv. Sci. Inst. Ser. C Math. Phys. Sci.* 396).

[8] E. D. Sontag. Neural nets as systems models and controllers. In *Proceedings of the Seventh Yale Workshop on Adaptive and Learning Systems*, Yale University, New Haven, CT, 1992, pp. 73–79.

[9] M. Matthews. A state-space approach to adaptive nonlinear filtering using recurrent neural networks. In *Proceedings of the 1990 IASTED Symposium on Artificial Intelligence Applications and Neural Networks*, Zürich, July 1990, pp. 197–200.

[10] M. M. Polycarpou and P. A. Ioannou. Neural networks and on-line approximators for adaptive control. In *Proceedings of the Seventh Yale Workshop on Adaptive and Learning Systems*, Yale University, New Haven, 1992, pp. 93–98.

[11] H. J. Sussmann. Uniqueness of the weights for minimal feedforward nets with a given input-output map. *Neural Networks* 5:589–593, 1992.

[12] F. Albertini and E. D. Sontag. For neural networks, function determines form. *Neural Networks* 6:975–990, 1993.

[13] F. Albertini and E. D. Sontag. Uniqueness of weights for recurrent nets. In *Proceedings of Mathematical Theory of Networks and Systems*, Regensburg, Germany, August 1993.

[14] F. Albertini and E. D. Sontag. State observability in recurrent neural networks. *Systems Control Lett.* 22:235–244, 1994.

[15] F. Albertini and P. Dai Pra. Forward accessibility for recurrent neural networks. *IEEE Trans. Automat. Control* 40:1962–1968, 1995.

[16] H. T. Siegelmann and E. D. Sontag. On the computational power of neural nets. *J. Comput. System. Sci.* 50:132–150, 1995.

[17] R. Koplon and E. D. Sontag. Using Fourier-neural networks to fit sequential input/output data. *Neurocomputing*, to appear.

[18] A. N. Michel, J. A. Farrell, and W. Porod. Qualitative analysis of neural networks. *IEEE Trans. Circuits Systems I Fund. Theory Appl.* 36:229–243, 1989.

[19] K. Romanik. Approximate testing and learnability. In *Proceedings of the Fifth ACM Workshop on Computational Learning Theory*, Pittsburgh, PA, July 1992.

[20] B. Dasgupta and E. D. Sontag. Sample complexity for learning recurrent perceptron mappings. *IEEE Trans. Inform. Theory* 42:1479–1487, 1996.

[21] P. Koiran and E. D. Sontag. Vapnik-Chervonenkis dimension of recurrent neural networks. Unpublished.

[22] E. D. Sontag. *Mathematical Control Theory: Deterministic Finite Dimensional Systems.* Springer-Verlag, New York, 1990.

[23] F. Albertini and P. Dai Pra. Observability of discrete-time recurrent neural networks coupled with linear systems. In *Proceedings of the European Control Conference*, Rome, September 5–8, 1995, pp. 1586–1589.

[24] F. Albertini and P. Dai Pra. Recurrent neural networks coupled with linear systems: observability in continuous and discrete time. *Systems Control Lett.* 27:109–116, 1996.

[25] F. Albertini, E. D. Sontag, and V. Maillot. Uniqueness of weights for neural networks. In *Artificial Neural Networks with Applications in Speech and Vision* (R. Mammone, Ed.), pp. 115–125. Chapman & Hall, London, 1993.

[26] R. Hermann and A. J. Krener. Nonlinear controllability and observability. *IEEE Trans. Automat. Control.* AC-22:728–740, 1977.

[27] H. Nijmeijer. Observability of autonomous discrete time non-linear systems: a geometric approach. *Internat. J. Control* 36:867–874, 1982.

[28] F. Albertini and D. D'Alessandro. Remarks on the observability of discrete-time nonlinear systems. In *Proceedings of the IFIP, System Modeling and Optimization*, Prague, July 10–14, 1995.

[29] H. J. Sussmann. Orbits of families of vector fields and integrability of distributions. *Trans. Amer. Math. Soc.* 180:171–188, 1973.

[30] E. D. Sontag and H. J. Sussmann. Complete controllability of continuous-time recurrent neural networks. *Systems Control Lett.* 30:177–183, 1997.

[31] R. B. Koplon. *Linear systems with constrained outputs and transitions.* Ph.D. Thesis, Rutgers University, New Brunswick, NJ, 1994.

[32] E. D. Sontag. Feedback stabilization using two-hidden-layer nets. In *IEEE Trans. Neural Networks* 3:981–990, 1992.

If, therefore, $x_{\setminus i}$ denotes $\{x_j: j \neq i\}$, then

$$\log \left\{ \frac{p(x_i = 1|x_{\setminus i})}{p(x_i = 0|x_{\setminus i})} \right\} = \sum_j w_{ij} x_j. \tag{2}$$

It is assumed that $w_{ij} = w_{ji}$, for all i, j, and that $w_{ii} = 0$, for all i. In practice, it may be that node i receives inputs from only a subset of the other units, corresponding to $w_{ij} > 0$. Such units form the *neighborhood* of i, denoted by ∂i, so that

$$\log \left\{ \frac{p(x_i = 1|x_{\setminus i})}{p(x_i = 0|x_{\setminus i})} \right\} = \sum_{j \in \partial i} w_{ij} x_j.$$

Suppose that at each stage a node is chosen at random for updating and is updated according to the above stochastic rule. Repetition of this procedure generates a sequence of states for the network of nodes that corresponds to a Markov chain, with stationary transition probabilities, on the 2^n-dimensional state space. At any given stage there is a positive probability that the state will remain unchanged, so that the chain is *aperiodic*. Furthermore, if the neighborhood system is also such that the chain is *irreducible*, that is, such that any state can be reached, with positive probability, from any other state, in finite time, then the chain is *ergodic*, and it follows that the Markov chain has a stationary probability distribution given by the Boltzmann–Gibbs distribution,

$$p(x) = \{Z(W)\}^{-1} \exp\{-E(x)\}, \tag{3}$$

for all x, where

$$E(x) = - \sum_{i > j} w_{ij} x_i x_j,$$

W denotes the matrix of weights $\{w_{ij}\}$, and

$$Z(W) = \sum_x \exp\{-E(x)\}$$

is the appropriate normalizing constant, called the *partition function,* a term from the literature in statistical physics. There are various other points of contact with statistical physics. Section 20.3.5 of Titterington and Anderson [1] briefly notes, with references, the relationship between Boltzmann machines and spin-glass models, and we allude to another interface later in Section V.G.

The plan of the rest of the chapter is as follows. In Section II we indicate the links between the dynamics of the Boltzmann machine with the Markov chain Monte Carlo techniques that are currently proving to be so useful in statistics and, in particular, in Bayesian methods. Section III reminds the reader of the Boltzmann machine's origins as stochastic versions of Hopfield nets, and Section IV introduces the feature of hidden nodes, which gives Boltzmann machines so much added flexibility. The main purpose of the chapter is to discuss methods that have been developed for training Boltzmann machines. These are outlined in Section V, which concentrates on the relationship of most of the algorithms to the statistical paradigm of parameter estimation by maximum likelihood. The particular algorithms are taken from both the neural computation literature and from modern publications in statistics. Sections VI and VII illustrate some of the algorithms in detail with examples without and with hidden units, respectively. The examples are, admittedly, of trivial dimensions, but this allows a comparatively detailed study. Section VIII describes a number of modifications of the basic Boltzmann machine, and Section IX briefly mentions a few possible developments for the future.

II. RELATIONSHIP WITH MARKOV CHAIN MONTE CARLO METHODS

One consequence of the above discussion is that, if the updating rule is applied many times, starting from any arbitrary state, then, in the long term, the procedure generates a realization from the probability distribution (3), by what is essentially a version of the so-called *Gibbs sampler,* which is one of a class of simulation procedures that have recently become known as *Markov chain Monte Carlo* (MCMC) methods. The method is also known as the *heat-bath method* and as *Glauber dynamics.* If n is large, it is not practicable to sample directly from (3), because of the size of the state–space (2^n elements) and the consequent infeasibility of computing the partition function. MCMC methods are designed to obviate this difficulty by constructing a Markov chain whose limiting distribution is the distribution of interest. In the case of the Gibbs sampler, the general rationale is as follows.

Of interest is the generation of a high-dimensional random vector $x = (x_1, \ldots, x_n)$ from a joint distribution $p(x)$. Instead of doing this directly, one generates a sequence of realizations of a Markov chain whose transition rules are based on the *n full conditional* distributions $\{p(x_i|x_{\setminus i})\}$. Typically, the full conditional distributions are much more manageable; in particular, the corresponding normalizing constant is easily computed. In the case where $p(x)$ is given by (3), the Gibbs sampler leads to the updating rule (2). The only minor difference between Gibbs sampling and the procedure described in Section I is that, in Gibbs sampling, the updating cycle usually cycles systematically through the elements of x, rather than choosing from them at random; the equilibrium behavior is not altered by this change in practice.

IV. HIDDEN UNITS

Although we shall regard the model introduced in Section I as a Boltzmann machine, the incorporation of *hidden nodes* is an important feature of Boltzmann machines as used in practice. In fact, the vector of node states, x, may well represent three types of variable, namely, *inputs, outputs,* and *hidden variables*. The inputs and outputs, which we shall denote by x_I and x_O, both correspond to *visible* units and represent physical quantities; we shall write $x_V = (x_I, x_O)$. The hidden units are created to add flexibility to the model, and we shall denote the corresponding set of variables by x_H. Thus, $x = (x_V, x_H) = (x_I, x_O, x_H)$. We shall denote the corresponding numbers of variables (i.e., nodes) by n_I, n_O, n_V and n_H, so that $n = n_V + n_H = n_I + n_O + n_H$.

When the Boltzmann machine is evolving, according to the stochastic updating rules, all units are treated in the same way, except in cases in which x_I is fixed (*clamped,* in the neural computing terminology), so that, in the long term, realizations are generated from the (joint) stationary distribution for x. However, the distribution of interest in practice is

$$p(x_V) = \sum_{x_H} p(x_V, x_H), \tag{4}$$

or, if x_I is clamped,

$$p(x_O | x_I) = \sum_{x_H} p(x_O, x_H | x_I).$$

Because (4) can be written in the mixture-distribution form,

$$p(x_V) = \sum_{x_H} p(x_V | x_H) p(x_H),$$

we can see that the hidden variables are what are called *latent variables* in statistics. They add flexibility to the structure of the models in the same way as mixture models, factor analysis models, and latent class models.

The features underlying the structure of Boltzmann machines are the numbers of nodes, visible and hidden; the pattern of internodal connections; and the connection weights. Recalling the relationship between Boltzmann machines and Gibbs distributions, we note that these features relate to statistical model building (in terms of the choice of the nodes and connections) and selection of parameter values (so far as the choice of weights is concerned). The art of model building involves the familiar objectives of balancing parsimony of structure with the complexity of the task that has been set; for instance, one may aim to "minimize," in some sense, the number of hidden nodes while ensuring that the model is sufficiently rich. So far as choice of weights is concerned, the approach depends on the objective of the whole exercise. When Boltzmann machines are used in the solution of optimization problems, the appropriate weights are determined by the particular task; see, for instance, Aarts and Korst [8] and Section 20.5 of Titterington and Anderson [1]. In this article, however, we shall concentrate mainly on the interpretation of Boltzmann machine learning as an exercise in statistical parameter estimation.

V. TRAINING A BOLTZMANN MACHINE

In this section, we consider what can be done if the parameters are unknown, although we do assume that the architecture (*i.e.*, the model) is given. We identify the Boltzmann machine with its stationary distribution, with the result that we are interested in estimating the parameters of a type of *exponential family distribution;* see, for instance, Cox and Hinkley [12, p. 12]. To see this, note that

$$\log p(x) = \sum_{i>j} w_{ij} x_i x_j + \text{constant},$$

where the constant does not depend on x. Thus the parameters, in W, and certain functions of the variables, which contribute to what are known as the *sufficient statistics,* are combined in a simple way.

The usual scenario is that a training set is available, which is assumed to come from the marginal stationary distribution for the visible variables, but we shall also consider the case in which a target distribution is prescribed for the visible variables and the objective is to find the best approximating Boltzmann machine with a given architecture. In statistical terms, this amounts to finding the best approximating exponential-family distribution, within a particular class, to the prescribed distribution.

We shall see that there are close relationships with Amari's information geometry of exponential family distributions, with maximum likelihood estimation and with the Iterative Proportional Fitting Procedure (IPFP) [13] used for fitting log-linear models to categorical data.

We shall denote the target distribution by $\{r(x): x \in \mathcal{X}\}$, and we shall denote the class of Boltzmann machines of a specified architecture by $\mathcal{B}$. Thus we envisage each $p \in \mathcal{B}$ to be of the form (3), but with parameters $\{w_{ij}\}$ to be chosen. Target distributions representing a training set D are simply the corresponding sets of relative frequencies. The training set itself is assumed to be a set of N independent n-dimensional realizations from $\mathcal{X}$:

$$D = \{x^{(1)}, \ldots, x^{(N)}\}.$$

We shall define

$$p_{ij} = \mathbb{E}_p(x_i x_j) = \text{Prob}_p(x_i = x_j = 1)$$

and similarly for r_{ij}, for all i, j, where $\mathbb{E}$ denotes expectation.

A. THE CASE WITHOUT HIDDEN UNITS

Ackley *et al.* [14] proposed the following rule for iteratively modifying the weights $\{w_{ij}\}$: w_{ij} changes to $w_{ij} + \Delta w_{ij}$, where

$$\Delta w_{ij} = \eta(r_{ij} - p_{ij}); \tag{5}$$

see also Hinton and Sejnowski [15]. Various remarks can be made about (5).

(i) In the terminology of exponential-family distributions, $\{w_{ij}\}$ are the *natural* parameters and $\{\sum_{k=1}^{N} x_i^{(k)} x_j^{(k)}\}$ are the associated *minimal sufficient statistics*, as revealed by the formula for the *likelihood function*, which is defined to be the joint probability function of all the data, regarded as a function of W:

$$\text{Lik}(W) = \prod_{k=1}^{N} p(x^{(k)}) = \{Z(W)\}^{-N} \exp\left\{ \sum_{i<j} w_{ij}\left(\sum_{k} x_i^{(k)} x_j^{(k)} \right) \right\}.$$

(ii) Expression (5) defines a gradient-descent rule for minimizing $I(r; p)$ with respect to W, where p is given by (3) and

$$I(q; p) = \sum_{x} r(x) \log\{r(x)/p(x)\}, \tag{6}$$

which is the Kullback–Leibler directed divergence between r and p; see also Luttrell [16]. (We assume in (ii) that $p(x) > 0$ whenever $r(x) > 0$ and that $0 \cdot \log 0 = 0$.)

Of course, minimizing $I(r; p)$ is equivalent to maximizing

$$\sum_{x} r(x) \log p(x),$$

which is the log-likelihood function in the case where r represents a training sample. To prove (ii), note that

$$\sum_{x} r(x) \log p(x) = \tfrac{1}{2} \sum_{x} r(x) x^T W x - \log Z(W)$$

$$= \sum_{x} r(x)\left(\sum_{i<j} w_{ij} x_i x_j \right) - \log Z(W)$$

$$= \sum_{i<j} r_{ij} w_{ij} - \log Z(W).$$

Thus

$$\frac{\partial I(r; p)}{\partial w_{ij}} = -\left(r_{ij} - \frac{\partial \log Z(W)}{\partial w_{ij}}\right) = (r_{ij} - p_{ij}),$$

by standard exponential-family theory, so that (5) can be written

$$\Delta w_{ij} = -\eta \frac{\partial I(r; p)}{\partial w_{ij}},$$

as required. The parameter η is the step size in the gradient descent algorithm, and, as usual, its choice will affect the convergence characteristics of the procedure.

The practical problem in implementing the algorithm is the calculation of p_{ij}. It is not a realistic proposition to compute this analytically, and in practice p_{ij} is estimated by $\tilde{p}_{ij}$, a relative frequency generated by simulation. This is in itself a time-consuming operation: each realization that contributes to $\tilde{p}_{ij}$ involves either iterating the relevant Gibbs sampler to stationarity or continuing a Markov chain Monte Carlo procedure long enough to nullify the effects of serial correlation; see, for instance, Besag and Green [17], Gelman and Rubin [18], and Geyer [19].

B. THE CASE WITH HIDDEN UNITS

The algorithm must be modified when there are hidden units. Recall that $x = (x_V, x_H)$, where x_V denotes the values of the visible units and x_H denotes those of the hidden units. Then the training data take the form $D = \{x_V^{(k)}, k = 1, \dots, N\}$ and the maximum likelihood estimation problem is to maximize, with respect to W,

$$\sum_{x_V} r_V(x_V) \log p_V(x_V),$$

where, for instance,

$$p_V(x_V) = p_V(x_V|W) = \sum_{x_H} p(x|W).$$

Equivalently, we have to minimize $I(r_V; p_V)$. In this case, the gradient descent rule is

$$\Delta w_{ij} = \eta\big(q_{ij}(W) - p_{ij}(W)\big), \qquad (7)$$

where p_{ij} is as before, and

$$q_{ij}(W) = \mathbb{E}\left\{N^{-1} \sum_{k=1}^{N} x_i^{(k)} x_j^{(k)} \Big| D, W\right\}.$$

When i and j correspond to visible units, $q_{ij} = r_{ij}$; otherwise, q_{ij} involves a conditional expectation. Thus, in general, both q_{ij} and p_{ij} involve expectations, which in practice must be estimated by simulation. The neural network terminology goes as follows. The updating of w_{ij} contains two phases: in the *positive phase* simulation (for q_{ij}), the visible units are *clamped* at the values given in the training set, so that the resulting realizations follow the required conditional distribution; the *negative-phase* simulation (for p_{ij}) is free-running, with no unit clamped.

Thus the complete training algorithm is iterative and each stage requires a large Monte Carlo exercise. As a result, it is notoriously slow to train a Boltzmann machine using a training set, although DeGloria *et al.* [20] indicate one way of speeding up the algorithm.

C. RELATIONSHIP WITH THE EM ALGORITHM

The case with hidden units fits naturally into the class of problems to which the EM algorithm [21] can be applied. The EM algorithm is a general iterative procedure for calculating maximum likelihood estimates in problems involving incomplete data. Suppose the log-likelihood of interest is $L(W)$, and that we seek to maximize this with respect to W. Let us expand the notation, writing $L(W; D)$ to indicate the dependence on the training data. Correspondingly, we write $L_c(W) = L_c(W; D_c)$ to denote the log-likelihood associated with the so-called *complete data*, D_c. In the context of Boltzmann machines, D_c includes the values for the hidden nodes for all of the realizations: $D_c = \{(x_V^{(k)}, x_H^{(k)}),$ $k = 1, \ldots, N\}$. Each iteration of the EM algorithm updates a current approximation, $W^{(s)}$, say, for the maximum likelihood estimate, to a better approximation, $W^{(s+1)}$. The iteration consists of an E-step and an M-step, defined as follows:

E-step: Compute $Q(W; D) = \mathbb{E}\{L_c(W; D_c)|D, W^{(s)}\}$
M-step: Find $W = W^{(s+1)}$ to maximize $Q(W; D)$

The EM algorithm has the appealing property of being monotonic, in that $L(W^{(s+1)}) \geq L(W^{(s)})$, so that the algorithm will converge to a local, if not necessarily a global, maximum of the log-likelihood of interest. In the case of the Boltzmann machine, the EM iteration turns out to have a particularly simple formulation, characteristic of exponential-family distributions, in that $W^{(s)}$ is updated to $W^{(s+1)}$, where $W^{(s+1)}$ solves

$$p_{ij}\left(W^{(s+1)}\right) = q_{ij}\left(W^{(s)}\right),$$

for all i, j; one computes, in the E-step, the expected values $q_{ij}(W^{(s)})$ of the sufficient statistics, given D and assuming that $W^{(s)}$ are the correct weights, and the M-step equates them to the unconditional expected values at the new set of weights, $W^{(s+1)}$. This gives, usually, a complicated set of equations. As before, each $q_{ij}(W^{(s)})$ usually must be computed using simulation.

D. DISCUSSION OF THE CASE WITH TRAINING DATA

The principal obstacle to the widespread use of Boltzmann machines and their associated stationary distributions in practice is the need for Monte Carlo methods, in both running and training the machines. Considerable parallelism is possible, but much benefit would be gained from faster Markov chain Monte Carlo methods and innovative maximum likelihood procedures.

An example of the latter is the work of Geyer and Thompson [22]. For simplicity, consider the case of no hidden unit, so that we are required to find W to maximize

$$L(W) = \tfrac{1}{2} \sum_{k=1}^{N} x^{(k)T} W x^{(k)} - N \log Z(W). \qquad (8)$$

Now,

$$Z(W) = \sum_{x} \exp\left(\tfrac{1}{2} x^{T} W x\right)$$
$$= Z(V) \sum_{x} \exp\left\{\tfrac{1}{2} x^{T} (W - V) x\right\} p(x|V),$$

where V is any set of weights. Thus,

$$\log Z(W) = \log Z(V) + \log d(W),$$

where

$$d(W) = \sum_{x} \exp\left\{\tfrac{1}{2} x^{T} (W - V) x\right\} p(x|V). \qquad (9)$$

If now $X^{(1)}, \ldots, X^{(s)}$ are realizations from $p(x|V)$, $d(W)$ can be estimated, for any W, by

$$d_s(W) = s^{-1} \sum_{l=1}^{s} \exp\left\{\tfrac{1}{2} X^{(l)T} (W - V) X^{(l)}\right\},$$

and the maximizer of

$$L_1(W) = \tfrac{1}{2} \sum_{k=1}^{N} x^{(k)T} W x^{(k)} - N \log d_s(W)$$

is used as an approximation to the maximizer of $L(W)$.

The rescaling procedure is explicit, it does not involve Monte Carlo, and it effectively fits a member of a class of log-linear models by maximum likelihood.

G. PARAMETER ESTIMATION USING MEAN-FIELD APPROXIMATIONS

The links with statistical physics bear fruit in the form of an approximate approach that can be used in various contexts including parameter estimation. This so-called Mean-Field Theory can be derived in various ways, one of which is the following. Suppose a random vector x has a probability distribution given by (3) and we wish to evaluate $\mathbb{E}(x_i)$, say. In view of the complicated partition function, $Z(W)$, this is usually not practicable, so an approximation, to be written $\langle x_i \rangle$, is defined as being $\mathbb{E}(x_i)$ evaluated as if all other x_j are fixed at their own mean-field approximations. Thus

$$\langle x_i \rangle = \mathbb{E}\{x_i | x_{\partial i} = \langle x_{\partial i} \rangle\},$$

that is,

$$\langle x_i \rangle = \sum_{x_i} x_i \exp\left\{x_i \sum_{j \in x_{\partial i}} w_{ij} \langle x_j \rangle\right\} \Big/ \sum_{x_i} \exp\left\{x_i \sum_{j \in x_{\partial i}} w_{ij} \langle x_j \rangle\right\}.$$

Because x_i can only take the values 0 and 1, we obtain

$$\langle x_i \rangle = \exp\left\{\sum_{j \in x_{\partial i}} w_{ij} \langle x_j \rangle\right\} \Big/ \left[1 + \exp\left\{\sum_{j \in x_{\partial i}} w_{ij} \langle x_j \rangle\right\}\right], \qquad \text{for all } i. \quad (15)$$

These equations can be solved numerically, for a given W, to give the set of values $\{\langle x_i \rangle\}$. One can similarly obtain corresponding equations for $\langle x_i x_j \rangle, i \neq j$, but it is common practice to make a further approximation and take

$$\langle x_i x_j \rangle = \langle x_i \rangle \langle x_j \rangle, \qquad (16)$$

with $\{\langle x_i \rangle\}$ obtained from (15). Values from (16) can then be used, instead of sample means from Monte Carlo simulation, in approximating, as appropriate, r_{ij} and p_{ij} in (5) or q_{ij} and p_{ij} in (7). The experience of Peterson and Anderson [25] is that the mean-field approach performs very well, with speed-up factors of up to 30 over the simulation approach.

It is also possible to define a mean-field approximation to $p(x)$ itself, by

$$p_{MF}(x) = \prod_i p(x_i | x_{\partial i} = \langle x_{\partial i} \rangle), \qquad (17)$$

which bears strong similarity to Besag's [26] pseudo-likelihood,

$$p_{PL}(x) = \prod_i p(x_i|x_{\partial i}).$$

Clearly, both (15) and (16) follow from (17).

Various aspects of Mean-Field Theory approximations are discussed in Amit [11], Hertz *et al.* [27], and Mezard *et al.* [28]. The theory is used by Geiger and Girosi [29] in image restoration, and Zhang [30] uses (17) as the basis of a practicable EM algorithm for dependent, incomplete data. Further applications of this type are mentioned later in Section VIII.C. However, the deterministic aspects of the method raise some concern about the statistical properties of resulting estimators; see, for instance, Dunmur and Titterington [31].

H. THE METHOD OF GELFAND AND CARLIN

Gelfand and Carlin [32] present a Monte Carlo method for obtaining maximum likelihood estimates when there are missing data. Geyer's [33] account of the method is as follows. Let the complete data be represented by $D_c = (D, D_m)$, where D_m denotes the missing data, and write

$$p(D_c|W) = p(D, D_m|W) = h(D, D_m|W)/Z_c(W),$$

where $Z_c(W)$ is the partition function and $h(D, D_m|W)$ is defined as appropriate. It turns out to be convenient to work in terms of likelihood ratios, relative to the model corresponding to an arbitrary set of weights V, say, so that the logarithm of the likelihood ratio, based on data x, is

$$l(W) = \log\left[\mathbb{E}_V\left\{\frac{h(D, D_m|W)}{h(D, D_m|V)}\Big|D\right\}\right] - \log\left[\mathbb{E}_V\left\{\frac{h(D, D_m|W)}{h(D, D_m|V)}\right\}\right].$$

In practice, the expectations are estimated by sample averages. Numerical maximization of $l(W)$ can then be undertaken. Note that Geyer [33] suggests that it is better to calculate the first term exactly, where possible, in contrast to Gelfand and Carlin's [32] suggestion that the calculation should be carried out iteratively, using successive estimates of W as the choice for V in the following iteration.

In the case of Boltzmann machine training, based on a sample of N realizations, we have $D_c = \{(x_1^{(k)}, \ldots, x_{n_V}^{(k)}, x_{n_V+1}^{(k)}, \ldots, x_{n_V+n_H}^{(k)}); k = 1, \ldots, N\}$, with n_V visible units and n_H hidden units, and

$$h(D, D_m)|W) = \exp\left(\sum_k \sum_{i<j} w_{ij} x_i^{(k)} x_j^{(k)}\right).$$

Thus,

$$\frac{h(D, D_m|W)}{h(D, D_m|V)} = \exp\left\{\sum_k \sum_{i<j} (w_{ij} - v_{ij})x_i^{(k)}x_j^{(k)}\right\}.$$

As a result, the Gelfand and Carlin log-likelihood ratio for training Boltzmann machines is

$$l(W) = \log\left[\mathbb{E}_V\left\{\exp\left(\sum_{k=1}^N \sum_{i<j} (w_{ij} - v_{ij})x_i^{(k)}x_j^{(k)}\right)\Big| D\right\}\right]$$

$$- \log\left[\mathbb{E}_V\left\{\exp\left(\sum_{k=1}^N \sum_{i<j} (w_{ij} - v_{ij})x_i^{(k)}x_j^{(k)}\right)\right\}\right].$$

In principle, this is now maximized numerically, with the expectations replaced by sample averages.

I. DISCUSSION

In both of the cases with and without hidden units, we have more than one possible algorithm for training a Boltzmann machine. For instance, if there is no hidden unit, we may use the gradient-descent algorithm (5) or the IPFP algorithm described in Section V.F. If there are hidden units, we may apply the gradient-descent algorithm (7) or the alternating minimization algorithm (11,12). To implement the gradient-descent algorithm, we must choose the step length, η, and a time-consuming aspect of the method is the need to carry out both simulation and iteration steps. With the IPFP/alternating minimization approach, also iterative, no simulation is necessary, apart from the possible need to estimate the $\{r_{ij}\}$. Byrne [24] reports a limited amount of numerical experimentation using the alternating minimization algorithm, but as yet no meaningful comparison has been carried out with the gradient-descent approach.

We now return to the EM algorithm. As Byrne [24] points out, the alternating minimization algorithm is an EM algorithm, with (11) representing the E-step and (12) the M-step. Indeed, this represents a particular version of a more general formulation of EM algorithms as alternating minimization algorithms based on the divergence $I(r; p)$.

The objective is to optimize p within some parametric class, $\mathcal{B}$, and r is constrained so as to be compatible with the observed data, i.e., $r \in \mathcal{D}$, say. Then the EM algorithm for updating p^t to p^{t+1} is

E-step: evaluate $I(r^t; p^t) = \min_{r \in \mathcal{D}} I(r; p^t)$
M-step: $p^{t+1} = \arg\min_{p \in \mathcal{B}} I(r^t; p)$.

Amari [34] prefers to refer to these two geometrically motivated steps in general as the *e-step* and *m-step* components of what he calls the *em algorithm*. He shows that, in many particular problems, including that of Boltzmann machines, the EM and em algorithms are identical, but that examples do exist for which the two algorithms are different. Another discussion of when the EM algorithm can be represented in 'em' terms appears in Csiszár and Tusnády [35], and the relationship is discussed by Neal and Hinton [36].

The EM algorithm also appears at a different level. As Anderson and Titterington [37] point out, each stage of the IPFP algorithm can be interpreted as an EM iteration, an observation that can be used to help establish the convergence of IPFP when used to solve (12).

VI. AN EXAMPLE WITH NO HIDDEN UNIT

In this and the following section, we provide numerical illustrations of the training algorithms described in Section V. The examples in this paper are of extremely small scale, so that the properties of the various estimation procedures can be assessed in detail.

First we consider Boltzmann machines with no hidden unit, so that the training problem is simplified. In fact, for this case, the surface in the parameter space defined by the Kullback–Leibler metric is concave when viewed from above [14], and so the log-likelihood surface, which is, up to an additive constant, the negative of the Kullback–Leibler distance between the empirical distribution from the data and the theoretical distribution, should be unimodal. Thus training procedures such as the simple gradient-descent rule defined by Ackley *et al.* [14] will not become trapped in local optima, and the results should be independent of the starting values.

The standard example we shall use in this section is a completely connected, three-node Boltzmann machine with one bias node, called node 0. This is shown in Fig. 1, with the values of the connection weights attached. A standard test data set (TD_1) was obtained by annealing the network to equilibrium and then running for 10,000 cycles, at each stage flipping the state of a random node and collecting the state vectors at the end of each cycle. Further versions of the data set, denoted by TD_k for various values of k, were generated by running the Boltzmann machine for a larger number $(10,000k)$ of iterations, but collecting a state vector only once every k iterations, so that successive state vectors should manifest lower serial correlation. Of course, with a network of this simplicity, it would be quite straightforward to calculate the corresponding set of multinomial probabilities and to simulate realizations directly, but the Boltzmann machine dynamics were implemented instead, to investigate informally the effects of serial correlation.

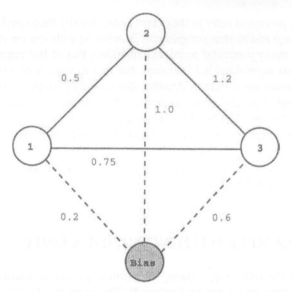

Figure 1 Architecture and weights for a simple Boltzmann machine with three nodes and bias node.

A. EXACT LIKELIHOOD ESTIMATION

As a result of the deliberately small scale of the example, it is possible to calculate and optimize the log-likelihood explicitly; exact computation of the partition function is feasible. As usual, w_{ij} denotes the connection weight between nodes i and j, and x_i^l denotes the particular binary (0/1) state of node i when the Boltzmann machine is represented by state vector x^l, where the eight possible state vectors are indexed in the order $\{0, 0, 0\}$, $\{0, 0, 1\}$, $\{0, 1, 0\}$, $\{1, 0, 0\}$, $\{1, 1, 0\}$, $\{1, 0, 1\}$, $\{0, 1, 1\}$, $\{1, 1, 1\}$. Then the log-likelihood for weights W is

$$L(W) = \sum_{l=1}^{8} N_l \left(\sum_{i<j} w_{ij} x_i^l x_j^l \right) - N \log Z(W), \qquad (18)$$

where N_l is the number of replications of the lth state in the complete set of n observations. The partition function $Z(W)$ takes the form

$$Z(W) = \sum_{l=1}^{8} \exp \left(\sum_{i<j} w_{ij} x_i^l x_j^l \right).$$

Both of the terms in (18) can be calculated very quickly once $\{N_l\}$ and $\{w_{ij}\}$ have been specified, and $L(W)$ can be maximized numerically by a routine from a sub-

Table I

True Weights, Maximum Likelihood Estimates, and Approximate 95% Confidence Intervals for the Network in Fig. 1, from 10,000 Realizations

Weight	True value	MLE[a]	Confidence interval
w_{12}	0.50	0.466	(0.311, 0.621)
w_{13}	0.75	0.715	(0.572, 0.858)
w_{23}	1.20	1.061	(0.884, 1.238)
w_{10}	0.20	0.246	(0.067, 0.425)
w_{20}	1.00	1.095	(0.913, 1.276)
w_{30}	0.60	0.777	(0.594, 0.959)

[a] MLE, Maximum likelihood estimate.

routine library; in our work we used the NAg Fortran Subroutine Library [38]. Table I displays the estimates that resulted from the application of this calculation to the data set TD_{50}. The table shows the upper triangle of the matrix of maximum likelihood estimates of the weights, along with the true weights. According to standard asymptotic theory for maximum likelihood estimation, the covariance matrix of the estimators can be approximated by the negative of the inverse of the matrix of second derivatives of $L(W)$, evaluated at the estimates. Approximate 95% confidence intervals for the true values of the parameters can then be calculated, assuming asymptotic Gaussianity, again as a consequence of standard theory. In this example, the corresponding intervals are quite wide (see Table I), and all intervals do cover the true values.

Table II contains the approximate, asymptotic correlation matrix of the estimators. The correlation structure results from the highly interconnected nature of

Table II

Approximate Correlation Matrix for the MLEs of the Weights in the Network in Fig. 1, from 10,000 Realizations

	w_{13}	w_{23}	w_{10}	w_{20}	w_{30}
w_{12}	−0.13	−0.13	−0.68	−0.50	0.18
w_{13}		−0.07	−0.59	0.14	−0.47
w_{23}			0.15	−0.71	−0.77
w_{10}				0.28	0.17
w_{20}					0.47

Table IV

True Weights Corresponding to the
Boltzmann Machine Models *BM*1 and *BM*2[a]

Weight	BM1	BM2
w_{12}	0.50	0.50
w_{13}	0.75	0.50
w_{14}	0.20	0.50
w_{23}	1.20	0.50
w_{24}	0.10	0.50
w_{34}	0.60	0.50
w_{15}	0.30	0.50
w_{25}	0.50	0.50
w_{35}	1.80	0.50
w_{45}	1.00	0.50
w_{10}	0.10	0.25
w_{20}	0.95	0.25
w_{30}	0.80	0.25
w_{40}	1.10	0.25
w_{50}	0.60	0.25

[a] Node 5 is a hidden node, and Node 0 is a bias node.

A value also must be selected for the learning rate, η. After some experimentation with $\eta \in \{0.2, 1.0, 2.0\}$, we decided to use $\eta = 0.2$, because, although the steps taken by the algorithm were quite small, this choice did seem to lead eventually to the largest value of the observed-data log-likelihood, $L(W)$. The algorithm was deemed to have converged if, in a given iteration, the change in each weight was less than a particular tolerance level; an "iteration" corresponds to a complete pass through the set of weights. An alternative way of measuring convergence would be to look at changes in the value of $L(W)$. The results of gradient-descent training for *BM*1 and *BM*2, using a convergence tolerance of 10^{-5}, are shown in Table V, along with the attained value of $L(W)$ and the number of iterations required for convergence.

Convergence is clearly slow, especially in the case of *BM*1. This may mean that we are still some way from the true optimum. Rather than decrease the convergence tolerance, we applied Steffensen's iteration [40, p. 152], which is a device, based on Aitken's δ^2 method, for accelerating the convergence of iterative algorithms. The results of this are also shown in Table V. They show a noticeable improvement in the *BM*1 data and a marginal change in *BM*2.

The objective of Boltzmann machine training is to estimate the joint probabilities of the states of the visible nodes. In Table VI we display, for each of the

Table V

**Estimates of Weights Obtained by Gradient Descent
for Data from *BM*1 and *BM*2, without and
with Accelerated Convergence**

Weight	BM1		BM2	
	Standard	Accelerated	Standard	Accelerated
w_{12}	0.458	0.471	0.594	0.596
w_{13}	0.824	0.840	0.359	0.363
w_{14}	−0.083	−0.077	0.435	0.434
w_{23}	1.401	1.374	0.505	0.507
w_{24}	0.664	0.571	0.428	0.428
w_{34}	0.284	0.146	0.575	0.574
w_{15}	0.449	0.405	0.538	0.495
w_{25}	0.664	0.719	0.485	0.476
w_{35}	1.737	1.777	0.538	0.505
w_{45}	1.382	1.417	0.497	0.501
w_{10}	0.186	0.194	0.314	0.349
w_{20}	1.081	1.312	0.230	0.238
w_{30}	0.719	0.827	0.307	0.334
w_{40}	1.544	1.731	0.243	0.244
w_{50}	0.690	0.647	0.263	0.276
Iterations	21461	1475	1856	1510
$L(W)$	−6453.201	−6453.036	−14955.013	−14955.005

16 possible state vectors, the observed frequencies and, rounded to the nearest integers, the estimated expected frequencies computed at the end of the various training algorithms. In these terms, accelerating the convergence of the algorithm did not have much effect.

The true weights were also used to initialize the algorithms. In practice this is not feasible, and we experimented with a variety of sets of initial estimates. It turned out that values attained for $L(W)$ and for estimated expected frequencies were not sensitive to the choice of initial values, but that the final values for some of the weights were. One example, based on the *BM*1 data, is shown in Table VII, along with the corresponding set of estimated expected frequencies. There is evidence of nonidentifiability of the weights connecting visible unit 4, the hidden unit, and the bias unit. However, the algorithm still serves its purpose of creating a set of estimates that optimizes $L(W)$. The identifiability of multidimensional categorical-data probability models is a complicated issue; see, for instance, Section 3.2.4 of Hagenaars [41] and Goodman [42].

Table VI

**Observed and Estimated Expected Frequencies, Based on Estimates
from Table V, in the Various States, for *BM*1 and *BM*2**

	*BM*1			*BM*2		
State vector	Obs.	Exp. (stan.)	Exp. (accel.)	Obs.	Exp. (stan.)	Exp. (accel.)
(0,0,0,0)	0	0	0	18	24	23
(0,0,0,1)	2	2	2	40	41	41
(0,0,1,0)	2	1	1	48	45	45
(0,0,1,1)	29	30	30	150	147	147
(0,1,0,0)	1	1	1	50	40	40
(0,1,0,1)	22	22	22	108	113	113
(0,1,1,0)	27	28	29	126	134	134
(0,1,1,1)	1321	1320	1319	704	701	702
(1,0,0,0)	0	0	0	51	45	45
(1,0,0,1)	4	3	3	129	129	129
(1,0,1,0)	4	5	5	128	131	132
(1,0,1,1)	117	116	116	692	694	695
(1,1,0,0)	1	2	2	137	148	148
(1,1,0,1)	60	59	59	676	671	671
(1,1,1,0)	192	189	190	751	742	743
(1,1,1,1)	8218	8220	8220	6192	6195	6195

C. DIRECT MAXIMIZATION

We applied the quasi-Newton algorithm E04JAF of the NAg Library [38] to the direct maximization of $L(W)$; the results are shown in Table VIII, with the estimated expected frequencies in Table IX.

For *BM*1, the results are comparable to those obtained by gradient descent, apart from the troublesome weights identified above, and the expected frequencies behave well, apart from those associated with state vectors $x = (0, 1, 1, 1)$ and $x = (1, 1, 1, 1)$. For *BM*2, however, some of the weights seem to have "blown up", although the estimated expected frequencies are acceptable and the attained value of $L(W)$ is the highest achieved so far.

D. APPLICATION OF THE EM ALGORITHM

Recall that each vector $x_V^{(k)}$ in the training set indicates the responses of n_V visible nodes, and we regard $x^{(k)}$ as consisting of $n = n_V + n_H$ components, with $x_V^{(k)}$ filling the first n_V components and the remaining components filled

Table VII

**Results for the *BM*1 Data, Based on a Different
Set of Initial Estimates for the Weights[a]**

Weight	Estimate	State vector	Obs.	Exp.
w_{12}	0.458	(0,0,0,0)	0	0
w_{13}	0.847	(0,0,0,1)	2	2
w_{14}	−0.083	(0,0,1,0)	2	1
w_{23}	1.495	(0,0,1,1)	29	29
w_{24}	0.592	(0,1,0,0)	1	1
w_{34}	0.187	(0,1,0,1)	22	22
		(0,1,1,0)	27	28
w_{15}	0.396	(0,1,1,1)	1321	1320
w_{25}	0.634	(1,0,0,0)	0	0
w_{35}	1.864	(1,0,0,1)	4	4
w_{45}	3.334	(1,0,1,0)	4	5
		(1,0,1,1)	117	116
w_{10}	0.212	(1,1,0,0)	1	2
w_{20}	1.082	(1,1,0,1)	60	59
w_{30}	0.545	(1,1,1,0)	192	190
w_{40}	−0.243	(1,1,1,1)	8218	8220
w_{50}	0.991			

[a] Achieved log-likelihood is −6453.075.

by the (unobserved) responses $x_H^{(k)}$ from the n_H hidden units. The complete-data log-likelihood, $L_c(W)$, is

$$L_c(W) = \tfrac{1}{2} \sum_{i=0}^{n} \sum_{j=0}^{n} w_{ij} \left(\sum_{k=1}^{N} x_i^{(k)} x_j^{(k)} \right) - N \log Z_c(W),$$

where $Z_c(W)$ is the appropriate partition function. If at stage s in the corresponding EM algorithm we have current estimates $W^{(s)}$ of the weights, then the next set of values, $W^{(s+1)}$, is obtained by maximizing, with respect to W,

$$\tfrac{1}{2} \sum_{i=1}^{n} \sum_{j=1}^{n} w_{ij} \left\{ \sum_{l=1}^{N} \mathbb{E}(x_i^{(k)} x_j^{(k)} | x_V^{(k)}, W^{(s)}) \right\} - N \log Z_c(W), \qquad (19)$$

in which the conditioning on the observed data only through $x_V^{(k)}$ is a consequence of the independence of the different observations. As suggested by Qian and Titterington, in the discussion of Geyer and Thompson [22], $Z_c(W)$ can be approximated by the type of Monte Carlo method described in Section V.D, and in principle, the conditional expectations can also be estimated, using Monte Carlo

Table X

**Estimates of Weights for *BM*1 Data,
Obtained with the EM Algorithm**

Weight	True	Estimates		
Tolerance		0.01	0.01	0.001
initialized		True	Random	True
w_{12}	0.50	0.457	0.589	0.483
w_{13}	0.75	0.816	0.831	0.606
w_{14}	0.20	−0.087	−0.090	−0.151
w_{23}	1.20	1.406	1.468	1.855
w_{24}	0.10	0.530	0.565	0.658
w_{34}	0.60	−0.170	−0.048	−1.304
w_{15}	0.30	0.304	−0.666	0.756
w_{25}	0.50	0.488	0.794	−25.611
w_{35}	1.80	1.800	−0.715	3.942
w_{45}	1.00	1.002	−0.087	2.457
w_{10}	0.10	0.344	0.932	0.143
w_{20}	0.95	1.384	1.259	26.868
w_{30}	0.80	1.141	2.713	0.118
w_{40}	1.10	2.512	3.388	2.173
w_{50}	0.60	0.606	0.320	23.463
Iterations		2	2	941
$L(W)$		−6452.913	−6452.916	−6452.655

applied, initializing at the true weights and with a convergence tolerance of 0.001, results were obtained as shown in Table XI. The weights have not blown up in the same way, although the estimates obtained for the weights are quite different from the values obtained by gradient descent. This, again, is a manifestation of nonidentifiability, a problem that does not arise if one exploits the structure of the model for *BM*2 by reducing the number of parameters that must be estimated. For instance, if we require the bias connections to have a common (unspecified) value, then the number of parameters to be estimated is reduced to 11. The second set of results in Table XI was obtained after five EM iterations, starting from the true weights and using a convergence tolerance of 0.01. These results were similar to those obtained by the gradient-descent algorithm.

When the parameters are unconstrained, the networks represent saturated models, and this seemed to represent too many parameters for the EM algorithm to estimate reliably. EM may therefore be more suitable for less fully parameterized networks, or for more sparsely connected networks.

Table XI

Estimates of Weights for *BM2* Data,
Obtained with the EM Algorithm

Weight	True	Estimates	
w_{i0} initialized		Unequal true	Equal true
w_{12}	0.50	0.807	0.598
w_{13}	0.50	0.010	0.363
w_{14}	0.50	0.333	0.436
w_{23}	0.50	0.691	0.508
w_{24}	0.50	0.535	0.424
w_{34}	0.50	0.498	0.577
w_{15}	0.50	1.452	0.554
w_{25}	0.50	−1.112	0.408
w_{35}	0.50	1.247	0.546
w_{45}	0.50	0.655	0.439
w_{10}	0.25	−0.310	0.297
w_{20}	0.25	1.234	0.297
w_{30}	0.25	−0.155	0.297
w_{40}	0.25	0.165	0.297
w_{50}	0.25	0.376	0.297
Iterations		860	5
$L(W)$		−14,954.167	−14,955.032

VIII. VARIATIONS ON THE BASIC BOLTZMANN MACHINE

In this section we collate remarks about extensions and variations on the binary Boltzmann machine and discuss possible future developments, particularly from a statistical point of view.

A. THE BOLTZMANN PERCEPTRON

The formulation of the Boltzmann–Gibbs distribution in (2) allows, in principle, for connections among all nodes in the Boltzmann machine, be they inputs, outputs, or hidden nodes. One way both to simplify the model and to structure it around particular activities, is to eliminate some of the connections—in other words, to insist that some of the weights be zero. In the Boltzmann perceptron, the only connections permitted are between input nodes and hidden nodes, and between hidden nodes and output nodes; no intralayer connection is permitted, or any direct link between inputs and outputs, so that the network does have the feed-forward character of the standard multilayer perceptron. In addition, the distribution of interest during training is $p(x_O|x_I)$: the input units are clamped, and it is therefore unnecessary to insist that they be binary. The concept of the Boltzmann perceptron was developed by Hopfield [43], and Yair and Gersho [44, 45] showed that the network was sparse enough and suitably structured for the equilibrium probabilities to be computable deterministically, without the need for Monte Carlo approximations. Kappen [46] further extends the development, introducing lateral inhibition among the output units that facilitates a practicable deterministic learning rule. Kappen [46] also shows that the Boltzmann perceptrons are universal classifiers, and designs a version, incorporating lateral inhibition among the hidden units, for use as an estimator of the joint probability distribution, $p(x_I, x_O)$. Finally, Kappen and Nijman [47] study a version of this network, dealing with continuous inputs by incorporating the features of radial basis function networks, for deriving classification tools that can deal with missing data.

B. POLYTOMOUS BOLTZMANN MACHINES

In statistical terms, the stationary distributions associated with Boltzmann machines provide a class of pairwise interaction models for multivariate binary data. A natural direction for generalization is to allow each x_i to be polytomous (that is, multicategory) or ordered polytomous. A real-life example of the latter might be the degree of pain felt by sufferers from backache, described as "nonexistent," "mild," "moderate," "bad," or "severe". Anderson and Titterington [37] work through the case of unordered, polytomous variables, concentrating mainly on showing that the theory and algorithmic development described by Byrne [24] carry over to this case. They note that the formulation (2) corresponds to a linear logistic regression model for the binary response, x_i, regressed on the other x_j, and carry over the corresponding approach in the statistical literature for dealing with a polytomous response; see, for instance, Anderson [48] and Cox and Snell [49, Chap. 5]. The key idea is to represent a d-category variable by $(d - 1)$ binary variables, so that, ultimately, all calculations are made in terms of binary variables.

Suppose $x_i \in \{q_1, \ldots, q_d\}$ is the output from the ith neuron, and that $z_i = (z_{i1}, \ldots, z_{i(d-1)})$ is a vector of $d - 1$ binary variables. We create a set of d such vectors, one of which is to represent each of the $\{q_l\}$. In particular, let e_l be a

$(d-1)$-vector with 1 in position l and zero elsewhere, and let e_d be the vector that consists of $(d-1)$ zeros. Then we represent x_i by z_i according to the code

$$x_i = q_l \Leftrightarrow z_i = e_l, \qquad i = 1, \ldots, n; \qquad l = 1, \ldots, d.$$

The state space for each z_i is $S = \{e_1, \ldots, e_d\}$, and the state space for $z = (z_1, \ldots, z_n)$ is $\mathcal{Z} = S^n$. (This assumes that all of the x_i can take the same number, d, of categories. This can be generalized at the expense of more tortuous notation.) If z_{iu} denotes the uth component of z_i, then

$$x_i = q_l \Leftrightarrow z_{iu} = \delta_{lu},$$

where δ_{lu} is the Kronecker delta, for all i and u, and for $l = 1, \ldots, d-1$. For $l = d$, of course, $z_{iu} = 0$ for all u.

With this formulation, the polytomous Boltzmann machine consists of a set of multicategory neurons linked by weighted connections, either completely interconnected or with the pattern of connections determined by the particular application, just as for the standard Boltzmann machine. However, each neuron is a composite "processing unit," consisting of $d-1$ binary subneurons, a maximum of one of which is active at any one time, to represent the vectors $\{e_1, \ldots, e_d\}$. There is no connection among the binary subneurons within one composite node, but the connection between two composite neurons consists of some or all of the possible connections between binary subneurons in different nodes; for an illustration see Figure 1 of Anderson and Titterington [37].

To describe the probabilistic mechanism for the Boltzmann machine, which in turn defines the activation function associated with a typical multicategory neuron, we specify a set of weights $W = \{w_{ij}^{lu}: i, j = 0, \ldots, n; l, u = 1, \ldots, d-1\}$. We assume that $w_{ii}^{lu} = 0$ for all i, l, and u, define the energy function

$$E(z) = -\sum_i \sum_{j<i} \sum_l \sum_u w_{ij}^{lu} z_{il} z_{ju},$$

and let

$$p(z) = c \exp\{-E(z)\}, \qquad z \in \mathcal{Z},$$

denote the corresponding normalized probabilities on $\mathcal{Z}$. For a particular i, denote by $z_{\backslash i}$ the set $\{z_j: j \neq i\}$. Then, for $l = 1, \ldots, d-1$ we obtain

$$\frac{p(z_i = e_l \mid z_{\backslash i})}{p(z_i = e_d \mid z_{\backslash i})} = \exp\left\{\sum_{j=0}^n \sum_{u=1}^{d-1} w_{ij}^{lu} z_{ju}\right\}. \tag{20}$$

Note that this notation caters for the inclusion of a bias term, by setting $z_0 = e_1$, perpetually. Note also that, because $w_{ii}^{lu} = 0$, the summation over j on the right-hand side of (20) can tidily run from 0 to n. From (20), therefore, the updating rule for the ith neuron is

$$z_i = e_l, \text{ with probability } \frac{\exp\{\sum_{j=0}^{n} \sum_{u=1}^{d-1} w_{ij}^{lu} z_{ju}\}}{1 + \sum_{r=1}^{d-1} \exp\{\sum_{j=0}^{n} \sum_{u=1}^{d-1} w_{ij}^{ru} z_{ju}\}},$$

$$l = 1, \ldots, d - 1, \quad (21)$$

and

$$z_i = e_d, \text{ with probability } \left[1 + \sum_{r=1}^{d-1} \exp\left\{ \sum_{j=0}^{n} \sum_{u=1}^{d-1} w_{ij}^{ru} z_{ju} \right\} \right]^{-1}. \quad (22)$$

In terms of the original expression of the neuron states in terms of x_i, we have that $x_i = q_l$, with probability given by (21), for $l = 1, \ldots, d - 1$, and $x_i = q_d$, with probability given by (22).

The updating rules (21) and (22) constitute the appropriate Gibbs sampler for the Boltzmann machine. With this framework, Anderson and Titterington [37] spell out the corresponding version of the theory and training algorithms used by Byrne [24] in the context of the binary Boltzmann machine. They also clarify the relationship between the EM algorithm and the IPFP.

C. NEAL'S APPROACH BASED ON BELIEF NETWORKS

The notoriously slow gradient-descent learning procedure for Boltzmann machines with hidden units was noted in Section VI.C: in the traditional approach, Monte Carlo simulation is required in both the so-called positive and negative phases of the iterative stage. In view of this, Neal [50] pointed out the use of *belief networks* [51] as creators of flexible probability distributions for multivariate binary data. The structure of the joint probabilities takes the simple form

$$p(x) = \prod_i p(x_i | \mathcal{X}_i),$$

where $\mathcal{X}_i$ is some subset of $\{x_j: j < i\}$. The underlying units are implicitly ordered, and it is a trivial matter, once $p(x)$ is specified, to generate a realization from the distribution. Furthermore, the problem of an intractable partition function has disappeared. The relationship of these models to Boltzmann machines is similar to that between causal Markov Mesh Random Field models [52] and Markov Random Fields. Neal [50] introduces a particular class of such networks, called *sigmoid belief networks,* characterized by the following assumption about $p(x_i|\mathcal{X}_i)$:

$$
x_i = \begin{cases} 1 & \text{with probability } \left[1 + \exp\left\{ -\sum_{j<i} w_{ij}x_j \right\} \right]^{-1} \\ 0 & \text{otherwise.} \end{cases}
$$

Note the similarity to, and minor but important difference from (1). The terminology derives from the use of the logistic sigmoid in defining the probabilities. However, the computation of *full conditional* probabilities, such as $P(x_i = 1|x_{\backslash i})$, is typically not possible, and they usually must be estimated by Gibbs sampling. Neal [50] estimates parameters from a training set by gradient ascent of the log-likelihood function. He shows that the gradient involves terms corresponding only to the "positive phase" of Boltzmann machine learning (based on conditional expectations), so that the computational burden is much less. He also describes *noisy-OR belief networks,* in which, conditional on $\{x_j: j < i\}$,

$$
x_i = \begin{cases} 1 & \text{with probability } 1 - \exp\left\{ -\sum_{j<i} w_{ij}x_j \right\} \\ 0 & \text{otherwise.} \end{cases}
$$

In a numerical study of some small-scale problems, Neal [50] finds that his models are as flexible as those corresponding to Boltzmann machines, but that training is much faster, and he suggests using them in medical prognosis.

Although, as commented above, the $p(x)$ associated with a belief network is easy to calculate, for a given x and a given set of weights, W, this is not true if some of the components of x correspond to hidden units, with the result that the probability distribution of real interest is $p(x_V) = \sum_{x_H} p(x)$. Unless the hidden variables "come after" all of the visible variables in the ordering defined by the x subscript, the summation cannot be done easily, and we are in a difficulty similar to that of being faced with an intractable partition function. An alternative to using Monte Carlo methods is to seek analytical approximations to $p(x_V)$, for given x and W. Saul *et al.* [53] use mean-field approximations to derive a lower bound, in the case of sigmoid belief networks, adapting an approach developed for the so-called Helmholtz machine by Dayan *et al.* [54] and Hinton *et al.* [55]. Jaakkola and Jordan [56] extend the method to the case of noisy OR networks and show how to obtain upper bounds for both types of belief network. In Jaakkola and Jordan [57], a way of obtaining upper and lower bounds is described for the Boltzmann machine itself, incorporating a process of pruning the corresponding network until a skeleton is left for which computation of the probability is tractable.

In related work, Saul and Jordan [58, 59] show how some Boltzmann machines do turn out to be computationally tractable. These are called Boltzmann trees, and

[16] S. P. Luttrell. The use of Bayesian and entropic methods in neural network theory. In *Maximum Entropy and Bayesian Methods* (J. Skilling, Ed.), pp. 363–370. Kluwer Academic, Dordrecht, 1989.

[17] J. Besag and P. J. Green. Spatial statistics and Bayesian computation. *J. Roy. Statist. Soc. Ser. B* 55:25–37, 1993.

[18] A. Gelman and D. B. Rubin. Inference from iterative simulation using multiple sequences. *Statist. Sci.* 7:457–472, 1992.

[19] C. J. Geyer. Practical Markov chain Monte Carlo. *Statist. Sci.* 7:473–483, 1992.

[20] A. De Gloria, P. Faraboschi, and M. Olivieri. Efficient implementation of the Boltzmann machine algorithm. *IEEE Trans. Neural Networks* 4:159–163, 1993.

[21] A. P. Dempster, N. M. Laird, and D. B. Rubin. Maximum likelihood from incomplete data via the EM algorithm (with discussion). *J. Roy. Statist. Soc. Ser. B* 39:1–38, 1977.

[22] C. J. Geyer and E. A. Thompson. Constrained Monte Carlo maximum likelihood for dependent data (with discussion). *J. Roy. Statist. Soc. Ser. B* 54:657–699, 1992.

[23] S. Amari, K. Kurata, and H. Nagaoka. Information geometry of Boltzmann machines. *IEEE Trans. Neural Networks* 3:260–271, 1992.

[24] W. Byrne. Alternating minimization and Boltzmann machine learning. *IEEE Trans. Neural Networks* 3:612–620, 1992.

[25] C. Peterson and J. R. Anderson. A Mean Field Theory learning algorithm for neural networks. *Complex Systems* 1:995–1019, 1987.

[26] J. Besag. Statistical analysis of non-lattice data. *The Statistician* 24:179–195, 1975.

[27] J. Hertz, A. Krogh, and R. G. Palmer. *Introduction to the Theory of Neural Computation.* Addison-Wesley, Reading, MA, 1991.

[28] M. Mezard, G. Parisi, and M.A. Virasoro. *Spin Glass Theory and Beyond.* World Scientific, Singapore, 1987.

[29] D. Geiger and F. Girosi. Parallel and deterministic algorithms from MRF's: surface reconstruction. *IEEE Trans. Pattern Anal. Machine Intell.* 13:401–412, 1991.

[30] J. Zhang. The Mean Field Theory in EM procedures for blind Markov random field image restoration. *IEEE Trans. Image Processing* 2:27–40, 1993.

[31] A. P. Dunmur and D. M. Titterington. Parameter estimation in latent structure models. *Technical Report 96-2*, Department of Statistics University of Glasgow, 1996.

[32] A. E. Gelfand and B. P. Carlin. Maximum likelihood estimation for constrained or missing data problems. *Canad. J. Statist.* 21:303–311, 1993.

[33] C.J. Geyer. On the convergence of Monte Carlo maximum likelihood calculations. *J. Roy. Statist. Soc. Ser. B* 56:261–274, 1994.

[34] S. Amari. Information geometry of the EM and em algorithms for neural networks. *Neural Networks* 8:1379–1408, 1995.

[35] I. Csiszár and G. Tusnády. Information geometry and alternating minimization procedures. In *Statistics and Decisions* (E. J. Dudewicz *et al.*, Eds.), Supplementary Issue no. 1, pp. 205–237, Oldenbourg, Munich, 1984.

[36] R. M. Neal and G. E. Hinton. A new view of the EM algorithm that justifies incremental and other variants. *Preprint, Department of Computer Science, University of Toronto,* 1993.

[37] N. H. Anderson and D. M. Titterington. Beyond the binary Boltzmann machine. *IEEE Trans. Neural Networks* 6:1229–1236, 1995.

[38] Numerical Algorithms Group. *NAG Fortran Library, Mark 13.* NAG Ltd., Oxford, 1988.

[39] S. E. Fienberg. *The Analysis of Cross-Classified Data.* MIT Press, Cambridge, MA, 1977.

[40] R. F. Churchhouse (Ed.). *Handbook of Applicable Mathematics,* Vol. III: *Numerical Methods.* Wiley, New York, 1981.

[41] J. A. Hagenaars. *Categorical Longitudinal Data.* Sage, London, 1990.

[42] L. A. Goodman. Exploratory latent structure analysis using both identifiable and unidentifiable models. *Biometrika* 61:215–231, 1974.

[43] J. J. Hopfield. Learning algorithms and probability distributions in feed-forward and feedback networks. *Proc. Nat. Acad. Sci. U.S.A.* 84:8429–8433, 1987.

[44] E. Yair and A. Gersho. The Boltzmann Perceptron network: a soft classifier. *J. Neural Networks* 3:203–221, 1990.

[45] A. Yair and A. Gersho. Maximum *a posteriori* decision and evaluation of class probabilities by Boltzmann Perceptron classifiers. *Proc. IEE* 78:1620–1628, 1990.

[46] H. J. Kappen. Deterministic learning rules for Boltzmann machines. *Neural Networks* 8:537–548, 1995.

[47] H. J. Kappen and M. J. Nijman. Radial basis Boltzmann machines and learning with missing values. In *Proceedings of the 1995 World Congress on Neural Networks*, Washington, DC, 1995.

[48] J. A. Anderson. Separate sample logistic discrimination. *Biometrika* 59:19–35, 1972.

[49] D. R. Cox and E. J. Snell. *Analysis of Binary Data*, 2nd ed. Chapman & Hall, London, 1989.

[50] R. M. Neal. Connectionist learning of belief networks. *Artificial Intelligence* 56:71–113, 1992.

[51] J. Pearl. *Probabilistic Reasoning in Intelligent Systems: Networks of Plausible Inference*. Morgan Kaufmann, San Mateo, CA, 1988.

[52] K. Abend, T. J. Harley, and L. Kanal. Classification of binary random patterns. *IEEE Trans. Inform. Theory* 4:538–544, 1965.

[53] L. K. Saul, T. Jaakkola, and M. I. Jordan. Mean field theory for sigmoid belief networks. *J. Artificial Intelligence Res.* 4:61–76, 1995.

[54] P. Dayan, G. E. Hinton, R. M. Neal, and R. S. Zemel. The Helmholtz machine. *Neural Comput.* 7:889–904, 1995.

[55] G. E. Hinton, P. Dayan, B. Frey, and R. M. Neal. The wake-sleep algorithm for unsupervised neural networks. *Science* 268:1158–1161, 1995.

[56] T. S. Jaakkola and M. I. Jordan. Computing upper and lower bounds on likelihoods in intractable networks. *AI Memo no. 1571*, MIT, 1996.

[57] T. S. Jaakkola and M. I. Jordan. Recursive algorithms for approximating probabilities in graphical models. *Computation Cognitive Science Technical Report 9604*, MIT, 1996.

[58] L. K. Saul and M. I. Jordan. Learning in Boltzmann trees. *Neural Computation* 6:1174–1184, 1994.

[59] L. K. Saul and M. I. Jordan. Boltzmann chains and hidden Markov models. In *Advances in Neural Information Processing Systems 7* (G. Tesauro, D. S. Touretzky, and T. K. Leen, Eds.). MIT Press, Cambridge, MA, 1995.

[60] S. Rüger, A. Weinberger, and S. Wittchen. Decimatable Boltzmann machines vs. Gibbs sampling. *Bericht 96-29 des Fachberichs Informatik der Technischen Universität Berlin*, 1996.

[61] R. A. Iltis and P.-Y. Ting. Data association in multi-target tracking: a solution using a layered Boltzmann machine. In *Proceedings of the International Joint Conference on Neural Networks, 1991*, Vol. 1, pp. 31–36. IEEE, New York, 1991.

[62] A. F. M. Smith and A. E. Gelfand. Bayesian statistics without tears: a sampling-resampling perspective. *Amer. Statist.* 46:84–88, 1992.

[63] J. A. Anderson. Regression and ordered categorical variables (with discussion). *J. Roy. Statist. Soc. Ser. B* 46:1–30, 1984.

[64] P. McCullagh. Regression models for ordinal data (with discussion). *J. Roy. Statist. Soc. Ser. B* 42:109–142, 1980.

[65] B. Cheng and D. M. Titterington. Neural networks: a review from a statistical perspective (with discussion). *Statist. Sci.* 9:2–54, 1994.

[66] B. D. Ripley. Neural networks and related methods for classification (with discussion). *J. Roy. Statist. Soc. Ser. B* 56:409–456, 1994.

highlight divergence from normality. Examples might include the detection of abnormal features in electroencephalographic data, the detection of abnormal cells on cervical smears, fault detection in machinery, the detection of abnormal tissue on magnetic resonance imaging scans, etc. Typically the normal data is used to construct a density function, and the novel or abnormal features are highlighted as outliers from this distribution. Estimation of a density function is a well-known topic in statistics, but is also extensively used in neural computing, particularly in unsupervised learning and radial basis function (RBF) networks, which form a distribution function covering the input data.

Classification and regression problems are usually handled by using multilayered neural network architectures. Networks trained with the Back Propagation algorithm and RBF networks are a common choice for these types of problem. For standard Back Propagation, the weights and biases of the nodes are found with a gradient descent procedure and the architecture of the network is found by experimentation. Usually the network is trained with several choices for the number of hidden nodes, and performance is evaluated against a validation set to determine the optimal number of hidden nodes. This step is computationally intensive, and therefore only a small fraction of the space of possible networks can be evaluated. For RBF networks it is similarly important to find the optimal choice of base functions for covering the density distribution of the input data.

Constructive algorithms determine the architecture of the network and the parameters (weights, thresholds, etc.) necessary for learning the data. Compared to algorithms such as Back Propagation, they have the following potential advantages:

- They grow the architecture of the neural network in addition to finding the parameters required.
- They can reduce the training to single-node learning, hence substantially simplifying and accelerating the training process. The learning speed of constructive algorithms such as Cascade Correlation are at least an order of magnitude faster than that of Back Propagation.
- Some constructive algorithms are guaranteed to converge, unlike the Back Propagation algorithm, for example.
- Algorithms such as Back Propagation can suffer from catastrophic interference when learning new data; that is, storage of new information seriously disrupts the retrieval of previously stored data. The incremental learning strategy of constructive algorithms offers a possible solution to this problem.

Constructive techniques are of interest for other reasons. To date, a great deal of effort has been directed toward finding efficient algorithms for determining the weights in a neural network. Standard Back Propagation is typical in that the procedure determines the weights but not the architecture of the network. On the other hand, for biological neural systems, the number of vesicles released at synaptic junctions suggests that the range of synaptic values is fairly limited and that the precision in these values can be expected to be poor. Learning in biological systems may be oriented toward setting up an appropriate connectivity rather than the determination of high-precision synaptic values. Evidence for this comes from the development of neural architectures in neonates, where neural structures are adapted through the branching of certain pathways, with pruning and decay of other neural circuits. This adaptive development may be essential for cognition in complex information-processing systems, because the category of learnable concepts is known to be very restricted [1], and therefore complicated concepts must be built up from simpler low-level concepts in a constructive fashion.

The major potential shortcoming of constructive algorithms is their aptitude for capturing noise and overfitting the training data. The objective of training is not to obtain an exact representation of the training data, but to construct a model of the rule or process that generated that data. Unfortunately, the ability to guarantee convergence can lead to the algorithm giving a perfect fit to the training data and therefore a perfect fit to the noise. We illustrate this idea in Fig. 1, where the solid line is supposed to represent the underlying rule and the crosses represent the training data that are drawn from this rule but corrupted by noise. The dashed line represents the solution found by a constructive algorithm in which all of the training data are correctly learned, but the solution found is poor. Plainly the solution is over-complex, does not accurately capture the underlying rule, and could be expected to give poor generalization for new data drawn from that rule. The generalization error of neural networks can be generally viewed as the sum of a bias term and a variance. A nonzero bias can arise because the function learned

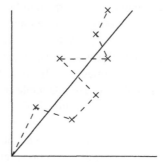

Figure 1 If the neural network has too many free parameters, it can fit the noise exactly (dashed line), giving a poor approximation to the underlying rule (solid line).

by the neural network differs on the average from the underlying rule or function generating that data. A nonzero variance can arise because the function implemented by the network may be very sensitive to the particular choice of the training data, as in Fig. 1. A neural network with too simple an architecture will be unable to learn the data correctly and will have a large bias. On the other hand, if the network is over-complex, the variance will be large, with the network exactly fitting any noise in the chosen data set, for example. Constructive algorithms can frequently generate too complex an architecture with too many hidden nodes or hidden layers, and consequently we need a strategy to reduce network complexity if required. The solution is to remove excess weights or hidden nodes during or after the training process, a topic we will discuss further in Section V.

Rather than growing neural networks and then pruning, it seems sensible to start with a network that is bound to solve the problem and then prune. However, such destructive algorithms have several disadvantages. First, a network with a small number of hidden nodes can be trained more rapidly, and therefore it makes sense to start with a small network and grow further hidden nodes. Having found a network that stores the data, we use this as a first approximation for beginning the pruning process. A second disadvantage is that it is difficult to guess the initial size of the network before running a destructive algorithm. Certain problems (e.g., N-parity or the Twin Spirals problem) require a substantial number of hidden nodes, and to avoid potential problems with a highly intermeshed data set, it would be necessary to start with a complex initial architecture.

In this review we will start with constructive algorithms for classification and regression tasks. Because networks with analog outputs can be readily adapted to give binary outputs, the latter category include classification as a subclass. In both of these cases network construction proceeds through the successive addition of single hidden nodes. Consequently, Section IV is devoted to constructive techniques that add entire subnetworks. In Section V we consider pruning techniques to reduce network complexity. Given the rapid expansion of this topic, we have had to be selective and make only brief reference to many interesting algorithms that have been proposed recently. We have also had to ignore evolutionary techiques that are closely related to this topic, for example, the use of genetic algorithms to determine the network architecture [2]. In addition to altering weights and architecture, it is also possible to use adaptable updating functions at hidden nodes to add a further degree of flexibility [3–6]. This additional freedom is achieved by introducing further trainable parameters at the hidden nodes. Consequently, these models tend to favor networks with a small bias and high variance compared to networks with fixed updating functions, and consequently we will not consider them here.

II. CLASSIFICATION

A. INTRODUCTION

In this section we will consider constructive algorithms for solving classification problems. We have also selected the algorithms to illustrate the different types of architectures that can be generated by constructive algorithms. Broadly speaking, there are two main classes: networks with a shallow structure, perhaps consisting of a single hidden layer that is grown laterally, and deeper architectures consisting of thin hidden layers (which may only have one hidden node each), with growth consisting of additional layers interposed between the input layer and the output.

During the training of a classifier, we want to identify input patterns with their correct category. We will use the object x_j^μ to represent these inputs to the networks where the index μ labels the pattern ($\mu = 1, \ldots, p$) and j ranges over the components ($j = 1, \ldots, N$ for N nodes in the input layer). Because these components will make up a vector, we will also sometimes write these objects $\mathbf{x}^\mu$. The corresponding targets are y_i^μ, where μ is the pattern label and i labels the output nodes. The output can also be viewed as a vector $\mathbf{y}^\mu$.

Weights leading from a node j to a node i will be denoted W_{ij}, and the threshold at a node i will be denoted T_i (the *bias* is the negative of this threshold, $-T_i$). Thus if the nodes in the network use a ± 1 updating function, the output at node i is related to the inputs by

$$y_i = \text{sign}\left(\sum_j W_{ij} x_j - T_i\right), \tag{1}$$

where we define the sign function as having an output of $+1$ if its argument is greater than or equal to zero and -1 otherwise. It is also common to use the quantization $(1, 0)$, in which case we use the Heaviside step function for the updating. For binary classification we will generally label the two target classes by P^+ and P^- (where P^+ represents the set with target $+1$ and P^- represents the set with targets -1 or 0). The separatrix in Eq. (1) can be viewed as an oriented hyperplane in an N-dimensional space:

$$\mathbf{W} \cdot \mathbf{x} = T. \tag{2}$$

For binary classification tasks, a constructive algorithm will typically try to separate the two classes of data, or if this is not possible, it will try to maximize the number of patterns on the correct sides of the hyperplane. If it is not possible to separate the two classes, then some of the patterns are incorrectly stored and the algorithm will proceed to grow further hidden nodes to store these patterns.

B. THE POCKET ALGORITHM

Because a data set may not be separable by a hyperplane, it is common to use a variant of the perceptron algorithm (called the *pocket algorithm*), which minimizes the number of errors for nonseparable data or finds a solution if the data is linearly separable (the perceptron algorithm and some alternatives to the pocket algorithm are considered in the Appendix).

As for the perceptron algorithm, the pocket algorithm only changes the weights if a pattern is incorrectly stored (*A1*). The patterns are presented in a random order, and a separate set of weights W_{ij}^p are kept (in one's pocket), along with the number of consecutive presentations for which these weights correctly classified the patterns. Because the patterns are presented randomly, a good set of weights will have a lower probability of being altered and hence remain unchanged for a longer time than weights that give rise to errors. Consequently, to find a good solution, we only replace the pocketed weights with a new set when the current sequence of correct classifications is longer than the previous sequence of correct classifications. It is possible to show that these pocketed weights will give the minimum possible number of errors with a probability approaching 1 as training increases. Formally, the Pocket Convergence theorem [7–9] states that for a finite set of patterns and a probability $P < 1$, their exists an m such that after m iterations, the probability of finding optimal weights exceeds P.

A1. The Pocket Algorithm.

1. Randomly initialize the initial weight vector W_{ij}^0.
2. Choose a training example at random (with input x_j^μ and corresponding target y_i^μ).
3. At iteration t, if the current weights correctly store the pattern, that is,

$$y_i^\mu \sum_j W_{ij}^t x_j^\mu > T_i, \tag{3}$$

   then go to 4; else update the weight vector,

$$W_{ij}^t = W_{ij}^{t-1} + y_i^\mu x_j^\mu, \tag{4}$$

   and go to 2.
4. If the current sequence of correct classifications with the new weights is longer than the sequence of correct classifications for the pocketed weights W_{ij}^p, then replace the pocketed weights by these weights and record the length of its run of correct classifications.
5. If the maximum number of iterations is exceeded, then **stop**; else go to step 2.

This algorithm improves the pocketed weights stochastically, and consequently there is a nonzero probability that a good set of weights could be overwritten by poor weights after a long sequence of the latter. An improvement is therefore to introduce a rachet mechanism such that every time the pocketed weights are replaced, the number of errors must decrease. Thus in addition to the pocketed weights and length of sequence, we must also record the number of errors made with each pocketed weight set. Suppose the current sequence length of the pocketed weights is L and the current set of perceptron weights has remained unchanged for more than L presentations; then we proceed to evaluate the number of errors for the current perceptron weights. If the number of errors is less than that for the current pocketed weights, then we replace the pocketed weights, with the weights from the perceptron rule, also recording the sequence length and this new minimum number of errors. Unfortunately, this evaluation of the number of errors for the new candidate weights substantially increases the computational load, although giving a better eventual solution.

C. TOWER AND CASCADE ARCHITECTURES

The classification algorithms we will describe in the following sections have guarranteed convergence if the pattern sets have a property that Frean [10] has called *convexity* (although this is not a necessary condition for convergence for some algorithms). A pattern set is convex if each pattern in the set can be separated from the other patterns by a hyperplane [9–11]. For example, suppose the inputs in the training patterns, x_j^μ, have components ±1 and let us further suppose that pattern $\mu = 1$ has target $+1$. If we use single-node learning with weights $W_j = x_j^1$ and a threshold $T = N$, then $u = \text{sign}(\sum_j W_j v_j - T)$ gives an output $u = +1$ if $v_j = x_j^1$ and -1 otherwise (the same construction is possible with $(1, 0)$ updating functions, of course). Geometrically, the patterns can be pictured as being located at some of the corners of an N-dimensional hypercube, and this solution amounts to a hyperplane that cuts off one corner from the rest of the hypercube. A second class of convex patterns arises with input vectors, x_j^μ, which have real-valued components satisfying the constraint

$$\sum_{j=1}^{N} \left(x_j^\mu\right)^2 = 1. \tag{5}$$

In this case the pattern vectors can be viewed as emanating from the origin and as being of constant length, so that they lie as labeled points on the surface of an N-dimensional hypersphere. It is again possible to separate one point from the rest by using a tangential hyperplane that separates this point from the rest of the hypersphere.

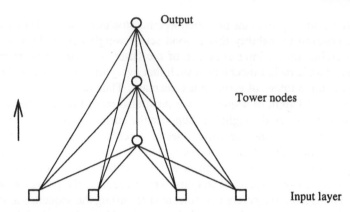

Figure 2   The architecture generated by the Tower algorithm. Each hidden node is connected to the input nodes and the previous hidden node.

For convex pattern sets it is possible to develop a number of constructive algorithms with guaranteed convergence. As an illustration, let us consider one of the first and simplest algorithms, namely the Tower algorithm shown in Fig. 2. There are N inputs in the initial input layer of the Tower, together with an additional node $(N+1)$, clamped at $+1$ to handle the bias. The lowest hidden node has input from all of the nodes in this layer (including the bias node), and each higher node in the Tower has contributions from this input layer and the hidden node directly below it. Each node is trained using the pocket algorithm with rachet, and then its weights are fixed and its output becomes a contribution to the next higher node.

If the hidden nodes use the binary quantization $(1, 0)$ and the pattern set is convex, it is straightforward to see that each new hidden node can be trained to make at least one less error than the immediately preceding hidden node. For example, suppose a hidden node is wrongly 0 when pattern v is presented. At the next higher node in the Tower, we can use the convexity of the pattern set to find weights and a threshold between the input layer and the hidden node such that this node will be 1 when pattern v is presented. If the weight between this hidden node and its predecessor in sufficiently large, it will respond correctly to the pattern set learned by the previous hidden node in addition to the vth pattern. For a finite pattern set this guarantees convergence (although with poor generalization, unless each hidden node can find a better solution, preferably correcting a number of errors).

Another early constructive technique, the Tiling Algorithm [12], similarly builds upward, using layers of hidden nodes consisting of a single master and several ancillary nodes to enforce learnable representations on the hidden layers. However, in the instance of master nodes with direct connections to all of the in-

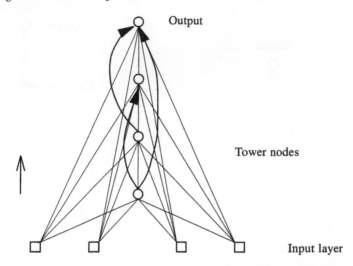

Figure 3 The cascade architecture generated by the Pyramid algorithm. Each hidden node is connected to the input nodes and all of the previous hidden nodes.

puts and the preceding master node [13], no ancillary nodes are required and this technique gives an alternative construction of the Tower architecture.

We can generalize the Tower algorithm by introducing additional connections between each hidden node and all preceding hidden nodes in addition to the inputs. This is the Pyramid architecture illustrated in Fig. 3. Following more recent usage, we will henceforth refer to the Pyramid model as an example of a *cascade* architecture. In terms of successful applications and popularity, the cascade architecture is most commonly used in the context of the Cascade Correlation algorithm (Section III.B), in which the new hidden node is trained to correlate with the magnitude of the residual error at the output node. For classification tasks, the cascade architecture has been investigated (and its convergence proved) in the context of the Perceptron Cascade algorithm [14–16]. In this algorithm the hidden nodes are trained to correct the two types of classification error at the output: wrongly off (a 0 instead of a 1) and wrongly on (1 instead of a 0). Each time a hidden node is constructed its weights are trained and it is added to the network and frozen; there is no subsequent training of its weights. The output nodes are connected to all of the input nodes and to all hidden nodes by weights that are retrained after the addition of each hidden node. As previously, a bias is also included, using a weight W_0 connected to an additional input node, which is clamped at $+1$ for all input patterns. Burgess *et al.* have successfully used this algorithm for 3D object recognition [15] and shown that it can converge for arbitrary real-valued inputs [14].

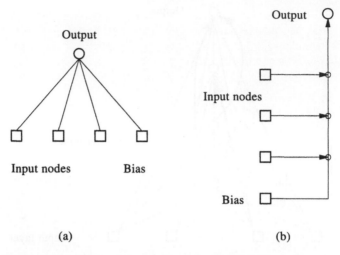

(a)   (b)

Figure 4 To simplify the drawing of Cascade Correlation networks, it is common to use a compact diagrammatic representation. The network in (a) is represented by (b), in which a link via directed lines to the right and upward represents connections and trainable weights in the network.

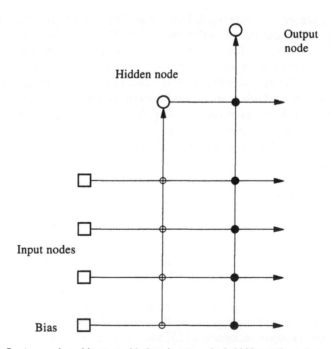

Figure 5 A cascade architecture with three inputs, a single hidden node, and one output.

The structure of connections in cascade architectures can easily become complicated if there are a large number of inputs or hidden nodes. This is especially true for hidden nodes higher in the tree, which will develop a large fan-in from all of the previous hidden nodes and all of the nodes in the input layer. Consequently, it is common to introduce a compact diagrammatic representation for the network (Fig. 4). Thus, for example, a network with three inputs, a bias node, and one hidden node would be represented as in Fig. 5.

D. TREE ARCHITECTURES: THE UPSTART ALGORITHM

1. The Algorithm

The Upstart algorithm [10, 17] is an efficient constructive procedure for building classifier networks. As noted above, there are two types of error that can occur at the output node ((1, 0) node quantization is required, as we will see):

- The output is 1 when it should have been 0. We call these patterns *wrongly on*.
- The output is 0 when it should have been 1. We call these patterns *wrongly off*.

The algorithm starts without hidden nodes and attempts to separate the two classes of data by using the Pocket algorithm, for instance. If it is not possible to separate the two classes, then the best solution is recorded and the corresponding weights and bias are used for the direct connections between the input layer and output (Fig. 9). To correct the remaining errors, we proceed as follows:

If the output makes wrongly *on* mistakes, we build a hidden node called a *corrector* (Fig. 6). The weight between this hidden node and the output is large and negative (the magnitude must exceed the sum of the positive weights into the output node from the inputs). We now use the pocket algorithm to find a set of weights from the inputs to this hidden node. Let T_o be the target value at the output and O_o be the actual output achieved for a given input pattern, then the target values we want at the hidden node are given by the entries in the table in Fig. 7.

Plainly if the target output value (T_o) is 1 and we are considering a negative weight between this hidden node and the output, then the target at the hidden node must be 0 so as not to introduce an error. If the target output (T_o) is 0 and the present output (O_o) is 1, then we must use a target of 1 at the hidden node to correct this error. Finally, if the target output is 0 (T_o) and the present output is 0 (O_o), then either a target of 0 or 1 is satisfactory at the hidden node, because 1 will reinforce this pattern, whereas 0 will have no effect (the output will remain correct). This entry has been denoted by a don't care symbol X (either 0 or 1), and the corresponding patterns can simply be dropped from the training set.

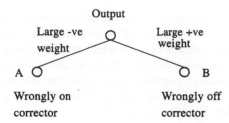

Output

Large -ve
weight

Large +ve
weight

A

B

Wrongly on
corrector

Wrongly off
corrector

Figure 6 The corrector nodes generated by the Upstart algorithm. Node A corrects wrongly on errors and has a large negative weight between it and the output node. Node B corrects wrongly off errors and has a large positive weight between it and the output node. There are connections into all three nodes not shown in this figure.

If the output makes wrongly off mistakes, we build a second corrector. The weight between this hidden node and the output is large and positive (again the magnitude must exceed the sum of the negative weights into the output node from the input). We now use the pocket algorithm to find a set of weights from the inputs to this hidden input, using the entries of the table in Fig. 8 as target values.

If errors exist at these correctors, then we introduce further correctors to remove these errors and keep repeating the process until no errors are left. At the end of the algorithm, we obtain a binary tree network (Fig. 9), with all hidden nodes having direct connections to the input layer nodes. Because some patterns will fall into the category of "don't care" targets, we see that the learning task becomes successively easier as we descend the tree. This does not ensure convergence, because it is conceivable that no patterns will fall into this state as we descend a limb of the tree. However, for a convex pattern set, we can always correctly store at least one pattern at each corrector, and this guarantees convergence for a finite pattern set. In Section II.F we will see that the tree structure of the Upstart algorithm is also reducible to a network with a single hidden layer.

Frean [17] performed numerical experiments with artificial tasks (N-parity, "2 or more clumps", etc.), and the generalization ability of the resulting networks

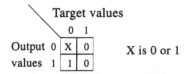

Target values

		0	1
Output	0	X	0
values	1	1	0

X is 0 or 1

Figure 7 The truth table for the wrongly on corrector (node A) in Fig. 6. The entries in the table are the desired target values for this corrector. The output values are those at the output node (O_o), and the target values are the desired outcome at the output node (T_o).

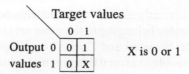

		Target values	
		0	1
Output	0	0	1
values	1	0	X

X is 0 or 1

Figure 8 The truth table for the wrongly on corrector (node B) in Fig. 6. The entries in the table are the desired target values for this corrector. The output values are those at the output node (O_o), and the target values are the desired outcome at the output node (T_o).

was good and much better than earlier algorithms such as the Tower and Tiling algorithms. However, the algorithm does not appear to have been used in practical classification tasks since its introduction.

E. CONSTRUCTING TREE AND CASCADE ARCHITECTURES BY USING DICHOTOMIES

Let us consider classification tasks where the input vectors have binary-valued components (quantized ±1) and the targets belong to two classes: patterns with target $y^\mu = 1$ (the set P^+) and those with target $y^\mu = -1$ (the set P^-) (this choice of target quantization is important, as we will see shortly). For input vectors with binary-valued components, it is always possible to find a set of weights

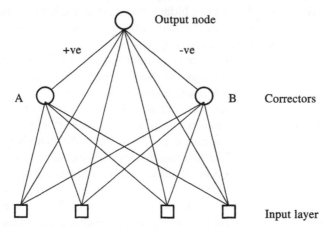

Figure 9 An example of a possible architecture generated by the Upstart algorithm with two corrector nodes. In contrast to this example, the tree will grow asymmetrically for most typical data sets.

and thresholds that will correctly store all of the patterns belonging to one of these sets and at least one member belonging to the other set (for target $y^1 = +1$, say, this was the construction $W_j = x_j^1$ and $T = N$ for an updating function such as Eq. (1)). Usually it is possible to exceed this minimal solution and store a number of patterns of one target sign in addition to all of the patterns of the other target sign. A set of weights and thresholds that correctly store all of the P^+ patterns and some of the P^- will be said to induce a $\oplus$-*dichotomy*, whereas a $\ominus$-*dichotomy* will correspond to correct storage of all of the P^- patterns and some of the P^+.

Let us consider a pair of nodes in a hidden layer with direct connections to the output node, with each connection having a weight value of $+1$. Let us assume the first of these nodes induces a $\oplus$-dichotomy and the second induces a $\ominus$-dichotomy (we will also refer to these hidden nodes as *dichotomy nodes* below). If the first node correctly stored a pattern belonging to P^- then the second node must similarly store this pattern correctly, and each hidden node contributes -1 to the output node. On the other hand, if the pattern belonging to P^- was not stored correctly, then the first node will contribute a $+1$ to the output, which is canceled out by the -1 from the second node (because the weights leading to the output node are both $+1$). In a similar fashion, if the second node successfully stores a pattern belonging to P^+, then both nodes will contribute $+1$ to the output node; otherwise the contributions from the two nodes cancel each other out. If the threshold at the output is zero, then the patterns contributing two $+1$ or two -1 to the output are stored correctly.

Now let us consider those patterns belonging to P^+ and P^- that remain unstored, that is, the contributions from the pair of hidden nodes cancel each other out. In the Target Switch algorithm [18], we handle these unstored patterns by introducing further hidden nodes alternately inducing $\oplus$- and $\ominus$-dichotomies. Patterns correctly stored at the first two hidden nodes are discarded from the training sets of subsequent hidden nodes. Consequently, we avoid disrupting previously stored patterns (at earlier dichotomies) by introducing further nodes between this hidden layer and the output. This can be achieved by using a cascade architecture of linear nodes or a tree architecture of thresholding nodes (we will call these additional hidden nodes *cascade nodes* and *tree nodes* below).

The topology of the cascade architecture is illustrated in Fig. 10. A link between two nodes indicates a connection with a corresponding weight value always fixed at $+1$, and the numbers indicate the order in which the dichotomy nodes are grown. Suppose the output of the first two dichotomy nodes is $(+1, +1)$. The first linear cascade node feeds a $+2$ to all subsequent cascade nodes and the output. This inhibits subsequent cascade nodes from sending an erroneous signal to the output node. For example, suppose the output is -1 for all dichotomy nodes after the first pair; then the corresponding outputs of the other cascade nodes will be 0. On the other hand, if a pattern is not stored correctly at the first pair, then the first

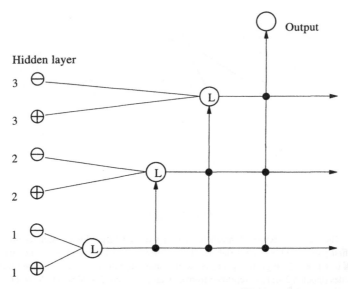

Figure 10 The cascade architecture for the Target Switch algorithm. The dichotomy nodes labeled 1 feed the first linear cascade node, which then feeds the second and third cascade nodes and the output node. If the output from this first pair of dichotomy nodes is $(+1, +1)$ or $(-1, -1)$, then the first cascade node inhibits the succeeding cascade nodes and hence determines the output; otherwise the first cascade node outputs 0, and the final output is determined by the succeeding dichotomy nodes. Reprinted from C. Campbell and C. P. Vincente *Neural Computation* [18], 1995, with permission of MIT.

cascade node outputs 0, and consequently the output of the network is influenced solely by the remaining dichotomy nodes. The number of dichotomy nodes in the hidden layer can be odd or even. If we have m dichotomy nodes, the number of linear cascade nodes is $m/2$ (m even) or $(m + 1)/2$ (m odd).

Instead of linear cascade nodes, we can use thresholding nodes between the dichotomy nodes and the output. The corresponding tree architecture is illustrated in Fig. 11, with the numbers indicating the order in which the dichotomy nodes are grown. This architecture is less economical in terms of the number of extra hidden nodes generated, with $\frac{1}{4}(m^2 - 2m)$ (m even) or $\frac{1}{4}(m - 1)^2$ (m odd) tree nodes for m dichotomy nodes.

To implement this method for storing the patterns, we need an efficient procedure for obtaining the dichotomies. The method we now outline starts by attempting to maximize the number of correctly stored patterns (using the pocket algorithm, for example). If separation is not possible, we then shift the threshold so that all of the $+1$ are stored correctly (for a $\oplus$-dichotomy), although some of the -1 are incorrectly stored. We then locate the most problematic pattern among

threshold value determined in step 2 above, and the weights directly connect the input and output nodes.

2. If target switching occurred, then a hidden node is created and the weights leading into this hidden node ($i = 1$) are set equal to the weights determined in 1 (similarly, the threshold T_1 is set equal to the threshold determined in 1). A second hidden node is created, $i = 2$, inducing a $\ominus$-dichotomy. The training sets P_2^+ and P_2^- are initially set equal to the original P^+ and P^-. We then determine the weights W_{2j} and threshold T_2.

3. If the previous pair of hidden nodes failed to store some of the pattern set, then we create training sets P_i^+, P_i^-, P_{i+1}^+, and P_{i+1}^- for a further two hidden nodes, inducing a $\oplus$- and $\ominus$-dichotomy, respectively. These training sets consist of patterns previously unstored at earlier hidden nodes. Step 3 is iterated until all patterns are stored (the final separation of the remaining pattern can occur at an odd-numbered node).

4. A cascade or tree architecture is created (as illustrated in Figs. 10 and 11).

It is also possible to handle arbitrary real-valued inputs by using the Target Switch algorithm [18]. The algorithm has been tried on several artificial problems and has compared well with other techniques such as Back Propagation and neural decision trees (Section IV.B). In further experimentation by the author, it has been found to perform best for Boolean problems and with reasonably balanced target sets.

Instead of using the above tree and cascade architectures, it is also possible to use weight pairs that are multiples of 2 between the hidden layer and output (Fig. 12). This architecture was outlined earlier by Marchand *et al.* [11] in 1990. However, the objective of Campbell and Perez [18] was to enhance generalization performance by reducing the number of trainable free parameters in

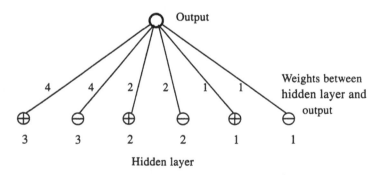

Figure 12   Instead of the cascade or tree architectures in Figs. 10 and 11, we can use a single hidden layer and weights that are multiples of 2 between the hidden layer and output.

the network. In particular, these authors were interested in training using binary-valued weights (quantized ± 1) between the inputs and hidden layer, and weights with value 1 between the hidden layer and the output. Apart from having good generalization properties [20], such weight values are straightforward to implement in hardware [18]. Although binary-valued weights would appear to be very restrictive, it is important to remember that they will give 2^N evenly distributed hyperplanes as candidates for a separatrix (about 10^{30} hyperplanes for a network with $N = 100$ input nodes, for example). This restriction only results in an approximate doubling of the number of hidden nodes generated compared to real weights for most data sets considered [18]. Binary weight implementations were found to be best for learning Boolean problems, in which case the improvement in generalization can sometimes be substantial (for example, a generalization performance of $91.4 \pm 3.4\%$ on a test set was achieved for a Boolean problem for which Back Propagation gave $67.3 \pm 5.7\%$). Other constructive approaches to generating feed-forward networks with binary-valued weights have been considered recently [21].

F. Constructing Neural Networks with a Single Hidden Layer

Instead of generating tree or cascade architectures, we can also use the dichotomy procedure to generate a shallower network with a single hidden layer and weights with a value of 1 between the hidden nodes and output. As for the Target Switch algorithm, we will use target values ± 1. Let P_i^+ and P_i^- be the local pattern sets at hidden node i; then we can generate the network as follows [22].

A4. Growing a Single Hidden Layer: Version 1.

1. Perform a $\oplus$-dichotomy with the current training set. For hidden node i the training set P_i^+ is equal to the original P^+, whereas P_i^- only consists of members of P^- previously unstored at earlier hidden nodes, inducing a $\oplus$-dichotomy. We repeatedly grow hidden nodes, iterating this step until all patterns belonging to P^- are stored.
2. Similarly, we construct a set of hidden nodes inducing $\ominus$-dichotomies. For hidden node i, the training set P_i^- is equal to the original P^-, whereas P_i^+ only consists of members of P^+ previously unstored at earlier hidden nodes inducing a $\ominus$-dichotomy. We repeatedly grow hidden nodes and iterate this step until all patterns belonging to P^+ are stored.
3. We use a threshold at the output node equal to the difference between the number of hidden nodes inducing $\oplus$-dichotomies and the number inducing $\ominus$-dichotomies.

Correlation, the hidden nodes are connected to all preceding hidden nodes in addition to the nodes in the input layer. The function of the hidden nodes is to correct the residual errors at the output. We are only interested in the magnitude of the correlation between the hidden node values and the residual error at the output because, if the hidden node correlates positively with the residual error, we can use a negative weight between it and the output, whereas if this correlation is negative, we can use a positive weight.

A6. The Cascade Correlation Algorithm.

1. We start without hidden nodes and with an architecture looking like that in Fig. 13 (we have chosen one output node and two inputs for purposes of illustration). We then perform gradient descent to minimize an error function such as

$$E = \tfrac{1}{2} \sum_{\mu} (y^{\mu} - O^{\mu})^2, \tag{6}$$

where O^{μ} is the output of the network and y^{μ} is the expected target. We can use the Delta rule with weight changes $\Delta W_j = -\eta \partial E / \partial W_j$, or a faster alternative, such as Quickprop [35] (Section VII.B). If the error falls below a certain tolerance, then we **stop**; the algorithm has found a solution without hidden nodes. If it reaches a plateau at a certain error value, then we end the gradient descent, recording the weights for the best solution found so far. It is now necessary to add hidden nodes to correct the error that remains in the output. Before doing so, we record the residual pattern errors,

$$\delta^{\mu} = (y^{\mu} - O^{\mu}), \tag{7}$$

for each pattern μ, where the output O^{μ} is calculated using those weights W_j which minimize E (we calculate the output from $O^{\mu} = f(\sum_{\mu} W_j(x_j^{\mu}))$ for our

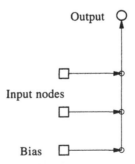

Figure 13 A cascade architecture with two input nodes, a bias, and no hidden nodes.

chosen updating function, such as $f(\phi) = \tanh(\phi)$, for example). We also calculate the average pattern error, $\bar{\delta} = (1/p)\sum_{\mu}\delta^{\mu}$, where p is the number of patterns.

2. We now grow a hidden node as in Fig. 14 and adjust the weights between the hidden node and the inputs so as to maximize the correlation S:

$$S = \left| \sum_{\mu} \left(H^{\mu} - \overline{H}^{\mu}\right)\left(\delta^{\mu} - \bar{\delta}\right) \right| \qquad (8)$$

where H^{μ} is the output of the hidden node and $\overline{H}$ is the average of these outputs over the pattern set, that is, $\overline{H} = (1/p)\sum_{\mu} H^{\mu}$. S is maximized by a gradient ascent. Suppose the weights leading from the input to the hidden node are J_j; then suitable weight changes are

$$\Delta J_j = \eta \frac{\partial S}{\partial J_j} = \eta\epsilon \sum_{\mu} \left(\delta^{\mu} - \bar{\delta}\right) f'\left(\phi^{\mu}\right) x_j^{\mu}, \qquad (9)$$

where η is the learning rate and $\phi^{\mu} = \sum_k J_k x_k^{\mu}$. $f'(\phi)$ is the derivative of $f(\phi)$ with respect to ϕ, for example, for an updating function $f(\phi^{\mu}) = \tanh(\beta\phi^{\mu}/2)$, $f'(\phi^{\mu}) = \beta[1 - [f(\phi^{\mu})]^2]/2$. ϵ is the sign of the correlation between the hidden node's value and the output node (this parameter arises from our earlier remark about the two sign choices for the weights between hidden nodes and output). We

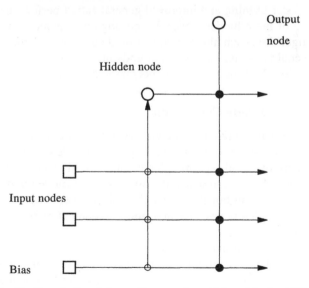

Figure 14 The Cascade Correlation architecture after addition of the first hidden node.

perform this gradient ascent until S stops increasing, at which point we freeze the weights belonging to this hidden node.

3. With the hidden node in place in the network, we now go back to step 1 and perform a gradient descent in the total error E, but now adjusting the weights from the hidden node(s) to the output in addition to the weights from the inputs to the output. Having reached a plateau as in 1, we may satisfy our stopping criterion, otherwise we grow a further hidden node and perform a gradient ascent in S, but now including the weights from the previous hidden node(s) in addition to the weights from the input layer. This step is repeated until the error E falls below a prescribed tolerance.

Instead of using one candidate hidden node, we can also have several candidates with different initial weight configurations. Because single-node learning is involved at each step, this algorithm is very fast, outperforming standard Back Propagation by about an order of magnitude in terms of training speed.

There are many variants on the original Cascade Correlation algorithm. For example, Phatak and Koren [36] have proposed a variant in which there is more than one hidden node in each layer, although the nodes in a new layer are only connected to those in the hidden layer immediately previous. This prevents the problem of steadily increasing fan-in to hidden nodes deep in the network, although the fixed fan-in of the hidden nodes may mean the network is not capable of universal approximation. Simon *et al.* [37] have investigated a cascade architecture in which each output node is connected to its own set of hidden nodes rather than having the hidden nodes connected to all of the output nodes. Simulations suggest this leads to faster training and improved generalization performance, although at the expense of more hidden nodes. In the original statement of the Cascade Correlation algorithm, each hidden unit is a single node with sigmoidal updating function. We could also use other types of updating function, such as radial basis functions (Section III.D) or entire networks rather than a single node [38–40].

2. Recurrent Cascade Correlation

Recurrent neural networks can generate and store temporal information and sequential signals. It is straightforward to extend the Cascade Correlation algorithm to generate recurrent neural networks. A commonly used recurrent architecture is the Elman model (Fig. 15), in which the outputs of the hidden nodes at discrete time t are fed back as additional inputs to the hidden layer at time $t + 1$. To store the output of the hidden nodes, Elman introduced context nodes, which act as a short-term memory in the system.

To generate an Elman-like network using Cascade Correlation, each added node has a time-delayed recurrent self-connection that is trained along with the other input weights to candidate nodes to maximize the correlation. When the candidate node is added to the network as a hidden node, this recurrent weight is frozen along with the other weights (Fig. 15).

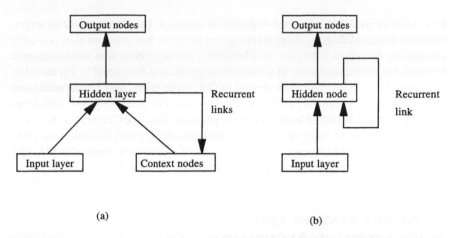

(a)

(b)

Figure 15 (a) The structure of an Elman network with recurrent links and feedback via context nodes to the hidden layer. (b) Recurrent Cascade Correlation constructs similar recurrent links to the hidden nodes.

Recently Giles *et al.* [41] have argued that this Recurrent Cascade Correlation (RCC) architecture cannot realize all finite state automata, for example, cyclic states of length more than two under a constant input signal. This result was extended to a broader class of automata by Kremer [42]. Indeed, apart from RCC, there has been very little other work on constructive generation of recurrent architectures [43] or investigations of their representational capabilities [44].

3. Applications of Cascade Correlation

The Cascade Correlation algorithm has been used in a wide variety of applications, and it is certainly the most popular choice of constructive algorithm for this purpose. A number of applications in machine vision have been reported. Masic *et al.* [45] have used the algorithm to classify objects in scanned images for an automatic visual inspection system. In this case, the network was used to classify five different objects with the feature vectors extracted from two-dimensional images of circularly scanned images. The system was able to classify partially occluded objects with a high degree of accuracy. Cascade Correlation has also been used in the segmentation of magnetic resonance images of the brain [46]. In this study the performance of the Cascade Correlation algorithm was compared to a fuzzy clustering technique. The latter algorithm was observed to show slightly better segmentation performance when compared on the raw image data. However, for more complex segmentations with fluid and tumor edema boundaries, the performance of Cascade Correlation was roughly comparable to the fuzzy clustering algorithm. Zhao *et al.* [47] used a Cascade Correlation neural network to classify facial expressions into six categories of emotion: happiness, sadness, anger, surprise, fear, and disgust. After training, the network was successful in correctly classifying 87.5% of a test set. In chemistry, the algorithm was used to train a network for both quantitative and qualitative prediction for complex ion mobility spectrometry data sets with 229 spectra of 200 input points and 15 output classes [48], achieving significantly better results compared to those obtained from other techniques, such as partial least-squares regressian. Cascade Correlation has been used in a number of other applications, such as cereal grain classification [49], learning the inverse kinematic transformations of a robot arm controller [37], the classification of cervical cells [50], and continuous speech recognition [51].

C. NODE CREATION AND NODE-SPLITTING ALGORITHMS

1. Dynamic Node Creation

The Dynamic Node Creation method of Ash [52] adds fully connected nodes to the hidden layer of a feed-forward neural network architecture trained using Back Propagation. Training starts with a single hidden node and proceeds until the functional mapping is learned (the final error is below a tolerance), or the error ceases to descend and a new hidden node is added. After addition of a new node, both the weights into the new node and previous weights are retrained.

The algorithm retains a history of width w for the error averaged over all output nodes and patterns. If this error ceases to descend quickly enough during the width of this history, a new node is added to the hidden layer. Thus if E is this average error, then a new node is added if

$$\frac{E^t - E^{t-w}}{E^s} < \epsilon, \tag{10}$$

where t denotes the current training epoch (number of presentations of the entire training set), s is the epoch after which the last training node was last added, and ϵ is the trigger slope parameter, which is the threshold for extra node addition.

Dynamic node creation has the advantage that the procedure starts with a small network that can be trained and evaluated quickly. As new nodes are added, the preexisting weights are generally in a favorable region of weight space for finding an eventual solution, so the algorithm spends the least time in the final training stages before convergence. For hard benchmark problems such as n-parity, mirror symmetry, and the encoder problem, the algorithm always converged on a solution that was frequently close to known best solutions. The algorithm does have the disadvantage that the trigger parameter must be found by experimentation, because there is no theoretical guidance for a good choice for this parameter.

2. Hanson's Meiosis Networks

Meiosis networks were proposed by Hanson [53] and construct a feed-forward neural network by using a node-splitting process in the single hidden layer, with the error dictating the splitting process. However, rather than just adding a new node to the hidden layer, a suitable hidden node is now selected and split. The selection is made on the basis of the ratio of variance/mean for a weight distribution at each hidden node. For nodes in the hidden layer, the summed inputs $\phi_j^\mu = \sum_k J_{jk} x_k^\mu$ are evaluated by using weights J_{jk} sampled from a distribution:

$$P(W_{jk} = J_{jk}) = \mu_{\mathbf{w}} + \sigma_{\mathbf{w}} N(0, 1), \tag{11}$$

where $\mu_{\mathbf{w}}$ and $\sigma_{\mathbf{w}}$ are the mean and standard deviation at weight W_{jk}, and $N(0, 1)$ is a random normal deviate with mean 0 and standard deviation 1.

Training is accomplished by modifying the means $\mu_{\mathbf{w}}$ and standard deviations $\sigma_{\mathbf{w}}$ for each weight distribution, using a error gradient procedure. The mean is modified by using a standard gradient descent procedure:

$$\mu_{\mathbf{w}}^{t+1} = \mu_{\mathbf{w}}^t - \eta \frac{\partial E}{\partial J_{ij}}, \tag{12}$$

where t is the iteration index, η is the learning rate, and $\partial E / \partial J_{ij}$ is the weight gradient evaluated with value J_{ij}. The standard deviations are updated in a similar fashion, so that errors will increase the variance:

$$\sigma_{\mathbf{w}}^{t+1} = \lambda \left(\beta \left| -\frac{\partial E}{\partial J_{ij}} \right| + \sigma_{\mathbf{w}}^t \right), \tag{13}$$

where β is a learning parameter and λ is a decay parameter that must be less than 1. If λ is smaller, the system settles faster, whereas if it is larger it will tend to jump around more before settling. Starting with one hidden node and initial means and variances chosen randomly, the algorithm is therefore as follows.

A7. Hanson's Meiosis Algorithm.

1. We present an input vector and make a forward pass to find the outputs.
2. We find the differences between outputs and targets and use these errors to update the means and variances of the weight distribution (the errors appear via the derivatives $\partial E / \partial J_{ij}$).
3. We evaluate the variance/mean ratio for each hidden node for both the input and output weights. If these ratios are greater than a predefined threshold, then the corresponding nodes are split.
4. Having split certain hidden nodes, the corresponding weights are assigned half the variance of the old nodes, and the new means for the split nodes are differentiated by introducing a small random noise $W_{ij} \to W_{ij} \pm \epsilon$.
5. Training ceases when the network error is below a given tolerance.

Based on experiments presented in [53], Meiosis seems to be reasonably effective, but it is rather slow when the number of input nodes is large. The parameters are also found by experimentation, and the performance can be quite sensitive to the choice of these parameters. For example, if the decay parameter λ is too small, node splitting may not occur, and if it is too high, then too many nodes may be generated. This experimentation to find the most suitable parameters adds to the computational load.

Hanson's Meiosis method gives a criterion for splitting nodes based on those weight distributions exhibiting a large variance. The magnitude of the divergence is well defined but the directions are not. This causes most splits to slip straight back to the original nodes position without any improvement in network performance.

3. Other Node-Splitting Algorithms

An alternative scheme has been proposed by Wynne-Jones [54], in which there is an attempt to find the best location for the two splitting nodes. In this scheme we freeze the current weights in the network and find the weight updates that would be made for each training pattern. The distribution of weight updates is illustrated in Fig. 16, where the bold line indicates the current vector of weights leading into the hidden node, and the arrows indicate the scatter of proposed new weight updates (which would average to zero at a minimum of the error). There may exist a clear clustering of new updates (indicated by the dashed arrows in Fig. 16). If

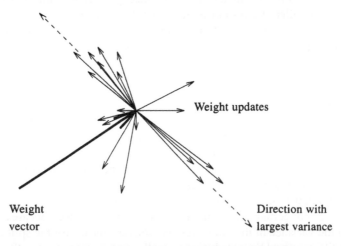

Figure 16   After the error has reached a plateau, the proposed weight updates form a distribution averaging to zero net displacement in weight space. The best node-splitting choice would be in the direction of largest variance.

this principal direction can be found, the algorithm of Wynne-Jones [54] finds the variance in this direction and new nodes are placed one standard deviation to either side of the old position. The direction for placing the new nodes and the magnitude of their distance from the tip of the current weight vector are calculated by principal component analysis.

To find this best direction, we evaluate the covariance matrix for the set of proposed weight updates $\Delta^\mu W_{ij}$:

$$C_{ij} = \sum_{\mu=1}^{p} \Delta^\mu W_{ij} \Delta^\mu W_{ij}. \tag{14}$$

The largest eigenvalue for this matrix is the variance for the split, and the corresponding eigenvector is the direction. There are a number of possible ways of performing principal component analysis, but because we have a large matrix, an iterative estimation procedure is most appropriate. We do not outline the method here, but refer to [55, 56] for a more complete discussion and outline of the methods.

Wynne-Jones [54] has experimented with a number of different splitting criteria and a variety of classification problems to evaluate this algorithm. Unfortunately, it was found that the node-splitting technique was frequently unable to improve on the performance of the network used as the seed for the initial split. The most likely reason for this is that the splitting may correct some misclassified patterns, but a greater number of new misclassifications may be introduced because of the long-range effects of these decision boundaries. Consequently, the newly created nodes may revert to the decision boundary of the node from which they were created, with no overall benefit in terms of classification performance. One way of circumventing this problem is to avoid long-range decision boundaries, and instead use a network of *localized* receptive fields such as the radial basis function (RBF) networks we now describe. In this case simulations suggest that the splitting technique works very well.

D. CONSTRUCTING RADIAL BASIS FUNCTION NETWORKS

RBF networks are a simple but powerful network architecture that has been used in a variety of applications. Whereas multilayer learning algorithms such as Back Propagation construct the architecture of the network by using separating hyperplanes, RBF networks develop functional approximations using combinations of local basis functions. The RBF network has a feed-forward architecture with a single hidden layer, with nonlinear updating functions that we will denote $f(\cdot)$. The output nodes usually have simple linear updating functions. If weights from hidden nodes j to the output nodes i are denoted W_{ij}, then the RBF mapping can be written

$$y_i^\mu = \sum_{j=1}^q W_{ij} f_j(\mathbf{x}^\mu) + W_{i0}. \tag{15}$$

As before, the bias W_{i0} can be included in the summation by incorporating an extra hidden node f_0 with updating fixed at $+1$, and consequently we can write the above equation compactly as $y_i^\mu = \sum_{j=0}^q W_{ij} f_j(\mathbf{x}^\mu)$. There are a number of possible choices for the basis functions on the single hidden layer. One obvious choice is to use Gaussian basis functions:

$$f_j(\mathbf{x}^\mu) = \exp\left(-\frac{\sum_k (x_k^\mu - r_{kj})^2}{2\sigma_j^2}\right), \tag{16}$$

where $\mathbf{x}^\mu$ is the input vector, $\mathbf{r}_j$ is a vector that determines the center of the basis function j, and the parameter σ_j controls the width of the basis function j. Training RBF networks therefore amounts to finding the hidden-to-output weights W_{ij} and the parameters $\mathbf{r}_j$ and σ_j for the hidden nodes (Fig. 17). Assuming an arbitrary number of basis functions and with minor restrictions on the choice of basis function, it has been shown that an RBF network is capable of universally approximating any arbitrary function. Girosi and Poggio [57] have also shown that RBF networks are capable of finding the unique function that has the minimum approximating error.

In early applications of RBF networks, the number of basis functions was selected arbitrarily and the positions of the centers were found by randomly selecting examples from the data set (this has the advantage that the centers are most

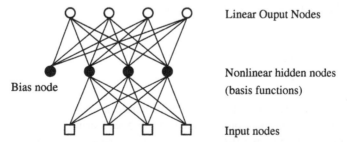

Figure 17 An RBF network consists of a single hidden layer interposed between the input nodes and the output. Each hidden node represents a basis function, and the lines from inputs k to hidden node j represent the trainable parameters $\mathbf{r}_j$ and σ_j. The lines from the hidden nodes to the output i represent the trainable weights W_{ij}. The bias in the output layer is handled by an extra "basis function" clamped at $+1$.

likely to be concentrated in the regions of highest data density). The variances could then be chosen to be half the distance to the nearest center, for example.

Rather than guessing the number of basis functions and their parameters, it makes more sense to follow a principled construction of the network through the growth of hidden nodes as required. The orthogonal least-squares (OLS) method proposed by Chen [58, 59] is such a constructive procedure which, starting from the empty set, adds one basis function at a time until the residual error is below a tolerance. The main idea is to select a subset of the input training vectors $\mathbf{x}^\mu$ as the centers of the basis functions $\mathbf{r}_j$ (we will select the σ_j so that the difference between $\mathbf{x}^\mu$ and $\mathbf{r}_j$ in (16) gives a Euclidean distance).

The selection of the best candidate basis function is based on minimization of an error function. If input $\mathbf{x}^\mu$ is presented to the RBF network, then the predicted output would be

$$O_i^\mu = \sum_{j=0}^{q} W_{ij} f_j(\mathbf{x}^\mu). \tag{17}$$

To train the network, we then minimize the difference between this and the expected outcome:

$$E = \sum_{\mu,i} \left(y_i^\mu - O_i^\mu\right)^2. \tag{18}$$

For linear updating functions at the output nodes, the minimization of this error function leads to a set of simultaneous linear equations for determination of the weights between the hidden layer and outputs:

$$\mathbf{W} = \left(\mathbf{F}^T\mathbf{F}\right)^{-1}\mathbf{F}^T\mathbf{y}, \tag{19}$$

in matrix notation, where $\mathbf{F}$ is the design matrix:

$$\mathbf{F} = \begin{bmatrix} 1 & f_1(\mathbf{x}^1) & f_2(\mathbf{x}^1) & \cdots & f_q(\mathbf{x}^1) \\ 1 & f_1(\mathbf{x}^2) & f_2(\mathbf{x}^2) & \cdots & f_q(\mathbf{x}^2) \\ \vdots & \vdots & \vdots & \vdots \\ 1 & f_1(\mathbf{x}^P) & f_2(\mathbf{x}^P) & \cdots & f_q(\mathbf{x}^P) \end{bmatrix}. \tag{20}$$

In matrix notation, we can therefore write $\mathbf{O} = \mathbf{FW}$, and by using Eq. (19), the difference between the expected and predicted output becomes

$$\mathbf{y} - \mathbf{O} = \mathbf{y} - \mathbf{F}\left(\mathbf{F}^T\mathbf{F}\right)^{-1}\mathbf{F}^T\mathbf{y} \tag{21}$$

$$= \left(\mathbf{I} - \mathbf{F}\left(\mathbf{F}^T\mathbf{F}\right)^{-1}\mathbf{F}^T\right)\mathbf{y} \tag{22}$$

$$= \mathbf{Py}, \tag{23}$$

performances are often good, at least on artificial data sets. However, node creation and splitting algorithms have been less successful in practical applications, possibly because the new hidden nodes do not always systematically decrease errors for some (although not necessarily all) of these approaches. In particular, they have also not been extensively used on real-life data sets, so their reliability is unknown. Recent algorithms include techniques that iteratively attempt to estimate the number of required hidden nodes from the dimensions of the input and output spaces [86] and algorithms that dynamically expand and shrink the network to fit the problem [87]. Constructive algorithms that use higher order weights have also been proposed in the context of regression problems [88, 89].

IV. CONSTRUCTING MODULAR ARCHITECTURES

A. INTRODUCTION

So far we have considered constructive methods in which single nodes are added to the network. We now consider techniques in which entire neural network modules are constructed during the training process. Mainly we will consider neural decision trees in which the modules are constructed as decision elements in a classification tree.

B. NEURAL DECISION TREES

Decision trees are a popular approach to pattern classification problems. Each branch node of a decision tree has a set of child nodes, each of which is also a decision tree, and so the structure is recursive. Information is presented at the root node and propagates down the tree until it reaches a terminal or leaf node. The leaf nodes perform no processing and only assign the appropriate class labels to the input patterns (Fig. 19).

The essential idea is to solve the problem by using a divide- and- conquer approach, with successive partitionings or splittings of the input space. The splitting procedure usually generates a list of possible splits and then searches through this set to find the best choice. This is continued until each leaf node corresponds to a particular class. Different ways of generating the search space of partitions and evaluating the goodness of a particular split lead to different types of decision tree algorithm. This approach to classification [90–92] has been successfully used in a number of applications, for example, [93, 94], and has the useful feature that a complex rule may be decomposed into a sequence of simpler local classification rules.

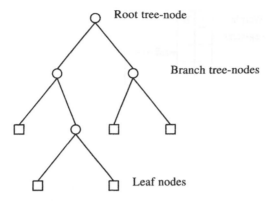

Figure 19 The structure of a decision tree. Each circle represents a decision node, and the squares represent leaf nodes, which assign class labels.

Decision trees can be straightforwardly combined with neural networks, because neural network modules can be used to make the decisions at the branch nodes in the tree. For this reason, a number of neural tree models have been proposed [95–102]. For neural computing the neural tree architecture has the advantage that it can be readily implemented in hardware because of its recursive nature. At a branch tree node in a classification tree, the outcome of the decision causes the loading of one of two sets of weights (Fig. 20). This process continues until a leaf node is reached (indicated perhaps by a flag in the weight register), at which point the result becomes the output for the entire tree.

A straightfoward way of generating a neural tree is as follows [95].

A8. Construction of a Neural Decision Tree.

1. Attempt to separate the pattern set using the pocket algorithm, etc. The solution will divide the data into two sets, S_1 and S_0, according to the outputs $+1$ and -1, respectively.
2. For the pattern set S_1, check if all of the patterns correctly belong to the same class. If this is the case, then we have arrived at a leaf node. If not, then repeat step 1 with this subset and a new node, thus creating two further subsets S_{10} and S_{11}.
3. We repeat the above step with the corresponding set S_0 if it also contains incorrectly classified patterns generating further subsets S_{00} and S_{01}.
4. Recursively repeat steps 2 and 3 for all subsets until leaf nodes are reached.

Neural decision trees can also be extended to the case of multiple output classes by generalizing the concept of separability. A two-class problem is linearly sep-

the desired output (a 1 for P^+ and a 0 for P^-), then the task of globally optimizing the performance of the trio reduces to minimization of a suitable error function, such as

$$E(\mathbf{x}) = \tfrac{1}{2}\big(o(\mathbf{x}) - o_D(\mathbf{x})\big)^2, \qquad (29)$$

and this can be achieved by a suitable gradient descent procedure (Section VII.B) in the parent and child weights [105]. To further optimize the performance of the neural tree, the authors also outline a further pruning procedure [105]. For a classification task involving handwritten character recognition, this algorithm consistently outperformed the standard neural tree (*A8*) for performance on unseen characters [105].

A second approach to improving the neural tree performance has been considered by Guo and Gelfand [106]. Many different splitting criteria have been proposed for decision trees, but it has been found that classification performance does not differ significantly between rules [92]. Instead the performance is substantially affected by the set of features chosen by the splitting rule [92]. In the approach considered by Guo and Gelfand, the branch nodes in the classification tree consist of small multilayered neural network modules, which are trained to extract local features. These authors also propose an efficient pruning algorithm to further improve performance. On handwritten character recognition and waveform recognition, the proposed method outperformed Back Propagation in simulations.

D. OTHER APPROACHES TO GROWING MODULAR NETWORKS

Apart from trees of networks it is interesting to consider the possibility of growing other modular structures. Modular arrangements would be beneficial in terms of hardware implementation, training speed, and the interpretational advantage of decomposing a complex problem into simpler subproblems. Furthermore, there is extensive evidence for modular processing in neural structures such as the neocortex. More generally, modular neural networks may be required for complex information tasks encountered in the real world, where the number of nodes could be very large.

Despite the appeal of modular neural networks, this remains a relatively undeveloped subject. Modular schemes have been proposed for fixed architectures with a single layer of modular subnetworks, for example, the mixture of experts model of Jacobs and Jordan [107, 108], and it would be interesting to develop constructive schemes along these lines.

V. REDUCING NETWORK COMPLEXITY

A. INTRODUCTION

In the Introduction we pointed out that constructive algorithms have the potential disadvantage that they can create over-complex networks. Pruning redundant weights and nodes will help reduce this complexity, apart from making implementation easier and highlighting the relevance of various input nodes. Minimization of an error function (or storing all of the data in a training set) is also an inappropriate measure for stopping the training process, because it may give an over-complex model. Thus we will consider a number of other performance measures that validate the performance of a network in terms of its ability to capture the function or rule generating the training data (Section V.C). Here we will only consider pruning after training. In this case pruning procedures fall in to two categories: weight pruning and node pruning. Node pruning can be further classified into input node pruning and hidden node pruning.

B. WEIGHT PRUNING

1. Magnitude-Based Pruning Algorithms

One of the simplest weight-pruning procedures is to successively remove weights according to their magnitude, starting with those with the smallest values. There is a theoretical justification for this rule from calculations based on the statistical mechanics approach to neural computation [109–111]. The rationale is that weights with small values generally have the least effect on the output, and they tend to arise from conflicting requirements imposed on the weights by different patterns. Although this is a simple procedure, it is also effective and often exhibits a performance comparable to that of more sophisticated approaches.

2. Optical Brain Damage

For many models (e.g., Cascade Correlation or dynamic node creation) learning involves the reduction of an error function. In this case more sophisticated procedures can be used. Let us consider the change in an error function due to a change in the value of one of the weights. Let us suppose the weight W_i is changed by an amount ΔW_i; then the corresponding change in the error function is

$$\Delta E = \sum_i \frac{\partial E}{\partial W_i} \Delta W_i + \frac{1}{2} \sum_{i,j} H_{ij} \Delta W_i \Delta W_j + \cdots, \qquad (30)$$

that is, $\lambda \mathbf{I}$. Consequently, the algorithm actually finds the inverse of $\mathbf{H} + \lambda \mathbf{I}$. The OBS algorithm can be summarized as follows.

A11. The OBS Algorithm.

1. Train the network until a minimum of the error function is found.
2. Find the inverse Hessian by using the iterative technique in Eq. (41).
3. Find the error changes ΔE_i for each weight value i and eliminate the weight or weights that give rise to the smallest increase in the error function.
4. After pruning, if a stopping criterion is met, **stop**; else go to step 1.

The OBS algorithm is more computationally intensive than OBD, and OBD is in turn more computationally intensive than straightforward weight elimination based on magnitudes. However, there is a reward for this greater effort in that numerical simulations suggest that the OBS technique is superior to OBD, which in turn is often superior to magnitude-based pruning techniques. This has been confirmed in simulations [112–115].

C. NODE PRUNING

Apart from eliminating weights, we can also eliminate entire input or hidden nodes. The most obvious way of assessing the relevance of a node is to consider how well the network would perform in the absence of that node, in particular what the change would be in the error after its elimination:

$$\Delta E = E_{\text{without node}} - E_{\text{with node}}. \tag{42}$$

To make this idea more mathematically precise, we can introduce [116] an attentional coefficient α_j for node j that can have a value of 0 or 1. Thus if v_j is the output of node j and it can feed node i (with output u_i), then

$$u_i = f\left(\sum_j W_{ij}\alpha_j v_j\right), \tag{43}$$

and the α_j gates the contribution of node j to node i. This arrangement is shown in Fig. 21. Plainly, if $\alpha_j = 0$, then node j has no effect on the rest of the network. Using these attentional coefficients, we can therefore write Eq. (42) as

$$\Delta E = E_{\alpha_j=0} - E_{\alpha_j=1}. \tag{44}$$

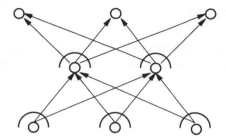

Figure 21 A feed-forward network. Semicircular arcs show the locations of the attentional coefficients. Each attentional coefficient gates all of the outputs of hidden or input nodes in a forward direction.

We can approximate this difference by the derivative of the error with respect to α_j:

$$\Delta E = \left.\frac{\partial E}{\partial \alpha_j}\right|_{\alpha_j}, \tag{45}$$

which can be computed by using an error back-propagation algorithm similar to the method used in the Back Propagation [116–118]. This approximation saves on the computation without much loss of accuracy in assessing the attentional strength of each node. In practice, this derivative fluctuates sharply, and it is best to moderate it with a component of the previous ΔE value during pruning:

$$\Delta E_j^{t+1} = 0.8\Delta E_j^t + 0.2\frac{\partial E^t}{\partial \alpha_j}. \tag{46}$$

Further details and examples are given by Mozer and Smolensky [116].

D. SUMMARY

These and other pruning techniques are surveyed further by Reed [119]. To complete the pruning process, we must also have an effective stopping criterion. So far we have suggested minimization of the training error to a less-than-prescribed tolerance. Although it is a common stopping criterion, the training error can introduce a bias due to the choice of data set. Instead, one could use a separate test set or generalized cross-validation [120]. Other criteria, such as the Bayesian evidence [121], or criteria such as generalized predicted error or predicted squared error can also be used [122] and can be more accurate.

This determines the weight vector, which maximizes the separation between the two clusters and gives a solution:

$$W_j = \frac{1}{N^+} \sum_{\mu \in P^+} x_j^\mu - \frac{1}{N^-} \sum_{\mu \in P^-} x_j^\mu. \tag{50}$$

This rule is fast to implement, but the assumption of a normal distribution for the two classes is generally unrealistic, and the solution found is far from optimal. Its use may be restricted to problems in which the number of inputs is large, and the methods below are too computationally intensive.

2. The Perceptron Algorithm

The perceptron algorithm is a much more efficient algorithm to use for single-node learning. The well-known Perceptron Convergence Theorem [23, 25] states that the perceptron algorithm will find weights for storing a pattern set after a finite number of iterations through the set, provided a solution exists. For single-node learning with an updating function as in (1), the perceptron algorithm is as follows.

A12. The Perceptron Algorithm.

1. At the first iteration $t = 0$, initialize the weights W_j^0 to random values.
2. Present the pattern set $\mu = 1, \ldots, p$. For each pattern evaluate
   $\lambda^\mu = y^\mu \sum_j W_j^t x_j^\mu$. If $\lambda^\mu \leq 0$, then update the weights according to
   $W_j^{t+1} = W_j^t + y^\mu x_j^\mu$.
3. If $\lambda^\mu > 0$ for all $\mu = 1, \ldots, p$, or a maximum number of iterations has been exceeded, then **stop**, else repeat step 2.

The perceptron rule is capable of storing patterns up to the optimal capacity. Given the simplicity of single-node learning, it has been possible to calculate the optimal properties of single-layered neural networks, though only for the idealized case of randomly constructed patterns with binary components [127–130]. We find that for p random patterns and N input nodes, it is theoretically possible to store up to $p = 2N$ pairs of patterns in a fully connected single-layered neural network by using the perceptron algorithm (strictly in the large N limit). By contrast, the Fisher rule can only store up to $p \simeq 0.14N$ patterns [131]. If $p > 2N$, the result is shown in Fig. 22, where the horizontal axis is the storage ratio $\alpha = p/N$, and the vertical axis is the storage error (minimum fraction of incorrectly stored patterns) [132, 133]. A nonzero error starts at $\alpha = 2$ and gradually increases as α increases. Constructive algorithms based on the Pocket algorithm utilize this curve: as successive hidden nodes are added, the algorithm iterates down this curve until the number of remaining patterns is sparse compared

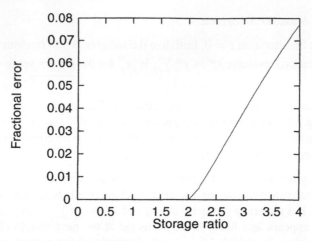

Figure 22 The theoretical minimum fractional error versus storage ratio for randomly constructed, unbiased, and uncorrelated patterns with binary components. The storage ratio is the number of stored patterns per node (in a fully connected network).

to the dimensionality of the space, and so it is possible to separate the remaining pattern set. The use of randomly constructed patterns is unrealistic, of course, but the same essential feature holds for real-life data sets.

Although the perceptron rule is efficient and capable of finding a quasi-optimal solution, there has been interest in rules that offer additional improvements. In particular, rules have been developed which are faster and not only store the patterns correctly ($\lambda^{\mu} = y^{\mu} \sum_j W_j^t x_j^{\mu} > 0 \ \forall \mu$), but embed them strongly so that the patterns are still recognized correctly, despite the presense of noise (by using the stronger bound $\lambda^{\mu} = y^{\mu} \sum_j W_j^t x_j^{\mu} > c|W|$, where $|W| = \sqrt{\sum_j W_j^2}$). Examples are the Minover algorithm [12] and the Adatron [134] (whereas the perceptron and Minover reduce the error as a power law, the Adatron approaches a solution exponentially fast [135]).

3. The Maxover Algorithm, the Thermal Perceptron, and Other Alternatives to the Pocket Algorithm

For constructive algorithms we often want to store as many patterns as possible if we cannot store the entire training set. If we want to maximize the number of stored patterns, then it makes sense to train on those patterns that are *closest* to being stored correctly. The Maxover algorithm [136] is an example of such an algorithm.

A13. The Maxover Algorithm.

1. At the first iteration $t = 0$, initialize the weights W_j^0 to random values.
2. At iteration t evaluate $\lambda^\mu = y^\mu \sum_j W_j^t x_j^\mu$ for the pattern set $\mu = 1, \ldots, p$. For those μ such that $\lambda^\mu \leq c|W|$, where $|W| = \sqrt{\sum_j W_j^2}$, find the λ^μ that is the maximum (most positive or closest to 0 if negative). Let this be pattern ν then update the weights according to $W_j^{t+1} = W_j^t + y^\nu x_j^\nu$.
3. If a maximum number of iterations is exceeded or no corrections were required, then **stop**; else return to step 2.

A similar procedure for finding the optimal linearly separable subset is the thermal perceptron rule proposed by Frean [137]. This rule is based on the following observation. If a pattern is correctly stored and $\lambda^\mu = y^\mu \sum_j W_j x_j^\mu$ is large, then this pattern appears less likely to be corrected at the next weight change compared to a pattern for which λ^μ is small. Similarly, if the pattern is incorrectly stored ($\lambda^\mu < 0$) the weight changes required to correct this pattern will be larger and therefore much more likely to disrupt the storage of other correctly stored patterns. Consequently, the weight changes should be biased toward correcting those patterns for which λ^μ is close to zero. An effective way of doing this is to bias the weight changes by using an exponential factor:

$$\Delta W_j = \eta y^\mu x_j^\mu e^{-|\lambda^\mu|/T}, \tag{51}$$

with the "temperature" T controlling the degree of bias against patterns with a large value of $|\lambda^\mu|$. For a large value of T, we have the usual perceptron algorithm, because the exponential is virtually unity for any input, whereas a small value of T would mean no appreciable changes unless $|\lambda^\mu|$ is nearly zero. Thus the best way of using this algorithm is to gradually anneal the system, that is, to reduce the temperature from a high T value where the usual perceptron algorithm is used toward small T, thereby biasing the algorithm toward those patterns with small $|\lambda^\mu|$ values. For best results it is also advisable to reduce the learning rate η from 1 to 0 while the temperature T is reduced. It is possible to show that this algorithm will converge by using the perceptron convergence theorem [25], which can be shown to hold at any given T value. This method compares well with the pocket algorithm and other techniques, such as gradient descent [137]. A further temperature-dependent algorithm for finding the maximum linearly separable subset is the Minierror algorithm of Raffin and Gordon [138].

B. CONTINUOUSLY-VALUED NODES

In the case of continuously valued data, gradient descent techniques offer the best approach to finding an approximately good solution, even if the data set is not linearly separable. Gradient descent techniques need little introduction [117, 118], but given their use in the Cascade Correlation algorithm and elsewhere, we briefly summarize them here. Suppose we wish to minimize an error function such as the standard quadratic form

$$E = \tfrac{1}{2} \sum_{\mu=1}^{P} \left(y^\mu - O^\mu \right)^2,$$ (52)

where $O^\mu = f(\phi^\mu)$ and $\phi^\mu = \sum_j W_j x_j^\mu$ (single-node learning is assumed). The simplest gradient descent technique involves iterative descent in weight space:

$$W_j' = W_j + \Delta W_j \qquad \Delta W_j = -\eta \frac{\partial E}{\partial W_j}.$$ (53)

This derivative can be straightforwardly evaluated by using the chain rule:

$$\Delta W_j = \eta \sum_{\mu} \left(y^\mu - O^\mu \right) f'(\phi^\mu) x_j^\mu,$$ (54)

if $f(\phi) = \tanh(\phi)$, then $f'(\phi) = [1 - f(\phi)^2]$, for example. A number of much faster variants are possible and should be used in practice. For example, rather than use a constant learning rate η, it is better to use adaptive step sizes. The adaptive learning rates can be different for different weights [107, 139, 140]:

$$\Delta W_j = -\eta_j \frac{\partial E}{\partial W_j}.$$ (55)

Second-order methods use a quadratic approximation to the error function and therefore try to use information about the shape of the error surface beyond the gradient. An algorithm along these lines is Quickprop [35], which was originally used with Cascade Correlation in Fahlman's original paper [35]. Many other algorithms using second-order information have also been proposed [141–143].

REFERENCES

[1] L. G. Valiant. A theory of the learnable. *Comm. Assoc. Comput. Machinery* 27:1134–1142, 1984.

[2] X. Yao. A review of evolutionary artificial neural networks. *Internat. J. Intelligent Systems* 8:539–567, 1993.

[3] J. H. Friedman. Adaptive spline networks. In *Advances in Neural Information Processing Systems,* Vol. 3. pp. 675–683. Morgan Kaufmann, San Mateo, CA, 1991.

[4] J. H. Friedman and W. Stuetzle. Projection pursuit regression. *J. Amer. Statist. Assoc.* 76:817–823, 1981.

[5] J. N. Hwang, S. R. Lay, M. Maechler, D. Martin, and J. Schimert. Regressian modelling in back-propagation and projection pursuit learning. *IEEE Trans. Neural Networks* 5:342–353, 1994.

[6] J. O. Moody and N. Yarvin. Networks with learned unit response functions. In *Advances in Neural Information Processing Systems*, Vol. 4, pp. 1048–1055. Morgan Kaufmann, San Mateo, CA, 1992.

[7] S. Gallant. *Neural Network Learning and Expert Systems*. MIT Press, Cambridge, MA, 1993.

[8] S. I. Gallant. Optimal linear discriminants. In *IEEE Proceedings of the 8th Conference on Pattern Recognition*, pp. 849–852, 1986.

[9] S. I. Gallant. Three constructive algorithms for network learning. In *Eighth Annual Conference of the Cognitive Science Society*, Amherst, MA, pp. 652–660, 1986.

[10] M. Frean. Small nets and short paths: optimising neural computation. Ph.D. Thesis, Center for Cognitive Science, University of Edinburgh, 1990.

[11] M. Marchand, M. Golea, and P. Rujan. A convergence theorem for sequential learning in two-layer perceptrons. *Europhys. Lett.* 11:487–492, 1990.

[12] M. Mezard and J.-P. Nadal. Learning in feedforward layered networks: the Tiling algorithm. *J. Phys. A* 22:2191–2203, 1989.

[13] J.-P. Nadal. Study of a growth algorithm for a feed-forward network. *Internat. J. Neural Systems* 1:55–60, 1989.

[14] N. Burgess. A constructive algorithm that converges for real-valued input patterns. *Internat. J. Neural Systems.* 5:59–66, 1994.

[15] N. Burgess, R. Granieri, and S. Patarnello. 3D object classification: application of a constructive algorithm. *Internat. J. Neural Systems* 2:275–282, 1991.

[16] N. Burgess, S. D. Zenzo, P. Ferragina, and M. N. Granieri. The generalisation of a constructive algorithm in pattern classification problems. *Second workshop on neural networks: from topology to high energy physics. Internat. J. Neural Systems* 3:65–70, 1992.

[17] M. Frean. The Upstart algorithm: a method for constructing and training feedforward neural networks. *Neural Comput.* 2:198–209, 1990.

[18] C. Campbell and C. Perez Vicente. The Target Switch algorithm: a constructive learning procedure for feed-forward neural networks. *Neural Comput.* 7:1221–1240, 1995.

[19] R. Zollner, H. Schmitz, F. Wunsch, and U. Krey. Fast generating algorithm for a general three-layer perceptron. *Neural Networks* 5:771–777, 1992.

[20] E. B. Baum and Y.-D. Lyuu. The transition to perfect generalization in perceptrons. *Neural Comput.* 3:386–401, 1991.

[21] E. Mayoraz and F. Aviolet. Constructive training methods for feedforward neural networks with binary weights. *Internat. J. Neural Networks* 7:149–166, 1996.

[22] C. Campbell and C. Perez Vicente. Constructing feed-forward neural networks for binary classification tasks. In *European Symposium on Artificial Neural Networks*, pp. 241–246. D. Facto Publications, Brussels, 1995.

[23] N. J. Nilsson. *Learning Machines*. McGraw-Hill, New York, 1965.

[24] C. Campbell, S. Coombes, and A. Surkan. A constructive algorithm for building a feed-forward neural network. In *Neural Networks: Artificial Intelligence and Industrial Applications*, pp. 199–202. Springer-Verlag, New York, 1995.

[25] M. Minsky and S. Papert. *Perceptrons*, 2nd Ed. MIT Press, Cambridge, MA, 1988.

[26] S. J. Nowlan and G. E. Hinton. Simplifying neural networks by soft weight-sharing. *Neural Comput.* 4:473–493, 1992.

[27] D. Martinez and D. Esteve. The Offset algorithm: building and learning method for multilayer neural networks. *Europhys. Lett.* 18:95–100, 1992.

[28] P. Rujan. Learning in multilayer networks: a geometric computational approach. *Lecture Notes in Phys.* 368:205–224, 1990.

[29] S. Knerr, L. Personnaz, and G. Dreyfus. Single-layer learning revisited: a stepwise procedure for building and training a neural network. In *Neurocomputing: Algorithms, Architectures and Applications* (J. Fogelman, Ed.). Springer-Verlag, New York, 1990.

[30] M. Biehl and M. Opper. Tiling-like learning in the parity machine. *Phys. Rev. A* 44:6888–6902, 1991.

[31] G. Barkema, H. Andree, and A. Taal. The Patch algorithm: fast design of binary feedforward neural networks. *Network* 4:393–407, 1993.

[32] F. M. F. Mascioli and G. Martinelli. A constructive algorithm for binary neural networks: the Oil-Spot algorithm. *IEEE Trans. Neural Networks* 6:794–797, 1995.

[33] N. J. Redding, A. Kowalczyk, and T. Downs. Constructive higher-order network algorithm that is polynomial in time. *Neural Networks* 6:997–1010, 1993.

[34] S. Mukhopadhyay, S. Roy, L. S. Kim, and S. Govel. A polynomial time algorithm for generating neural networks for pattern classification: its stability properties and some test results. *Neural Comput.* 5:317–330, 1993.

[35] S. Fahlman and C. Lebiere. The cascade correlation architecture. In *Advances in Neural Information Processing Systems*, Vol. 2, pp. 524–532. Morgan Kaufmann, San Mateo, CA, 1990.

[36] D. S. Phatak and I. Koren. Connectivity and performance tradeoffs in the cascade correlation learning architecture. *IEEE Trans. Neural Networks* 5:930–935, 1994.

[37] N. Simon, H. Cororaal, and E. Kerckhoffs. Variations on the cascade correlation learning architecture for fast convergence in robot control. In *Proceedings of the Fifth International Conference on Neural Networks and Their Applications*, Nimes, France, pp. 455–464, 1992.

[38] E. Littmann and H. Ritter. Cascade LLM networks. In *Artificial Neural Networks* (I. Aleksander and J. Taylor, Eds.), Vol. 2, pp. 253–257. Elsevier, Amsterdam, 1992.

[39] E. Littman and H. Ritter. Cascade network architectures. In *Proceedings of the International Joint Conference on Neural Networks*. Baltimore, MD, 1992, Vol. 2, pp. 398–404.

[40] E. Littman and H. Ritter. Learning and generalisation in cascade network architectures. *Neural Comput.* 8:1521–1540, 1996.

[41] C. L. Giles, D. Chen, G.-Z. Sun, H.-H. Chen, Y.-C. Lee, and M. W. Goudreau. Constructive learning of recurrent neural networks: limitations of recurrent cascade correlation and a simple solution. *IEEE Trans. Neural Networks* 6:829–836, 1995.

[42] S. Kremer. Constructive learning of recurrent neural networks: limitations of recurrent cascade correlation and a simple solution—comment. *IEEE Trans. Neural Networks* 7:1047–1049, 1996.

[43] P. J. Angeline, G. M. Saunders, and J. B. Pollack. An evolutionary algorithm that constructs recurrent neural networks. *IEEE Trans. Neural Networks* 5:54–65, 1994.

[44] D. Chen and C. Giles. Constructive learning of recurrent neural networks: limitations of recurrent cascade correlation and a simple solution—reply. *IEEE Trans. Neural Networks* 7:1045–1051, 1996.

[45] N. Masic and S. D. Ristov, and B. Vojnovic. Application of the cascade correlation network to the classification of circularly scanned images. *Neural Comput. Appl.* 4:161–167, 1996.

[46] L. O. Hall, A. M. Bensiad, L. P. Clarke, R. P. Velthuizen, M. S. Silbiger, and J. C. Bezdek. A comparison of neural network and fuzzy clustering techniques in segmenting magnetic resonance images of the brain. *IEEE Trans. Neural Networks* 3:672–682, 1992.

[47] J. Zhao, G. Kearney, and A. Soper. Classifying expressions by cascade correlation neural network. *Neural Comput. Appl.* 3:113–124, 1995.

[48] P. Zheng, P. D. Harrington, and D. M. Davis. Quantitative analysis of volatile organic compounds using ion mobility spectrometry and cascade correlation neural networks. *Chemometrics Intelligent Lab. Systems* 33:121–132, 1996.

[49] B. Dolenko, H. Card, M. Neuman, and E. Shwedyk. Classifying cereal grains using back propagation and cascade correlation networks. *Canad. J. Electrical Comput. Engrg.* 20:91–95, 1995.

[50] S. J. McKenna, I. W. Ricketts, A. Y. Cairns, and K. A. Hussein. Cascade correlation neural networks for the classification of cervical cells. In *IEE Colloqium on Neural Networks for Image Processing Applications*, London, pp. 1–4, 1992.

[100] T. Sanger. A tree-structured adaptive network for function approximation in high-dimensional spaces. *IEEE Trans. Neural Networks* 2:285–293, 1991.

[101] J. Sirat and J.-P. Nadal. Neural trees: a new tool for classification. *Network* 1:198–209, 1990.

[102] M. Marchand and M. Golea. Greedy heuristics for halfspace intersections and neural decision lists. *Network* 4:67–86, 1993.

[103] L. Hyafil and R. L. Rivest. Constructing optimal decision trees is NP-complete. *Inform. Process. Lett.* 5:15–17, 1976.

[104] A. Sankar and R. J. Mammone. *Neural Tree Networks*, pp. 281–302. Academic Press, San Diego, 1991.

[105] F. D'Alche-Buc, D. Zwierski, and J.-P. Nadal. Trio learning: a new strategy for building hybrid eural trees. *Internat. J. Neural Systems* 5:259–274, 1994.

[106] H. Guo and S. B. Gelfand. Classification trees with neural network feature extraction. *IEEE Trans. Neural Networks* 3:923–933, 1992.

[107] R. Jacobs. Increased rates of convergence through learning rate adaptation. *Neural Networks* 1:295–307, 1988.

[108] R. Jacobs, M. Jordan, S. Nowlan, and G. Hinton. Adaptive mixtures of local experts. *Neural Comput.* 3:79–87, 1991.

[109] M. Bouten. Storage capacity of diluted neural networks. *Lecture Notes in Phys.* 368:225–236, 1990.

[110] M. Bouten, A. Engel, A. Komoda, and R. Serneels. Quenched versus annealed dilution in neural networks. *J. Phys. A* 23:4643–4657, 1990.

[111] P. Kuhlmann, R. Garces, and H. Eissfeller. A dilution algorithm for neural networks. *J. Phys.* 25:L593–L598, 1992.

[112] Y. Le Cunn, J. S. Denker, and S. A. Solla. Optimal brain damage. In *Advances in Neural Information Processing Systems*, Vol. 2, pp. 598–605. Morgan Kaufmann, San Mateo, CA, 1990.

[113] B. Hassibi and D. G. Stork. Second order derivatives for network pruning: optimal brain surgeon. In *Advances in Neural Information Processing Systems*, Vol. 5, pp. 164–171. Morgan Kaufmann, San Mateo, CA, 1993.

[114] N. Tolstrup. Pruning of a large network by optimal brain damage and surgeon: an example from biological sequence analysis. *Internat. J. Neural Systems* 6:31–42, 1995.

[115] J. Gorodkin, L. K. Hansen, A. Krogh, C. Svarer, and O. Winther. A quantitative study of pruning by optimal brain damage. *Internat. J. Neural Systems* 4:159–170, 1993.

[116] M. C. Mozer. Skeletonization: a technique for trimming the fat from a network via relevance assessment. *Neural Inform. Process. Systems* 1:107–115, 1989.

[117] J. Hertz, A. Krogh, and R. Palmer. *Introduction to the Theory of Neural Computation*. Addison-Wesley, Redwood City, CA, 1991.

[118] S. Haykin. *Neural Networks: A Comprehensive Foundation*. Macmillan Co., New York, 1994.

[119] R. Reed. Pruning algorithms—a survey. *IEEE Trans. Neural Networks* 4:740–747, 1993.

[120] G. Golub, M. Heath, and G. Wahba. Generalised cross-validation as a method for choosing a good ridge parameter. *Technometrics* 21:215–223, 1979.

[121] D. J. C. MacKay. Probable networks and plausible predictions—a review of practical Bayesian methods for supervised neural networks. *Network* 6:469–505, 1995.

[122] J. Moody. Prediction risk and architecture selection for neural networks. In *From Statistics to Neural Networks: Theory and Pattern Recognition Applications, NATO ASI Series F136* (J. H. Friedman and H. Wechsler, Ed.), pp. 147–165. Springer-Verlag, New York, 1994.

[123] H. H. Thodberg. Ace of bayes: application of neural networks with pruning. Technical Report no. 1132E, Danish Meat Research Institute, Roskilde, Denmark, 1993.

[124] D. J. C. MacKay. A practical Bayesian framework for back propagation networks. *Neural Comput.* 4:448–472, 1992.

[125] D. J. C. MacKay. The evidence framework applied to classification networks. *Neural Comput.* 4:720–736, 1992.

[126] C. M. Bishop. *Neural Networks for Pattern Recognition.* Oxford Univ. Press, 1995.

[127] T. Cover. Geometrical and statistical properties of systems of linear inequalities with applications in pattern recognition. *IEEE Trans. Electron. Comput.* 14:326–334, 1995.

[128] E. Gardner. Maximum storage capacity of neural networks. *Europhys. Lett.* 4:481–485, 1987.

[129] E. Gardner. The space of interactions in neural network models. *J. Phys. A* 21:257–270, 1988.

[130] E. Gardner and B. Derrida. Optimal storage properties of neural network models. *J. Phys. A* 21:271–284, 1988.

[131] D. Amit, H. Gutfreund, and H. Sompolinsky. Spin-glass models of neural networks. *Phys. Rev. A* 32:1007–1018, 1985.

[132] J. K. Fontanari and W. K. Theumann. On the computational capability of a perceptron. *J. Phys. A* 26:L1233–L1238, 1993.

[133] W. Whyte and D. Sherrington. Replica-symmetry breaking in perceptrons. *J. Phys. A* 29:3063–3073, 1996.

[134] J. K. Anlauf and M. Biehl. *Properties of an Adaptive Perceptron Algorithm,* pp. 153–156. North-Holland, Amsterdam, 1990.

[135] W. Kinzel. Statistical mechanics of the perceptron with maximal stability. *Lecture Notes in Phys.* 368:175–188, 1990.

[136] A. Wendemuth. Learning the unlearnable. *J. Phys. A* 28:5423–5436, 1995.

[137] M. Frean. A thermal perceptron learning rule. *Neural Comput.* 4:946–957, 1992.

[138] B. Raffin and M. Gordon. Learning and generalisation with Minierror, a temperature-dependent learning algorithm. *Neural Comput.* 7:1206–1224, 1995.

[139] F. Silva and L. Almeida. Speeding up backpropagation. In *Advanced Neural Computers.* pp. 151–156. North-Holland, Amsterdam, 1990.

[140] M. Riedmiller and H. Braun. A direct adaptive method for faster backpropagation learning: the Rprop algorithm. In *IEEE International Conference on Neural Networks,* San Francisco, CA, 1993, pp. 586–591.

[141] R. Battiti. First and second order methods for learning: between steepest descent and Newton's method. *Neural Comput.* 4:141–166, 1992.

[142] S. Becker and Y. Le Cun. Improving the convergence of back-propagation learning with second order methods. In *Proceedings of the 1988 Connectionist Models Summer School* (D. Touretzky, G. Hinton, and T. Sejnowski, Eds.), pp. 29–37. Morgan Kaufmann, San Mateo, CA, 1989.

[143] A. I. Shepherd. *Second-Order Methods for Neural Networks. Fast and Reliable Training Methods for Multi-Layer Perceptrons.* Springer-Verlag, London, 1997.

Modular Neural Networks

Kishan Mehrotra
Department of Electrical Engineering
and Computer Science
Center for Science and Technology
Syracuse University
Syracuse, New York 13244-4100

Chilukuri K. Mohan
Department of Electrical Engineering
and Computer Science
Center for Science and Technology
Syracuse University
Syracuse, New York 13244-4100

I. INTRODUCTION

Modularity is perhaps the most important principle underlying modern software engineering methodologies. Although all complex systems consist of interconnected parts, a system is considered modular only if each part has clearly defined and distinguishable internal structure and purpose, and the linkages between different parts are sparse and well defined. This allows each module to be designed, analyzed, and understood separately; it is a maxim among software developers that modularity is essential to the synthesis and analysis of complex systems.

Modularity also allows us to grapple successfully with physical and biological systems that are too complex to be understood in their entirety by single individuals: a physician who specializes in understanding the digestive system, for instance, abstracts away from most of the rest of the complexity of human anatomy and physiology, and refers to other specialists if it becomes necessary to do so. The digestive system may be considered a module of the human body, weakly coupled with other modules such as the circulatory system, via a relatively small number of interconnections. Within each such module, we may again find further evidence of specialization by using submodules, for example, the functioning of the stomach may be understandable more or less separately from that of the intestines and the rest of the esophagus, to which it is connected.

It therefore comes as no surprise that the most marvelous of human organs, the brain, itself exploits the principle of modularity. For instance, different parts of the brain specialize for different tasks, and groups of neurons interact in complex ways. There is no general agreement on the precise number of modules in the brain, the precise function of each module, and the precise nature of interaction between modules. It is believed that further specialization does occur within a high-level module such as the visual cortex, devoted to processing and understanding images. Minsky [1] describes a model that views the human brain as a collection of interacting modules called *agents*. In Minsky's model, each agent is capable only of performing simple actions, but intelligence emerges from the collective behavior of such agents.

Artificial neural networks and connectionist models have been inspired by studies of the behavior of animal brains. Hence it is logical that such networks must also exploit the principles of modularity that find expression in biological brains, to solve problems of significant complexity. Traditional neural network learning algorithms and models focus on small subtasks, mimicking low-level behavior of small numbers of neurons, and making assumptions such as exhaustive interconnectivity between all neurons in adjacent layers. Although these algorithms are vital to the foundation of learning systems, a practical approach must necessarily address issues such as modular design, if there is to be a good chance of being able to solve complex tasks. To use an engineering analogy: constructing an edifice needs careful design, understanding the edifice as composed of high level substructures, each of which is constructed from various building blocks and bricks. Similarly, developing an elaborate neural network for a practical application is best done by designing the system in terms of modules, which, of course, invoke learning algorithms that serve as the building blocks for connectionist systems. A building is more than a heap of bricks glued together—yet many neural network practitioners attempt to solve complex tasks by pushing data through a "black box" that is essentially a mass of interconnected neurons.

Neural networks may be modular at different conceptual levels. In a trivial sense, each node or each layer can be thought of as a module. However, our primary concern is with networks that consist of several loosely interconnected components, where each component (module) is itself a neural network.

Many successful real-world applications of neural networks have been achieved by using modular architectures. Several papers exist in the literature that address the construction of modular networks, often oriented toward solving a specific task by using a specific architecture; Plaut and Hinton [2] and Jacobs *et al.* [3] were among the first to address this issue explicitly, although other networks, such as those of Fukushima [4], have also used modular neural networks for difficult problems.

In this chapter, we survey modular connectionist systems, analyzed from the viewpoint of system architecture, with examples of successful applications of modular networks. We describe how modularity may be achieved in neural networks, and how modular neural networks are useful in practice, achieving faster and better quality results for complex tasks, even though a single neural network is theoretically capable of achieving the desired goal. In most such networks, modularity is planned by the network builder, who is explicitly attempting an optimal use of resources. Such optimality may not be achieved easily by self-organizing networks whose structure develops via evolutionary mechanisms, because progress is constrained by past history and current configurations.

Section II outlines some of the advantages of using modular neural networks. Various possible modular neural network architectures are described in Section III. Each of these architectures is discussed in greater detail in Sections IV to VII, along with examples. Adaptive modular networks, the internal structure of which evolves during the training process, are discussed in Section VIII. The last section contains a summary and presents issues for further study.

II. WHY MODULAR NETWORKS?

Modularity is the central tenet of modern software engineering practice, and ought to be rigorously applied when neural network software is to be used in applications where the networks may change with time. Maintaining, improving, and enhancing the functionality of a system are known to be much easier if a software system is designed to be modular, and this holds for neural networks as well. Modular neural networks have several advantages when compared to their counterparts among nonmodular networks: training is faster, the effects of conflicting signals in the weight modification process can be diminished, networks generalize better, the network representation is more meaningful to the user (i.e., the behavior of the network can be interpreted more easily by the user), and practical hardware constraints are met more easily. These advantages are discussed in the remainder of this section.

A. COMPUTATIONAL REQUIREMENTS

In theory, a sufficiently large neural network can always be trained to accomplish any function approximation task [5–8]. In practice, however, the learning algorithm invoked may not succeed in the training task in a reasonable amount of time. The task of learning is much easier if the function to be learned can be decomposed naturally into a set of simple functions, where a separate network can be trained easily to approximate each of the simple functions. Improvements in training time can be attributed to three reasons:

1. Each module often addresses a simpler task, and hence can be trained in fewer iterations than the unimodular network.

III. MODULAR NETWORK ARCHITECTURES

A system with complex input/output relationships can be decomposed into simpler systems in many ways. What are the various possible ways of putting modules together to form a modular neural network? We categorize modular network architectures as follows:

1. *Input decomposition.* Each first-level module processes a different subset of input attributes (dimensions). These subsets need not be disjoint, that is, each input attribute may be fed into several modules. Sparse connectivity is achieved if each input node is connected only to a small number of higher level nodes.

2. *Output decomposition.* The output vector is separated into its components, and different modules are invoked for each component or subset of components. This is a popular decomposition procedure, particularly in many-class classification problems.

3. *Hierarchical decomposition.* Modules are organized into a treelike structure, the leaves of which are closest to the inputs, and the root of which generates the system outputs. Each module performs some operations, and each higher level module processes the outputs of the previous level module. "Pipelining" may be considered a special case of hierarchical decomposition, with a sequence of operations performed on the input vectors by different modules.

4. *Multiple experts.* In this architecture, the "opinions" of multiple expert modules (operating independently) are combined in a final decision-making module. Different modules may be specialized for different subtasks, or trained to perform similar tasks. In human decision making in the medical domain, for instance, experts with different expertise may be consulted, and (in some cases) different experts with the same specialization may be consulted to have a high level of confidence in the final decision-making step. The decision-making module may form a consensus or probabilistic combination of the outputs of these modules, or may use a competitive approach, determining which of the modules has its say for any given element of the input space.

These architectures are examined in greater detail in the next four sections, with example applications.

IV. INPUT DECOMPOSITION

A system with multiple inputs may be decomposable into subsystems in such a way that the inputs of each subsystem constitute a proper subset of the inputs of the entire system, as illustrated in Fig. 1. Each subsystem's outputs depend only on its own inputs. The inputs of different subsystems need not be completely

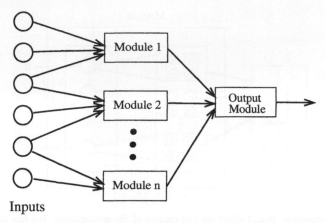

Inputs

Figure 1 Input modularity: each first-level module processes a different subset of inputs.

disjoint. For instance, different parts of the human retina and early visual system are devoted to different input regions, although they overlap to some extent.

A. NEOCOGNITRON

In some situations, it is to our advantage to decompose a large input array into several small arrays because it is easier to understand and process smaller arrays. Information from smaller arrays can be combined at a later stage. This is the essential feature of Neocognitron, developed by Fukushima for visual pattern recognition [4, 10–12]. In a Neocognitron, the input images are two-dimensional arrays, and the final result of pattern recognition indicates which high-level feature or shape has been found in the entire input image, activating the appropriate output node. The network uses a sequence of many modules, with each module extracting features from the previous module. Each network module consists of two layers of nodes. The first layer in each module, known as the S-layer, searches for the presence of a feature in a specific region of the input image U. For a character recognition problem, for instance, one S-layer node may search for a vertical line segment in the top left corner of the input image, as shown in Fig. 2, whereas another may search for a horizontal line segment in the lower left corner of the input image. Modules that are farther away from the input array perform successively higher level pattern recognition, abstracting away from details such as precise positions of features.

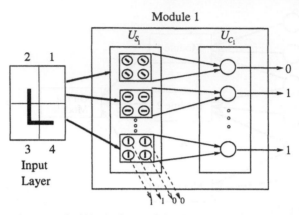

Figure 2 Connections to and within the first module of the neocognitron. The four outputs of the lowermost array in U_{S_1} indicate which quadrants of the input image contain vertical line segments.

B. DATA FUSION

In some applications, different kinds of inputs are available to the system, and each kind of input must be processed separately by a separate module before information (from different kinds of inputs) can be meaningfully combined. For instance, audio and visual inputs may be available, which must first be processed separately (by a specialized audio module and a specialized visual module). This yields better results than invoking a single complex module that attempts to process raw audio and visual inputs simultaneously. For another example, in the medical diagnosis of a patient, some conclusions can be derived from results of blood tests, and others from sources such as physical symptoms, X-rays, or a patient's verbal description of his condition. In this case it would be desirable to train one network for recognition based on results of the blood test, another neural network would learn from results of the X-rays, and so on.

V. OUTPUT DECOMPOSITION

Sometimes a task can be seen to consist of several subtasks that can be learned independently. For instance, many practical applications of neural networks address classification tasks in which each subtask can be thought of as learning the characteristics of a single class. A neural network can be designed for each subtask, and the overall result is a collection or combination of the results of smaller neural network modules. The basic architecture is illustrated in Fig. 3. In this

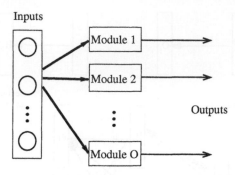

Figure 3 Output modularity. Each first-level module processes a different subset of outputs.

approach to modularity, a training set with its own input and output vectors is obtained for each subtask. For instance, in attempting to recognize letters of the English alphabet, it is often desirable to group similar letters together, and train one network for each group of letters.

Rueckl *et al.* [13] have studied the problem of analyzing images in which one of a number of known objects could occur anywhere. They found that training time was shorter when separate networks were used for two tasks:

(a) to identify the location of the object in the image, and
(b) to recognize the object in the image.

The problem of modularity has been approached from a more pragmatic viewpoint in the area of speech recognition. Waibel [14] has devised a technique called *connectionist glue* to train modules for different tasks and then connect them together, as shown in Fig. 4. Waibel [14] trained one neural network for recognition of phonemes B, D, and G (voiced stops) and another neural network to recognize phonemes P, T, and K (voiceless stops), using separate data sets. The individual neural networks achieved 98.3% and 98.7% correct recognition, respectively, whereas naively combining them into a single neural network achieved only 60.5% correct recognition for the six phonemes mentioned above. Fixing the (previously trained) weights from the inputs to the hidden nodes, and retraining the rest of the weights improved the performance of the combined neural network was to 98.1%. Next, four new nodes were introduced into the hidden layer, with attached connection weights trained along with all weights from the hidden layer to the output nodes. These new nodes act like "glue" to join the previously trained neural networks. Performance of the network was improved from 98.1% to 98.4% by addition of these extra hidden-layer nodes. Some additional training of this modular neural network further improved the performance to 98.6%, illus-

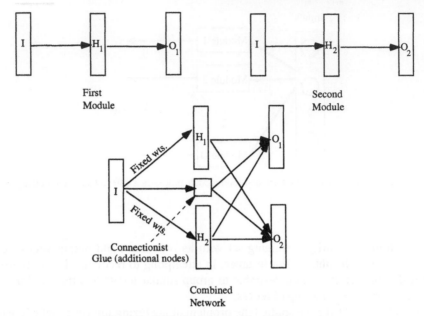

Figure 4   Waibel's connectionist modular network.

trating that it helps to add new hidden nodes, and to perform additional training with the entire training data set on some or all weights that connect hidden nodes to output nodes.

Anand *et al.* [15] exploit output modularity for problems involving the classification of input vectors into K disjoint classes, where $K > 2$. When compared to a monolithic network with K output nodes, a modular network with K one-output modules is easier to train and is more likely to succeed in reaching desired error rates. A module for class C_i is trained to distinguish between patterns belonging to classes C_i and its complement $\overline{C_i}$.

Because a training set for a K-class problem may be expected to contain approximately equal numbers of exemplars for all classes, the training set for module i will contain many more exemplars for class $\overline{C_i}$ than for C_i. Anand *et al.* [16] provide a training algorithm that performs better than back-propagation on such "imbalanced" problems. The relative performance of the modular network improves as the number of classes increases. The performance of modular and nonmodular networks has been compared on three problems: classifying iris flowers [17], a speech recognition example, and a character recognition example. The training process was faster for the modular network by a factor of 3 for the first two data sets, when compared to a monolithic network. For the third task, the modular network yielded a speedup of about 2.5 when the target mean square error was relatively high (0.007). However, the nonmodular network was unable to converge to a lower target mean square error (0.003), whereas the modular network did succeed in achieving this criterion.

VI. HIERARCHICAL DECOMPOSITION

A system with multiple outputs and multiple inputs can sometimes be decomposed into simpler multi-input multi-output modules arranged in a hierarchy, as illustrated in Fig. 5. The outputs of lower level modules act as inputs to higher level modules. The simplest kind of modularity involves pipelining, shown in Fig. 6, which is useful when the task requires different types of neural network modules at various stages of processing.

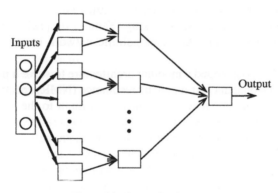

(a) Hierarchical organization

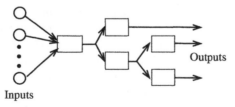

(b) Successive refinement

Figure 5 (a) Hierarchical organization. Each higher level module processes the outputs of the previous level module. (b) Successive refinement. Each module performs some operations and distributes tasks to the next higher level modules.

use for function approximation, radial basis function (RBF) networks also construct the system output as a weighted average of some of the node outputs. The same principle can be extended to modular networks: each module is associated with a prototype or reference vector whose proximity to an input vector is used to determine the relative importance of the module for that input vector. Often each node in an RBF network computes a Gaussian function, suggesting that the approach may be evaluated in the context of previous statistical work on Gaussian distribution functions.

An interesting inference problem in statistics, often observed in industrial applications as well as in nature, involves parameter estimation in a mixture of distributions. The problem may be formally stated as follows:

Let d be a random vector. Let p_i denote the *a priori* probability that the density function of d is given by $f(d; \theta_i)$, for $i = 1, \ldots, m$, with $\sum_{i=1}^{m} p_i = 1$. Then the sum

$$g(d; p_1, \ldots, p_m, \theta_1, \theta_2, \ldots, \theta_m) = \sum_{i=1}^{m} p_i f(d; \theta_i)$$

is also a density function. It is known as the mixture density[1] function and represents the unconditional density of d. Unknown *a priori* probabilities $(p_1, \ldots, p_m)$ and unknown parameters $(\theta_1, \ldots, \theta_m)$ are estimated by using a sample (set of available vectors) $\{d_1, d_2, \ldots, d_n\}$ from $g(d; p_1, \ldots, p_m, \theta_1, \theta_2, \ldots, \theta_m)$.

The maximum likelihood method, discussed in Section VII.A, is a favorite estimation procedure among statisticians. We discuss its neural network implementation in Section VII.B. Another possible statistical estimation procedure is the EM algorithm. This method and its neural networks implementation are discussed in Section VII.D.

A. MAXIMUM LIKELIHOOD METHOD

For notational convenience, we use Θ to denote the vector of all θ_i's, $\mathcal{X}$ to denote the sample $\{d_1, d_2, \ldots, d_n\}$, and p to denote the vector $(p_1, \ldots, p_m)$. Assuming that $d_1, \ldots, d_n$ are chosen independently and randomly with density $g(d; p, \Theta)$, the "likelihood function" of Θ and p is given by the joint density

$$L(\Theta, p \mid \mathcal{X}) = \prod_{j=1}^{n} g(d_j; p, \Theta) = \prod_{j=1}^{n} \left\{ \sum_{i=1}^{m} p_i f(d_j; \theta_i) \right\}.$$

[1]We have formulated the problem in terms of continuous random variables and densities, but a similar definition applies for discrete random variables as well.

In the maximum likelihood method, estimates of the unknown parameters are obtained by maximizing the above function or (equivalently) its logarithm. Using the classical maximization approach, it suffices to solve the following system of equations:

$$\frac{\partial}{\partial \theta_k} \log L(\Theta, p \mid \mathcal{X}) = 0, \text{ for } k = 1, \ldots, m,$$

$$\frac{\partial}{\partial p_k} \log L(\Theta, p \mid \mathcal{X}) = 0, \text{ for } k = 1, \ldots, m.$$

It is easy to verify which solutions of these equations give the maxima (instead of the minima). Because each p_i is constrained to satisfy $0 \le p_i \le 1$ and $\sum_{i=1}^{m} p_i = 1$, the relation

$$p_k = \frac{\exp(u_k)}{\sum_{i=1}^{m} \exp(u_i)} \tag{1}$$

gives unconstrained parameters $(u_1, \ldots, u_m)$ that are easier to estimate. The log-likelihood function (ℓ) is given by

$$\ell \equiv \log L = \sum_{j=1}^{n} \left[\log\left(\sum_{i=1}^{m} \exp(u_i) f(d_j; \theta_i) \right) - \log\left(\sum_{i=1}^{m} \exp(u_i) \right) \right], \tag{2}$$

maximized by solving the following system of equations:

$$\frac{\partial}{\partial \theta_k} \ell = \sum_{j=1}^{n} \frac{\exp(u_k)}{\sum_{i=1}^{m} \exp(u_i) f(d_j; \theta_i)} \frac{\partial}{\partial \theta_k} f(d_j; \theta_k) = 0, \tag{3}$$

$$\frac{\partial}{\partial u_k} \ell = \sum_{j=1}^{n} \left\{ \frac{\exp(u_k) f(d_j; \theta_k)}{\sum_{i=1}^{m} \exp(u_i) f(d_j; \theta_i)} - \frac{\exp(u_k)}{\sum_{i=1}^{m} \exp(u_i)} \right\} = 0. \tag{4}$$

The system of equations in (3) and (4) is nonlinear and can be solved by iterative methods. In the following, we specialize the above general formulation to an important special case of multivariate Gaussian densities, give a few more details from the statistical viewpoint, and illustrate its neural network implementation as developed by Jordan *et al.* [3, 23–26].

B. MIXTURE OF EXPERTS NETWORKS

Consider the problem of supervised learning. The training set $T = \{(x_j, d_j): j = 1, \ldots, n\}$ consists of n pairs of observations where x_j denotes an I-dimensional input vector and d_j denotes the associated O-dimensional output

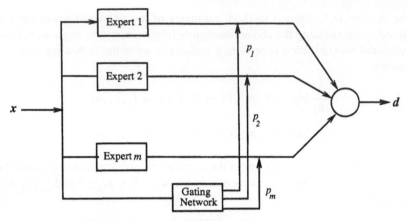

Figure 8   Basic structure of mixture of experts networks.

vector. The probabilistic model that relates an input x_j to its output d_j is described below:

Given an input vector x, a parameter θ is chosen randomly with probability $p_i(x)$, where $0 \le p_i \le 1$ and $\sum_{i=1}^{m} p_i = 1$. The desired output (d) represents a random variable satisfying the probability density function $f(\cdot; \theta_i)$. Finally, the functional relation $F_i(x) = \theta_i$ completes the relation between x and d.

The data come from a mixture of densities $g(d; \Theta) = \sum_{i=1}^{m} p_i f(d; \theta_i)$. Although m is an unknown integer in most real world-problems, it is often possible to make a reasonable guess for its value during the design of the network.

In the above model, parameters $\theta_1, \ldots, \theta_m$ and $p_1, \ldots, p_m$ are unknown. In a mixture of experts network, one expert (a neural network) is dedicated to learn the probability density function $f(\cdot; \theta_i)$ or the associated parameters for each i, and a gating network is assigned to learn p_i for $i = 1, \ldots, m$. Figure 8 shows the basic structure of this network, extensively discussed by Jordan, Jacobs, and their co-workers.

C. MIXTURE OF LINEAR REGRESSION MODEL AND GAUSSIAN DENSITIES

We illustrate the above-described modular structure, examining an important special case in greater detail. Let θ_i represent the expected value of d, conditional on the selected density. Assume that θ_i is a linear combination of x; that is,

$$\theta_i = F_i(x) = \text{E}(d \mid x, i) = W_i x$$

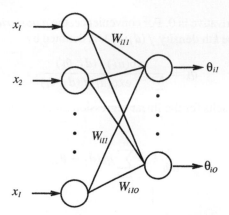

Figure 9 Structure of an experts network for linear regression model.

where W_i is a matrix of weights. The statistical implication is that the vector observation, d, is a linear combination of the input x and a random (vector) component. Its neural network implication is that the ith expert network is a simple network without any hidden layer, as shown in Fig. 9.

In addition, let f be the probability density function of a multivariate Gaussian random variable with independently distributed components, that is,

$$f(d; \theta_i) = \frac{1}{(2\pi)^{O/2}} \exp\left(-\frac{1}{2}(d - \theta_i)^T (d - \theta_i)\right),$$

for $i = 1, \ldots, m$, where $\theta_i = F_i(x) = W_i x$, and O is the output vector dimensionality. This mixture of experts is called an *associative Gaussian mixture model*. Recall that the gating frequencies p_i are expressed through the unconstrained parameters u_j; the latter are related linearly to the inputs, with

$$u_i \equiv v_i x.$$

Estimates of weights W_k and v_k can be obtained from Eqs. (3) and (4), differentiating θ_k with respect to W_k, and u_k with respect to v_k. Because the vector θ_k and the matrix W_k are related by $\theta_k = W_k x$, it follows that

$$\frac{\partial \theta_k(i)}{\partial W_k(i, j)} = x_j, \tag{5}$$

and every other such derivative is 0. Similarly, because $u_k = \sum_j v_{k,j} x_j$, it follows that

$$\frac{\partial u_k}{\partial v_{k,j}} = x_j, \tag{6}$$

every other such derivative is 0. For convenience, the *a posteriori* probability, that d_j is drawn from the kth density $f(d_j; \theta_k)$, is denoted by

$$q_k = \frac{\exp(u_k) f(d_j; \theta_k)}{\sum_{i=1}^{m} \exp(u_i) f(d_j; \theta_i)}.$$
(7)

Summarizing the results for the linear regression model, from Eqs. (3) and (4) we obtain

$$\frac{\partial}{\partial \theta_k} \ell = \sum_{j=1}^{n} q_k (d_j - \theta_k)$$

and

$$\frac{\partial}{\partial u_k} \ell = \sum_{j=1}^{n} (q_k - p_k).$$

The chain rule of derivatives allows us to estimate the weights. The following algorithm emerges from these observations:

1. *Initialization*: Assign randomly chosen uniformly distributed values between 0 and 1, to all elements of W_k and v_k, for each k.
2. *Iterative Modification*: Repeatedly perform the following weight modifications:

$$\Delta W_k(i, j) = -\eta q_k \big(d_i - \theta_k(i)\big) x_j$$

and

$$\Delta v_k = -\eta (q_k - p_k) x_j,$$

where η is a small positive real number.

D. THE EM ALGORITHM

The EM algorithm, proposed by Dempster *et al.* [27], is an iterative technique for obtaining maximum likelihood estimates in the presence of incomplete data. There are two types of sample sets: $\mathcal{X}$, which represents the data that can be observed, and $\mathcal{Y}$, the data that we desire to observe. The main difference between $\mathcal{X}$ and $\mathcal{Y}$ is the missing data, $\mathcal{Z}$.

First we reexamine the mixture of distributions case mentioned above. Suppose that when we observe the sample element d_j we also know which of the m density functions generates it. That is, suppose that it is possible to observe (d_j, z_j), where $z_j = (z_{j1}, \ldots, z_{im})$, and precisely one element $z_{j,i}$ equals 1; each of the rest equals 0. If $z_{j,i} = 1$, then the true density function of d_j is $f(d_j; \theta_i)$, and the joint density function of (d_j, z_j) can be expressed as

$$g^*(d_j, z_j; \Theta) = \prod_{i=1}^{m} \left[p_i f(d_j; \theta_i) \right]^{z_{j,i}}.$$

Consequently, the likelihood function associated with $\mathcal{Y} = \{(d_j, z_j): j = 1, \ldots, n\}$ is given by

$$\mathrm{L}_c(\Theta \mid \mathcal{Y}) = \prod_{j=1}^{n} g^*(d_j, z_j; \Theta)$$

$$= \prod_{j=1}^{n} \prod_{i=1}^{m} \left[p_i f(d_j; \theta_i) \right]^{z_{j,i}},$$

and the log-likelihood function is given by

$$\ell_c(\Theta \mid \mathcal{Y}) = \sum_{j=1}^{n} \sum_{i=1}^{m} z_{j,i} \left[\log f(d_j; \theta_i) + \log p_i \right]. \tag{8}$$

A comparison of the above equation with Eq. (2) indicates why this log-likelihood estimation is easier; the logarithm is now inside the second summation sign.

Knowledge of $z_{j,i}$ values facilitates the estimation problem considerably. However, in practice, $\mathcal{Z} = (z_1, \ldots, z_n)$ is unobservable, that is, $\mathcal{X}$ is the observable data, $\mathcal{Y}$ represents what we wish we could observe, and $\mathcal{Z}$ represents the missing data. In this setting, the EM algorithm proposes the following solution to estimate Θ and p (via u):

1. Choose an initial estimate $\widehat{\Theta}_0$ of Θ.
2. Until the estimates stabilize, repeatedly perform the following computation steps, where α denotes the iteration number and E denotes the expectation:

    (a) *Expectation step*. Find the expected value of the log-likelihood ℓ_c associated with $\mathcal{Y}$, from Eq. (8), conditional upon observed data $\mathcal{X}$ and the current estimate $\widehat{\Theta}_\alpha$ of Θ.
    (b) *Maximization step*. Find the "improved" estimate $\widehat{\Theta}_{\alpha+1}$ of Θ by using the above expected log-likelihood function.

To apply the EM algorithm to the mixture of densities problem, we need

$$\mathrm{E}\ell_c = \sum_{j=1}^{n} \sum_{i=1}^{m} \mathrm{E}\big(z_{j,i} \left[\log f(d_j, \theta_i) + \log p_i \right] \mid \mathcal{X}, \widehat{\Theta}_\alpha\big),$$

module when it is introduced adaptively. The main questions to be addressed in developing adaptive modular networks are

- When is a new module to be introduced?
- How is each module to be trained?
- What is the network architecture?
- How does the network output depend on the existing modules?
- How are existing modules to be modified when a new module is introduced?

The first of these questions has a straightforward answer: new modules can be generated when the performance of current modules is inadequate. No *a priori* information would then be needed regarding the number of modules needed for a specific problem. The remaining questions posed above are answered differently by different adaptive modular network approaches. This section outlines four such algorithms that adaptively introduce modules into a network.

1. The Attentive Modular Construction and Training Algorithm (AMCT) [33] successively introduces and trains new modules on small portions of the data set, steadily extending the "window" of data on which a module has been trained. A complete network is then constructed, with all of the modules constituting a "hidden layer" (of modules), and the weights (including those from the modules to an output node) are then trained, using a small number of iterations of the back-propagation algorithm.

2. Ersoy and Hong [34] propose a network consisting of multi-output percep-tron modules. In their model, later modules are invoked only if it is obvious from the output of earlier modules that they "reject" an input vector (i.e., do not gen-erate a reasonable output vector). The training process involves the successive addition of new modules. The input vectors are subjected to nonlinear transfor-mations before being fed into the new modules. Note that the outputs of the earlier modules are not directly supplied as inputs into later modules, allowing for greater parallelism in execution.

3. The Adaptive Multi-Module Approximation Network (AMAN) [35] asso-ciates multiple "prototypes" or reference vectors with each module in the network; the network output depends on the output of the module whose reference vector is nearest an input vector. A competitive learning mechanism is used to associate the module with reference vectors identifying cluster centroids. The introduction of a new module may necessitate readjusting the reference vectors of existing modules, but not their internal connection weights.

4. Some existing nonmodular adaptive training algorithms can be modified so that the adaptive process successively introduces neural network modules into the network, instead of individual nodes. For instance, the "Blockstart" algorithm [37] adaptively develops a multilayer hierarchical neural network for two-class classification problems, following the principles of Frean's "Upstart" algorithm

[37]. Each module is a small feedforward network, trained by an algorithm such as back-propagation.

A. ATTENTIVE MODULAR CONSTRUCTION AND TRAINING

Theoretically, multilayered feedforward neural networks can approximate any continuous function to an arbitrary degree of accuracy [5–7, 38–40]. However, these networks are often difficult to train, possibly because of local minima, inadequate numbers of hidden units, or noise. Discontinuous functions and functions with sharp corners are particularly difficult for feedforward networks to approximate, as recognized by Sontag [41]. Such functions arise naturally in problems such as multicomputer performance modeling: a typical communication cost curve is flat for one range of input parameter values, then jumps steeply whenever a parameter such as message length reaches certain thresholds. Some work on discontinuity approximation has been carried out in surface reconstruction in 3-D images [42]. Current neural network methods that are successful for this problem [43–45] can only deal with the case of a discretized domain where function values (intensity or pixel values) are defined at a finite number of pixel locations. These networks have limitations in interpolation because each output node approximates the function value at a single (x, y) location. Moreover, they are designed to work only in two-dimensional input space.

Lee *et al.* [33, 46] developed a new algorithm to solve this problem. In general, the number of discontinuities in a problem may previously be unknown; hence the neural network is constructed incrementally. Because discontinuities are local singularities and not global features, modules are trained by using small neighborhoods of data space. Partitioning an input space for better performance has been suggested for other applications by various researchers [47–50]. In the approach of Choi and Choi [49], for instance, the entire input space is tessellated into a large number of cells, for each of which a separate network "granule" is trained; however, the computational needs and number of parameters of the resulting system are excessively high. Ideally, the number of "cells" should be variable, with nonuniform sizes, and determined adaptively by the algorithm.

In the network constructed by the AMCT algorithm, each module is a one-hidden-layer network containing a small number of hidden nodes, trained on a small subset of training samples. The need for a new module is automatically recognized by the system. This algorithm performs very well on low-dimensional problems with many discontinuities, and requires fewer computations than traditional back-propagation. The success of the algorithm relies on independent scaling of training data and window management. Modular training is followed by merging and finding weights of the top layer connections. The weights of the top

AMCT algorithm was found to require roughly 30% fewer weight changes than a nonmodular network trained by back-propagation.

B. ADAPTIVE HIERARCHICAL NETWORK

Algorithms have been designed to solve classification problems by using an adaptively developing hierarchical neural network. These algorithms first use a "simple" neural network module, attempting to classify correctly as many input/output pairs as possible. If the resulting error exceeds a preassigned threshold, then a new neural network component is trained on the incorrectly classified data. This step is repeated until all or most data are correctly classified. An example of this approach is the nonmodular "tiling algorithm" of Mezard and Nadal [51], in which new nodes are successively introduced to separate samples of different classes that cannot be distinguished by existing nodes in the current layer.

Ersoy and Hong [34] develop a similar adaptive neural network, based on the premise that most errors occur because of input/output pairs that are linearly non-separable, and that a nonlinear transformation of the inputs can improve the separability between two classes. Inputs and outputs are presumed to be binary, and the applications explored so far are primarily in signal processing. Each module is a multi-output perceptron (without any hidden layer) containing one layer of weights trained by the delta rule (gradient descent), attempting to classify correctly the data for which previously existing modules were unsuccessful. The output vector generated by the module is examined to determine if the module has been successful in producing the desired output vector. After a reasonable training period, the remaining data vectors (on which the current module is unsuccessful) are piped through a nonlinear transform and then into a newly spawned module, on which the training process is again applied. The nonlinear transform most used by Ersoy and Hong consists of a real discrete Fourier transform followed by the sign function. Figure 13 illustrates the architecture of a network that develops in this manner.

The training process continues until a prespecified stopping criterion, such as an error bound, is achieved. In applying the network to new test data, the modules are successively applied to the input data (along with the relevant nonlinear transforms) until one is found whose output is considered satisfactory.

Ersoy and Hong [34] have observed that the performance of their self-organizing hierarchical neural networks is better than the performance of the usual feedforward back-propagation neural networks with one or two hidden layers. They also report that this modular network model has better fault-tolerant properties.

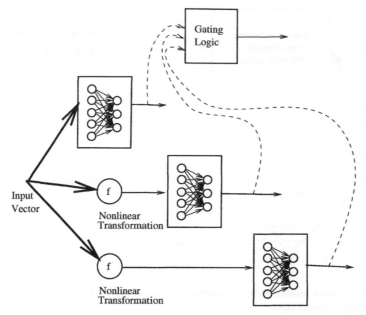

Figure 13 Adaptive modular network of Ersoy and Hong.

C. ADAPTIVE MULTIMODULE APPROXIMATION NETWORK

Kim *et al.* [35] propose an adaptive modular neural network in which each module is associated with one or more adaptively determined reference vectors that identify when the module is to be invoked. The connection weights of that module are used to generate the appropriate output vector. Unlike the other adaptive modular algorithms, each module may be appropriate for more than one small region in data space, because each module may be associated with multiple reference vectors. This network model is successful in solving problems involving the approximation of a collage of several different simpler functions; it is much more difficult to train unimodular networks for such tasks. The network architecture is illustrated in Fig. 14.

In using the notion of "reference vectors," the relative proximity of which is used to determine the choice of the appropriate module, the AMAN algorithm bears an analogy with learning vector quantization (LVQ) [52] and counterpropagation [53] algorithms. However, those algorithms are not adaptive or modular, and were developed for classification and pattern association tasks, and not for arbitrary function approximation problems.

time an order of magnitude less than the unimodular network, reaching lower error levels.

D. BLOCKSTART ALGORITHM

Frean's "Upstart" algorithm [37] adaptively adds nodes to a network, successively invoking the algorithm recursively on smaller subsets of the training data. The "Blockstart Algorithm" [36] extends this approach, adaptively developing a multilayer hierarchical neural network for two-class classification problems, as illustrated in Fig. 15. Each module is a small feedforward network, trained by an algorithm such as back-propagation. The first module is trained on the entire training set, with the initial invocation of the algorithm being

$$N = \text{Blockstart}(T_1, T_0),$$

where T_1 is the subset on which the desired output is 1 and T_0 is the subset on which the desired output is -1. The current invocation of the algorithm terminates if perfect (or acceptable) classification performance is obtained by this module. Otherwise, if $T_1^- \subset T_1$ and $T_0^- \subset T_0$ constitute the misclassified samples, the algorithm is recursively invoked twice:

$$N_1 = \text{Blockstart}(T_1^-, T_0),$$
$$N_0 = \text{Blockstart}(T_0^-, T_1).$$

In the complete network, all inputs are supplied to each of N, N_1, N_0; in addition, there are also connections from the output nodes of N_1, N_0 to the output node of

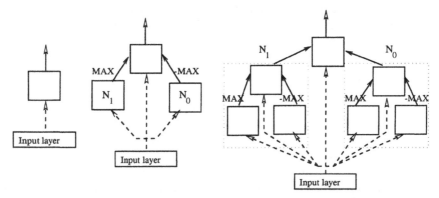

Figure 15 Blockstart algorithm. Connections from lower level module outputs lead directly into the outermost node of the next higher level module, carrying a weight of MAX or −MAX.

N, with connection weights MAX and $-$ (MAX), respectively, where MAX is sufficiently large, say exceeding $| \sum_k w_k i_k^p |$, where w_k is the connection weight from the kth input to N and i_k^p is the kth element of the pth input pattern.

The resulting network has many layers, but the training process is not computationally expensive, because each module is small, and the weights within a module are trained exactly once. Termination of the algorithm is ensured because each successive recursive call addresses fewer training patterns.

IX. CONCLUSIONS

This chapter has surveyed the topic of modular neural networks, examining various modular network architectures. In the first model, different modules process different subsets of input attributes. In the second, the problem being addressed is partitioned into subtasks that are solved by using different modules. The third model includes a number of different levels of modules, with results from one level feeding into the next. The fourth model invokes a decision-making method to combine the results of various "expert" modules. This is followed by a discussion of adaptive modular networks, in which modules are automatically added by the learning algorithm. The construction of such modular networks allows us to conduct successful training of networks for large problems with reasonably small computational requirements.

If a problem can be solved easily by using a small neural network whose number of weights is one or two orders of magnitude less than the number of input samples, then there is no need to resort to a modular architecture. In practice, this is rarely the case. Modular neural networks can be used in many practical applications for which training a single large monolithic neural network is infeasible or too computationally demanding, or leads to poor generalization because of the large number of weights in the network. The choice of the network architecture depends on the problem, and on the nature of the *a priori* information available about the problem. When fault tolerance is a major concern in an application, each module may be trained once and then duplicated, yielding the redundancy needed for the network in operational use.

The research area of modular neural networks is far from exhausted. To begin with, it may be possible to formulate other modular network architectures for various problems. Few adaptive modular algorithms exist, providing scope for further exploration, especially in the context of applications characterized by a continually changing problem environment. Of particular interest are new adaptive network training algorithms for association and optimization tasks. Several algorithms also beg for a clear theory that indicates why modular networks are better than nonmodular ones of equal size. It may be conjectured, for instance, that the presence of a larger number of weights in a nonmodular network leads to the existence of a larger number of local optima of the mean square error than in the case of the modular network. Similarly, when compared to nonmodular networks with the same number of nodes, modular networks are capable of implementing only a proper subset of the set of functions that produce desired results on the training data.

When domain knowledge is available, the main task is that of embedding such knowledge in the network structure, and deciding whether a connectionist or hybrid model is appropriate for the problem. In the absence of clear *a priori* domain-specific knowledge, a difficult issue bearing serious study involves determining how best to break down a complex task into simpler subtasks. The learning process would be accelerated considerably if one can find ways to reduce the complexity of the function to be learned by the neural network.

We end this chapter by noting that a modular connectionist system may include some modules that are not neural networks. For instance, such a system may contain rule-based expert system modules, or may contain specialized hardware components for tasks such as signal processing. The overall architecture of the system may again follow one of the schemes discussed in Section III. For instance, Zhao and Lu [54] use a hybrid pipelining architecture with two modules for classifying the depth of burn injury, using inputs extracted from multiple-wavelength spectra of visible and infrared radiation used to evaluate burn injuries, which is first preprocessed to have zero mean and unit variance. The first module in the system is a statistical analyzer that performs principal components analysis, and the second module is a feedforward neural network trained by back-propagation. A classification accuracy of 87.5% is reported by the authors. Another example of a hybrid neural network is the face recognition system of Lawrence *et al.* [55], which combines local image sampling, a self-organizing map neural network, and a convolutional network that resembles the neocognitron.

REFERENCES

[1] M. Minsky. *The Society of Mind.* Simon & Schuster, New York, 1985.
[2] D. C. Plaut and G. E. Hinton. Learning sets of filters using back-propagation. *Comput. Speech Language* 2:35–61, 1988.
[3] R. A. Jacobs, M. I. Jordan, and A. G. Barto. Task decomposition through competition in a modular connectionist architecture: the what and where vision task. *Cognitive Sci.* 15:219–250, 1991.
[4] K. Fukushima. Neocognitron: a self-organizing neural network model for a mechanism of pattern recognition unaffected by shift in position. *Biol. Cybernet.* 36:193–202, 1980.
[5] R. Hecht-Nielsen. Theory of the backpropagation neural network. *Proc. Internat. Joint Conference Neural Networks* 1:593–611, 1989.
[6] G. Cybenko. Approximation by superpositions of a sigmoidal function. *Math. Control Signals Systems* 2:303–314, 1989.
[7] K. Hornik, M. Stinchcombe, and H. White. Multilayer feedforward networks are universal approximators. *Neural Networks* 2:359–366, 1989.

[8] V. Kurkova. Kolmogorov's theorem and multilayer neural networks. *Neural Networks* 5:501–506, 1992.

[9] R. E. Robinson, H. Yoneda, and E. Sanchez-Sinencio. A modular CMOS design of a Hamming network. *IEEE Trans. Neural Networks* 3:117–124, 1992.

[10] K. Fukushima, S. Miyake, and T. Ito. Neocognitron: a neural network model for a mechanism of visual pattern recognition. *IEEE Trans. System Man Cybernet.* SCM-13:826–834, 1993.

[11] K. Fukushima. Neural network model for selective attention in visual pattern recognition and associative recall. *Appl. Optics* 26:193–202, 1987.

[12] K. Fukushima. Neocognitron: a hierarchical neural network capable of visual pattern recognition. *Neural Networks* 1:119–130, 1988.

[13] J. G. Rueckl, K. R. Cave, and S. M. Kosslyn. Why are 'What' and 'Where' processed by separate cortical visual systems? A computational investigation. *J. Cognitive Neurosci.* 1:171–186, 1989.

[14] A. Waibel. Connectionist glue: modular design of neural speech systems. Technical report, Carnegie Mellon University, Pittsburgh, PA, 1989.

[15] R. Anand, K. G. Mehrotra, C. K. Mohan, and S. Ranka. Efficient classification for multiclass problems using modular networks. *IEEE Trans. Neural Networks* 6:117–124, 1995.

[16] R. Anand, K. G. Mehrotra, C. K. Mohan, and S. Ranka. An improved algorithm for neural network classification of imbalanced training sets. *IEEE Trans. Neural Networks* 4:962–969, 1993.

[17] R. A. Fisher. The use of multiple measurements in taxonomic problems. *Ann. Eugenics* 7: 179–188, 1936.

[18] M.-C. Yang, K. Mehrotra, C. K. Mohan, and S. Ranka. Partial shape matching with attributed strings and neural networks. In *Proceedings of the Conference on Artificial Neural Networks in Engineering (ANNIE)*, November 1992, pp. 523–528.

[19] M. Flasinsski. On the parsing of deterministic graph languages for syntactic pattern recognition. *Pattern Recognition* 21:1–16, 1993.

[20] R. Anand, K. G. Mehrotra, C. K. Mohan, and S. Ranka. Analyzing images containing multiple sparse patterns with neural networks. *Pattern Recognition* 26:1717–1724, 1993.

[21] T. Kohonen. Self-organized formation of topologically correct feature maps. *Biol. Cybernet.* 43:59–69, 1982.

[22] S.-W. Lee. Multilayer cluster neural networks for totally unconstrained handwritten numeral recognition. *Neural Networks* 8:783–792, 1995.

[23] R. A. Jacobs and M. I. Jordan. A competitive modular connectionist architecture. In *Advances in Neural Information Processing Systems*, Vol. 4, pp. 767–773. Morgan Kaufmann, San Mateo, CA, 1991.

[24] R. A. Jacobs, M. I. Jordan, S. J. Nowlan, and G. E. Hinton. Adaptive mixtures of local experts. *Neural Comput.* 3:79–87, 1991.

[25] R. A. Jacobs and M. I. Jordan. Hierarchies of adaptive experts. In *Advances in Neural Information Processing Systems* (J. E. Moody, S. J. Hanson, and R. P. Lippmann, Eds.), Vol. 4, pp. 985–992. Morgan Kaufmann, San Mateo, CA, 1991.

[26] R. A. Jacobs and M. I. Jordan. Hierarchical mixtures of experts and the EM algorithm. *Neural Comput.* 6:181–214, 1994.

[27] A. P. Dempster, N. M. Laird, and D. B. Rubin. Maximum likelihood from incomplete data via the EM algorithm. *J. Roy. Statist. Soc. Ser. B* 39:1–38, 1977.

[28] M. I. Jordan and L. Xu. Convergence results for the EM approach to mixtures of experts architectures. *Neural Networks* 8:1409–1432, 1995.

[29] S. P. Singh. The efficient learning of multiple task sequence. In *Advances in Neural Information Processing Systems* (J. E. Moody, S. J. Hanson, and R. P. Lippmann, Eds.), Vol. 5, pp. 251–258. Morgan Kaufmann, San Mateo, CA, 1992.

[30] H. Gomi and M. Kawata. Recognition of manipulated objects by motor learning. In *Advances in Neural Information Processing Systems* (J. E. Moody, S. J. Hanson, and R. P. Lippmann, Eds.), Vol. 5, pp. 547–554. Morgan Kaufmann, San Mateo, CA, 1992.

[31] J. Fritsch. Modular neural networks for speech recognition. Diploma Thesis, Interactive Systems Laboratory, Carnegie Mellon University, Pittsburgh, PA, 1996.

[32] S. E. Fahlman and C. Lebiere. The cascade-correlation learning architecture. In *Advances in Neural Information Processing Systems II (Denver 1989)* (J. E. Moody, S. J. Hanson, and R. P. Lippmann, Eds.), Vol. 3, pp. 524–532. Morgan Kaufmann, San Mateo, CA, 1990.

[33] H. Lee, K. Mehrotra, C. K. Mohan, and S. Ranka. An incremental network construction algorithm for approximating discontinuous functions. In *Proceedings of the International Conference on Neural Networks (ICNN)*, Vol. 4, pp. 2191–2196, 1994.

[34] O. K. Ersoy and D. Hong. Parallel, self-organizing, hierarchical neural networks. *IEEE Trans. Neural Networks* 2:167–178, 1990.

[35] W. Kim, K. Mehrotra, and C. K. Mohan. Adaptive multi-module approximation network (AMAN). In *Proceedings of the Conference on Artificial Neural Networks in Engineering*, 1997.

[36] D. Anton. Block-start neural networks. Technical report, personal communication, 1994.

[37] M. Frean. The upstart algorithm: a method for constructing and training feedforward neural networks. *Neural Computation* 2:198–209, 1990.

[38] R. Hecht-Nielsen. *Neurocomputing.* Addison-Wesley, Reading, MA, 1989.

[39] A. N. Kolmogorov. On the representation of continuous functions of many variables by superposition of continuous functions of one variable and addition. *Dokl. Akad. Nauk USSR* 114:953–956, 1957.

[40] K. I. Funahashi. On the approximate realization of continuous mappings by neural networks. *Neural Networks* 2:183–192, 1989.

[41] E. D. Sontag. Capabilities of four- vs. three-layer nets, and control applications. In *Proceedings of the Conference on Information Science and Systems*, Johns Hopkins University, Baltimore, MD, March 1991.

[42] S. S. Sinha and B. G. Schunck. A two-stage algorithm for discontinuity-preserving surface reconstruction. *IEEE Trans. Pattern Analysis Machine Intelligence* 14:36–55, 1992.

[43] C. Koch, J. Marroquin, and A. Yuille. Analog "neuronal" networks in early vision. *Proc. Natl. Acad. Sci. U.S.A.* 83:4263–4267, 1986.

[44] J. G. Harris. The coupled depth/slope approach to surface reconstruction. Technical Report TR-908, Artificial Intelligence Laboratory, MIT, 1986.

[45] J. G. Marroquin. Deterministic Bayesian estimation of Markovian random fields with applications to computational vision. In *Proceedings of the First International Conference on Computer Vision*, June 1987, pp. 597–601.

[46] H. Lee. *Neural network modeling approaches in performance evaluation of parallel applications.* Ph.D. Thesis, Syracuse University, Syracuse, New York, 1993.

[47] J. E. Moody and C. Darken. Learning with localized receptive fields. In *Proceedings of the 1988 Connectionist Models Summer School* (D. Touretzky, G. Hinton, and T. Sejnowski, Eds.), pp. 133–143. Morgan Kaufmann, San Mateo, CA, 1988.

[48] J. E. Moody and C. Darken. Fast learning in networks of locally-tuned processing units. *Neural Comput.* 1:281–294, 1989.

[49] C. Choi and J. Y. Choi. Construction of neural networks for piecewise approximation of continuous functions. In *Proceedings of the International Conference on Neural Networks*, 1993, pp. 428–433.

[50] J. H. Friedman. Adaptive spline networks. In *Advances in Neural Information Processing Systems* (J. E. Moody, S. J. Hanson, and R. P. Lippmann, Eds.), Vol. 3, pp. 675–683. Morgan Kaufmann, San Mateo, CA, 1991.

[51] M. Mezard and J.-P. Nadal. Learning in feedforward networks: the tiling algorithm. *J. Phys. A* 22:2191–2204, 1989.

[52] Tuevo Kohonen. Improved versions of learning vector quantization. In *Proceedings of the International Joint Conference on Neural Networks,* San Diego, CA, 1990, Vol. 1, pp. 545–550.

[53] R. Hecht-Nielsen. Counterpropagation networks. *IEEE Internat. Conf. Neural Networks* 2:19–32, 1987.

[54] S. X. Zhao and T. Lu. The classification of the depth of burn injury using hybrid neural network. Technical Report, Physical Optics Corporation, Torrance, CA, 1996.

[55] S. Lawrence, C. L. Giles, A. C. Tsoi, and A. D. Back. Face recognition: a hybrid neural network approach. Technical Report UMIACS-TR-96-16, University of Maryland Institute for Advanced Computer Studies, April 1996.

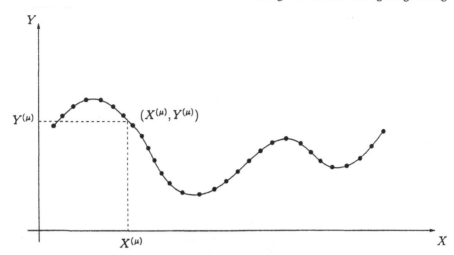

Figure 2   Schematic illustration of a function-mapping associative memory. A set of 50 one-dimensional pattern pairs $(X^{(\mu)}, Y^{(\mu)})$ was used.

This type of memory was initially studied by Taylor [7] in 1956, followed by the introduction of the learning matrix by Steinbuch [8]; the correlation matrix memories by Anderson [9], Kohonen [10], and Nakano [11]; and the pseudo-inverse memories by Wee [12], Kohonen [13], and others [14–18]. All of these models use linear functions **F** (i.e., **F** are matrices). Gabor *et al.* were probably the first to introduce nonlinear function to the study of memory [19]. Since then, various nonlinear models were developed. Some of the most significant models include the perceptron of Rosenblatt [20, 21], the adaline of Widrow and Hoff [22], the madaline of Widrow and his students [23], the sparsely distributed memory of Kanerva [24], the back-propagation algorithm of Rumelhart *et al.* [25], and the radial basis function layered feedforward networks of Broomhead and Lowe [26].

The above type of associative memories will henceforth be referred to as Function Mapping Associative Memories (FMAMs).

Principle 2: Attractors of Dynamic Systems

The most striking feature of a dynamic system is the existence of attractors. There has been increasing evidence in biology that the attractors of a biological memory function as storage [27]. This suggests that an associative memory can

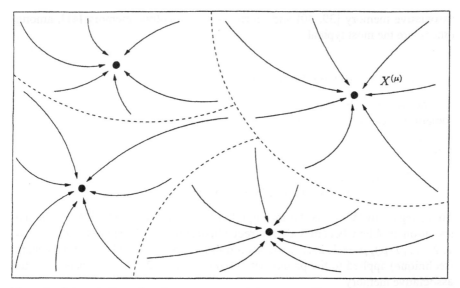

Figure 3 Schematic illustration of an attractor associative memory. Three point attractors (patterns) were assumed.

be developed as a dynamic system, say $\mathbf{Q} : \mathbf{X} \times \{t\} \rightarrow \mathbf{X}$, such that each $X^{(\mu)}$ isan attractor of the system $\mathbf{Q}$, for example,

   (i) each $X^{(\mu)}$ is an equilibrium point of $\mathbf{Q}$ ($\mu = 1, 2, \ldots, p$) and
   (ii) each $X^{(\mu)}$ is attractive

Here $\mathbf{X}$ is again the pattern state space, and t is the time (usually $t \in [0, \infty)$).

Figure 3 shows schematically the principle of this kind of associative memory. Each pattern to be stored is an (point) attractor of the constructed dynamic system. Because of this, the memory is named an Attractor Associative Memory (AAM). Two striking characteristics of an AAM are (1) every stored memory pattern can be recalled from its nearby vectors—an implicit error-correction capability; (2) the retrieval process of the stored pattern is not a direct mapping computation, but an evolution of the memory's orbit as time goes by. We will present a detailed analysis of this type of memory in this chapter.

Attractor neural networks have been intensively studied during the past two decades. The additive model [27–30], the correlograph model [31], the brain-state-in-a-box [32], Hopfield models [33–35], the Cohen–Grossberg model [36], the Boltzman machine [37], the mean-field-theory machine [38], the bidirectional

dressed. The emphasis here is placed on some new powerful encoding techniques. In Section III we investigate a new type of continuous AAM—the competitive associative memory, which is based on simulating the competitive persistence of biological species and aimed at excluding the spurious stable points. By applying the general theories developed in Section II, the neural network model and its neurodynamics are analyzed. As a demonstration of the effectiveness of the proposed model, we also derive in this section a novel neural network memory that can always respond to input reliably and correctly. Section IV is devoted to the study of a class of discrete AAMs—the asymmetric Hopfield-type networks. We first demonstrate the convergent dynamics of the networks by developing various convergence principles in a unified framework. We then conduct a quantitative analysis of the network's error-correction capability by establishing a classification theory of energy functions associated with the networks. The established theories are applied to the formulation of a "skill" (called the *complete correspondence modification skill*), for improving the error-correction capability of the symmetric Hopfield-type networks. Numerical simulations are used to demonstrate the effectiveness and power of the developed theories. We conclude the chapter with a summary of results in Section V.

II. POINT ATTRACTOR ASSOCIATIVE MEMORIES

Loosely speaking, a dynamical system is a system whose state varies with time (such as those governed by a set of differential or difference equations). In this section we study a special type of dynamical system, feedback neural networks functioning as associative memories.

From the dynamic system point of view, a feedback neural network is a large-scale, nonlinear, and dissipative system. This last property implies that the state trajectories of the system may converge to manifolds of low dimensions [5, 47–50]. If the manifold is a single point, we call it a *point attractor*. If the trajectory is in the form of a periodic orbit, we call it a *stable limit cycle*. A dynamic system whose attractors are all point attractors is said to be a *point attractor* (dynamic) *system*. A point attractor system is an associative memory or, more precisely, a point attractor associative memory (PAAM), if the system's attractors correspond to or contain the prototype patterns to be memorized.

The PAAMs have been extensively studied because of their usefulness in modeling associative memory processes in both biological and artificial systems. In the following, the basic models and the related theories are reviewed and generalized in a unified framework. New techniques for design and analysis of the PAAMs are then developed.

A. Neural Network Models

1. Generalized Model and Examples

Neural networks with dynamics are generally referred to as *dynamic neural networks* (DNNs). A DNN is usually described by a system of differential equations,

$$\frac{d}{dt} x_i(t) = F_i(t, x(t)), \quad i = 1, 2, \ldots, N, \tag{1}$$

or a set of difference equations,

$$x_i(t + 1) = G_i(t, x(t)), \quad i = 1, 2, \ldots, N, \tag{2}$$

where $x(t) = (x_1(t), x_2(t), \ldots, x_N(t))^T \in \Omega_N$ is the state variable, Ω_N is the underlying state space, and $F_i, G_i : \Omega_N \times (0, \infty) \to \mathbf{R}$ are, in general, nonlinear functions of their arguments. The state space Ω_N can be the Euclidean space or its subset. It can also be a non-Euclidean space such as a circle, a sphere, or some other differentiable manifold.

A neural network is a system that consists of a large number of processing units, called *neurons*, which are fully interconnected to each other. To see how a neural network can be modeled by either system (1) or by system (2), let us first consider possible models of a single neuron that accepts a set of stimuli (inputs) $x_1, x_2, \ldots, x_N$ and outputs a signal y_i.

The model of McCulloch and Pitts [51] is given by

$$y_i = \varphi_i(u_i),$$

with

$$u_i = \sum_{j=1}^{N} w_{ij} x_j - \theta_i, \tag{3}$$

where φ_i, called the *activation function*, is a sigmoid nonlinearity (i.e., a continuous, increasing, range-bounded function); $W_i = (w_{i1}, w_{i2}, \ldots, w_{iN})^T$ is the so-called synaptic weights, with w_{ij} representing the strength of the stimulus x_j acting on the ith neuron, and θ_i is a threshold attached to the neuron. Alternatively, Hopfield [34], aiming at processing spatial-temporal inputs, treated the neuron function as a RC circuit described by

$$y_i = \varphi_i(u_i),$$

where $v(t + 1)$ satisfies

$$v_i(t + 1) = \varphi_i\big(u_i(t + 1)\big) = \varphi_i\big(H_i\big(t, W_i, \Phi(u(t))\big)\big). \qquad (13)$$

In either case, E is said to be an energy of the PAAM.

The conditions (11) and (12) here mean nothing but the dissipation property of the PAAMs. Equation (11) implies

$$\left.\frac{dE(u(t))}{dt}\right|_{(8)} = \sum_{i=1}^{N} \frac{\partial}{\partial u_i} E(u(t)) \frac{d}{dt} u_i(t)$$

$$= \sum_{i=1}^{N} \frac{\partial}{\partial u_i} E(u(t)) H_i\big(t, W_i, \Phi(u(t))\big) \le 0,$$

and Eq. (12) implies

$$\Delta E\big(v(t)\big)\big|_{(9)} = E\big(v(t + 1)\big) - E\big(v(t)\big)$$

$$= E\big(\Phi(u(t + 1))\big) - E\big(v(t)\big) \le 0;$$

both indicate that the energy E decreases monotonically along the trajectories of the PAAMs.

The following is a set of PAAM examples that encompass most of the well-known neural network memories in the literature:

- Cohen–Grossberg Model [36]:

$$\frac{du_i}{dt} = a_i(u_i)\left[b_i(u_i) - \sum_{j=1}^{N} c_{ij}\varphi_j(u_j) \right], \quad j = 1, 2, \ldots, N, \qquad (14)$$

where $a_i(u_i) \ge 0$, $c_{ij} = c_{ji}$ and

$$E(u) = \tfrac{1}{2}\sum_{i=1}^{N}\sum_{j=1}^{N} c_{ij}\varphi_j(u_j) - \sum_{i=1}^{N} \int_0^{v_i} b_i(\lambda)\varphi_i'(\lambda)d\lambda. \qquad (15)$$

- Hopfield Model [34]:

$$C_i\frac{du_i}{dt} = \frac{u_i}{R_i} + \sum_{j=1}^{N} w_{ij}\varphi(u_j) + I_i, \quad i = 1, 2, \ldots, N,$$

where $w_{ij} = w_{ji}$ and

$$E(v) = -\tfrac{1}{2}\sum_{i=1}^{N}\sum_{j=1}^{N} w_{ij} v_i v_j - \sum_{i=1}^{N} \frac{1}{R_i}\int_0^{v_i} \varphi_i^{-1}(\lambda)d\lambda + \sum_{i=1}^{N} I_i v_i.$$

- Little–Hopfield Model [35, 53]:

$$v_i(t+1) = \text{sgn}\left[\sum_{j=1}^{N} w_{ij} v_j(t) - I_i\right], \qquad (16)$$

where $w_{ij} = w_{ji}$, sgn $(\cdot)$ is a signum function, and

$$E(v) = -\tfrac{1}{2}\sum_{i=1}^{N}\sum_{j=1}^{N} w_{ij} v_i v_j + \sum_{i=1}^{N} I_i v_i. \qquad (17)$$

- Brain-State-in-a-Box Model [32]:

$$v_i(t+1) = \text{sat}\left[v_i(t) + \beta \sum_{j=1}^{N} w_{ij} v_j(t)\right] \qquad (18)$$

where $w_{ij} = w_{ji}$, sat$(\cdot)$ is a saturation function, and

$$E(v) = -\frac{\beta}{2}\sum_{i=1}^{N}\sum_{j=1}^{N} w_{ij} v_i v_j.$$

- Recurrent Back-Propagation Algorithm [54]:

$$\frac{dx_i(t)}{dt} = -x_i(t) + \varphi\left[\sum_{i=1}^{N} w_{ij} x_j(t)\right] + K_i, \quad i = 1, 2, \ldots, N,$$

or, equivalently,

$$\frac{du_i(t)}{dt} = -u_i(t) + \sum_{j=1}^{N} w_{ij}\varphi\big(u_j(t)\big) + \sum_{j=1}^{N} w_{ij} K_j, \quad i = 1, 2, \ldots, N,$$

where $w_{ij} = w_{ji}$, $\varphi(\cdot)$ is sigmoid function, and

$$E(v) = -\tfrac{1}{2}\sum_{i=1}^{N}\sum_{j=1}^{N} w_{ij} v_i(v_j + 2K_j) + \sum_{i=1}^{N}\int_{0}^{v_i} \varphi^{-1}(\lambda)d\lambda.$$

We will further suggest some new PAAM structures in Sections III and IV of the present chapter.

It should be noted that among all of the examples listed above, the Cohen–Grossberg model is the most general [5, 49, 55–58] (hence, in the following, any general result will be illustrated by and applied to this model). Nevertheless, it was the Hopfield model that first manifested the physical principle of storing informa-

We find

$$
\frac{dE(x)}{dt}\Big|_{(32)} = \sum_{i=1}^{N} \xi_i \big[d_i(x_i)\big]^{-1} \mathrm{sign}(x_i - \bar{x}_i) \frac{d}{dt} x_i
$$

$$
= \Big\langle S(x - \bar{x})\xi, D(x)^{-1} \frac{dx}{dt} \Big\rangle = \langle S(x - \bar{x})\xi, F_1(x) \rangle.
$$

We express $F_1(x)$ at $\bar{x}$ as $F_1(x) = DF_1(\bar{x})(x - \bar{x}) + o(x - \bar{x})$, where $o(x - \bar{x})$ denotes the remaining nonlinear-order terms of $F_1(x)$. Substituting this into the above equation gives

$$
\frac{dE(x)}{dt}\Big|_{(32)} = \langle S(x - \bar{x})\xi, A(x - \bar{x}) + o(x - \bar{x}) \rangle
$$

$$
= \sum_{i=1}^{N} \xi_i \, \mathrm{sign}(x_i - \bar{x}_i) \sum_{j=1}^{N} a_{ij}(x - \bar{x}_j) + o\big(\|x - \bar{x}\|\big)
$$

$$
\leq \sum_{j=1}^{N} \Big[\xi_j a_{jj} + \sum_{i \neq j}^{N} \xi_i |a_{ij}| \Big] |x_j - \bar{x}_j| + o\big(\|x - \bar{x}\|\big)
$$

$$
\leq \max \Big\{ \xi_j a_{jj} + \sum_{i \neq j}^{N} \xi_i |a_{ij}| \Big\} \|x - \bar{x}\|_1 + o\big(\|x - \bar{x}\|\big).
$$

In light of Eq. (33), the last term of the above inequality is negative whenever x is in a small neighborhood of $\bar{x}$. The asymptotic stability of $\bar{x}$ then follows from Theorem 2 by applying the Liapunov method.

The conditions in Theorem 6 can be shown to be strict in the sense that no inequality signs can be reversed (i.e., replacing the "larger than" sign with the "smaller than" sign). If we impose the reversion, Theorem 3 shows that $\bar{x}$ is indeed unstable [59].

To split a system into a form of (32) is of particular significance. Whenever it can be done, the stability of the original system is characterized by its simplified system, $dx/dt = F_1(x)$. For example, we can recast the Cohen–Grossberg model Eq. (14) in the splitting form

$$
\frac{dv}{dt} = D(v)F_1(v) \tag{34}
$$

where

$$
D(v) = \mathrm{diag}\big\{a_1\big(\varphi^{-1}(v_1)\big)\varphi_1'\big(\varphi^{-1}(v_1)\big), \ldots, a_N\big(\varphi^{-1}(v_N)\big)\varphi_N'\big(\varphi^{-1}(v_N)\big)\big\},
$$
$$
F_1(v) = B(v) - Cv,
$$
$$
B(v) = \big(b_1\big(\varphi^{-1}(v_1)\big), b_2\big(\varphi^{-1}(v_2)\big), \ldots, b_N\big(\varphi^{-1}(v_N)\big)\big)^T.
$$

Theorem 6 can then be applied directly to yield the stability of Cohen–Grossberg PAAM, as follows.

THEOREM 7 (Asymptotic Stability of the Cohen–Grossberg Model). *Assume that the PAAM is the Cohen–Grossberg model in which φ_i^{-1} exist, $a_i(u_i) > 0$ and $\varphi_i'(u_i) > 0$ for any i and u_i. If $\bar{v}$ is an equilibrium state of (34), then $\bar{v}$ is asymptotically stable provided*

(i) $c_{ii} - b_i'(\varphi^{-1}(v_i)) := b_{ii} > 0, i = 1, 2, \ldots, N$, *and*
(ii) $B = (b_{ij})_N \times N$ *with* $b_{ij} = -|c_{ij}| \ (i \neq j)$ *is an M-matrix.*

There exists a great number of well-known results for M-matrices that can be applied to derive the specific conditions for B to satisfy (ii). An example is the quasi-diagonal dominance of B:

$$\xi_i |b_{ii}| > \sum_{\substack{j \neq i}}^{N} \xi_j |b_{ij}|, \qquad i = 1, 2, \ldots, N, \tag{35}$$

where $(\xi_1, \xi_2, \ldots, \xi_N)$ is a set of N positive numbers. When this specification is used, we obtain, from Theorem 7, the following.

COROLLARY 2. *In the setting of Theorem 7, any $\bar{v} \in F^{-1}(0)$ is asymptotically stable if there are N positive constants $\xi_1, \xi_2, \ldots, \xi_N$ such that*

(p1): $B(\bar{v}) = C\bar{v}, \forall \bar{v} \in F^{-1}(0)$
(p2): $c_{ii} - \xi_i^{-1} \sum_{j \neq i}^{N} \xi_j |c_{ij}| > \max\{b_i'(\varphi^{-1}(\bar{v}_i)): \bar{v} \in F^{-1}\}, i = 1, \ldots, N$

Corollary 2 underlies the synthesis techniques of the Cohen–Grossberg model [60–62].

C. ENCODING STRATEGIES

Suppose we are given a set of M N-dimensional prototype patterns $\{X^{(\mu)}: \mu = 1, 2, \ldots, p\}$ that we wish to store as asymptotically stable equilibrium states of an N-neuron PAAM of the form (8). An encoding strategy is a method or rule to specify the configuration of such a PAAM system.

Encoding is an "inverse" problem in the sense that, given the set of point attractors, we are asked to construct a dynamic system (PAAM) that possesses these attractors. The solution is not unique in general. To simplify the subsequent exposition, we assume in this subsection that the PAAMs are given as the Cohen–Grossberg model in which the functions $a_i(\cdot)$ and $b_i(\cdot)$ are also prespecified (particularly, we assume $b_i(u_i) = u_i$, as in the Hopfield model). Thus only the connection weights c_{ij} and the neuron activation function $\varphi_i(\cdot)$ have to be deter-

If one assumes Eq. (41) holds for any $1 \le k \le L - 1$ with some $L \ge 1$, then, for $k = L$, (38) becomes

$$H_L(\mathbf{X}, \mathbf{Y})X^{(\mu)} = H_{L-1}(\mathbf{X}, \mathbf{Y})X^{(\mu)} + \frac{\eta_{L-1}(\mathbf{X}, \mathbf{Y})\epsilon_{L-1}^T(\mathbf{X})X^{(\mu)}}{\epsilon_{L-1}^T(\mathbf{X})X^{(L)}}, \qquad (42)$$

where $\epsilon_{L-1}^T(\mathbf{X})X^{(L)} \neq 0$, because of the definiteness of $H_{L-1}(\mathbf{X}, \mathbf{Y})$. Because the matrix $P_{L-1}(\mathbf{X})$ is the best approximation of $\mathbf{R}^N$ in $\mathbf{X}_{L-1} = \mathrm{span}\{X^{(1)}, \ldots, X^{(L-1)}\}$, which means $\langle X - P_{L-1}(\mathbf{X})X, Y \rangle = 0$ for any $X \in \mathbf{R}^N$ and $Y \in \mathbf{X}_{L-1}$ [61], we deduce that, for any $\mu \le L - 1$,

$$\epsilon_{L-1}^T(\mathbf{X})X^{(\mu)} = \langle X^{(L)} - P_{L-1}(\mathbf{X})X^{(L)}, X^{(\mu)} \rangle = 0.$$

It follows from Eq. (42) that $H_L(\mathbf{X}, \mathbf{Y})X^{(\mu)} = H_{L-1}(\mathbf{X}, \mathbf{Y})X^{(\mu)} = Y^{(\mu)}$ for any $\mu \le L - 1$. Furthermore, a direct calculation with Eqs. (42) and (40) gives

$$H_L(\mathbf{X}, \mathbf{Y})X^{(L)} = H_{L-1}(\mathbf{X}, \mathbf{Y})X^{(L)} + \eta_{L-1}(\mathbf{X}, \mathbf{Y}) = Y^{(L)}.$$

The equality (41) follows for $i = L$. By induction, the proof is completed.

Some remarks on Algorithm 1 are useful.

(i) The algorithm proposed here is a direct generalization of the Hebbian learning rule:

$$H_M = \sum_{\mu=1}^{M} Y^{(\mu)}\left(X^{(\mu)}\right)^T. \qquad (43)$$

To see this, let us suppose that $\{X^{(1)}, X^{(2)}, \ldots, X^{(M)}\}$ and $\{Y^{(1)}, Y^{(2)}, \ldots, Y^{(M)}\}$ are both normalized and orthogonal. Then Algorithm 1 implies that $P_1(\mathbf{X}) = (X^{(1)})(X^{(1)})^T$ and $H_1(\mathbf{X}, \mathbf{Y}) = (Y^{(1)})(X^{(1)})^T$. If we assume that

$$P_k(\mathbf{X}) = \sum_{\mu=1}^{k} X^{(\mu)}\left(X^{(\mu)}\right)^T, \qquad H_k(\mathbf{X}, \mathbf{Y}) = \sum_{\mu=1}^{k} Y^{(\mu)}\left(X^{(\mu)}\right)^T \qquad (44)$$

for some $k \ge 1$, then by definition (Eqs. (39)–(40)),

$$\epsilon_k(\mathbf{X}) = X^{(k+1)} - \sum_{\mu=1}^{k} X^{(\mu)}\left(X^{(\mu)}\right)^T X^{(k+1)} = X^{(k+1)},$$

$$\eta_k(\mathbf{X}, \mathbf{Y}) = Y^{(k+1)} - \sum_{\mu=1}^{k} Y^{(\mu)}\left(X^{(\mu)}\right)^T X^{(k+1)} = Y^{(k+1)},$$

and hence, Eqs. (37) and (38) imply, respectively,

$$P_{k+1}(\mathbf{X}) = P_k(\mathbf{X}) + \frac{(X^{(k+1)})(X^{(k+1)})^T}{(X^{(k+1)})^T(X^{(k+1)})} = \sum_{\mu=1}^{k+1} X^{(\mu)}(X^{(\mu)})^T,$$

and

$$H_{k+1}(\mathbf{X}, \mathbf{Y}) = H_k(\mathbf{X}, \mathbf{Y}) + \frac{(Y^{(k+1)})(X^{(k+1)})^T}{(X^{(k+1)})^T(X^{(k+1)})} = \sum_{\mu=1}^{k+1} Y^{(\mu)}(X^{(\mu)})^T.$$

Thus the identities (44) are also valid for $\mu = k + 1$. This is true for any $k = 1, 2, \ldots, M - 1$. In particular, we obtain the Hebb's rule (43) when $k + 1 = M$.

(ii) The Hebb's rule has been regarded as a learning algorithm with biological plausibility [4, 65–67]. Apart from this, the most distinctive advantage of the rule is its "accumulation" feature in learning, that is, a new pattern can be learned by accumulating (adding) it directly to the existing memory. This accumulation property is very useful in problems in which the patterns to be stored are presented on-line. Clearly the much generalized Algorithm 1 retains this distinguished feature of the Hebb's rule.

(iii) Let $\mathbf{X} = [X^{(1)}, X^{(2)}, \ldots, X^{(M)}]$ and $\mathbf{Y} = [Y^{(1)}, Y^{(2)}, \ldots, Y^{(M)}]$. Then $H_M(\mathbf{X}, \mathbf{Y})$, defined by Algorithm 1, can also be expressed as

$$H_M(\mathbf{X}, \mathbf{Y}) = \mathbf{Y}\mathbf{X}^+,$$

where $\mathbf{X}^+$ is the Moore–Penrose inverse of $\mathbf{X}$. This is a direct encoding known as the *pseudo-inverse method* [12, 13, 39]. However, as noted by many authors, the accumulation property will be lost if such a direct encoding method is adopted. This reveals a fundamental difference between the proposed Algorithm 1 and the pseudo-inverse method.

The successive interpolating encoding developed in this section is a very fundamental learning rule that can be applied to general PAAM research [64, 68–71]. An example is shown in the following subsection.

2. A Sparsely Connected Encoding

The matrix W to be encoded represents the connection weights among the neurons of the PAAM. The sparseness of W therefore reflects the connection complexity and the storage efficiency of the network [57, 64, 72]. All elements of the matrix $H_p(\mathbf{X}, \mathbf{Y})$ encoded according to Algorithm 1 are nonzero in general, which corresponds to a fully connected neural network. However, if the given pattern set $\mathbf{X}$ is known to be "decomposable" in certain way, we may obtain a very sparsely connected encoding. This subsection is devoted to this study. We begin with a fundamental definition.

where $H_M(\cdot, \cdot)$ is the interpolation operator constructed according to Algorithm 1.

The so constructed matrix W is clearly very sparse—each row or column contains only one nonzero block (hence the name "sparsely connected encoding"), for example,

$$W = \begin{pmatrix} 0 & W_{12} & 0 & \cdots & 0 \\ 0 & 0 & W_{23} & \cdots & 0 \\ \cdots & \cdots & \cdots & \cdots & \cdots \\ W_{K1} & 0 & 0 & \cdots & 0 \end{pmatrix}. \tag{46}$$

In contrast with the fully connected encoding that requires $N \times N$ connections, the number of connections of a neural network using sparsely connected encoding is

$$C(s_1, s_2, \ldots, s_K) = \sum_{k=1}^{K} \left\{ n(k) \times n(s_k) \right\},$$

which may be far less than $N \times N$, because $N = n(1) + n(2) + \cdots + n(K)$. This shows that the sparsely connected encoding can yield a PAAM of much lower connection complexity than any other fully connected encoding. Based on this observation, a complexity reduction principle has been developed in [64] for the Litter–Hopfield model.

EXAMPLE 2 (Bidirectional Associative Memories). Consider the heteroassociation problem $\{(\xi^{(\mu)}, \zeta^{(\mu)}); \mu = 1, 2, \ldots, p\}$, where $\xi^{(\mu)} \in (-1, 1)^N$, $\zeta^{(\mu)} = (-1, 1)^M$. As explained in Section I, the problem can be converted into an autoassociation problem $\{X^{(\mu)}: \mu = 1, 2, \ldots, p\}$ with $X^{(\mu)} = (\xi^{(\mu)}, \zeta^{(\mu)})$ in the product space $(-1, 1)^{N+M}$. The pattern set $\mathbf{X} = \{X^{(\mu)}: \mu = 1, 2, \ldots, p\}$ is clearly decomposable at 2-level whenever $\{\xi^{(\mu)}: \mu = 1, 2, \ldots, p\}$ and $\{\zeta^{(\mu)}: \mu = 1, 2, \ldots, p\}$ are both in general position. The decomposition is given by, for example,

$$\{1, 2, \ldots, N + M\} = N_1 \cup N_2,$$

with

$$N_1 = \{1, 2, \ldots, N\} \text{ and } N_2 = \{N + 1, N + 2, \ldots, N + M\}.$$

In the decomposition framework, $X^{(\mu)} = (X_1^{(\mu)}, X_2^{(\mu)})$ is specified by

$$X_1^{(\mu)} = \xi^{(\mu)} \text{ and } X_2^{(\mu)} = \zeta^{(\mu)}.$$

Therefore, $\mathbf{X}_1 = \{\xi^{(\mu)}: \mu = 1, 2, \ldots, p\}$ and $\mathbf{X}_2 = \{\zeta^{(\mu)}: \mu = 1, 2, \ldots, p\}$.

Now if we apply sparely connected encoding with the permutation $(s_1, s_2) = (2, 1)$, we obtain

$$W = \begin{pmatrix} O & H_p(\mathbf{X}_2, \mathbf{X}_1) \\ H_p(\mathbf{X}_1, \mathbf{X}_2) & O \end{pmatrix}.$$

Using this encoding in the Cohen–Grossberg model gives rise to the following PAAM system:

$$\frac{d}{dt}\begin{pmatrix} \xi \\ \zeta \end{pmatrix} = A\begin{pmatrix} \xi \\ \zeta \end{pmatrix}\left[B\begin{pmatrix} \xi \\ \zeta \end{pmatrix} - \begin{pmatrix} O & H_p(\mathbf{X}_2, \mathbf{X}_1) \\ H_p(\mathbf{X}_1, \mathbf{X}_2) & O \end{pmatrix} \Phi\begin{pmatrix} \xi \\ \zeta \end{pmatrix} \right],$$

where

$$A(X) = \big(a_1(x_1), a_2(x_2), \ldots, a_{N+M}(x_{N+M})\big)^T,$$

$$B(X) = \big(b_1(x_1), b_2(x_2), \ldots, b_{N+M}(x_{N+M})\big)^T,$$

$$\Phi(X) = \big(\varphi_1(x_1), \varphi_2(x_2), \ldots, \varphi_{N+M}(x_{N+M})\big)^T.$$

Note that A, B, and Φ are all diagonally dependent only, so that we can express the system in the following form:

$$\frac{d}{dt}\xi = A(\xi)\big[B(\xi) - H_p(\mathbf{X}_2, \mathbf{X}_1)\Phi(\zeta)\big],$$

$$\frac{d}{dt}\zeta = A(\zeta)\big[B(\zeta) - H_p(\mathbf{X}_1, \mathbf{X}_2)\Phi(\xi)\big],$$

which is seen to be a generalization of the bidirectional associative memory model proposed by Kosko [39, 73].

III. CONTINUOUS PAAM: COMPETITIVE ASSOCIATIVE MEMORIES

In the design of a PAAM there are two major considerations: the storage capacity and the error-correction capability. We would like to attain both large storage capacity and high error-correction capability. However, these two requirements are incompatible. The reason is that a large storage capacity requires a small attraction basin for each stored pattern, whereas a high error-correction capability asks for a large-size attraction basin for each stored pattern; hence the number of patterns that can be stored is limited. The existence of the so-called spurious attractors is the major obstacle to extending the storage limit.

over, if $M = N$, $\alpha_i(t) = \lambda_i(t) > \epsilon > 0$ and $\|X^{(i)}\| = 1$ for any $t \geq 0$ and $i = 1, 2, \ldots, M$, the solution $u(t, u_0)$ has the following properties:

(i) $\|u(t, u_0)\| = 1$ *for any $t \geq 0$ provided $\|u_0\| = 1$*
(ii) $\|u(t, u_0)\|$ *increases monotonically to 1 provided $0 < \|u_0\| < 1$*
(iii) $\|u(t, u_0)\|$ *decreases monotonically to 1 provided $\|u_0\| > 1$*
(iv) *If $u_0 \neq 0$, then $u(t, u_0) \neq 0$ for any $t > 0$*

Theorem 9 shows that the system (51) can be considered as a third-order continuous Hopfield-type network without second-order connections [76, 77]. In fact, with $u = (u_1, u_2, \ldots, u_N)^T$,

$$B(t) = H_M(\mathbf{X}\mathbf{\Lambda}_\lambda(t), \mathbf{X}) = (b_{ij}(t))_{N \times M}, \tag{52}$$

$$C(t) = H_M(\mathbf{X}\mathbf{\Lambda}_\alpha(t), \mathbf{X}) = (c_{kl}(t))_{N \times M}, \tag{53}$$
$$P_M(\mathbf{X}) = (p_{ij})_{N \times N},$$

we can rewrite the model (51) as

$$\frac{du_i}{dt} = \sum_{j=1}^{M} b_{ij}(t) v_j + \sum_{j=1}^{M} \sum_{k=1}^{M} \sum_{l=1}^{M} (p_{ij} b_{kl}(t)) v_j v_k v_l, \qquad i = 1, 2, \ldots, N,$$

where $v_i = \text{sat}(u_i)$ is the saturation nonlinearity:

$$\text{sat}(u_i) = \begin{cases} +1, & u_i > 1 \\ u_i, & u_i \in [-1, 1] \\ -1, & u_i < 1 \end{cases} . \tag{54}$$

The competition mechanism embodied in Eq. (51) is uniquely characterized by the parameters $\lambda_i(t)$ and $\alpha_i(t)$, and their selection is, in general, problem dependent. For example, when the model (51) is used to perform distance-based recognition, $\lambda_i(t)$ can be taken as a constant or the reciprocal of the distance between the pattern $X^{(i)}$ and the initial guess u_0, that is,

$$\lambda_i = \lambda_i^D = \frac{\|u_0 - X^{(i)}\|^{-1}}{\|u_0 - X^{(1)}\|^{-1} + \cdots + \|u_0 - X^{(M)}\|^{-1}}. \tag{55}$$

On the other hand, when the network is used for "criminal recognition" or "spelling check in writing" applications [74], $\lambda_i(t)$ should be chosen to effect both the distance-based and the recurrence-frequency-based competitions. For instance, $\lambda_i(t)$ may be specified as

$$\lambda_n^P = P_i \tag{56}$$

or

$$\lambda_i = \lambda_i^D \lambda_i^P, \tag{57}$$

where P_i is the recurrence probability (frequency) of the pattern $X^{(i)}$ (obtained by, say, experience or statistics). Alternatively, $\lambda_i(t)$ may be taken as the solution of a specific differential or difference equation, if the competition does obey such an equation.

It is seen that many different competition rules can be incorporated into the model (51), which may embrace more than one competition principle. However, no network training is necessary once the competition principle (equivalently, the parameters $\lambda_i(t)$ and $\alpha_i(t)$) is specified.

B. Competition-Winning Principle

The competitive recognition mechanism of the model (51) is elucidated in this subsection through a detailed stability analysis of the system. We will show, in particular, the following distinctive features of the model:

- Provided that the competitive and inhibitive parameters are suitably chosen, there will be no nontrivial spurious stable state and only the prototype patterns are stored in the memory.
- There holds a competition-winning principle: if there exists a unique winner, the pattern corresponding to the winner is almost asymptotically stable in global, and hence it can be retrieved from almost any input vector in the underlying state space.

Without loss of generality, we assume that $M = N$ (hence $P_M = I$ according to (50)), so that the model (51) can be analyzed in the whole space $\mathbf{R}^N$. We also take $X^{(i)}$ and $-X^{(i)}$ be identical, because it is well known that an associative memory cannot distinguish a pattern and its complement in general (see, e.g., [78–80]).

1. Nonexistence of Spurious Stable State

The following theorem asserts the nonexistence of nontrivial spurious stable states in the model (51).

THEOREM 10.   *If* $\alpha_i(t) = \lambda_i(t)/(X^{(i)})^T(X^{(i)})$ *and* $\lambda_i(t) \neq \lambda_j(t)$ *whenever* $i \neq j$ *for any* $i, j = 1, 2, \ldots, M$, *then the model* (51) *has only* $2M + 1$ *equilibria given by the zero vector and the prototype patterns* $\mp X^{(1)}, \mp X^{(2)}, \ldots, \mp X^{(M)}$.

We show by contradiction that no other equilibrium state exists except the said $2M + 1$ states. Assume that Eq. (51) has an equilibrium point u^* that is not in $\{0, \mp X^{(1)}, \mp X^{(2)}, \ldots, \mp X^{(M)}\}$. We apply the transformation

$$u = \sum_{i=1}^{M} y_i X^{(i)} = XY, \tag{58}$$

$\pm Y^{(i_0)} = \{y_{i_0} = \pm 1, \ y_j = 0, \ \forall j \neq i_0\})$. Thus system (59) can be written accordingly as

$$\frac{d}{dt}(y_i) = \lambda_i(t)y_i - [Y^T X^T B(t) X Y]y_i, \qquad i = 1, 2, \ldots, N. \qquad (63)$$

Furthermore, by using (52), the system (51) can be rewritten as

$$\frac{du}{dt} = B(t)u(t) - [u^T(t)B(t)u(t)]Pu(t), \qquad (64)$$

which, by Theorem 8, has a unique solution $u(t)$ for any initial state $u(0)$. Moreover, $\|u(t)\| \to 1$ as t goes to infinity. Define a zero-measure set $\Im_0$ by

$$\Im_0 = \{Y \in \mathbf{R}^N : \ y_{i_0} = 0\}.$$

We proceed to show that the solution $Y(t)$ of the system (64) will converge to $\pm Y^{(i_0)}$ from any initial value $Y(0) \in \mathbf{R}^N \setminus \Im_0$. Actually, for any given initial value $Y(0)$, there is a unique solution $y_i(t)$ of the system (64). Moreover, if $y_i(t_0) = 0$ for some t_0, then $y_i(t) = 0$ for all $t \geq t_0$. Assume that $Y(0)$ is not in $\Im_0$; then $y_{i_0}(0) \neq 0$. It follows from Eq. (64) that

$$\frac{1}{2}\frac{d}{dt}(y_{i_0})^2 = \left\langle y_{i_0}, \frac{d}{dt}(y_{i_0}) \right\rangle = \{\lambda_{i_0}(t) - [Y^T X^T B(t) X Y]\}(y_{i_0})^2. \qquad (65)$$

Because $\|u(t)\| \to 1$, $[Y^T X^T B(t) X Y] = u^T(t)B(t)u(t) \leq \max\{\lambda_i(t); \ i = 1, 2, \ldots, N\}\|u(t)\|^2 \to \lambda_{i_0}$, which means that there exists a $T > 0$ such that

$$\lambda_{i_0}(t) - [Y^T X^T B(t) X Y] \geq 0, \qquad \forall t \geq T.$$

We conclude from Eq. (65) that $d(y_{i_0})^2/dt \geq 0$ $(t \geq T)$, and so $y_{i_0}(t) \neq 0$ $(t \geq T)$. For any $t \geq T$, let $z_i(t) = y_i(t)/y_{i_0}(t)$. By Eq. (64) and

$$\frac{d}{dt}(z_i) = \left\{ \frac{d}{dt}(y_i)(y_{i_0}) - \frac{d}{dt}(y_{i_0})(y_i) \right\} \Big/ (y_{i_0})^2,$$

we obtain

$$\frac{d}{dt}(z_i) = \big(\lambda_i(t) - \lambda_{i_0}(t)\big)z_i,$$

the solution of which is

$$z_i(t) = \exp\left(\int_0^t [\lambda_i(s) - \lambda_{i_0}(s)]ds \right) z_i(0).$$

Because, by assumption, $\lim_{s \to \infty} \lambda_i(s) - \lambda_{i_0}(s) = \lambda_i^* - \lambda < 0$, the above equality gives $z_i(t) \to 0$ as $t \to \infty$ for any $i \neq i_0$. Thus, $y_i(t) \to 0$ $(i \neq i_0)$ and

$$u(t) = XY = \sum_{i=1}^{N} y_i(t)X^{(i)} \to \lim_{t \to \infty} y_{i_0)}(t)X^{(i_0)}.$$

This shows $\lim_{t \to \infty} y_{i_0}(t) = \pm 1$ because $\|u(t)\| \to 1$, that is, $Y(t)$ converges to $\pm Y^{(i_0)}$.

In Theorem 11, the assumption that the competition winner parameter λ_{i_0} is unique is fundamental. If this assumption does not hold, the dynamic behavior of the system (61) may become more complicated. The following example helps understanding this phenomenon.

EXAMPLE 3 (Equal Competitive Parameters Imply Limit Cycle) [73]. Assume two 2-D prototype patterns $X^{(1)} = (x_1^{(1)}, x_2^{(1)})^T$ and $X^{(2)} = (x_1^{(2)}, x_2^{(2)})^T$, which are assumed to be orthonormal. We let $\lambda_1(t) = \lambda_2(t) = c_0$ and specialize the competitive associative memory model (51) to

$$\frac{du(t)}{dt} = Cu(t) - [u^T(t)Cu(t)]u(t), \qquad u = (u_1, u_2) \in \mathbf{R}^2, \qquad (66)$$

where

$$C = c_0[(X^{(1)})(X^{(1)})^T + (X^{(2)})(X^{(2)})^T].$$

Then, with

$$U = x_1^{(1)}u_1 + x_2^{(1)}u_2, \qquad V = x_1^{(2)}u_1 + x_2^{(2)}u_2,$$

the system (66) can be expressed as

$$u_1' = c_0[1 - (U^2 + V^2)](x_1^{(1)}U + x_1^{(2)}V),$$

$$u_2' = c_0[1 - (U^2 + V^2)](x_2^{(1)}U + x_2^{(2)}V).$$

Under the polar coordinate transformation $U = r\cos\theta$, $V = r\sin\theta$, we obtain

$$\frac{dr}{dt} = c_0(1 - r^2)r, \qquad \frac{d\theta}{dt} = 1. \qquad (67)$$

From Eq. (67) we easily see that $\{r = 1, \theta = t\}$ is a nontrivial limit cycle of the system (76). This limit cycle is also asymptotically stable, because, starting from any (r_0, θ_0), the phase trajectory of the first equation of (67) must approach the solution $r = 1$ from either the outside or the inside of the circle $r = 1$, depending on whether $r > 1$ or $r > 1$. Therefore,

$$\{u(t) = (u_1(t), u_2(t)): (x_1^{(1)}u_1 + x_2^{(1)}u_2)^2 + (x_1^{(2)}u_1 + x_2^{(2)}u_2)^2 = 1\}$$

is an asymptotically stable limit cycle of the system (66).

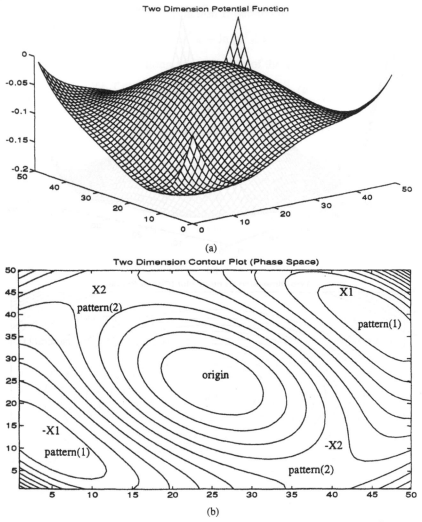

(a)

(b)

Figure 6   The landscape of the energy E with $\lambda_1 = 0.7$ and $\lambda_2 = 0.3$. (b) The corresponding contour plot of E.

For the given initial guess, no stored patterns can be recognized by the conventional "competitive recognition in distance" associative memories, because the initial input has the same distance to all patterns of "House," "Palette," "Tools," "No Smoking," "Clock," and "Lens." However, the introduction of the competitive parameters $\{\lambda_n\}$ in the associative memory model (51) allows not only competitions of stored patterns in distance, but also other factors that could improve

Figure 7 The prototype patterns of six pictures, each composed of 64 × 64 pixels.

the recognition (e.g., the recurrence probabilities of the stored patterns). We have taken in the simulations the parameters $\{\lambda_n\}$ to be

$$\lambda_n = \lambda_n^D \lambda_n^A, \qquad n = 1, 2, \ldots, 6, \tag{70}$$

Figure 8 The initial input composed of $(1/6)$[House] $+$ $(1/6)$[Palette] $+$ $(1/6)$[Tools] $+$ $(1/6)$[No Smoking] $+$ $(1/6)$[Clock] $+$ $(1/6)$[Lens].

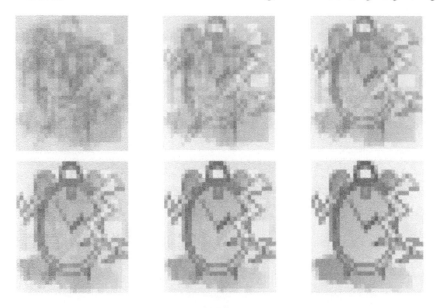

(c)

Figure 9 (*Continued*)

D. Application: Perfectly Reacted PAAM

As demonstrated in the previous example, the competitive associative memory may have important applications in pattern recognition, especially when particular pattern must be recognized from a set of stored patterns and the recognition process is governed by certain known competition mechanism. In this section, we apply the developed method to the original association problem to yield a new, "perfectly reacted" PAAM.

For most associative memory applications, it is natural to devise a system in a way that it can respond to any initial input u_0 by producing a vector u^* nearest to u_0 in distance. Usually u_0 is a distorted or incomplete version of the output u^*, the latter being one of the stored prototype patterns in the memory. We have named the system that uses the above distance-based recognition process as "non-competitive" associative memory. We ask if the competitive associative memory model (61) can also apply to this case.

One straightforward way is to specify the competitive parameters $\lambda_i(t)$ as that in Eq. (55). However, in doing that, all of the stored prototype patterns must be examined, which is certainly undesirable (because the method will degenerate to the classical recognition of comparing the input directly with every given prototype vector). In contrast, we would prefer a way of assigning $\lambda_i(t)$ that is based purely on the initial key.

Such a new strategy is motivated by the following observations. In the competitive associative memory (cf. Eq. (63)), each competitive parameter $\lambda_i(t)$ is in fact an eigenvalue of $B(t)$, with the stored prototype pattern $X^{(i)}$ as its associated eigenvector (cf. (49)). From this point of view, we propose:

1. By associating with each prototype pattern $X^{(i)}$ a specific family of $\{\lambda_i(t)\}$, the memory stores the pattern $X^{(i)}$ as a common eigenvector associated with the eigenvalue $\lambda_i(t)$ of $B(t)$.
2. The dynamics of the memory is described by an algorithm for finding the eigenvector associated with the largest eigenvalue of $B(t_\infty)$, where $B(t_\infty) = \lim_{t\to\infty} B(t)$.
3. The variation of the eigenvalues $\{\lambda_i(t)\}$ plays a role in performing the competitive recognition of the stored memories.

We suggest the following new PAAM model to implement the above proposal.

Algorithm 3 (A Perfectly Reacted PAAM Model).   Given a set of M prototype patterns $\{X^{(i)}: i = 1, 2, \ldots, N\}$, we denote $\Lambda = \text{diag}\{N, N-1, \ldots, 1\}$.

(i) Let $B = H_N(\mathbf{X}, \mathbf{X}\Lambda)$ be generated by Algorithm 1.
(ii) Set $R(u_0) = (u_0^T B u_0)/(u_0^T u_0)$ and $\rho = $ the integer nearest to $R(u_0)$.
(iii) Take

$$
B(u_0) = \begin{cases} (R(u_0) - B)^{-1} - (R(u_0) - \lambda_{\rho-1})^{-1} + 1; & \text{if } R(u_0) > \rho \\ (B - R(u_0))^{-1} + (\lambda_{\rho+1} - R(u_0))^{-1} + 1; & \text{if } R(u_0) < \rho \end{cases},
$$

$$(73)$$

and construct

$$
\frac{du}{dt} = B(u_0)u(t) - \left[u^T(t)B(u_0)u(t)\right]u(t) \tag{74}
$$

$$
u(0) = u_0. \tag{75}
$$

The feasibility of the above algorithm can be explained as follows. Definition (73) ensures that the matrix $B(u_0)$ takes all prototype patterns $X^{(i)}$ as its eigenvectors as B does. The eigenvalues of $B(u_0)$ are

$$
\lambda_j\big(B(u_0)\big) = \begin{cases} (R(u_0) - j)^{-1} - (R(u_0) - \rho + 1)^{-1} + 1, & \text{if } R(u_0) > \rho \\ (j - R(u_0))^{-1} + (\rho + 1 - R(u_0))^{-1} + 1, & \text{if } R(u_0) < \rho \end{cases},
$$

which are clearly positive. Then by the competition-winning principle (Theorem 11), the unique solution $u(t)$ of the system (74) and (75) must converge to the pro-

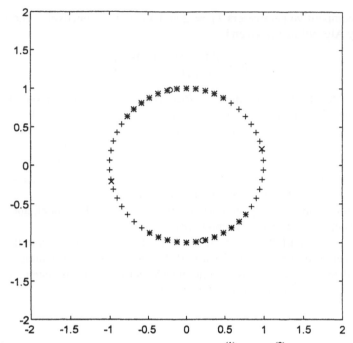

Figure 12   The attraction basins of the stored memories $\pm X^{(1)}$ and $\pm X^{(2)}$ when all initial states are limited to the unit circle. Again, all of the points marked with an $*$ are attracted to $\pm X^{(1)}$, and the points marked with a $+$ are attracted to $\pm X^{(2)}$.

IV. DISCRETE PAAM:
ASYMMETRIC HOPFIELD-TYPE NETWORKS

The Cohen–Grossberg model, the Hopfield model, and the competitive associative memory model in the previous two sections represent important examples of PAAMs with continuous dynamics. In this section we consider another important class of PAAMs that are modeled by discrete dynamic systems.

One of most successful and influential discrete PAAM model is the Little–Hopfield model (16, 17). Many other discrete PAAM models such as bidirectional associative memories [39], recurrent neural networks [82], and Q-state attractor neural networks [73, 83], are its variants or generalizations. The model has been extensively studied (see, e.g., [60–62], [78–80], [84–101]), because of its usefulness both as associative memory and optimization problem solver. In most of the previous studies, the symmetry of the connection weight of the network is commonly assumed. In this section we develop a unified theory that is valid not only for networks with symmetric connections, but also for networks with asymmetric connections. Henceforth we refer to the Little–Hopfield model with asymmetric (symmetric) connections as the asymmetric (symmetric) Hopfield-type network.

We begin with some equivalent definitions of Hopfield-type networks.

A. NEURAL NETWORK MODEL

A Hopfield-type network of order N comprises N neurons, which can be represented by a weighted graph $\mathcal{N} = (W, I)$, where $W = (w_{ij})_{N \times N}$ is an $N \times N$ matrix, with w_{ij} representing the interconnection weight from neuron j to i, and $I = (I_i)_{N \times 1}$ is an N-dimensional real vector with I_i representing the threshold attached to the neuron i. There are two possible values for the state of each neuron: $+1$ or -1. Denote the state of neuron i at time t as $v_i(t)$; the vector $V(t) = (v_1(t), v_2(t), \ldots, v_N(t))^T$ is then the state of the whole network at time t.

According to Eq. (16), the state of a neuron is updated according to the following first-order difference equation:

$$v_i(t+1) = \text{sgn}(u_i(t+1)) = \begin{cases} 1, & \text{if } u_i(t+1) \geq 0 \\ -1, & \text{if } u_i(t+1) < 0 \end{cases}, \qquad (76)$$

where $\text{sgn}(\cdot)$ is the signum activation function, and

$$u_i(t+1) = \sum_{j=1}^{N} w_{ij} v_j(t) - I_i. \qquad (77)$$

If only one neuron is allowed to change state at any time, the network is said to be operating in the *serial mode*. Otherwise, the network is operating in the *parallel mode* (or *fully parallel mode*), in which all of the neurons are updated simultaneously.

Let

$$\epsilon_i = \min \left\{ I_i - \sum_{j=1}^{N} w_{ij} v_j : v_j \in \{-1, 1\}, \ \sum_{j=1}^{N} w_{ij} v_j < I_i \right\}$$

$$\tilde{I} = I - \tfrac{1}{2}(\epsilon_1, \epsilon_2, \ldots, \epsilon_N)^T = (\tilde{I}_1, \tilde{I}_2, \ldots, \tilde{I}_N)^T$$

and define

$$\tilde{u}_i(t+1) = \sum_{j=1}^{N} w_{ij} v_j(t) - \tilde{I}_i.$$

DEFINITION 4 (Generalized Potential of a Hopfield-type Network).   Let the mapping $H(R): \mathbf{R}^N \rightarrow \mathbf{R}^N$ be defined by Eq. (80). The operator $H(R)$ is said to be a *subdifferential mapping restricted to the orbit* Γ_0, if there is a functional g such that

$$g\big(V(t+1)\big) - g\big(V(t)\big) \geq \langle H(R)(V(t)),\ V(t+1) - V(t)\rangle, \qquad t \geq 0.$$

In this case the functional $-g$ is called a generalized potential of the Hopfield network (79) with respect to the orbit Γ_0.

The following theorem reveals that a generalized potential can provide a general construction of the strict Liapunov function of the network.

THEOREM 13.   *Any generalized potential of the system* (79) *is a strict Liapunov function.*

To prove the theorem we assume, for instance, that $-g$ is a generalized potential of the network (79) with respect to its orbit Γ_0. Then, denote $E(V) = -g(V)$ and using Definition 4, we have

$$\begin{aligned}
\Delta E(V)|_{\Gamma_0} &= g\big(V(t)\big) - g\big(V(t+1)\big) \\
&\leq \langle H(R)V(t),\ V(t) - V(t+1)\rangle \\
&= -\langle R\big(WV(t) - I\big),\ V(t+1) - V(t)\rangle \\
&= \sum_{i \in I(t)} (-\alpha_i)\big[u_i(t+1)\big]\big[v_i(t+1) - v_i(t)\big] < 0,
\end{aligned}$$

which vanishes if and only if $V(t)$ is an equilibrium state of (79) from some time t_0 on. This last inequality follows because $v_i(t+1) = \operatorname{sgn}(u_i(t+1))$ implies $[u_i(t+1)][v_i(t+1) - v_i(t)] = 2|u_i(t+1)| > 0$, and $I(t) = \emptyset$ implies $V(t+1) = V(t)$. Therefore $V(t)$ is an equilibrium state of (79).

The significance of Theorem 13 is that it shows how a strict Liapunov function of the system (79) can be obtained by finding a generalized potential of the system; the latter can be done easily by using the special form of H(R) (Definition 4). In fact, Definition 4, together with (80), suggests that the generalized potential $-g$ should obey

$$\partial g(V) = R(WV - I), \qquad \forall V \in \mathbf{H}^N. \tag{84}$$

It follows that such a functional g must be quadratic:

$$g(V) = \tfrac{1}{2}\big(V^T A V\big) - V^T b \tag{85}$$

for some $A = (a_{ij})_{N \times N}$ and $b = (b_1, b_2, \dots, b_N)^T$.

We proceed to specify A and b so that g defined by Eq. (85) does become a generalized potential of a Hopfield-type network. Express $g(V)$ at $V(t)$ in a

Taylor series,

$$g(V) = g(V(t)) + [\tfrac{1}{2}(A + A^T)V(t) - b](V - V(t))$$
$$+ \tfrac{1}{4}(V - V(t))^T(A + A^T)(V - V(t)),$$

and bring this into Eq. (84). We see that $-g$ is a generalized potential of the system (79), provided

$$[\tfrac{1}{2}(A + A^T)V(t) - b](V(t + 1) - V(t))$$
$$+ \tfrac{1}{4}(V(t + 1) - V(t))^T(A + A^T)(V(t + 1) - V(t))$$
$$\geq \langle R(WV(t) - I), V(t + 1) - V(t) \rangle.$$

Or, equivalently,

$$\left\langle \left(RW - \frac{A + A^T}{2} \right)V(t) - (RI - b), V(t + 1) - V(t) \right\rangle$$
$$\leq \frac{1}{2}(V(t + 1) - V(t))^T\left(\frac{A + A^T}{2} \right)(V(t + 1) - V(t)).$$

Let $\Delta V(t) = V(t + 1) - V(t)$ and take $b = RI$ in the last inequality. Then the above inequality is equivalent to

$$Q(R)V(t) := \left\langle \left(RW - \frac{A + A^T}{2} \right)V(t), \Delta V(t) \right\rangle$$
$$- \frac{1}{4}\langle (A + A^T)\Delta V(t), \Delta V(t) \rangle \leq 0,$$

which also amounts to

$$\sum_{i \in I(t)} \sum_{j=1}^{N} \left[\alpha_i w_{ij} - \frac{a_{ij} + a_{ji}}{2} \right] v_j(t)\Delta v_i(t)$$
$$\leq \frac{1}{2} \sum_{i \in I(t)} \sum_{j \in I(t)} \frac{a_{ij} + a_{ji}}{2} \Delta v_i(t)\Delta v_j(t). \tag{86}$$

Note that $v_j(t) = -\tfrac{1}{2}\Delta v_j(t)$ for any $j \in I(t)$. A sufficient condition for the above inequality to hold is

$$\sum_{i \in I(t)} \sum_{j \in J(t)} \left| \alpha_i w_{ij} - \frac{a_{ij} + a_{ji}}{2} \right| [\Delta v_i(t)]^2 \leq \sum_{i \in I(t)} \sum_{j \in I(t)} (\alpha_i w_{ij})\Delta v_i(t)\Delta v_j(t), \tag{87}$$

where $J(t) = \{1, 2, \ldots, N\} \backslash I(t)$. We can rewrite (87) in the form

$$\sum_{i \in I(t)} \sum_{j \in I(t)} \bar{w}_{ij}\Delta_i(t)\Delta v_j(t) \geq 0, \tag{88}$$

Recall that the stored pattern is a dynamic procedure aimed at minimizing the energy where the valley becomes a basin of attraction. It turns out that the error-correction capability of the memory is characterized by the "width" of the valleys of the energy function. Our theory is based exactly on a quantitative measurement of the width of these valleys.

The analysis conducted in the last subsection reveals that the most natural energy function associated with the Hopfield-type network (79) is given by

$$E(V) = -\frac{1}{2} \sum_{i=1}^{N} \sum_{j=1}^{N} a_{ij} v_i v_j + \sum_{i=1}^{N} b_i v_i = -\frac{1}{2} \left(V^T A V \right) + V^T b. \qquad (93)$$

We are therefore considering the following combinatorial optimization problem:

$$\text{Minimize} \{ E(V) : V \in \mathbf{H}^N \}. \qquad (94)$$

Notice that the problem (94) is itself a model of many important combinatorial optimization problems such as TSP or MIS [61, 62, 99–101]. This in turn suggests the application of the Hopfield-type networks in solving these problems. However, we will not, go into this topic in this chapter.

To quantify the valley of a minimizer of E, some precise definitions are needed.

DEFINITION 5 (k-Local Minimizer). A vector $V^* \in \mathbf{H}^N$ is said to be a k-local minimizer of E if $E(V^*) \leq E(V)$ for any

$$V \in B_H(V^*, k) = \{V : d_H(V, V^*) \leq k\},$$

where $d_H(V, V^*)$ denotes the Hamming distance between V and V^* (i.e., the number of different components in V and V^*). A 1-local minimizer of E is simply called a local minimizer of E.

DEFINITION 6 (Classification of Energy). Let $\Omega_k(E)$ be the set of all k-local minimizers of E and $\Omega(\mathcal{N})$ be the set of all stable states of the Hopfield-type network $\mathcal{N}$.

(i) E is called a regular energy of $\mathcal{N}$ if $\Omega_k(E) \subseteq \Omega(\mathcal{N})$ (i.e., any k-local minimizer of E is a stable state of $\mathcal{N}$). In this case, $\mathcal{N}$ is said to have a regular correspondence property.

(ii) E is called a normal energy of $\mathcal{N}$ with order k if $\Omega_k(E) \supseteq \Omega(\mathcal{N})$ (i.e., any stable state of $\mathcal{N}$ is a k-local minimizer of E). In this case, $\mathcal{N}$ is said to have a normal correspondence property.

(iii) E is called a complete energy of $\mathcal{N}$ with order k, if $\Omega_k(E) = \Omega(\mathcal{N})$ (i.e., there is a one-to-one correspondence between the k-local minimizers of E and the stable states of $\mathcal{N}$). In this case, $\mathcal{N}$ is said to have a *complete correspondence* property. Thus E is both regular and normal if it is complete.

It is known that Definition 6 plays an important role in using the Hopfield-type network as a minimization algorithm for the problem (93) [96]. In brief, whereas the regularity of the energy function E characterizes the reliability of the deduced Hopfield-type network algorithm, the normality ensures the algorithm's high efficiency. We further remark that normality can be used to characterize the error-correction capability of the corresponding Hopfield-type network and that regularity is an indicator of nonexistence of states that are not asymptotically stable. Accordingly, Definition 6 also plays an important role in the stability analysis of Hopfield-type networks.

We now proceed to find general conditions under which the energy E of the form (93) becomes regular, normal, or complete. To this end, we let $\Delta V^* = V - V^*$ for any fixed $V \in B_H(V^*, k)$, and let

$$I^* = \{i \in \{1, 2, \ldots, N\}: \Delta V_i^* \neq 0\}, \quad J^* = \{1, 2, \ldots, N\}\backslash I^*$$

(hence $\Delta V_i^* = -2v_i^*$ if and only if $i \in I^*$). By expanding the energy E, we obtain

$$
\begin{aligned}
E(V) - E(V^*) &= -\langle H(R)V^*, \Delta V^* \rangle + \{\langle H(R)V^*, \Delta V^* \rangle \\
&\quad - [\tfrac{1}{2}(A + A^T)V^* + b]^T \Delta V^* - \tfrac{1}{4}\langle (A + A^T)\Delta V^*, \Delta V^* \rangle\} \\
&= -\langle H(R)V^*, \Delta V^* \rangle + Q(R)(V^*),
\end{aligned}
\tag{95}
$$

where

$$
Q(R)(V^*) = \left\{ \left\langle \left(RW - \frac{A + A^T}{2} \right) V^*, \Delta V^* \right\rangle - \frac{1}{4}\langle (A + A^T)\Delta V^*, \Delta V^* \rangle \right\}.
\tag{96}
$$

By Eq. (80),

$$
-\langle H(R)V^*, \Delta V^* \rangle = \sum_{i \in I^*} \alpha_i (WV^* - I)_i (2v_i^*).
$$

Identity (95) can then be written as

$$
E(V) - E(V^*) = \sum_{i \in I^*} 2\alpha_i (WV^* - I)_i v_i^* + Q(R)(V^*).
\tag{97}
$$

If $V^* \in \Omega_k(E)$ is a k-local minimizer, then it is also a local minimizer. So taking $I^* = \{i\}$ in the last identity gives $(WV^* - I)_i v_i^* > 0$ (i.e., $V^* \in \Omega(N)$) provided $Q(R)(V^*) \leq 0$. Conversely, if $V^* \in \Omega(N)$ is an equilibrium state of the network N, then $E(V) \geq E(V^*)$ as long as $Q(R)(V^*) \geq 0$.

Theorem 17 may be very powerful in the quantitative measurement of the error-correction capability of a particular Hopfield-type network. The following are two examples.

EXAMPLE 4 (Error-Correction Capability of Little–Hopfield Network).   Assume that $\xi^{(\mu)} = (\xi_1^{(\mu)}, \xi_2^{(\mu)}, \ldots, \xi_N^{(\mu)})^T \in \mathbf{H}^N$, $\mu = 1, 2, \ldots, p$, are p orthogonal prototype patterns, and $\mathcal{N} = (W, 0)$ is a Hopfield-type network, with W encoded by the Hebbian rule:

$$w_{ij} = \frac{1}{N} \sum_{\mu=1}^{p} \xi_i^{(\mu)} \xi_j^{(\mu)}, \qquad i, j = 1, 2, \ldots, N.$$

Then $|w_{ij}| \le p/N$, $W\xi^{(\mu)} = 1\xi^{(\mu)}$, and W is symmetric. Hence, with $R = \mathrm{diag}\{1, 1, \ldots, 1\}$, $A = W$ (so $k_i(\alpha_i) = 0$), and $\lambda^* = 1$,

$$1 \ge k\frac{p}{N} \ge \sum_{i \in I} |w_{ij}|.$$

Consequently, the condition (98) is satisfied if

$$k \le \frac{N}{p},$$

that is, each stored memory $\xi^{(\mu)}$ is at least a $\lceil N/p \rceil$-local minimizer, where $\lceil \cdot \rceil$ denotes the integer part of N/p. Similarly, the condition (99) is met whenever

$$k \le \frac{N}{2p},$$

that is, $\xi^{(\mu)}$ can be retrieved from any key with maximum $N/2p$ error bits. Note that this error estimate coincides with the well-known result $k = \lceil N/2p \rceil$ of Cottrel [86]. This demonstrates the great power of the theory developed in this section.

EXAMPLE 5 (Error-Correction Capability of the Hopfield Network with Pseudoinverse Encoding).   We still assume that $\xi^{(\mu)} = (\xi_1^{(\mu)}, \xi_2^{(\mu)}, \ldots, \xi_N^{(\mu)})^T \in \mathbf{H}^N$, $\mu = 1, 2, \ldots, p$, are the prototype patterns. However, instead of the orthogonal assumption, $\{\xi^{(\mu)}\}$ are now in general position. Consider the Hopfield-type network $\mathcal{N} = (W, 0)$, with W encoded by the pseudo-inverse rule:

$$W = X(X^T X)^{-1} X^T = (w_{ij})_{N \times N},$$

where $X = [\xi^{(1)}, \xi^{(2)}, \ldots, \xi^{(p)}]$.

Because W is an orthogonal projector, we have $W\xi^{(\mu)} = \xi^{(\mu)}$, and

$$\max\{|w_{ij}|, \ i, j = 1, 2, \ldots, N\} = \max\{w_{ii} \colon i = 1, 2, \ldots, N\}.$$

Denote $\max\{w_{ii}\} = \max\{w_{ii}: i = 1, 2, \ldots, N\}$. Then, as long as

$$k \leq \frac{1}{2\max\{w_{ii}\}}, \tag{100}$$

the condition (99) is satisfied with $\lambda^* = 1$, $A = W$, and $R = \text{diag}\{1, 1, \ldots, 1\}$.

The estimate (100) reveals an important fact: for the Hopfield network with pseudo-inverse encoding, the smaller the diagonal elements of W, the stronger is the network's error-correction capability. This also supports the general conclusion stated in Theorem 16.

D. APPLICATION: COMPLETE-CORRESPONDENCE ENCODING

Based on the theoretical results of the last two subsections, we develop encoding techniques for a Hopfield-type network $\mathcal{N} = (W, I)$ by requiring that W and I satisfy the following requirements:

    (i) Equilibrium-state requirement: $S(W\xi^{(\mu)} - I) = \xi^{(\mu)}$, $\mu = 1, 2, \ldots, p$
    (ii) Convergence requirement: **(P1)** or **(P2)** in Theorem 14
    (iii) Stability requirements: **(P3)** in Theorem 17.

The condition **(P3)** clearly implies the equilibrium-state requirement. So we can, instead of (i), ask the pair (W, I) to satisfy

$$W\xi^{(\mu)} - I = \lambda_{(\mu)}\xi^{(\mu)}, \quad \mu = 1, 2, \ldots, p, \tag{101}$$

where $\{\lambda_{(\mu)}\}$ are any prefixed set of positive real parameters.

In practice, by taking any one of the given patterns $\{\xi^{(\mu)}: \mu = 1, 2, \ldots, p\}$, say $\xi^{(p)}$ as a reference vector, and then letting

$$I = W\xi^{(p)} - \lambda_{(p)}\xi^{(p)}, \tag{102}$$

we can transform (101) into the following standard form:

$$WX^{(\mu)} = \tilde{\lambda}_{(\mu)}X^{(\mu)}, \qquad \mu = 1, 2, \ldots, p - 1, \tag{103}$$

where $X^{(\mu)} = \xi^{(\mu)} - \xi^{(p)}$ and $\tilde{\lambda}_{(\mu)} = \lambda_{(\mu)} - \lambda_{(p)}$ for any $\mu \neq p$. Denote

$$\mathbf{X} = \left[X^{(1)}, X^{(2)}, \ldots, X^{(p-1)}\right]$$

and

$$\mathbf{\Lambda} = \text{diag}\left\{\tilde{\lambda}_{(1)}, \tilde{\lambda}_{(2)}, \ldots, \tilde{\lambda}_{(p-1)}\right\}.$$

The equations (103) can also be rewritten as

$$WX = X\Lambda. \tag{104}$$

A general solution to this equation is given by

$$W = X\Lambda X^+ + Y[I_d - XX^+], \tag{105}$$

where X^+ is the Moore–Penrose inverse of X, I_d is the $N \times N$ identity matrix, and Y is an arbitrary matrix. It is known that XX^+ is the orthogonal projection of R^N onto the subspace

$$L_{p-1} = \text{span}\{X^{(1)}, X^{(2)}, \ldots, X^{(p-1)}\}.$$

Hence XX^+ can be computed recursively by means of Algorithm 1 presented in Section II.C.1. Note also that $X\Lambda X^+ = H_{(p-1)}(X, X\Lambda)$ can be calculated according to Algorithm 1.

Thus, except for Λ and Y, the encoding (105) can be easily obtained. Now different specifications of Λ and Y in Eq. (105) correspond to different encoding schemes. For example, $\Lambda = I$ and $Y = 0$ correspond to the projection scheme [62] or the pseudo-inverse method [12, 13]; $Y = 0$ corresponds to the spectrum method [102]; and $\Lambda = I$ and $Y = \tau I$ (τ is a real parameter [67]) correspond to the eigenstructure methods [103–108].

In principle, the parameters Λ and Y should be chosen in such a way that the resulting network can fully satisfy the convergence and stability requirements. More preferably, the network's performance in terms of error-correction capability is also optimized. It is of course, a difficult, although not impossible task to find such a solution in general. In the following we will confine ourselves to the case of symmetric encodings. For this particular but commonly assumed case, we show how all of the currently known encodings can be dramatically improved by applying the new theories developed in this chapter.

From Eq. (105), the symmetry of W requires that $\Lambda = \alpha I$, where α is a real constant, and that Y should satisfy $Y[I_d - XX^+] = [I_d - XX^+]Y^T$. This last requirement can be met for any arbitrary pattern set X, if and only if $Y = \tau I$, where τ is a real constant. Consequently, we conclude that a symmetric encoding W must have a general form $W = \alpha XX^+ - \tau[I_d - XX^+]$. The parameter α can be assumed to be 1. Thus a general symmetric encoding W is of the form

$$W(\tau) = XX^+ + \tau(I_d - XX^+) = (1 - \tau)XX^+ + \tau I_d. \tag{106}$$

It is observed that for Eq. (106), $W(0)$ is exactly the pseudo-inverse rule (or projection rule) commonly used in the current literature, and $W(-1^-)$ is the eigenstructure rule suggested in [103–108], where 1^- means a real number less than and very near 1. We will define an optimal τ^* so that the network $\mathcal{N} = (W(\tau^*), I)$ encoded by (106) will outperform those encoded by other existing rules.

The completeness theorem (Theorem 16) can serve as the basis of recognizing such an optimal parameter τ^*. This is because, once the τ^* is specified in this way, the network $\mathcal{N} = (W(\tau^*), I)$ will have the complete correspondence property (CCP), that is, each pattern $X^{(i)}$ stored in the network is at least a 1-local minimizer of an energy (hence the attraction basin of $X^{(i)}$ at least contains the Hamming ball $B_H(X^{(i)}, 1)$, and no equilibrium state in the network is not asymptotically stable, resulting in fewer spurious states). Such a network therefore has stronger error-correction capability.

Given any symmetric Hopfield-type network $\mathcal{N} = (W, I)$, an equivalent network with the CCP is obtained by forcing the diagonal elements of W to zero. This is referred to as a *complete correspondence modification skill* [68]. We call an encoding with such a skill a *complete-correspondence encoding*.

From Eq. (106), a complete-correspondence encoding for the symmetric Hopfield-type network $\mathcal{N}$ can be constructed according to the following algorithm.

Algorithm 4 (Complete-Correspondence Encoding).

(i) Given the pattern set $\{\xi^{(\mu)}: \mu = 1, 2, \ldots, p\}$, let $X^{(\mu)} = \xi^{(\mu)} - \xi^{(p)}$, $\mu = 1, 2, \ldots, p - 1$, and let $\mathbf{X} = [X^{(1)}, X^{(2}, \ldots, X^{(p-1)}]$.

(ii) Set $P^+ = \mathbf{X}\mathbf{X}^+ = (p_{ij})_{N \times N}$, and $p^* = \min\{p_{11}, p_{22}, \ldots, p_{NN}\}$.

(iii) With $-(1 - p^*)^{-1}p^* < \tau^* < 1$, define

$$M(\tau^*) = P^+ + \tau^*(I_d - P^+). \tag{107}$$

(iv) Let

$$D(\tau^*) = \text{diag}\{(1-\tau^*)p_{11}+\tau^*, (1-\tau^*)p_{22}+\tau^*, \ldots, (1-\tau^*)p_{NN}+\tau^*\}$$

and define the symmetric Hopfield network $\mathcal{N} = (W(\tau^*), I)$ by

$$W(\tau^*) = M(\tau^*) - D(\tau^*) \tag{108}$$

$$I = W\xi^{(p)} - \xi^{(p)}. \tag{109}$$

From Eqs. (107) and (108), the so defined symmetric Hopfield-type network assuredly has the CCP. Hence it takes all of the prototype patterns $\xi^{(\mu)}$ ($\mu = 1, 2, \ldots, p$) as its asymptotically stable states, with the attraction basin not less than $B_H(\xi^{(\mu)}, 1)$. By Corollary 3, the network is also globally convergent whenever it is operated in the serial mode. Furthermore, write $P^- = (I_d - \mathbf{X}\mathbf{X}^+)$

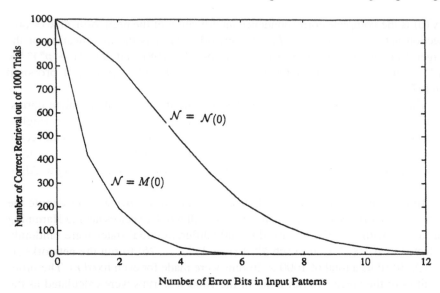

Figure 14   Comparison of error-correction capability between the network $\mathcal{N} = M(0)$ with the pseudo-inverse rule and its complete correspondence modification $\mathcal{N} = \mathcal{N}(0)$. The task is to recognize the 26 English letters.

V. SUMMARY AND CONCLUDING REMARKS

Associative memories have been one of the most active research fields in neural networks; they emerged as efficient models of biological memory and powerful techniques in various applications related to pattern recognition, expert systems, optimization, and intelligent control.

We have shown that almost all existing neural network models can function as associative memories in one way or another. According to the principle of performing the association, these models can be put into three categories: Function-Mapping Associative Memories (FMAMs), Attractor Associative Memories (AAMs), and Pattern-Clustering Associative Memories (PCAMs). Each of the different types of neural networks has its own advantages and shortcomings. However, we argued that the Point Attractor Associative Memories (PAAMs) in AAMs are the most natural and promising.

A PAAM is a dissipative, nonlinear dynamical system formed by a large number of connected dynamic neurons. In most cases the system is modeled either as a set of differential equations like Eq. (8) (the continuous PAAM), or as a set of difference equations like Eq. (9) (the discrete PAAM). A unified definition of PAAM system has been presented (Definition 1), which generalizes the well-known PAAM networks such as the Cohen–Grossberg model, the Hopfield model, the Litter–Hopfield model, the Brain-State-in-a-Box model, and the recurrent back-propagation algorithm. A PAAM is featured by the convergence of its trajectories in state space to its point attractors. Because of that, the basic principle of the PAAM is characterized by its dynamics, which maps initial network states to the final states of the network. Whereas the final states are the point attractors identified with the memorized items, any initial state of the network is a probe vector, representing a complete or partial description of one of the memorized items. The evolution of the network from an initial state to an attractor then corresponds to pattern recall, information reading, or pattern recognition.

Two fundamental issues of PAAM technique are (i) encoding: how to store the given prototype patterns as the attractors of a PAAM, and (ii) decoding: how to retrieve the stored memories according to a certain recognition principle. The encoding specifies the synaptic interconnections of a PAAM network, which then, together with the recall dynamics, determines the decoding mechanism. Therefore the neurodynamics of a PAAM provides the basis for both encoding and decoding.

For a PAAM to be useful, two kinds of dynamics have been shown to be imperative: global convergence dynamics and asymptotic stability dynamics. We have presented in Section II a unified account of the methodologies for conducting such convergence and stability analysis. Several generic criteria for establishing these two kinds of dynamics for the continuous PAAMs are developed in Theorems 4–6, with specialization to the Cohen–Grossberg model stated in Corollary 1 and Theorem 7. It is concluded that the famous LaSalle invariance principle provides the general mathematical framework for the convergence analysis, whereas the classical Liapunov method and the linearization method underlie the stability analysis. Nevertheless, the full use of the generalized gradient system structure defined in Eq. (28) has been shown to be very helpful in all analyses.

Based on the neurodynamics analysis for the general PAAM systems, two general-purpose encoding schemes have been proposed (Algorithms 1 and 2). The successive interpolating encoding defined by Algorithm 1 is a generalization of the well-known Hebb's rule, which retains the "accumulation" feature of the latter and at the same time ensures the restorability of any set of linear independent prototype patterns. Therefore the algorithm can be widely employed to supersede the encoding schemes using the pseudo-inverse, projection, or eigenstructure methods. On the other hand, the sparsely connected encoding described in Algorithm 2 gives us a flexible framework within which not only can the heteroassociation problems be tackled as autoassociative problems (as illustrated by Example 2), but many different complexity reduction strategies for PAAMs can also be deduced.

As special cases of the general PAAM theories developed in Section II, two important examples are studied in Sections III and IV.

In Section III a continuous PAAM model, the competitive associative memory, is investigated. It is deduced from the successive interpolating encoding scheme and is a three-order nonautonomous differential equation. With the aim of incorporating certain competitive recognition principles into the information reading procedure, such a memory treats the prototype patterns as being stored as a set of different biological species. Then the model mimics the competitive persistence of the species in performing the pattern recall from the stored memories. In Theorems 10 and 11, it is shown that the memory performs very well in competitive recognition, in the sense that, as long as the competitive and inhibitive parameters are appropriately specified, no nontrivial spurious attractor exists in the network (i.e., only the prototype patterns to be stored are in its memories). Furthermore, whenever the competitive parameters eventually lead to a unique winner, only the prototype pattern corresponding to the winner is almost asymptotically stable globally, and hence can be retrieved from almost anywhere in the underlying state space. Owing to these features, the memory can be very efficient and reliable in pattern recognition tasks, especially when a specific pattern must be recognized from a set of stored memories and when the recognition process is governed by certain known competition mechanism.

By applying this principle and regarding the pattern recall as recognizing a particular pattern (from among the given set of prototypes) that is the closest in distance to the given probe u_0, a novel PAAM model called perfectly reacted PAAM is formulated in Algorithm 3. This PAAM model can always find the best matching of the given probe from the memories in the Rayleigh quotient distance $R^{1/2}(\cdot)$. More precisely, for any given probe, the network can yield the best approximation of the probe when projected onto the unit sphere $B^N = \{x \in R^N: \|x\| = 1\}$. Thus, whenever the prototype patterns are normal (i.e., with norm one), this kind of memory can be perfectly applied.

As a discrete PAAM example, the asymmetric Hopfield-type networks are examined in detail in Section IV. The symmetric version of the model has been extensively studied in the past. Yet a deep understanding of the general asymmetric case is yet to be achieved. To this end, we have developed a theory for the asymmetric networks with a general convergence principle and a novel classification theory of energy functions. The convergence principle (Theorem 14), which characterizes the conditions under which the networks have convergent dynamics, generalizes the previous results for symmetric network and yields a series of new criteria (Corollaries 3 and 4). The classification theory provides us with a fresh and powerful methodology for the asymptotic stability analysis of the networks. Through the categorization of the traditional energy functions into regular, normal, and complete classes, we have found that the normality (and furthermore, completeness) of an energy function can quantitatively characterize the error-correction capability of the corresponding networks, and hence underlies the asymptotical stability.

By applying this new theory, a generic modification strategy called complete-correspondence modification skill has been formulated, which dramatically improves the performance of the existing symmetric Hopfield-type networks in terms of error-correction capability. Incorporating this skill into the general encoding technologies then yields a new useful symmetric encoding scheme, the complete-correspondence encoding defined in Algorithm 4. It is seen that all of the known encoding schemes like the projection rule, the pseudo-inverse rule, and the eigenstructure rules all are naturally embodied in and improved by this new encoding.

The exposition of the present chapter has been restricted to the point attractor-type neural associative memories in which the monotonic neurons (i.e., the activation function is monotonic) are applied (e.g., sigmoid, signum, or saturation neurons). It should be noted, however, that PAAMs with nonmonotonic neurons exist and have attracted increasing interest in recent years. Interested readers are referred to [41], [109], and [110]. In addition, except for the point attractor associative memories, other dynamic neural associative memories such as the chaotic and the oscillatory associative memories are drawing much attention. A comprehensive exposition of these memories can be found in [111] and [112].

ACKNOWLEDGMENT

The artwork (Fig. 1, Figs. 7–9) produced by Joseph C. K. Chan and the computing assistance provided by W. L. Yeung are gratefully acknowledged.

REFERENCES

[1] T. J. Teyler. Memory: Electrophysiological analogs. In *Learning and Memory: A Biological View* (J. L. Martinez, Jr., and R. S. Kesner, Eds.), pp. 237–265. Academic Press, Orlando, FL, 1986.

[2] J. A. Anderson. What Hebb synapses build. In *Synaptic Modification, Neuron Selectivity, and Nervous System Organization* (W. B. Levy, J. A. Anderson, and S. Lehmkuhle, Eds.), pp. 153–173. Erlbaum, Hillsdale, NJ, 1985.

[3] H. Wechaler and G. L. Zimmerman. 2-D invariance object recognition using distributed associative memory. *IEEE Trans. Pattern Anal. Machine Intelligence* 20:811–821, 1988.

[4] J. A. Hertz, A. Krogh, and R. G. Palmer. *Introduction to the Theory of Neural Computation.* Addison-Wesley, Reading, MA, 1994.

[5] S. Haykin. *Neural Networks: A Comprehensive Foundation.* Macmillan, New York, 1994.

[6] A. Fuchs and H. Haken. Pattern recognition and associative memory as dynamic processes in a synergetic system. *Biol. Cybernet.* 60:17–22, 1988.

[7] W. K. Taylor. Electrical simulation of some nervous system functional activities. In *Information Theory* (E. C. Cherry, Ed.), Vol. 3, pp. 314–328. Butterworth, London, 1956.

[8] K. Steinbuch. Die Lernmatrix. *Kybernetik.* 1:36–45, 1961.

[9] J. A. Anderson. A simple neural network generating an iterative memory. *Math. Biosci.* 14:197–220, 1972.

[10] T. Kohonen. Correlation matrix memories. *IEEE Trans. Comput.* C-21:353–359, 1972.

[11] K. Nakano. Association—a model of associative memory. *IEEE Trans. Systems Man Cybernet.* SMC-2:380–388, 1972.

[62] S. I. Sudharsanan and M. Sundareshan. Equilibrium characterization of dynamic neural networks and a systematic synthesis procedure for associative memories. *IEEE Trans. Neural Networks* 2:509–521, 1991.

[63] B. Widrow and S. D. Stearns. *Adaptive Signal Processing*. Prentice-Hall, Englewood Cliffs, NJ, 1985.

[64] Z. B. Xu and C. P. Kwong. A decomposition principle for complexity reduction of artificial neural networks. *Neural Networks* 9:999–1016, 1996.

[65] L. Personnaz, I. Guyon, and G. Dreyfus. Collective computational properties of neural networks: New learning mechanisms. *Phys. Rev. A*. 34:4217–4228, 1986.

[66] S. Grossberg. Nonlinear neural networks: Principles, machines and architectures. *Neural Networks* 1:15–57, 1988.

[67] H. Haken. Neural and synergetic computer. *Springer Ser. Synergetics* 42:2–28, 1988.

[68] Z. B. Xu, G. Q. Hu, and C. P. Kwong. Some efficient strategies for improving the eigenstructure method in synthesis of feedback neural networks. *IEEE Trans. Neural Networks* 7:233–245, 1996.

[69] Z. B. Xu and C. P. Kwong. Global convergence and asymptotic stability of asymmetric Hopfield neural networks. *J. Math. Anal. Appl.* 191:405–427, 1995.

[70] Z. B. Xu, Y. Leung, and X. W. He. Asymmetric bidirectional associative memories. *IEEE Trans. Systems Man Cybernet* 24:1558–1564, 1994.

[71] Z. Y. Chen, C. P. Kwong, and Z. B. Xu. Multiple-valued feedback and recurrent correlation neural networks. *Neural Comput. Appl.* 3:242–250, 1995.

[72] F. Paper and M. N. Shirazi. A categorizing associative memory using an adaptive classifier and sparse coding. *IEEE Trans. Neural Networks* 7:669–675, 1996.

[73] B. Kosko. Adaptive bidirectional associative memories. *Appl. Optics*. 26:4947–4960, 1987.

[74] X. W. He, C. P. Kwong, and Z. B. Xu. A competitive associative memory model and its dynamics. *IEEE Trans. Neural Networks* 6:929–940, 1995.

[75] Z. B. Xu and Y. Leung. Competitive associative memory: The extended model and its global stability analysis. *IEEE Trans. Neural Networks*. To appear.

[76] C. L. Giles and T. Maxwell. Learning, invariance, and generalization in high-order neural networks. *Appl. Optics*. 26:23, 1987.

[77] A. N. Michel, J. A. Farrell, and H. F. Sun. Analysis and synthesis techniques for Hopfield type synchronous discrete time neural networks with application to associative memory. *IEEE Trans. Circuits Systems* 37:1356–1366, 1990.

[78] S. V. B. Aiyer, M. Niranjan, and F. Fallside. A theoretical investigation into the performance of the Hopfield model. *IEEE Trans. Neural Networks* 1:204–215, 1990.

[79] J. Bruck and V. P. Roychowdhury. On the number of spurious memories in the Hopfield model. *IEEE Trans. Inform. Theory* 36:393–397, 1989.

[80] J. Bruck and M. Blaum. Neural networks, error correcting codes and polynomials over binary n-cubes. *IEEE Trans. Inform. Theory* 35:976–987, 1989.

[81] Y. Leung and Z. B. Xu. An associative memory based on key management and competitive recognition. *IEEE Trans. Neural Networks*. To appear.

[82] T. D. Chiueh and R. M. Goodman. Recurrent correlation associative memories. *IEEE Trans. Neural Networks* 2:275–284, 1991.

[83] G. A. Kohring. On the Q-state neuron problem in attractor neural networks. *Neural Networks* 6:573–581, 1993.

[84] J. Bruck and J. W. Goodman. A generalized convergence theorem for neural networks. *IEEE Trans. Inform. Theory* 34:1089–1092, 1988.

[85] J. Bruck. On the convergence properties of the Hopfield model. *Proc. IEEE* 78:1579–1585, 1990.

[86] M. Cottrel. Stability and attractivity in associative memory networks. *Biol. Cybernet*. 58:129–139, 1988.

[87] S. Dasgupta, A. Ghosh, and R. Cuykendall. Convergence in neural memories. *IEEE Trans. Inform. Theory* 35:1069–1072, 1989.

[88] E. Goles, F. Fogelman, and D. Pellegrin. Decreasing energy functions as a tool for studying threshold networks. *Discrete Appl. Math.* 12:261–277, 1985.

[89] E. Goles. Antisymmetrical neural networks. *Discrete Appl. Math.* 13:97–100, 1986.

[90] R. J. McEliece, E. C. Posner, E. R. Rodemich, and S. S. Venkatesh. The capacity of the Hopfield associative memory. *IEEE Trans. Inform. Theory* 33:461–482, 1987.

[91] S. Porat. Stability and looping in contortionist models with asymmetric weights. *Biol. Cybernet.* 60:335–344, 1989.

[92] I. Pramanick. Parallel dynamic interaction—an inherently parallel problem solving methodology. Ph.D. Thesis, Department of Electrical and Computer Engineering, University of Iowa, 1991.

[93] Y. Shrivastava, S. Dasgupta, and S. M. Reddy. Guaranteed convergence in a class of Hopfield networks. *IEEE Trans. Neural Networks.* 3:951–961, 1992.

[94] L. Personnaz, I. Guyon, and G. Dreyfus. Information storage and retrieval in spin-glass like neural networks. *J. Physique Lett.* 46:359–365, 1985.

[95] A. N. Michel, J. A. Farrell, and W. Porod. Qualitative analysis of neural networks. *IEEE Trans. Circuits Systems* 36:229–243, 1989.

[96] Z. B. Xu, G. Q. Hu, and C. P. Kwong. Asymmetric Hopfield-type networks: Theory and applications. *Neural Networks* 9:483–510, 1996.

[97] A. Crisanti and H. Sompolinsky. Dynamics of spin systems with randomly asymmetric bonds: Langevin dynamics and a spherical model. *Phys. Rev. A.* 36:4922–4936, 1987.

[98] I. Kanter and H. Sompolinsky. Associative recall of memory without errors. *Phys. Rev. A* 36:444–445, 1987.

[99] J. J. Hopfield and D. W. Tank. Neural computation of decisions in optimization problems. *Biol. Cybernet.* 52:141–152, 1985.

[100] E. D. Dahl. Neural network algorithms for an NP-complete problem: Map and graph coloring. In *Proceedings of the Second IEEE International Conference on Neural Networks,* 1988, Vol. 3, 113–120.

[101] V. Wilson, and G. S. Pawley. On the stability of the TSP problem algorithm of Hopfield and Tank. *Biol. Cybernet.* 58:63–78, 1988.

[102] R. J. Marks, II, S. Oh, and L. E. Atlas. Alternating projection neural networks. *IEEE Trans. Circuits Systems* 36:846–857, 1989.

[103] J. H. Li, A. N. Michel, and W. Porod. Qualitative analysis and synthesis of a class of neural networks. *IEEE Trans. Circuits Systems* 35:976–986, 1988.

[104] J. H. Li, A. N. Michel, and W. Porod. Analysis and synthesis of a class of neural networks: Variable structure systems with infinite gain. *IEEE Trans. Circuits Systems* 36:713–731, 1989.

[105] J. H. Li, A. N. Michel, and W. Porod. Analysis and synthesis of a class of neural networks: Linear systems operating on a closed hypercube. *IEEE Trans. Circuits Systems* 36:1405–1422, 1989.

[106] A. N. Michel, J. Si, and G. Yun. Analysis and synthesis of a class of discrete-time neural networks described on hypercubes. *IEEE Trans. Neural Networks* 2:32–46, 1991.

[107] G. Yun and A. N. Michel. A learning and forgetting algorithm in associative memories: Results involving pseudo-inverse. *IEEE Trans. Circuits Systems* 38:1193–1205, 1991.

[108] G. Yun and A. N. Michel. A learning and forgetting algorithm in associative memories: The eigenstructure method. *IEEE Trans. Circuits Systems* 39:212–225, 1992.

[109] S. Yoshizawa, M. Morita, and S. Amari. Capacity of associative memory using a nonmonotonic neuron model. *Neural Networks* 6:167–176, 1993.

[110] S. Yoshizawa. In *The Handbook of Brain Theory and Neural Networks* (M. A. Aribib, Ed.), pp. 651–654. MIT Press, Cambridge, MA, 1996.

wide applicability. Here, however, the goal is to introduce a new way of thinking about a new, or perhaps very old, type of neural network.

Our objective is to design a rational device. We should therefore try to quantify what we mean by *rational*. The word *rational* is defined in the dictionary as "having or exercising the ability to reason" and is derived from the Latin word *rationalis*, which, in turn, is derived from the Latin word *ratio*, meaning computation. The dictionary defines the word *ratio* as "a relation in degree or number between two similar things." We shall see that the ILU is a rational device in every regard stated above, in that it indeed computes a relation that is a ratio and which describes a relative degree between two similar things. The computed ratio is used by the ILU to determine the most logical questions to ask as well as dictating the most rational decisions to give.

We will see that the ILU arises as a natural consequence of a rational argument. This makes sense because the ILU is itself a rational device and hence should easily be understood by another rational device, just as digital computers can efficiently and precisely simulate other digital computers. As a rational device, the ILU learns, reasons, asks questions, and makes decisions. Even though a single ILU is a very powerful computational device, it should be construed as part of a larger device called an inductive logic computer or ILC. This chapter will focus on the ILU, but ultimately, the ILU will typically be but one of many similar components comprising an ILC that is configured to perform some useful task.

Why use the adjective "inductive"? What exactly is it that distinguishes inductive logic from, say, deductive logic? The answer is that inductive logic generalizes the concept of deductive logic. Most are familiar with deductive logic and its consequences, such as engineering realizations that rely on digital logic. Conventional digital computers are deductive. That is, digital computers are supplied with digital (binary) information upon which they, at their most fundamental level, operate using standard Boolean operators such as AND, OR, and NOT, or other Boolean functions arising from combinations thereof. Furthermore, a deductive logical process evolves rigorously and causally through the use of decision operators such as IF, THEN, and OR ELSE logical constructs. A common deductive statement might take the form "If a is true and b is true, then c is true." Decision operators have a fundamental element that is causal in nature and tends to drive the discrete trajectory of a deductive process in time. There is no intrinsic uncertainty associated with decisions derived through a deductive reasoning process. All of the information necessary to form a conclusion and then assert a decision at each critical juncture is present.

Unfortunately, life outside the digital computer does not typically admit or permit the use of deductive logic, because all of the information required to make a deductive decision is rarely present. A deductive system confronted with such a dilemma could not evolve along its discrete deductive trajectory, and the causal flow of information would cease.

Alternatively, the fact that decisions must typically be made in the face of uncertainty is intrinsic to inductive logic. Decisions might be thought of as actions arising from a "participant" through inductive reasoning processes, whatever such processes might consist of or however they might be formulated. Information can be promulgated, although the quality of the information may not be on a par with that arising from a deductive decision-making process. In some intuitive sense, we would like to maximize the quality of the information that is promulgated within any notional inductive reasoning process. Here the term "inductive" is meant to describe a process whereby the "best" possible decisions are made and promulgated regarding a measure of "goodness" that is also derived through a logical reasoning process.

Again, the main purpose of this chapter is to provide a qualitative and engineering-oriented overview of how the inductive reasoning process can be practically realized and implemented. This is done through the construct of the ILU. Furthermore, we will see that the ILU shares much in common with biological neurons, indeed, much more than described here.

The logical theory behind our approach has origins going back as far as Aristotle and perhaps earlier. That is to say, much of the following material is basically not new, although the interpretations given may be novel. The history of logic is both interesting and technically valuable for obtaining deeper insights into the analyses given here. Logic is by far the most rigorously developed quantification of any philosophical thought or idea. Indeed, philosophers have consistently formulated basic questions that at first may seem vain, but evolve with understanding to provide fundamentally new insights and new mathematical perspectives with practical utility. More precisely, many questions, although initially thought vain, become quantified after a time through the tools of mathematics, which are but mechanized and logically self-consistent expressions of our thoughts. Of course, we cannot know with certainty whether a question is vain or not, and if forced to decide, we are unable to do so. We are indecisive. But what is interesting is that our indecision can be quantified, as we will see. Such is the nature of inductive logic.

The more fundamental theory of logic is obviated here, but acknowledged through citations, references, and to a large extent, supplied logical tables. Logical arguments and examples are given instead. Indeed, we ratiocinate, that is, we reason methodically and logically, but do not resort to a mathematical rigor. Our problem is that the presented logical concepts are very basic and require the use of extremely precise language and logical meaning. This is not to say that the approach we describe cannot be rigorously formulated, but rather that we abandon this rigor in an effort to convey insight.

Key to reading this chapter is the fact that the ideas described are very fundamental, so fundamental, in fact, that there is often no precise word or expression to sufficiently and succinctly convey the intended concept. Consequently, one is

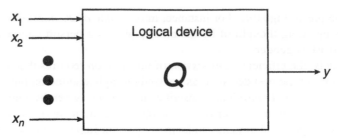

Figure 1 The logical device, denoted Q, represents a general system that supports causal information flow; that is, it can observe presented input assertions $x_1, x_2, \ldots, x_n$ that originate externally to the system while simultaneously supporting the assertion of a single output decision y, which may, in turn, be observed by another logical device.

constructs to conduct decision points in time. At these decision points, supplied information is logically combined, operated upon, and then used to generate new information. The device Q can even be a conventional digital computer if it operates deductively. However, if Q were truly a deductive device, any input x_i that was missing or somehow in error would likely cause the output y of the device to be in error as well. Imagine a digital computer with an operating system with a size of 100 million bits. If even 1 bit were inadvertently changed, the operating system would likely fail at some point. Such is the unforgiving nature of deductive logic. From now on, we will assume that Q operates on the basis of inductive logic.

Missing or erroneous inputs are easily tolerated and furthermore assumed by an ILC. It is the nature of an ILC to simply make the best possible decisions given all observable and relevant information while simultaneously asking the best possible questions, given the time allowed, with the criterion of *best* still to be defined.

Returning to Fig. 1, we will restrict the inputs x_i and the output y to be Boolean or, more precisely, *distinctions*, because they can take on only one of two possible values. Alternatively, each input x_i and the output y can be thought of as being binary-valued, but this represents a too restrictive point of view for our purposes. However, a Boolean interpretation is consistent with the function of a digital device and is consistent with our objective to design an ILU that will not only function inductively, but will compute and then transmit decisions. The ILUs considered in this chapter must abide by the standard rules of Boolean algebra, which we will summarize, and in the limit of complete knowledge, operate deductively. Furthermore, ILU operation should be based on principles that are a logical and unique generalization of Boolean algebra. These two assumptions form the basis of the discussions for the remainder of this section.

Boolean algebra is a logic of propositions. Propositions represent distinctions on the part of an observer, because it is the observer who defines the distinctions. That is, we distinguish things by giving them names. If two things are indistinguishable, they are not distinct relative to the observer who says they are not, and they therefore can be represented by the same proposition by this same observer. If we know only two things and these two things are not the same, then we can distinguish them from one another because whatever one thing is, the other is not. These observations are very simple and very fundamental.

Observability and assertability can be viewed as complementary logical constructs. Regarding assertability, a decision maker who gives the same answer twice when asked a question will provide no new information to the person posing the question. Regarding observability, an observer posing a question twice will obtain no new information from the same source. Consider the following example.

Let the concept "apple" be denoted by the proposition a. Now a is defined more or less universally by most adults. The operative word here is "defined." We define the distinction a, having learned it previously from someone in conjunction with our experiences. Suppose we observe the *world* (i.e., our external environment) while at the same time *exclusively* looking for apples. That which we observe and is asserted to us will be distinguished, by us who define apple, as either a or not a, with the latter denoted by $\sim a$. The operator "$\sim$" denotes the logical operator NOT, but physically should be interpreted as "distinguished from."

Now suppose we see "a bushel of apples." Well, we are not looking for a proposition b = "a bushel of apples," because we have no defining distinction for this concept. However, what we may observe and what is asserted to us are many apples *with* one another. This is denoted by the logical expression $a = a \vee a \vee \cdots \vee a$, where "$\vee$" denotes the Boolean inclusive OR function and is the logical operator associated with the physical observation "apple *with* apple *with* $\cdots$ *with* apple" for each observable apple in the bushel. Even if all apples but one were to disappear, the last remaining apple would guarantee the answer "yes" to the observer. Thus the logical operator "$\vee$" represents physical superposition in that all of the presented quantities are *with* one another. Another physical analogy would be the measurement of the fluid level in a cylindrical glass of water in which ice and liquid were originally combined in some unknown proportion. After the ice melts, the measured level is the sum of the original water level without ice plus the additional water level attributable to the melted ice. The measurement is made on a superposition of the two fluid sources, which cannot be distinguished.

Hence observation and measurement have a physical description through the logical operators "$\sim$" and "$\vee$." For instance, it is well known that $a = a \vee a$ is always logically true. As interpreted here, when you ask a particular and specific question, you can only get an answer at the point in time when you pose that question. Therefore, when you ask the precise and sole question "Do I see an apple?" it is immaterial whether a single apple or a bushel of apples is seen, and the answer to this question can still only be "yes."

As a more practical example, suppose you have lost your car keys in your house and are looking desperately for them. Going from room to room, you look for your keys, but see only *nothing*. Finally, you spot them on the television. They are *presented* to you, enabling you to assert the answer, "Yes, I finally found them." A major point here is that a physical interpretation of logic that deals with Boolean 0s and 1s can be misleading in a physical sense. In physical systems, assertions either *are* or *are not*. One either obtains the answer "yes" or "nothing," because nature never explicitly tells you "no." For example, a biological neuron either receives an action potential or does not, and in turn, either generates one or does not.

Now returning to our previous example, suppose we are looking for $b = $ "Two apples." While looking, we sight an apple a_1, and *then* turn around *and* see another apple a_2. Because our sole purpose in life (at this moment) is to search for b, we observe the answer $b = a_1 \wedge a_2$. Here "$\wedge$" denotes the logical AND function. This case differs from the "bushel of apples" case in that the conjunctive operator "$\wedge$" must physically and explicitly be carried out by the observer. The disjunctive operator is opposite the conjunctive operator in the sense that disjunction logically describes physical superposition, which is a property of the external world observed by the system posing the question. For the conjunctive case, the observer must be able to grasp that he or she has made two separate observations and has, in fact, performed coincidence detection. The conjunctive case represents an added level of complexity on the part of the observer and requires the consideration of the notion of *time* in making multiple measurements. Hence, "Time is that which keeps everything from happening at once" [7], or more precisely, time is that which keeps us from making all measurements at once and giving all answers at the same time.

The perspective of this chapter is that we can describe the world about us as having a Boolean structure that is imposed by its inherent physical properties and our own. The famous logician Emil Post [8] published a remarkable paper in which he exhaustively examined many of the essential properties of logic and noted the amazing similarity between logic, geometry, and the physical world about us. Upon understanding the extreme simplicity of this structure, one must agree with Post's logical interpretations.

From the perspective described so far, we can state that the information we receive has a Boolean structure dictated by its logical characteristics and our own. Historically, Boolean logic has been used to characterize the transmission of information through assertions. However, as described earlier, information flow requires the simultaneous consideration of transmission and transduction. With this in mind, consider the complementary nature and the interrelationships between questions and assertions as captured in the following two definitions:

(1) A question is defined by the possible answers derived through its posing and as obtained in response to presented assertions.

(2) An assertion is defined by the posable questions answered through its presentation and as generated in response to answers obtained.

Although innocuous enough, these two definitions are extremely important and form the basis for all that follows. Definitions (1) and (2) provide for a logical factorization of causal information flow into the separate processes of transduction and transmission, respectively. These definitions bring to mind the example of a sterogram. Sterograms are flat, two-dimensional figures, which when viewed properly (slightly out of focus with your eyes crossed), "come to life" as a three-dimensional figure. This rendering is only possible through a cooperative interaction of the observer and the properties of the sterogram.

Many metaphors and philosophical arguments capture the essence of (1) and (2) in one manner or another, for example, "Beauty is in the eye of the beholder" or "If a tree falls in the forest, does it make a sound?" Regarding the latter question, and from the previous descriptions, the answer is a resounding "No!" in that quantities that are not observable, that is, do not enter as arrows into the device shown in Fig. 1, cannot be considered information by that device. We adopt the definitions given by Cox [6] and call questions that cannot be answered relative to an inquiring observer *vain*. The term *vain* contrasts with the notion of *real* questions, that is, questions that can be answered. *Real* and *vain* have a logical significance to questions that is analogous to the significance of the terms *true* and *false* to assertions. The following examples and discussions describe in further detail notions regarding real, vain, and the logical meaning of definitions (1) and (2).

Suppose one person wants to convey to another person which card, out of a standard deck of 52, is being thought of. The person thinking of the card will answer any posed question except for the direct question, "What card is it?" which is therefore deemed a *vain* question, that is, a question that cannot be answered on the part of the person trying to guess the card. One could, for instance, ask the suit of the card, the color of the card, or even a very specific question like "Is it is the queen of hearts?" Let us denote the questions relating to suit and color by B and C, respectively. We maintain the convention that *questions* are denoted by capital italicized letters, whereas *assertions* are denoted by lowercase italicized letters. For example, one can obtain the answer $b =$ "The card is a club" as one possible response to posing B and hearing the *presentation* made by the other player, which might take the form "The suit of the card has the shape of a clover." The answer is logically distinct from the presentation made to the relevant observer regarding the question that is posed.

The person trying to guess the card can ask B and then C, which together will convey what these questions convey *jointly* to the observer. Asking both questions can be logically denoted $B \wedge C$, signifying that both B *and* C have been posed separately. Furthermore, $B \wedge C = B$, because knowing the suit will also indicate the color. The condition that $B \wedge C = B$ is the condition of logical implication, in that it signifies that the question B implies the question C, or $B \rightarrow C$. The practical interpretation is that if B is answered, then C is also answered. Alternatively, one can ask for the information that the questions B and C convey in *common*. This is described by the question $B \vee C$. Because both questions yield the color of the card, one can see that $B \vee C = C$. This condition also signifies the logical implication of C by B and is logically equivalent to the condition $B \wedge C = B$. One can derive one relation from the other. For instance, if we disjoin each side of $B \wedge C = B$ with C and note that because $C \vee C = C$, $(B \wedge C) \vee C = (B \vee C) \wedge (C \vee C)$, and $(B \vee C) \wedge C = C$, we can then obtain the expression $B \vee C = C$ (see Table I).

Logical identities such as those just described are listed in Table I for both questions and assertions. A one-to-one correspondence is seen between identities and properties in the *logical domain of questions* and the *logical domain of assertions*. For instance, either condition, $b \wedge c = b$ or $b \vee c = c$, describes the condition that assertion b implies assertion c, or $b \rightarrow c$. This can be interpreted as the condition that "If c answers the question, then b also answers the same question." For example, one can ask $F = $ "Is the plant just delivered a flower?" In this case, $r \rightarrow f$, where r and f are the responses "It is a rose" and "It is a flower," respectively. We will discuss Table I in more detail in the next section.

Table I

List of Corresponding Logical Identities for Assertions and for Questions

Assertions		Questions	
$a \wedge a = a$	$a \vee a = a$	$A \vee A = A$	$A \wedge A = A$
$a \wedge b = b \wedge a$	$a \vee b = b \vee a$	$A \vee B = B \vee A$	$A \wedge B = B \wedge A$
$(a \wedge b) \wedge b$ $= a \wedge (b \wedge b)$	$(a \vee b) \vee b$ $= a \vee (b \vee b)$	$(A \vee B) \vee C$ $= A \vee (B \vee C)$	$(A \wedge B) \wedge C$ $= A \wedge (B \wedge C)$
$(a \wedge b) \vee c$ $= a \vee c) \wedge (b \vee c)$	$(a \vee b) \wedge c$ $= (a \wedge c) \vee (b \wedge c)$	$(A \vee B) \wedge C$ $= A \wedge C) \vee (B \wedge C)$	$(A \wedge B) \vee C$ $= (A \vee C) \wedge (B \vee C)$
$(a \wedge b) \vee b = b$	$(a \vee b) \wedge b = b$	$(A \vee B) \wedge B = B$	$(A \wedge B) \vee B = B$
$(a \wedge \sim a) \wedge b$ $= a \wedge \sim a$	$(a \vee \sim a) \vee b$ $= a \vee \sim a$	$(A \vee \sim A) \vee B$ $= A \vee \sim A$	$(A \wedge \sim A) \wedge B$ $= A \wedge \sim A$
$(a \wedge \sim a) \vee b = b$	$(a \vee \sim a) \wedge b = b$	$(A \vee \sim A) \wedge B = B$	$(A \wedge \sim A) \vee B = B$
$\sim(a \wedge b)$ $= \sim a \vee \sim b$	$\sim(a \vee b)$ $= \sim a \wedge \sim b$	$\sim(A \vee B)$ $= \sim A \wedge \sim B$	$\sim(A \wedge B)$ $= \sim A \vee \sim B$
	$\sim\sim a = a$		$\sim\sim A = A$

In discussing the implication of assertions, one replaces *asks* with *tells* and *answered* with *answers*. Logical implication is important in the consideration of ILUs and ILCs and plays a role analogous to IF, THEN, and OR ELSE logical constructs in deductive computers.

In posing the question $B \vee C$, an additional burden is placed on the interrogator to compute the question $B \vee C$ in advance of its posing. This case, therefore, has added complexity on the part of the observer relative to the posing of $B \wedge C$. In the latter case, the observer simply poses both B and C. The question $B \vee C$, for instance, corresponds to the example in which the observer was looking for more than one apple and then sighted two and took explicit note of this fact. In that example, the question $B = A_1 \vee A_2$ was effectively posed and the corresponding answers to A_1 and A_2 were compressed into one observation, that is, $b = a_1 \wedge a_2$.

The duality between the properties of questions and the properties of assertions is intrinsic to the formulation given here. Acknowledging this duality to be the case can greatly facilitate understanding. This is one reason why we use the term *assertion* instead of *proposition*, because an assertion is more nearly the complement to the concept of a *question*. A question leads to the ingestion of information by an observer in the form of realized answers obtained through assertions presented to it that are subsequently transduced. Alternatively, an answer can lead to transmission of information in the form of an assertion by a decision maker. This assertion can then be presented to another observer, thereby completing a full information transaction. Such information transactions represent quantized steps of causal information flow.

The main purpose of this discussion is to demonstrate that assertions and questions each represent logical entities and that both are needed to support information flow. Figure 1 explicitly shows assertions as comprising external inputs x_i and a generated output y. The presence of questions as logical entities in Fig. 1 is implicit. A question X_i is associated with each assertion x_i. These questions must be present and associated with each input. Regarding the output, at least one other logical device (not shown) must exist with the potential for posing the real question Y and which therefore can receive the assertion y through its posing. If this were not so, the transmission of information from Q could not occur. Furthermore, through the assertions of other logical devices (also not shown), Q can receive inputs through the questions $X_1, X_2, \ldots, X_n$ that it poses. If this were not so, the transduction of information would be interrupted. The symmetry and duality between transduction and transmission are perfect. Answers are obtained on the basis of questions posed in response to presented assertions. Assertions are made on the basis of answers to questions that were posed and are presented to other questions. Again, the causal element of time must be acknowledged.

In this chapter we are interested in developing a methodology for the design of a device that operates inductively. This device will use assertions and questions as a substrate. Alone, however, these logical constructs can only support the design

determining the measurement that will maximize the information extracted from X that is common to Y.

In optimizing the transmission of information, we mean that another device having the capacity for observing the outputs of the subject ILU can maximize the information received by posing the question Y. The *transmission* of information deals with the exchange of information *between* devices, whereas the *transduction* of information deals with the processing of information *within* a device. Another device that can optimally receive the output y of the subject ILU must be able to ask the specific question Y. In maximizing the totality of forward information flow, the second observer must have the same issue A that the source ILU has (that is, exactly the same level of ignorance) and have as one of its computational goals the determination of the original input x to the first ILU. By having the same issue A, the second observer would essentially be approximating the optimized transduction process implemented within the first device. An engineer designing a communications channel implicitly incorporates the assumption of a shared issue when matching a receiver to the possible codes generated by the intended source.

Ideally, the first stage of information transfer described by $X \vee Y$ should be optimally matched to the second stage of information transfer Y. This strategy would support minimizing overall information loss, or equivalently, maximizing information throughput or flow. However, the determination of the input x by a second device is, in general, impossible because a second, physically separate device cannot even know the inputs to the first ILU, as this information cannot be transmitted. Hence it is up to the first device to also ask Y, thereby emulating the second receiver by having access to the same logical issue A implicit in the transduction process.

Because the issue A of the subject ILU cannot be transmitted without incurring additional inefficiency or information loss, the best that can be done is for the source ILU to attempt to optimize itself as a source of information. This can be achieved if the source ILU can measure its own output and hence have the ability to ask Y, as might any subsequent ILUs to which it may be connected. More specifically, the ILU must try to maximize the bearing of the question Y on the issue A, for in doing so it is attempting to optimize its efficiency as an information source by incorporating aspects of any other hypothetical receiver, thereby supporting the local evaluation of transmission quality. Therefore, the ILU must use $b(Y|A)$ as a numerical measure of the amount of information that is transmitted while realizing that it is itself receiving this same information, but in a feedback fashion. Because the ILU can ask Y, it can measure all of the physical quantities necessary for maximizing the bearing of the question Y on the issue A and hence hypothetically support the reconstruction of inputs arising from other physically separate devices.

So what is this measure called *bearing*? In attempting to resolve an issue, one must obtain answers to a thorough list of posed questions. If the list of questions is exhaustive on the subject issue, then the issue will be resolved. As mentioned previously, *the game of 20 questions* is a good example of the concept of bearing. In this game, one player thinks of something (just about anything). The *issue* of the other player is to resolve what this thing is. To do so, the second player poses up to 20 "yes or no" questions to the first player. A good player poses questions with significant bearing on his issue. This issue evolves with each posed question and each new piece of information obtained. The objective of the game is to resolve the issue by posing a minimum number of questions. For instance, knowing that the thing is a person, a good question would be M = "Is the person male?" because this has considerable bearing on the prevailing issue of "Which particular person?" is being thought of. This intuitive notion of bearing is quantified in the next section.

Again, the computational goals of the ILU require that its architecture lend itself to the numerical computation of both $b(Y|A)$ and $b(X \vee Y|A)$. The bearing $b(Y|A)$, or some monotonic function of $b(Y|A)$, must be computed to maximize transmission from the subject ILU to any subsequent ILUs to which it is connected. The bearing $b(X \vee Y|A)$, or some monotonic function of $b(X \vee Y|A)$, must be computed by the same ILU to maximize transduction between input and output. In both instances, logic requires that computation be performed on measurable quantities relative to the issue of the ILU. To reiterate, the issue A of the ILU is the conjunction of "What is my input?" = X, where $X = X_1 \wedge X_2 \wedge \cdots \wedge X_n$, *and* the output question, "What is my output?" = Y. The X_i represents the individual questions that correspond to "What is my ith input?"

All of this is a bit terse. A great depth of logical formalism underpins the described logical structure. Fortunately, and as it should be, the basic ideas are all logical and become intuitively obvious once recognized. Upon accepting the foregoing computational objectives, all that remains to computationally realize the ILU is to specify a quantitative measure for *bearing* that is useful for inquiry and measurement. In turn, we must specify a complementary measure for assertions useful for guiding decision making and inference. This second measure corresponds to *probability*.

III. LOGIC, PROBABILITY, AND BEARING

The stated motive of the ILU is to maximize the forward flow of information. As discussed in the previous section, this can be done by simultaneously maximizing both $b(Y|A)$ and $b(X \vee Y|A)$, where $b(Y|A)$ describes the transmitted component and $b(X \vee Y|A)$ describes the transduced component of information flow. Both $b(Y|A)$ and $b(X \vee Y|A)$ are computed by the ILU in response to having observed a sequence of L vector-valued inputs $\{x_1, x_2, \ldots, x_L\}$, where each $x_i = x_{i1} \wedge x_{i2} \wedge \cdots \wedge x_{il}$ for $l = 1, 2, \ldots, L$, in addition to the ILU having ob-

answered by a *true* assertion. An assertion is *false* if it answers a *vain* question and *true* if it answers a *real* question. A question may change from vain to real and back again over the course of *time*. For instance, asking what will happen tomorrow is vain until tomorrow comes, at which point the question becomes real. Answers received today regarding this question are false. The answers that will arise tomorrow can be true. *Time* itself plays the role of a synchronizing agent within the process of information flow and is itself a manifestation of it.

Perhaps the most important logical property of both questions and assertions is that of logical implication. If an assertion a implies another b, then if b answers a question, then a also answers the same question (both will give a true answer to the subject real question). For instance, if we ask the question, "What color is the apple?" the answer "dark red" implies that the answer "red" will also answer the question. We have denoted the logical implication of assertions by $a \rightarrow b$, which formally corresponds to either of the two logical identities $a \wedge b = a$ or $a \vee b = b$. The two are equivalent and each can be obtained from the other, for example, $a \wedge b = a$ can be disjoined on each side by b to obtain $a \vee b = b$ in much the same way as discussed earlier regarding the logical implication of questions.

Therefore, implication represents a possible logical relationship that may exist between two assertions. It also describes, in a complementary fashion, a possible logical relationship between two questions. If question A implies B, then question B is answered if A is answered. We already saw an example of the implication of questions where $B =$ "Are you female?" and $A =$ "Are you my sister?" Similarly, for assertions, if a implies b, then any question answered by b is also answered by a. Here the statement $a =$ "She is my sister" and the statement $b =$ "She is a female" both answer the question B, and hence $a \wedge b = a$ relative to the question B. Alternatively, if questions A and B are both answered by the statement a, then $A \vee B = B$ relative to assertion a. This example demonstrates the symmetry that exists within and between the logical domain of assertions and the logical domain of questions. It is instructive to work through several such practical exercises to firmly understand these interrelationships.

Logical implication forms the basis for deductive logic. For instance, Sherlock Holmes would use a train of logical implication to *deduce* a decision. Such logical constructs are easily realized in a digital computer and have formed the traditional basis for artificial intelligence through the IF, THEN, and OR ELSE logical constructs discussed earlier. However, deductive logic demands complete knowledge to complete a logical train of inference. In real life, we rarely have such complete knowledge and are typically forced to make rational guesses.

So if logical implication forms the basis of deductive logic, what then should form the basis for inductive logic? Richard Cox [2, 4] has shown that, for reasons of logical consistency, inductive logic must, in the limit of complete knowledge, tend to the deductive reasoning process. In addition, decisions reached inductively must be based on probability. More specifically, probability is a real-valued measure of the degree to which an implicant a implies an implicate b. Therefore, the degree of implication in this case is $p(b|a)$, which can be read as either the "probability of b given the premise a" or "the logical degree to which $a \rightarrow b$." Furthermore, the properties of any objective probability that can be derived must be consistent with every property listed on the left side of Table I. An objective derivation of probability [2, 4, 5] has shown it to be the same unique function with properties that we ascribe as belonging to conventional probability.

The implication of questions, as well as the implication of assertions, has a unique and complementary measure in an inductive framework. Just as probability is the unique measure describing the extent to which a prevailing state of knowledge implies each candidate decision, another measure, which we call *bearing*, describes the extent to which a question B resolves the issue A of an observer having a prevailing state of ignorance. This has been formally expressed as $b(B|A)$. We will see that the measures $p(b|a)$ and $b(B|A)$ together are adequate to derive and describe the operation of the ILU.

Consistent with Fig. 1, the ILU will operate in such a manner as to maximize its information throughout. The ILU will do so by giving the best decisions via inferences, while asking the best questions through interrogation to efficiently resolve its issue. As discussed, one can show that any "degree of implication" of one assertion by another must formally and uniquely correspond to probability. Alternatively, any such degree of implication of one question by another must formally and uniquely correspond to bearing [6].

The reader is undoubtedly familiar with the properties of probability. The properties of bearing are likely less familiar, although they have a one-to-one corre-

Table II

Some Selected Properties of Probability as a Unique Measure of Degree of Implication of One Assertion by Another

Selected properties of probability	Comment
$p(b \wedge c|a) = p(b|a)p(c|a \wedge b)$ $= p(c|a)p(b|a \wedge c)$	Conjunctive rule (Bayes' theorem)
$p(b|a) + p(\sim b|a) = 1$	The premise $a = b \vee \sim b$
$p(b \vee c|a) = p(b|a) + p(c|a)$ $- p(b \wedge c|a)$	Disjunctive rule
$\sum_{i=1}^{n} p(b_i|a) = 1$	The premise is $a = b_1 \vee b_2 \cdots \vee b_n$, where the b_i are exhaustive and mutually exclusive, i.e., $\bigvee_{i=1}^{n} b_i$ is true while $b_i \wedge b_j$ is false for all i and j relative to the premise a, respectively.
$p(b \wedge c|a) + p(b \wedge \sim c|a) = p(b|a)$	Partial sum decomposition rule

in response to having observed these inputs?" We reemphasize that the ILU can observe $x = x_1 \wedge x_2 \wedge \cdots \wedge x_n$ in response to asking $X = X_1 \wedge X_2 \wedge X_3 \wedge \cdots \wedge X_n$. That is, while the ILU asks "X_1 *and* X_2 *and* $\cdots$ X_n" and is presented with "x_1 *with* x_2 *with* $\cdots$ *with* x_n," it then observes "x_1 *and* x_2 *and* $\cdots$ *and* x_n."

In having A as its issue, the ILU is asking $n + 1$ elementary questions. All of these questions must be asked by the ILU to resolve its issue A. Implicitly, the ILU must also provide an assertion y to Y, because this question is only *real* if the ILU can participate in response to the observed presentations x to answer the question regarding its own output. Because the ILU can ask Y, it contains a computational mechanism whereby it can change what it asks of X while simultaneously changing how it decides. Together, these adaptations provide for *learning* by the ILU and overall modulation of ILU information throughput. Learning characterizes an organizational structure that can, in response to all observable information, modify how it generates assertions to questions it has posed and how it adapts questions in response to assertions it has given.

In addition to having the issue A, the ILU also has the premise a regarding the possible inputs it can be presented with and what possible outputs it can generate. The premise a of the ILU is directly obtained from its issue A through the process of *transformation*. The issue is $A = X_1 \wedge X_2 \wedge X_3 \wedge \cdots \wedge X_n \wedge Y$, which, through the process of *transformation*, yields the premise $a = x_1 \vee x_2 \vee x_2 \cdots \vee x_n \vee y$. The premise a represents every possible combination of things the ILU can anticipate as possible states of nature. Conversely, the issue A represents all things that the ILU can resolve based on what has been presented to it. Because a question is defined by the set of possible answers that can be obtained through its posing, it can be seen that the ILU can pose $n + 1$ elementary questions as represented by the issue A and obtain 2^{n+1} possible answers as delineated by the premise a. The domain of questions described by A is a logarithmic domain relative to the domain of assertions described by a in the sense that $|A| = \log_2 |a|$, where $| \cdot |$ denotes the number of elements comprising either an issue or a premise. This numerical property is a fundamentally important relationship between a *system of questions* and its corresponding *system of assertions* and is the underlying reason why probability and bearing have the exponential and logarithmic forms to be described.

In summary, we have characterized a logical structure for the ILU which corresponds to that of Q as shown in Fig. 1, with one important exception: the ILU can observe its own output y in addition to its external inputs x_i. With the general logical structure of the ILU and its computational objectives in place, we can finally proceed with its design. The computational objectives will serve to drive the ILU to maximize the total flux of information associated with and under its control. In particular, we require that the ILU pursue the strategy suggested earlier, and stated here more quantitatively. In particular, the ILU should

(1) optimize the transduction of information by maximizing the bearing of the question $X \vee Y$ on the issue A, that is, the measure $b(X \vee Y|A)$, or a monotomic function thereof, and

(2) independently of (1), optimize its transmission of information to other logical devices that can pose Y (this should be accomplished by maximizing the bearing of Y on the issue A, that is, $b(Y|A)$ or a monotomic function thereof).

Remember that *bearing* addresses how well the argument question resolves the relevant issue with the prevailing state of ignorance, whereas *probability* measures the extent to which the premise and prevailing state of knowledge support inference. The ILU defines both its issue A and its premise a. Logically it is more proper to say that the issue and the corresponding premise define the ILU.

From the partial sum decomposition rule in Table III, it can be seen that $b(Y \vee \sim X|A) = b(Y|A) - b(X \vee Y|A)$, and if $b(Y|A)$ and $b(X \vee Y|A)$ can independently be maximized and have the same numerical maximum, then one is tempted to simply minimize $b(Y \vee \sim X|A)$, provided that the global minimum occurs at a common global maximum of $b(Y|A)$ and $b(X \vee Y|A)$. Minimizing $b(Y \vee \sim X|A)$ can be accomplished by a simpler mathematical derivation than one that chooses to separately maximize $b(Y|A)$ and $b(X \vee Y|A)$. However, such an approach does not yield the degree of insight given by the individual optimizations of $b(Y|A)$ and $b(X \vee Y|A)$.

Before proceeding, a more detailed consideration of complementary questions can provide additional insight into the logic of questions and assertions described here. Let A correspond to the issue of which room in your home contains the car keys that you lost. Let X represent things you can ask to see within the room you are in. Then let the question $\sim X$ represent things you can ask to see in all other rooms of your house, except for the room you are in. Thus, while standing in the subject room, $\sim X$ is a vain question and can yield no directly observable result until you go to another room. Even then, only a partial answer to $\sim X$ can be obtained. You must travel, in succession, to every other room in the house to resolve the issue A by asking $\sim X$.

Thus one can view the logical property which states $Y = (X \vee Y) \wedge (\sim X \vee Y)$ as equivalent to saying that the information obtained by asking Y is the same as the information obtained by asking the two questions $X \vee Y$ *jointly* with $\sim X \vee Y$. The question $X \wedge \sim X$ asks everything relative to the ILU because $X \wedge \sim X$ will always resolve any issue, including A. One can equivalently say that $b(X \wedge \sim X|A) = 1$, because logically $X \wedge \sim X \rightarrow A$.

Upon acceptance of goals (1) and (2) in this section as comprising the computational objectives of the ILU, all that is necessary to derive its architecture is to specify a functional form for bearing. We claimed earlier that bearing is con-

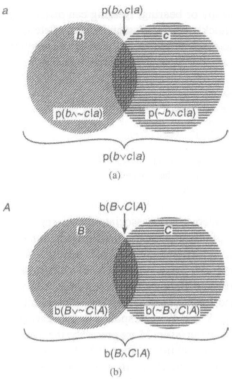

Figure 2 Familiar Venn diagrams such as that shown in (a) really only make sense in the context of a dual diagram, such as that shown in (b). (a) describes standard propositional logic, which in the present context consists of logical assertions. (b) describes the corresponding interrogative logic and must coexist with the Venn diagram in (a). *Probability* represents a natural measure for the implication of assertions, whereas *bearing* (entropy) represents a natural measure for the implication of questions.

measures meaningful to the implicit observer. In information theory, B and C represent random variables, that is, set theoretic quantities upon which an entropic measure has been defined. There is fundamentally no mathematical problem in using the logical methodology described here instead of a Kolomogorov-based approach, which deals with probability or entropy triples [10, 11] of the form $\{\Omega, F, \mu\}$, where Ω is the universal set, F is a finite Borel field, and μ is the established relevant measure on elements of this field. In Fig. 2a, the natural measure is probability. In Fig. 2b, the natural measure is entropy.

We interpret B and C as questions upon which bearings are defined relative to an issue A. Although a Kolomogorov-based approach and the mathematical framework we propose lead to the same results, the conceptual difference between the two should be understood because of additional insights gained and the resulting mathematical courses upon which one may be led. The relationships depicted in Fig. 2b have been noted by other authors, including Papoulis [10] and Yeung [11]. Yeung calls Fig. 2b an I-diagram.

Mutual information is not essentially different from any other entropic measure. More specifically, mutual information corresponds to the bearing of the information common to two questions on an underlying issue. Furthermore, one can consider and easily interpret the significance of bearing on many other logical combinations of questions that otherwise would defy meaningful interpretation in an information-theoretic context. For instance, $b(B \lor C \lor D|A)$ has no information-theoretic analog, but in the present context it is an easily interpreted construct.

Now returning to our issue, we want to consider how the ILU can implement its optimization strategy as described earlier by the simultaneous and independent maximization of both $b(X \lor Y|A)$ and $b(Y|A)$. This presumes that the ILU can ask $(X \lor Y) \land Y$ relative to the issue A. We now know that bearing can be equated numerically to entropy or mutual information, depending on the logical argument of the bearing function. Furthermore, logic dictates that the ILU be capable of directly computing or estimating monotonic functions of $b(X \lor Y|A)$ and $b(Y|A)$ in the execution of its optimization strategy. Knowing this and the mathematical form of entropy, we can write explicit formulas for both $b(Y|A)$ and $b(X \lor Y|A)$. In particular,

$$b(Y|A) = - \sum_{y \in Y} \mathrm{p}(y|a) \ln \mathrm{p}(y|a) \tag{1}$$

and

$$b(X \lor Y|A) = \sum_{x \in X} \sum_{y \in Y} \mathrm{p}(y \land x|a) \ln \frac{\mathrm{p}(y \land x|a)}{\mathrm{p}(x|a)\mathrm{p}(y|a)}, \tag{2}$$

respectively, where for brevity we have written $x = x_1 \land x_2 \land \cdots \land x_n$. The scale factor K needed to convert entropy into bearing has not been included, because it does not change our results in that it is a fixed constant. In Eqs. (1) and (2), the respective *bearings* are found by summing over all possible answers to the question Y and the question X. Because each of these answers is Boolean in nature, we can take answers as being either "0" or "1," or *nothing* or *true*, respectively. As discussed earlier, *true* and *nothing* represent descriptions of the types of *answers* that can arise from a posed question in response to a presented *assertion* as well as the two classes of answers that can arise from any physical question. Alternatively, *vain* and *real* describe the possible types of questions as contingent upon whether the relevant question can be answered. Surprisingly, there is no reference to *false*

process providing the logical *transformation*. When necessary, we will explicitly make the distinction between these two flavors of *x* clear.

Let us ask the following question: What probability distribution $p(x \wedge y|a)$ maximizes the normalization factor $K = H(A)$, given that the ILU must make the measurements *y* and $x \wedge y$? The factor *K* represents the total ignorance of the ILU and is necessary to convert standard entropy to normalized bearing. By maximizing *K* over $p(x \wedge y|a)$, we are effectively asking, What can we optimally infer, given that we have ignorance $H(A)$? That is, what exactly and truthfully can be said about all that we know without saying any more or any less? The maximization of *K* formally corresponds to the principle of maximized entropy [3, 5, 12].

In the notation $p(x \wedge y|a)$, *x* is in the conjunctive form because it is available to the ILU for use in the physical computation of this probability and can support the causal inference of *y*. Regarding the measurement $x \wedge y$, *x* is in the disjunctive form because this represents a potential presentation to the ILU. The total ignorance $b(A|A)$ of the ILU is given by

$$b(A|A) = -\sum_{y \in Y} \sum_{x \in X} p(y \wedge x|a) \ln p(y \wedge x|a). \tag{3}$$

Over its operational life, the ILU will have many presentations *y* and $x \wedge y$ made to it. It cannot be expected to maintain an inventory or otherwise store every answer to these presentations, but rather, it can retain a memory of these answers. We assume that the ILU can store a memory or some other type of reconstruction of the expected values of *y* and $x \wedge y$. These expected values are denoted here by $\langle y \rangle$ and $\langle x \wedge y \rangle$, respectively. The assumption that these expected values (or a mathematical equivalent) are stored within the ILU requires some type of internal storage mechanism for $n + 1$ real-valued parameters. There must be exactly $n + 1$ values because each $\langle x_i \wedge y \rangle$ for $i = 1$ to *n* requires a separate storage area, as does $\langle y \rangle$. We will be satisfied if the ILU can store $n + 1$ quantities that could, in principle, be used to compute $\langle y \rangle$ and $\langle x \wedge y \rangle$. This will be the case for the subject ILU.

Now, the $n + 1$ expectations $\langle y \rangle$ and $\langle x \wedge y \rangle$ are defined by the joint input–output distribution $p(x \wedge y|a)$, the determination of which was our original problem. Therefore, in addition to the optimization of Eq. (3), we can add that the ILU must measure $\langle y \rangle = E\{y\}$ and $\langle x \wedge y \rangle = E\{x \wedge y\}$, where the expectation operations denoted by E are with respect to $p(x \wedge y|a)$, that is, the knowledge state of the ILU regarding inference. Incorporating these constraints into Eq. (3) serves to acknowledge exactly that information which the ILU obtains by posing the questions $X \vee Y$ and Y, that is, $(X \vee Y) \wedge Y$, thereby constraining its architecture to those structures that admit the possible answers $x \wedge y$ with *y* or $(x \wedge y) \vee y$.

The optimization of Eq. (3) subject to the measurable quantities $\langle y \rangle$ and $\langle x \wedge y \rangle$ can be accomplished by introducing Lagrange multipliers with one multiplier assigned to each measurement function that the ILU must perform. We assume n Lagrange multipliers $\lambda = (\lambda_1, \lambda_2, \ldots, \lambda_n)$ for each element of $\langle x \wedge y \rangle = E\{x \wedge y\}$ and one additional multiplier μ for $\langle y \rangle = E\{y\}$. By introducing these Lagrange multipliers, we can effectively turn the constrained optimization of Eq. (3) into the unconstrained problem of finding the extrema of

$$
\begin{aligned}
b'(A|A) = & -\sum_{y \in Y} \sum_{x \in X} p(x \wedge y|a) \ln p(x \wedge y|a) \\
& + \lambda^T \left[\sum_{y \in Y} \sum_{x \in X} p(x \wedge y|a)(x \wedge y) - \langle x \wedge y \rangle \right] \\
& - \mu \left[\sum_{y \in Y} \sum_{x \in X} p(x \wedge y|a)y - \langle y \rangle \right] \\
& + \lambda_0 \left[\sum_{y \in Y} \sum_{x \in X} p(x \wedge y|a) - 1 \right],
\end{aligned}
\tag{4}
$$

where $\langle x \wedge y \rangle$ is treated as a column vector. Note also that we have included one additional Lagrange multiplier λ_0, which introduces another important and fundamental constraint, namely that the probabilities $p(x \wedge y|a)$ must sum to unity over $x \in X$ and $y \in Y$. Strictly speaking, we also must introduce constraints on each of the 2^{n+1} values that $p(x \wedge y|a)$ can have over $x \in X$ and $y \in Y$ to ensure that each value is positive. Fortunately, the form of the solution to Eq. (4) will implicitly guarantee that this is true, thereby making the explicit introduction of this large number of additional constraints unnecessary.

Because Eq. (3) has been made unconstrained by the introduction of additional dimensions to the problem through the Lagrange multipliers, we can optimize Eq. (4) by finding its partial derivative with respect to $p(x \wedge y|a)$ for each answer $x \in X$ and each $y \in Y$. In doing so, and by setting these derivatives to zero, we obtain

$$
-\ln p(x \wedge y|a) - 1 + \lambda^T (x \wedge y) - \mu y + \lambda_0 = 0.
\tag{5}
$$

By combining $-1 + \lambda_0$ into just $-\lambda_0$, Eq. (5) can be solved to give

$$
p(x \wedge y|a) = \exp[\lambda^T (x \wedge y) - \mu y - \lambda_0],
\tag{6}
$$

where, because Eq. (6) must sum to 1, we can define λ_0 in terms of the other Lagrange factors λ and μ by forming the sum

$$
\lambda_0 = \ln \sum_{y \in Y} \sum_{x \in X} \exp[\lambda^T (x \wedge y) - \mu y] = \ln Z,
\tag{7}
$$

time instant. In particular, the expression $\zeta(x) = \lambda^T x - \mu$ corresponds to the logarithm of the posterior odds of deciding $y = 1$, given observed information x as shown by the linear terms present in a logarithmic form of Bayes' theorem given by

$$\ln \frac{p(y = 1 | a \wedge x)}{p(y = 0 | a \wedge x)} = \ln \frac{p[x | a \wedge (y = 1)]}{p[x | a \wedge (y = 0)]} + \ln \frac{p(y = 1 | a)}{p(y = 0 | a)}$$

$$= \lambda^T x - \mu = \zeta(x). \tag{11}$$

In other words, the new information for decision making equals the original information for decision making plus newly observed information for decision making. The prior evidence for decision making is given by the decision threshold μ, and $\lambda^T x$ represents newly measured information.

Figure 4 summarizes the inferential architecture of the ILU. Note that the reason for incorporating the question Y has not been discussed. The question Y will be seen to support ILU question formation and adaptation regarding both optimized transduction and optimized transmission. In the next section, we will develop adaptation algorithms to be implemented by this architecture that will optimize its transduction and transmission through separate optimizations of $b(X \vee Y | A)$ and $b(Y | A)$, respectively. Both of these optimizations intrinsically require that the ILU ask the question Y.

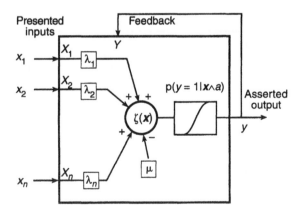

Figure 4 Architectural layout of the ILU for supporting inference and forward information flow. Asserted inputs x are measured through λ and then combined with μ to compute the evidence $\zeta(x)$. Subsequently, $\zeta(x)$ can be used to generate a probabilistic decision y. The decision y is measured by the ILU through feedback to support subsequent optimization of transmission and transduction.

V. OPTIMIZED TRANSMISSION

In attempting to optimize the *transmission* of information by the ILU, we effectively want to generate and *present* the *best assertions* to *questions* that other observers can ask regarding the ILU output. Regarding the source ILU, this optimization corresponds to maximizing $b(Y|A)$ with respect to the decision threshold μ, given that the ILU can measure presented inputs x through λ.

The decision threshold μ dictates what answers will be given in response to the measurement $\lambda^T x$ and therefore realizes the question Y, because questions are intrinsically defined by their possible answers. The threshold μ cleaves the space of possible assertions that the ILU can generate while simultaneously forming the output premise of the ILU.

Qualitatively, maximizing transmission corresponds to maximizing $b(Y|A)$ over μ for fixed λ, with no inherent constraints placed on μ, except that it is real-valued. The problem then becomes that of solving

$$\frac{\partial b(Y|A)}{\partial \mu} = 0, \tag{12}$$

where

$$b(Y|A) = \sum_{y' \in Y} p(y'|a) \ln \frac{1}{p(y'|a)}. \tag{13}$$

From Appendix, the marginal distribution of the output assertion y is

$$p(y|a) = \frac{\sum_{x' \in X} \exp[\lambda^T x' y - \mu y]}{Z}. \tag{14}$$

Now let us define S_x according to

$$S_x = \sum_{x' \in X} \exp[\lambda^T x']. \tag{15}$$

Then

$$b(Y|A) = \frac{1}{\ln 2} \left\{ \frac{2^n}{Z} \log_2 \frac{Z}{2^n} + \frac{S_x \exp[-\mu]}{Z} \log_2 \frac{Z}{S_x \exp[-\mu]} \right\}. \tag{16}$$

We incorporate the factor $1/\ln 2$ in Eq. (16) to evaluate it in terms of base 2, which is overall a more natural base for the consideration of computations performed by the ILU. This factor can be eliminated because it will not change the location of the extrema of Eq. (16). The factor Z in equation (16) is the normalization factor

VI. OPTIMIZED TRANSDUCTION

In attempting to optimize the *transduction* of information by the ILU, we effectively want to determine the *best questions* to ask based on *assertions* previously *presented* to it. The determination of the best question to ask should be achieved through the maximization of $b(X \vee Y|A)$ with respect to each element λ_i in the vector λ subject to the constraint $|\lambda|^2 = \gamma^2$ that arose during the optimization of ILU transmission.

The parameter vector λ dictates what answers can arise through inputs x as interrogated by the question X. Good measurements will maximize the information common to the output and the input, that is, that which can be asked of the input x and that which can be asked of the output y. These measurements will emphasize the λ_i whose coincidences $x_i \wedge y$ are most frequent. If $x_i \wedge y \approx x_i$, then $x_i \to y$, which even for a single-input ILU would minimize information loss. Because γ^2 must be bounded below unity to satisfy the maximization of $b(Y|A)$, we maintain this as an explicit constraint for optimizing $b(X \vee Y|A)$.

The quantitative mathematical problem then becomes that of finding the extremum of the objective function J by solving

$$\frac{\partial J}{\partial \lambda_i} = 0 \tag{22}$$

for $i = 1, 2, \ldots, n$, where n is the number of input elements in x and where

$$
\begin{aligned}
J &= b\big(X \vee Y|A\big) + \frac{1}{2}\alpha|\lambda|^2 \\
&= \sum_{x' \in X} \sum_{y' \in Y} p(x' \wedge y'|a) \ln \frac{p(y'|x' \wedge a)}{p(y'|a)} + \frac{1}{2}\alpha|\lambda|^2.
\end{aligned}
\tag{23}
$$

The factor α in Eq. (23) is a Lagrange multiplier introduced to explicitly enforce the condition $|\lambda|^2 = \gamma^2$. One can prove the so-called Gibbs' mutual information theorem or GMIT [13], which states that if the mutual or common information between a question X and a question Y is extremized for a joint probability distribution with an exponential form, the resulting condition for the extremal solution has an especially simple form. Basically, the theorem states that if one has a Gibbs or exponential distribution of the form $p(x \wedge y|a; \nu) = \exp[-\nu_1 f_1(x, y) - \nu_2 f_2(x, y) - \nu_n f_n(x, y)]/Z$, then the common information or $b(X \vee Y|A)$ is extremized over the parameter set ν when

$$\sum_{x' \in X} \sum_{y' \in Y} p(x' \wedge y'|a; \nu) \ln \frac{p(y'|x' \wedge a)}{p(y'|a)} [\langle f_j(x', y') \rangle - f_j(x', y')] = 0 \tag{24}$$

for $j = 1, 2, \ldots, n$. Here $\nu = (\lambda, \mu)$, $f_j(x, y) = x_j \wedge y$, and $\langle f_j(x, y) \rangle = \langle x_j \wedge y \rangle$ is the expected value of this coincidence, that is, the answers to the common question $X_j \vee Y$, and is given by

$$\langle f_j(x, y)\rangle = \sum_{x'\in X}\sum_{y'\in Y} x_j y \mathrm{p}(x' \wedge y'|a; \lambda, \mu), \tag{25}$$

with $\mathrm{p}(x \wedge y|a; \lambda, \mu) = \mathrm{p}(x \wedge y|a)$ given by Eq. (8). We have replaced the conjunction operator with the multiplication operator in making the substitution $x_i \wedge y = x_i y$ in Eq. (8), because for Boolean numbers, multiplication and conjunction are equivalent. It is worthwhile to note that rescaling the problems here from the Boolean values of 0 and 1 to 0 and any other number will not change any results because discrete entropy is invariant to scale.

The computational objective is to solve Eq. (23) and to find the conditions under which Eq. (22) holds. One can go through the rigorous mathematical detail, but using the GMIT, using Eqs. (22) through (25), and noting that

$$\frac{\partial}{\partial \lambda_i}\left[\frac{\alpha}{2}|\lambda|^2\right] = \alpha\lambda_i, \tag{26}$$

the optimization condition stated by Eq. (22) becomes

$$\frac{\partial J}{\partial \lambda_i} = \mathrm{E}\left\{\ln \frac{\mathrm{p}(y|x \wedge a)}{\mathrm{p}(y|a)}[x_i y - \langle x_i y\rangle]\right\} + \alpha\lambda_i. \tag{27}$$

As one can see from Eqs. (22) and (23), the partial derivatives are only taken with respect to the Lagrange factors of the n elements $\{x_1 y, x_2 y, \ldots, x_n y\}$ contained in the vector $x y = x \wedge y$.

From the Appendix, the forms of $\mathrm{p}(y|x \wedge a)$ and $\mathrm{p}(y|a)$ are known. When these are substituted into Eq. (27), one obtains the equation

$$A_i(\lambda, \mu) + B_i(\lambda, \mu) + \alpha\lambda_i = 0 \tag{28}$$

for $i = 1, 2, \ldots, n$. This equation must be simultaneously satisfied for all i, where A_i and B_i are defined according to

$$A_i(\lambda, \mu) = \mathrm{E}\left\{[x_i y - \langle x_i y\rangle][\lambda^T x y - \mu y]\right\} \tag{29}$$

and

$$B_i(\lambda, \mu) = \mathrm{E}\left\{[x_i y - \langle x_i y\rangle]\ln \frac{\mathrm{p}(y = 0|x \wedge a)}{\mathrm{p}(y|a)}\right\}, \tag{30}$$

respectively. $A_i(\lambda, \mu)$ can be simplified by remembering that $\mu = \lambda^T \langle x|y = 1\rangle$. Furthermore, $\lambda^T \langle x|y = 1\rangle\langle y\rangle = \lambda^T \langle xy\rangle$. With this last substitution, Eq. (29) becomes

$$A_i(\lambda, \mu) = \lambda^T \langle x x_i y\rangle - \mu\langle x_i y\rangle. \tag{31}$$

where we have taken account of the fact that $\mu = \langle \lambda^T x | y = 1 \rangle$ and where the matrix $\mathbf{R}$ is defined by

$$\mathbf{R} = \langle [x - \langle x | y = 1 \rangle][x - \langle x | y = 1 \rangle]^T | y = 1 \rangle. \tag{37}$$

Because the Lagrange factor α for the constraint $|\lambda|^2 = \gamma^2$ has not been specified, Eq. (37) can be written as the eigenvector equation

$$\mathbf{R}\lambda = \alpha'\lambda \tag{38}$$

by letting $\alpha' = -4\alpha$. One can go back and solve for α to find that α' must be the largest eigenvalue and hence λ the largest eigenvector of the covariance matrix $\mathbf{R}$. Note that $\mathbf{R}$, being a covariance matrix for the input x present during an output decision corresponding to $y = 1$, has full rank as long as none of the inputs are perfectly correlated. This condition is guaranteed if one of the elements of a perfectly correlated pair forces $\lambda_i \to 0$ through the optimized transduction adaptation algorithm. Forcing $\lambda_i \to 0$ essentially eliminates input x_i from any further consideration by the ILU, subsequently reducing the number of input dimensions from n to $n - 1$. In summary, finding the largest eigenvector of the matrix $\mathbf{R}$ defined by Eq. (37) represents the computational goal of the ILU regarding the optimized transduction of information.

VII. ILU COMPUTATIONAL STRUCTURE

Now that we know the computational objectives of the ILU, we must consider how to efficiently achieve them for both transmission and transduction. The optimized transmission, or inferential structure, has been described through the computation of the evidence $\zeta(x)$ for inference and decision making. The optimized transduction or interrogational structure must be addressed to modify the questions asked by the ILU. The simultaneous or individual modification of the inferential and interrogational structures of the ILU corresponds to learning.

As derived in the previous section, the computational objectives were found to include

$$\mu = \langle \lambda^T x | y = 1 \rangle \tag{39}$$

for optimized transmission and to find the largest eigenvector solution of

$$\mathbf{R}\lambda = \alpha'\lambda \tag{40}$$

for optimized transduction, where again, $\mathbf{R} = \langle [x - \langle x | y = 1 \rangle][x - \langle x | y = 1 \rangle]^T | y = 1 \rangle$. It is significant that Eqs. (39) and (40) only hold for presented inputs x that causally yield $y = 1$. This is fundamental to our development of an efficient algorithm for simultaneously achieving the computational objectives given by Eqs. (39) and (40). We assume that "on-line learning" occurs as driven by the sequential presentation of input patterns $\{x_1, x_2, \ldots\}$.

The function *evidence* was defined to be $\zeta(x) = \lambda^T x - \mu$. The ILU must compute *evidence* to support inference and decision making. The conditional expectation of $\zeta(x)$ given an output positive decision $y = 1$ is given by

$$\langle \zeta(x)|y = 1 \rangle = \langle \lambda^T x|y = 1 \rangle - \mu = 0. \tag{41}$$

Because Eq. (39) holds, Eq. (41) states that the average evidence for decision making, given that a positive decision is made, is 0! Equation (39) basically states that the decision threshold μ is just the conditional average of the measurement $\lambda^T x$, given that a positive decision $y = 1$ has been made. The ILU output decision conditionalizes the validity of both Eqs. (39) and (40).

The simplest conceivable way of computationally realizing Eq. (39) is to numerically average the induced measurement $\lambda^T x$ conditionalized on a previously made decision $y = 1$ and, internal to the ILU, adjust the parameter μ accordingly. This computation can practically be realized through a simple differential equation of the form

$$\frac{d\mu}{dt} = (1 - \tau_1)\mu + \tau_1(\lambda^T x) \tag{42}$$

implemented with time constant $1 - \tau_1$ for $\tau_1 \in (0, 1)$ and only implemented when $y = 1$. Equation (42) realizes an exponential window averaging of the past quantities $\lambda^T x$ measured by the ILU, which induced the decision $y = 1$. The width of the exponential window is controlled by the parameter τ_1. Now we consider Eq. (40), which optimizes transduction.

In 1982, Erikki Oja [14] derived and discussed a very important and simple adaptation equation which he proposed as a biologically plausible adaptation algorithm for neurons. Basically, Oja's adaptation equation takes as input a sequence of real-valued vectors upon which it operates. For a statistically stationary input, the equation computes and identifies the largest eigenvector of the correlation (not covariance) matrix of the input sequence. The form of Oja's adaptation equation is given by

$$\frac{d\lambda(t)}{dt} = \pi_1 \eta(x)\big[\pi_2 x(t) - \pi_3 \eta(x)\lambda(t)\big], \tag{43}$$

where $\eta = \lambda^T x$, π_1 is a time constant analogous to τ_1, and π_2, π_3 are two scaling factors for the solution. For a sequence of inputs $\{x_1, x_2, \ldots\}$, this equation will compute the largest eigenvector λ of the autocorrelation matrix $\mathbf{R}' = \text{E}[xx^T]$. This is almost exactly the same problem we have here, except for the following

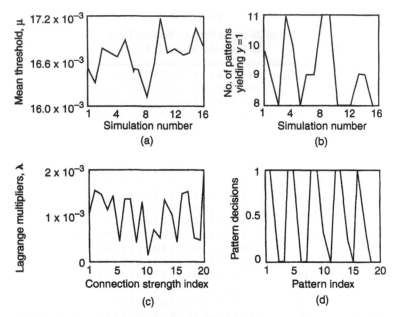

Figure 7 The decision threshold μ in (a) varies by only a few percent between simulations. (b) describes the number of input patterns that induce the decision $y = 1$ across simulations. A plot of the averaged Lagrange vectors λ over the 16 training sessions is given in (c). The specific input patterns x that induce the decisions $y = 0$ and $y = 1$ are described in (d).

tently the largest in each training session. This finding is counterintuitive from an information-theoretic standpoint, because this input offers no distinguishability among the training patterns. However, this interpretation is improper because the computational objective is to compute the magnitude of each λ_i based on the degree to which there is common information $X_i \vee Y$ as described by $x_i \wedge y$. Therefore, outputs y that are consistently asserted when input x_i is asserted will weight λ_i more heavily, because this condition is a stronger indicator of the implication $y \rightarrow x_i$ implying reconstructability of inputs.

Figure 7d indicates which training patterns give rise to the decisions $y = 0$ and $y = 1$ by letting the computational temperature T tend to 0, where inference was performed based on $p(y = 1|x) = 1/1 + \exp[-\zeta(x)/T]$. The parameter T essentially models additive measurement noise. As the noise tends to 0, T tends to 0, and the decision rule is deterministic and consists of the simple rule in which the ILU decides $y = 1$ if $\zeta(x) > \mu$. As T becomes large, the decision rule is completely random and is independent of the measured quantity $\zeta(x)$. In this case $p(y = 1|x)$ and $p(y = 0|x)$ each approach $1/2$.

IX. SUMMARY

We must conclude our discussion without producing a practical utility, although a single ILU has shown biomedical application for the screening of cataracts. Nor have we dealt with the issue of timing and synchronization between multiple ILU configurations, or even considered such configurations. It is a straightforward exercise to extend the analysis we have described to such configurations, which have more practical use than a single ILU.

We have, however, described an analytically tractable, intuitive, and rational methodology for the design of artificial neural networks that operate inductively rather than deductively. In this sense, the proposed ILU and any realized ILCs represent a computational generalization of conventional digital computers and deductive logic.

As stated in the beginning of the paper, many of the ideas we have presented here are not new. A logical legacy can be traced back quite far. Limited space does not permit a complete account of all participants. George Spencer-Brown [15] was the first to ascertain the logical origins of Boolean algebra and to emphasize the essential nature of distinguishability as a basis for logic. Edwin Jaynes [3], Myron Tribus [5], and Richard Cox [6] are major contemporary contributors to the field of inductive logic. Jaynes established the connectivity between thermodynamics and information theory. In doing so, he showed that thermodynamics is not an arbitrary theory, but rather a theory of theories. The work of Jaynes provided a Rosetta stone to Tribus [5], who extended the practical utility of inductive logic and advanced its logical underpinnings. It was Tribus who first conceived of a set of *desiderata* for the design of an ILC, which provided the basis for the approach described here. Finally, Cox, in his unassuming and profoundly insightful manner, realized the fundamental and physical nature of assertions, questions, probability, and entropy. It is to him that this chapter is dedicated, in that it is but a more detailed rendering of his account.

APPENDIX: SIGNIFICANT MARGINAL AND CONDITIONAL ILU DISTRIBUTIONS

Complete joint input–output distribution for x and y:

$$p(x \wedge y|a) = \frac{\exp[\lambda^T(x \wedge y) - \mu y]}{Z}. \tag{A1}$$

Partition function Z required for normalization:

$$Z = \sum_{y' \in Y} \sum_{x' \in X} \exp[\lambda^T(x' \wedge y) - \mu y']. \tag{A2}$$

ACKNOWLEDGMENTS

My gratitude to my wife for taking on more than her share of the load in keeping things running smoothly at home while I was distracted from the family with the writing of this chapter. Also, my gratitude to The Johns Hopkins University Applied Physics Laboratory for its support through the Janney Fellowship in completing this chapter. And finally, my sincere thanks to Myron Tribus for his thoughts and inspirations that assisted in the final preparation of this chapter.

REFERENCES

[1] C. E. Shannon and W. Weaver. *The Mathematical Theory of Communication.* Univ. of Illinois Press, Urbana, IL, 1949.

[2] R. T. Cox. Probability, frequency, and reasonable expectation. *Amer. J. Phys.* 14:1-13, 1946.

[3] E. T. Jaynes. Information theory and statistical mechanics. *Phys. Rev.* 106:620-630, 1957.

[4] R. T. Cox. *The Algebra of Probable Inference.* Johns Hopkins Univ. Press, Baltimore, MD, 1961.

[5] M. Tribus. *Rational Descriptions, Decisions, and Designs.* Pergamon Press, New York, 1969.

[6] R. T. Cox. Of inference and inquiry. In *Proceedings of the 1978 Maximum Entropy Formalism Conference,* pp. 119-167. MIT Press, Cambridge, MA, 1979.

[7] J. A. Wheeler. Information, physics, quantum: The search for links. In *Proceedings of the Workshop on Complexity, Entropy and the Physics of Information,* pp. 3-28. Addison-Wesley Publishers, Redwood City, CA, 1990.

[8] R. T. Cox. Introduction to a general theory of elementary propositions. *Amer. J. Math.* 163-185, 1931.

[9] Lao Tzu. *Tao Te Ching.* New York, 1972. (A contemporary translation by Gia-Fu Feng and Jane English. Originally traced to around the sixth century B.C.)

[10] A. Bruckner. *Foundations of Modern Analysis* (to revise). McGraw-Hill, New York, 1956.

[11] R. W. Young. A new outlook on Shannon's information measures. *IEEE Trans. Inform. Theory* 37:466-474, 1991.

[12] A. Papoulis and S. H. Kazarian. *Communication Systems: Principles with Applications.* Academic Press, New York, 1992.

Neural Networks Applied to Data Analysis

Aarnoud Hoekstra
Pattern Recognition Group
Faculty of Applied Physics
Delft University of
Technology
2600 GA Delft,
The Netherlands

Robert P. W. Duin
Pattern Recognition Group
Faculty of Applied Physics
Delft University of
Technology
2600 GA Delft,
The Netherlands

Martin A. Kraaijveld
Shell International
Exploration and
Production
Research and Technical
Services
2280 AB Rijswijk,
The Netherlands

I. INTRODUCTION

The analyst who has to find an automatic data classifier has to solve a set of problems. On one hand there are the data, objects, which have to be classified as well as possible; on the other hand, one has numerous classifiers to choose from. The question that arises is: How to choose the best classifier for the given set of objects? There is no general recipe in training a neural classifier on a data set. The best one can do is to obtain as much information as possible from the data available. This can be used to match against the capabilities of the classifier one has chosen. The techniques presented in this chapter can be used to study the neural classifier in relation to the data it has to classify. Neural networks have significantly increased the possibilities of analyzing and classifying data sets. The adaptive nonlinear property of these networks are of primary importance. Herewith they can be used for describing and generalizing almost any data set that can be represented in a continuous space. This property is directly related to the fact that neural networks can be given an arbitrary complexity by their architectural design, for example, the number of neurons and the number of layers, provided that the learning scheme is sufficiently powerful. Therefore in this chapter we will study how the properties of neural network classifiers can be used to analyze data.

The chapter will start off with an overview of different techniques available in the literature for the analysis of unlabeled data. This includes not only neural techniques but also nonneural techniques that are generally accepted. These techniques give an insight into the complexity of the available data. However, one is also interested in how labeled data can be analyzed. Moreover, if one has labeled data, how can these data be investigated to apply the appropriate (neural) classifier? Section III introduces a technique with which we can investigate the separability of the available data. By visualizing the scatter of the data in the feature space, it is possible to gain insight into its separability. The method maps the high-dimensional space onto a two-dimensional plane. This enables us to visually inspect the high-dimensional space and choose an appropriate classifier.

However, in practice many classifiers will solve a classification problem after having applied a separability analysis. Therefore, in Section IV a technique is introduced that can be used for classifier selection. By estimating the reliability, or confidence, of a classifier, a selection can be made. A classifier that has a bad confidence, that is, a low probability of correct classification, is likely to be rejected as a possible solution. Comparing different classifiers, either by confidence or test set performance, requires an independent set that can be used for testing. Generally these sets are not available; therefore validation sets are used for comparing the different classifiers. This implies that a method is required to generate these sets; Section IV also introduces a technique to generate such sets. An advantage of such validation sets is that they share the same characteristics as an independent test set.

A next step is to train a classifier on a given classification problem. Neural network classifiers are well known for their ability to solve almost any classification problem. This constitutes a problem in training a classifier on a particular task. If the classifier is trained too long it may not generalize at all. Section V introduces a measure that can be used to keep track of the network's generalization behavior during training. This behavior is strongly determined by the complexity of the classifier, for example, the number of hidden units, in relation to the data it is trained on. By examining this measure, the appropriate moment to stop training the classifier can be determined. The last section goes into the problem of classifier stability. During the training of a classifier its decision regions are frequently changing. This behavior can be characterized by the stability of a classifier. The more stable the classifier that is yielded, the better it is for solving a particular problem.

The general line of this paper follows the solution of a given classification problem with data by the following steps. Analyze the data using general techniques to get an indication of its complexity. Next, analyze the separability to be able to select an appropriate classifier. Having several appropriate classifiers, select from these classifiers those that have the most confidence. In training a classifier on a particular classification problem, keep track of its generalization behavior and stability to yield an optimal solution.

II. DATA COMPLEXITY

The most basic form is which data can be observed is as unlabeled data. This type of data is obtained, for instance, from measured signals belonging to unknown categories. Several new techniques have been developed to gain insight into the data. In this section an overview will be presented of different methods. It is not our intention to give a full and exhaustive list of algorithms. We will merely give an indication of how they can be placed in the entire field. Numerous methods can be found in the literature [1–14]. They belong to one of the main categories we distinguish below.

Although the techniques were mainly developed for unlabeled data, they can be applied to labeled data as well. One can distinguish between algorithmic and descriptive complexity. Algorithmic complexity describes the methods in terms of computing power needed to perform the algorithms. The more power that is needed, the more complex a method is. However, this complexity measure depends on the implementation of a method and the available computing power, and is therefore a subjective one.

Descriptive complexity is concerned with describing the method in terms of abilities, for instance, generalization capacity and the number of free parameters. We distinguish three main categories to which the data analysis algorithms may belong:

1. Prototype vector methods
2. Subspace or projection methods
3. Density estimation methods

The distinction is based on an increasing complexity of the methods, starting with the techniques with the lowest complexity. Our ordering is based on a descriptive complexity, the *data need*. The more data (objects) are needed to perform an algorithm accurately, the more complex it is. For example, to estimate the density of a set of objects and their a priori probabilities, far more objects are needed than for finding the cluster centers of the objects.

Now the different categories a studied in more detail.

A. PROTOTYPE VECTORS

As indicated, methods belonging to this category have the lowest descriptive complexity, that is, in terms of data need. The prototype methods are also known as vector quantization algorithms and determine cluster centers in the data. The available objects can be divided into (separate) clusters, and each of these clusters can be represented by a single vector called a *prototype*. Depending on the method, the number of prototypes is either fixed or can be increased during learning. In general, the more prototypes that are used, the better the data can be represented. However, too many prototypes may lead to an "overrepresentation," the extreme case in which each object is represented by a single prototype. The problem when applying these algorithms is how to choose the number of prototypes. In the literature many vector quantization algorithms can be found. We distinguish the following four algorithms:

Vector Quantization [15]

This algorithm starts with a fixed number of prototypes randomly initialized. At each update step, a prototype that is closest to the object under investigation is updated toward this object. This results in a set of prototypes that are centered in the clusters present in the data.

Isodata/K-Means Clustering [1, 14, 16]

These methods are basically the same as vector quantization. They differ from the previous methods in the sense that they apply batch updating. At each update step the available objects are assigned to a prototype. This prototype is thereafter updated by taking the mean of the feature vectors of the objects assigned to that prototype.

Self-Organizing Map [10, 15, 17]

This method is more complex than the previous one because it takes the neighborhood relations between the different prototypes into account. This implies that more data are needed for an accurate performance of the algorithm. The self-organizing map is described in more detail in one of the next sections.

The ART Network [18–20]

This method is similar to the vector quantization method, although it is described in the literature in a rather complicated way. It differs from vector quantization in the sense that it is able to increase the number of prototypes, at least up to a certain limit. An object that is fed to the network is either added to a matching prototype or rejected, that is, no prototype was available to assign the object to. If the object is rejected, a new prototype can be created.

There are also more traditionally oriented, that is, nonneural, techniques used to gain insight into data complexity. We can distinguish two types of algorithms, although in the literature variations can be found:

Hierarchical Clustering [1, 14, 16]

This type of data analysis algorithm builds a tree structure (dendrogram) of the objects available. The tree is built according to rules that state how objects can be clustered. This tree can be inspected visually to get an indication of how the data are clustered.

Minimal Spanning Tree [1, 14]

Minimal spanning trees are pruned versions of cluster trees such that the neighbor relations between objects are preserved.

The methods presented in this section have a low complexity. In general not many objects are needed for an accurate performance of the algorithms [8].

B. SUBSPACE OR PROJECTION METHODS

Subspace approaches differ from prototype algorithms because these methods try to determine which components in the data are important. In contrast to vector quantization methods, subspace or projection algorithms describe the data in terms of a reduced set of components. This requires more objects. The number of objects needed must be at least as large as the dimension of the subspace. For example, to locate a two-dimensional subspace in a three-dimensional space, we need at least three objects. Here five methods are described; more can be found in the literature:

Karhunen–Loève Transform [3]

The Karhunen–Loève transform is a linear mapping method that describes the data by using principal components. These principal components are derived from the available objects by transforming them to a space of lower dimensionality. By determining the eigenvalues and eigenvectors, a description of the data is obtained. The larger an eigenvalue, the more important that direction is for the description of the data.

Oja Neuron [21, 22]

This is also a linear mapping method; it is the neural variant of the Karhunen–Loève transform. As in the previous method, principal components are derived. In contrast to the Karhunen–Loève transform, a learning algorithm is used to find the principal components.

Sammon's Projection [23]

This method preserves all of the neighbor relations between the objects as much as possible, in contrast to the methods from the previous subsection, where a minimum number of neighbor relations are preserved. Sammon's method is explained in more detail in Section III.

Self-Organizing Map [10, 15, 17]

The self-organizing map is not only a vector quantization method; it is also a nonlinear projection method. Because neighborhood relations are preserved by using a fixed, usually two-dimensional grid of prototype vectors, a mapping is performed onto a two-dimensional space. By this type of mapping, possible subspace properties of the data are revealed. More details regarding this type of mapping algorithm can be found in Section III.

Auto-Associative Feedforward Neural Network [3, 7]

In contrast to the self-organizing map, the auto-associative network is able to project from a high-dimensional space onto a arbitrary lower dimensional space. This is done using a feedforward neural network with a "bottleneck." The number of neurons in the hidden layer is much smaller than the number of input neurons. By using auto-associative learning (that is, the network is taught to reproduce the input), the network is forced to compress the high-dimensional input into the bottleneck. Another major difference with the self-organizing map is that this network performs a global mapping, whereas the previous method preserves local neighborhood relations.

As stated earlier, these methods require more objects than vector quantization methods, and are therefore more complex.

C. Density Estimation Methods

The last category of methods for data analysis is density estimators. This category contains the most complex methods. To estimate the densities in the data, many objects are needed. We distinguish the following three methods:

Radial Basis Functions [3, 9]

This type of neural network uses a Gaussian function as activation function in the hidden units. The output is constituted by a linear combination of the Gaussian functions in the hidden layer, thus resulting in a global density estimation of the data. Because this method makes a global estimate (in the sense that a kernel encloses several objects, in contrast to Parzen) of the data density distribution, it is less complex than the Parzen method.

Parzen Method [6, 24]

In Parzen estimation, a superposition of Gaussian kernels located on the objects is used as the density estimate. These kernels are combined by linear summation, as in the radial basis functions, to find a probability density function of the objects. This method is very accurate but requires a huge number of objects, especially when estimating in a high-dimensional space.

Boltzmann Neural Networks [25]

This type of network is a so-called stochastic network. The objects are fed to the network, and after learning the neurons in the network represent the probability distribution of the objects. A drawback, however, is that the Boltzmann machine can only handle binary coded inputs.

The methods described in the previous sections can be used to analyze the data given. Depending on the degree of analysis, one of the methods from a category may be used. However, the accuracy of a method is restricted to the number of objects available. If, for instance, only a few objects are available, a vector quantization might be more informative than a Parzen estimation, which requires a lot of objects.

This section has introduced some general methods available in the literature that can be used to gain insight into the data. Depending on the information one needs to build a (neural) classifier, any one of these methods can be chosen. However, one must bear in mind that the number of available objects restricts the different methods in their applicability. The more objects that are available, the more information that can be extracted. Prototype vector approaches are suited to investigating whether the data are clustered in one way or another, whereas projection methods map the data onto a space of lower dimensionality and thus extract information on how the data are located. The last class of methods gives insight into the distribution of the data in terms of probability density estimations. It gives an indication of the probability of finding an object at a particular place. The next step is to find out how separable the data are. The more separable a set of objects is, the less complex the classifiers that can be used to solve a problem. In general, less complex classifiers are easier to find and analyze. The next section will deal with this separability problem.

III. DATA SEPARABILITY

As illustrated in the previous section, there are many methods for analyzing unlabeled data. However, in practical situations where one is dealing with a classification problem, this implies the use of labeled data. In this section we will focus on the problem of data separability. A method will be discussed for estimating the separability of the data. Knowing the separability of the data enables one to choose an optimal classifier that solves the problem, or at least one that is better than a random choice. Some data sets are more complex in the sense that they need a more complex classifier for classification. More complex classifiers are, for instance, neural classifiers with a large number of hidden units, or nearest-neighbor classifiers with a small k.

Let us consider the following classification problem. Figure 1 shows two classes with equal covariances but different means, which are separated using the k-nearest neighbor classifier, that is, a classifier that takes the k nearest neighbors around an object to determine its class membership. These two classes are separable with a small error, and therefore it does not appear to be a hard to separate the data set. However, if we increase the variance of both classes in the y direction (Fig. 1), and keep the number of objects fixed, it becomes more complex. Applying again the nearest-neighbor method to these classes now results in a classifier that performs worse, although the increase in the variance does not contribute to a better separation. The classes, however, are still separable with a small error. Figure 2 shows how the error depends on k for the different, stretched data sets. The error made by the classifier differs for each set, although the discriminating direction of the data set (the x direction) does not change.

Consequently, from the viewpoint of the classifier, the data have become more complex, inasmuch as they appear to be harder to separate. Therefore, knowing the separability of the data will give an indication of which classifier to use (k in Fig. 2). For large variance a small k should be selected, whereas small variances require a relatively large k. Another complexity problem, related to separability, is the problem of dimensionality. In two-dimensional problems, like the one in Fig. 1, it is easy to see how separable the data are. In higher dimensions it is not so clear how the data are distributed. To determine this, a method for inspecting the space is needed. The remainder of this section is devoted to the problem of visualizing the high-dimensional data, such that their separability can be investigated. It will be shown that a high-dimensional data space can be mapped onto a two-dimensional plane such that the separability of the data can be visualized. A nonlinear mapping method, the self-organizing map (SOM), is used to map the space onto a grid. This method is topology preserving, that is, neighbor relations in the high-dimensional space are preserved, as much as possible, in the lower dimensional grid. This property is used to inspect the scatter of the data.

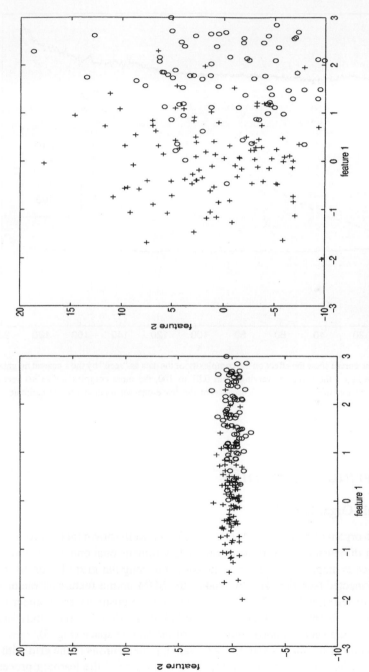

Figure 1 The data sets with increasing complexity from left to right. The overlap between the classes remains the same whereas the variance in the y direction increases.

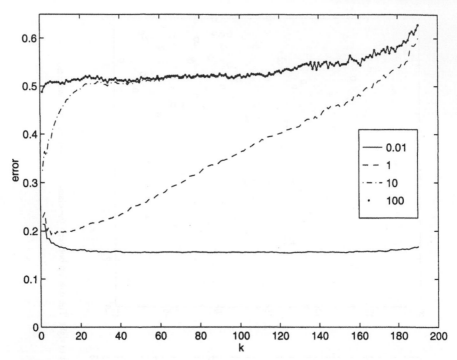

Figure 2   The curves show the effect on the complexity of the data as "seen" by the k nearest neighbor classifier. The larger the variance, varying from 0.01 to 100, the more complex a data set seems. The error of the classifier approaches 1 because of the leave-one-out method used to estimate the performance.

A. MAPPING ALGORITHMS

The Self-Organizing Map

The self-organizing map (SOM) [10, 15, 17] is a well-known method for mapping a high-dimensional feature space onto a low-dimensional one. In general the feature space is mapped onto a two-dimensional rectangular grid of neurons that are interconnected (see Fig. 4). This makes the SOM both a feature extractor as well as a clustering method. The map is trained in an unsupervised manner using competitive learning. Each neuron in the low-dimensional grid (usually 2) is assigned a feature vector representing a part of the feature space (Fig. 3).

The training of the map is started by initializing the neurons in the grid with a small random feature vector, or weight, $\vec{m}$. In every step of the learning process this weight is updated in such a way that it represents a part of the feature space as

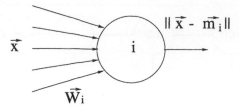

Figure 3 A neuron from the rectangular grid of the self-organizing map.

accurately as possible. Three steps in the learning procedure can be distinguished:

1. Presentation of a randomly selected object from the input feature space
2. Evaluation of the network
3. Updating of the weight vectors of the network

The first step is to randomly select an input object, although in practice the procedure is such that all objects are used at least once. This object is then mapped by the network. Each unit in the grid computes the distance of its weight vector $\vec{m}_i$ to the input vector $\vec{x}$ by using the Euclidean distance (Fig. 3). The neuron having the least distance is selected as "winner" s:

$$\left\| \vec{x}(t) - \vec{m}_s(t) \right\| = \min_i \left(\left\| \vec{x}(t) - \vec{m}_i(t) \right\| \right). \tag{1}$$

Note that the iteration step is indicated with t. The winning neuron is used as a starting point for updating all of the other neurons in the grid. All neurons within a certain neighborhood $N_c(t)$ (for a graphical interpretation of $N_c(t)$ see Fig. 4) of the winning neuron receive an update toward the presented input object. The update rule is as follows:

$$\vec{m}_i(t+1) = \begin{cases} \vec{m}_i(t) + \alpha(t)[\vec{x}(t) - \vec{m}_i(t)] & \text{if } i \in N_c(t) \\ \vec{m}_i(t) & \text{if } i \notin N_c(t) \end{cases}. \tag{2}$$

The neighborhood size $N_c(t)$ decreases monotonically in time; fewer neurons around the winning neuron must be updated because the objects are better represented each time an update is performed. The learning parameter $\alpha(t)$ in Eq. (2) linearly decreases in time to ensure that after a certain number of steps the network stops training. In the original formulation of the network [10, 15], a neighborhood parameter $h_{si}(t)$ was used. This $h_{si}(t)$ is in contrast to $N_c(t)$, a continuous value modeled by a Gaussian that has a kernel shrinking in time:

$$h_{si} = h_0(t) \exp\left(-\frac{\|r_i - r_s\|}{\sigma(t)^2} \right), \tag{3}$$

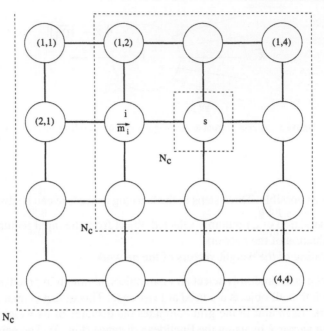

Figure 4 The two-dimensional grid of neurons in the self-organizing map.

where r_i and r_s are the coordinates of the neurons in the grid, and $\|r_i - r_s\|$ is a suitable distance measure between those neurons. For instance, if the coordinates were numbered as in Fig. 4, then the distance between i and s would be $\max(|r_{i_1} - s_{i_1}|, |r_{i_2} - s_{i_2}|)$. The size of the Gaussian function, determined by $\sigma(t)^2$, decreases as the network reaches convergence. The parameter $h_0(t)$ has the same role as the learning parameter $\alpha(t)$ in Eq. (2). The update rule stated in Eq. (2) now changes into

$$\vec{m}_i(t + 1) = h_{si}(t)\big[\vec{x}(t) - \vec{m}_i(t)\big]. \tag{4}$$

After training the network has reached convergence (see [26–30]) and can be used for classification. Here we will use the final values of the neuron weights to compute the interneuron distances [31]. This will make it possible to visualize the scatter of the data set.

Sammon's Projection

Sammon's projection [23] is a nonlinear projection method of maping a high-dimensional space onto a space of lower dimensionality. The algorithm maps the original space onto the projection space in such a way that the interobject distances in the original space are preserved in the projected space, just as in the SOM. However, experiments show that Sammon's algorithm usually outperforms any other mapping algorithm [32].

Let us denote the distance between an object i and an object j in the feature space by d_{ij}^*, and let d_{ij} be the distance between the same objects in the projected space. Sammon's algorithm tries to minimize the following error term, that is, the distortion of the projection:

$$E = \frac{1}{\sum \sum_{i<j} d_{ij}^*} \sum \sum_{i<j} \frac{(d_{ij}^* - d_{ij})^2}{d_{ij}^*}. \tag{5}$$

This equation can be minimized by using, for instance, a gradient descent as proposed by Sammon [23]. Although in principle Sammon's projection is not neural network oriented, it can be modeled by using a neural network as shown by [33].

B. Visualizing the Data Space

Two methods for maping a high-dimensional space onto a low-dimensional one have been introduced. However, to be able to display the structure of the feature space, the visualization of the feature vectors is modified. We do not display the feature vector values when inspecting the SOM, but the feature vector distances. By displaying the distances of the feature vectors of neighboring neurons, one is able to get an indication of how the feature vectors of the objects are distributed. Figure 5 shows a data set (for a description of this set see the experimental section) as it is mapped onto the SOM grid. The distances between the neurons in the grid are depicted as gray values. Because each neuron has eight surrounding neighbors, at least in the two-dimensional grid, eight distances are calculated. The gray value that is finally displayed is the maximum of these distances. Large distances result in a high gray value, and consequently a bright "color" in the map, and small distances result in dark areas in the image. The picture clearly shows a white area across the grid. This indicates that the data are clustered in at least two separable clouds of objects. Note·that because of the high dimensionality of the feature space (ten-dimensional) and the low dimension of the network grid (two-dimensional), the network is not able to show all of the differences between the clusters.

These kinds of images can be obtained from any trained SOM by using the distances of neighboring neurons in the grid [31]. Because the mapping algorithm is topology preserving, neurons that are neighbors in the grid are also expected to represent neighboring clusters of objects. Neurons in the grid at a large distance from each other, in terms of Euclidean distance, are expected to be separated by a large distance in the feature space. Therefore, the SOM can be used to visualize the data separability.

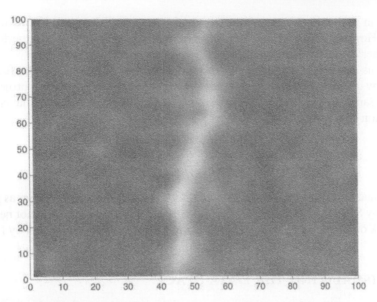

Figure 5   Mapping of the ten-dimensional data on a two-dimensional SOM grid. The data are divided into two parts, just as would be expected.

C. EXPERIMENTS

To judge the method introduced in the previous section, several experiments have been conducted. Here we will examine three experiments; in the tables more experiments are mentioned, two conducted on artificial data sets and one conducted on a real-life data set. More experiments and their results can be found in [31]. The two artificial data sets were used to verify the method because the properties of these sets are well known. The three sets are:

Data set 1: A ten-dimensional data set consisting of two standard normally distributed clusters of 500 objects each. Both sets have as covariances the identity matrix, and have means of $\vec{1}$ and $-\vec{1}$, respectively. They have a small overlap (only 0.078% Bayes error) and are therefore suited to displaying the mapping property of the SOM.

Data set 2: A three-dimensional artificial data set as depicted in Fig. 6. The classes have an equal number of objects (500) and were generated by a standard procedure [31]. As can be observed from the figure, the data have an intrinsic dimension of almost 2; therefore it is expected that they map very well onto the two-dimensional network grid.

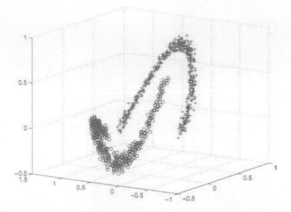

Figure 6   The data set in three dimensions, with an intrinsic dimensionality of 2.

Data set 3:   A real-life data set consisting of the IRIS [34] data. These data are four-dimensional and consist of 150 objects in three classes; each class has an equal number of objects (50).

For each of the data sets 10 different SOMs with different initialization were trained, in order to obtain statistics about the SOM performance. Each of these maps consisted of 100×100 units. Before training all the objects were randomized to cancel out any preferences in the data. Randomization was also performed to be able to cyclically train the data. Furthermore, the maps were trained for 100,000 epochs. The exact experimental conditions can be found in [31].

Figures 5, 7 and 8 show the mapping results for data sets 1, 2, and 3, respectively. The artificial data sets are clearly mapped onto the two-dimensional SOM grid. The white areas denote a large distance between neighboring neurons. The darker an area, the less distance there is between two neighboring neurons. Figure 5 shows a bright white line across the map. This line separates the feature space into separate clusters, which is in agreement with the data, since they consists of two ten-dimensional normally distributed clusters. The same holds for data set 2, which was intrinsically almost two-dimensional. Figure 7 shows that the SOM grid represents the two clusters very well, and indeed extracts its two-dimensional nature. More interesting is to investigate the behavior of the SOM on a real-life data set such as the IRIS set. The mapping shown in Fig. 8 shows the mapping on the IRIS data. Remarkably, only two clusters are detected, whereas the data can be classified into three different classes. When we have a look at the Sammon mapping, shown in Fig. 9, it turns out that two classes are mapped close to each other. Because the Sammon mapping has less distortion than the SOM [32], it can be expected that the SOM shows only two clusters.

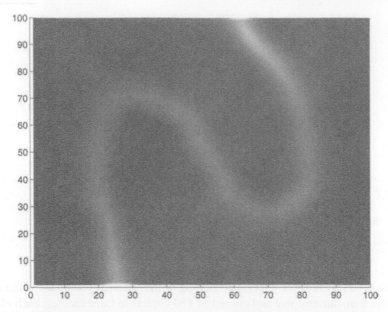

Figure 7   Mapping of the three-dimensional data set on the SOM grid. The intrinsic two-dimensional nature of the data is clearly extracted. The data can be found in Fig. 6.

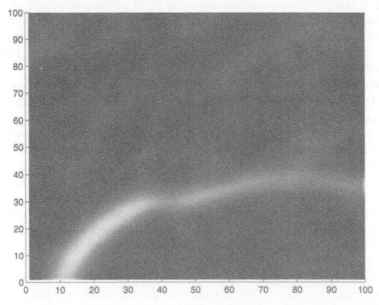

Figure 8   Mapping of the IRIS data on a two-dimensional SOM grid. The data are divided into two parts, whereas the number of classes is three.

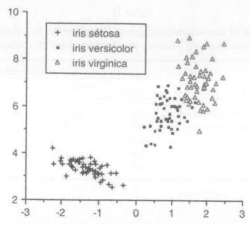

Figure 9 Mapping of the IRIS data set using Sammon's mapping method. Reprinted with permission from M. A. Kraajveld, J. Mao, and A. K. Jain, *IEEE Trans. Neural Networks* 6:548–559, 1995 (©1995 IEEE).

Table I summarizes the distortion of the two mappings for the three data sets. Sammon's projection generally results in less distortion when mapping from the high dimension onto the lower one. However, if the mappings are used for classification, then it shows that the SOM preserves the classes much better than Sammon's mapping. Tables II and III show the classification results from the mappings.

In conclusion, the proposed method indeed shows how separable a set of objects is. However, because of the high dimensionality of certain spaces, information is lost during the nonlinear mapping. The advantage of the visualization

Table I

The Average Sammon Distortion (in %) for the Different Data Sets

		Sammon distortion[a]	
Set	Description	SOM	Sammon
1	Ten-dimensional separated normal clusters	34.6 (1.2)	6.0 (0.1)
2	Two elongated clusters in 3D space	0.51 (0.0)	2.7 (1.2)
3	IRIS data	3.4 (0.4)	0.6 (0.1)
—	16 texture data	42.0 (6.9)	5.7 (0.1)
—	80X data	49.3 (2.2)	5.3 (0.4)

[a] Standard deviations are in parentheses.

Table II

The Average Error of the Nearest-Neighbor Classifier (in %), Estimated with the Leave-One-Out Method and Its Standard Deviation

Set	Description	Classification error		
		Input space	SOM projection[a]	Sammon projection[a]
1	Ten-dimensional normal clusters	0.2	0.3 (0.1)	0.3 (0.1)
2	Two clusters in 3D space	0.0	0.0 (0.0)	0.3 (0.4)
3	IRIS data	4.0	4.1 (0.7)	5.5 (1.8)
—	16 texture data	3.6	4.6 (0.9)	27.0 (2.5)
—	80X data	4.4	4.9 (2.2)	11.8 (4.0)

[a] Standard deviations are in parentheses.

method is that it enables one to actually have a look in the high-dimensional feature space. Neurons separated by a large distance in the map represent objects separated by a large distance in the feature space. The experiments shown in this section indeed confirmed this. Furthermore, the mapping distortion of the SOM is generally worse than Sammon's method (see Table I), but when the map is used as input to a classifier, it performs better.

The method introduced in this section enables us to visually inspect the labeled data located in some feature space. By visual inspection one gets an indication of the separability and therefore an appropriate classifier can be selected to classify the data. For instance, in the case of the IRIS data set, it can clearly be seen that two large clusters exist. This indicates that a simple classifier can be used to sepa-

Table III

The Average Error of the Nearest Mean Classifier (in %), Estimated with the Leave-One-Out Method and Its Standard Deviation

Set	Description	Classification error		
		Input space	SOM projection[a]	Sammon projection[a]
1	Ten-dimensional normal clusters	0.1	3.1 (3.5)	0.1 (0.1)
2	Two clusters in 3D space	13.3	13.5 (0.1)	13.4 (1.2)
3	IRIS data	8.0	6.6 (1.8)	7.7 (1.3)
—	16 texture data	6.5	8.8 (1.4)	28.4 (0.9)
—	80X data	4.4	12.9 (2.2)	16.0 (5.4)

[a] Standard deviations are in parentheses.

rate the "sétosa" from the "versicolor" and "virginica" simultaneously, but a more complex classifier is needed to separate "versicolor" from "virginica" (see also Fig. 9). The next section introduces the concept of confidence values. This enables us, for instance, to select the best classifier from a set of appropriate classifiers.

IV. CLASSIFIER SELECTION

In the previous section we introduced a method for estimating and inspecting the separability of labeled data. Suppose one has found a classifier (for example, a neural network) to separate these data in the feature space. In general there are many classifiers that can be used to build a function that separates the data. A selection must be made from among these classifiers. The problem is, however, deciding on the criterion for selection. In general, a classifier is selected by looking at the empirical error. That is, select the classifier with the lowest empirical error or the one that gives the most reliable estimate of the empirical error. In this section a technique is introduced that can be used to select a classifier based on the reliability of classification.

This reliability of classification, referred to as *confidence*, can be used to judge the classifier's classifications. By evaluating the levels of confidence for the different classifiers, the one in which we have the most confidence can selected as our final classifier. This section only introduces the tools for classifier selection, because at this moment there are no actual results on classifier selection. We do show some experimental results in which the confidence levels were used as a reject criterion.

Confidence values are not restricted to classifier selection, but can also be used to reject objects to increase the performance of a classifier. The confidence can also be used to construct new, multistage classifiers [35–37], based on the confidence assigned to an object by different classifiers. Note that the concept of confidence values holds for a particular classifier and data set; it is highly problem dependent.

This section is divided as follows. Next the concept of confidence values is introduced (what exactly do we define as a confidence value and how can it be computed?). The following subsection deals with the different methods for estimating confidence. Four methods will be introduced that can be used to estimate the confidence of a network classification. These different estimators must be tested by using a test set. However, this constitutes a problem, because independent test sets are hard to get or are not available at all. Subsection IV.C introduces a method for generating validation sets that share the same characteristics as independent test sets. The section ends with the results obtained from several experiments.

A. CONFIDENCE VALUES

When a trained neural network is used to classify an unknown object, one would like to know what the reliability of the classification is, that is, how certain we are the network classification is correct [6, 38–40]. In this section it is shown how the probability that an estimate of the class label is correct can be estimated. The reliability, or confidence, and its corresponding estimators will be introduced next.

Suppose that a network finds a discriminant function $S : \vec{x} \rightarrow \hat{\omega}$. This discriminant function S assigns a class label $\hat{\omega}$ to an object $\vec{x}$. For each object $\vec{x}$ the classification based on S is either correct or incorrect. Therefore, a correctness function $C(\vec{x}, \omega)$ is defined:

$$C(\vec{x}, \omega) = \begin{cases} 1, & \text{if } S(\vec{x}) = \omega \\ 0, & \text{if } S(\vec{x}) \neq \omega \end{cases}, \tag{6}$$

where ω is the true class label of object $\vec{x}$. When an unknown object is classified, the confidence of the estimate of the class label is the probability that the classification is correct. Given a classifier (a feedforward neural network classifier in our case) for an (in general unknown) object, the confidence $q(\vec{x})$ is given by

$$q(\vec{x}) = P\big(C(\vec{x}, \omega) = 1 | \vec{x}\big). \tag{7}$$

The classification confidence is thereby the a posteriori probability for the estimated class. For known distributions and given S, only the errors due to the class overlap as well as those due to imperfect training influence $q(\vec{x})$; therefore it can be expressed as

$$q(\vec{x}) = \frac{P_{\hat{\omega}} f_{\hat{\omega}}(\vec{x})}{f(\vec{x})}, \tag{8}$$

where $f_{\hat{\omega}}$ is the class conditional density function for class $\hat{\omega}$ (the class with the highest a posteriori probability) as a function of the object $\vec{x}$, and $P_{\hat{\omega}}$ is the a priori class probability. The function $f(\vec{x})$ denotes the joint probability density for $\vec{x}$, $f(\vec{x}) = \sum_{\omega} P_{\omega} f_{\omega}(\vec{x})$. However, in practice the distributions of the objects are unknown. Consequently, the confidence $q(\vec{x})$ must be estimated somehow. The next section introduces several possibilities for estimating $q(\vec{x})$.

Assume that $q(\vec{x})$ can be estimated by a $\hat{q}_i(\vec{x})$. Because there are many different $\hat{q}_i(\vec{x})$ possible, a criterion function is needed to compare them. This criterion function J_i is defined as follows:

$$J_i = \frac{1}{N_T} \sum_T \left[C(\vec{x}, \omega) - \hat{q}_i(\vec{x}) \right]^2, \tag{9}$$

where T is an independent test set, N_T is the number of objects in the test set, and the index i is used to indicate the J for the ith estimator used for $q(\vec{x})$. The lower bound of J_i is usually not zero, because of class overlap. However, when the underlying class densities are known, $J_{\min}$ can be determined by substituting Eq. (7) for each object in Eq. (9). The aim is to minimize J_i over different estimators $\hat{q}_i(\vec{x})$ for a certain independent test set, yielding the best estimator for the confidence $q(\vec{x})$.

Using an estimator for the confidence, the classifier we want can be selected. This is, of course, only useful if we have classifiers with the same performance on a test set. Otherwise we would just select that classifier with the best performance on the test set. Suppose the total confidence for a classifier is calculated by averaging $\hat{q}(\vec{x})$ over all objects $\vec{x}$ in the test set:

$$Q_S = \frac{1}{N_T} \sum_{\vec{x} \in T} \hat{q}(\vec{x}), \qquad (10)$$

where the symbols N_T and T have the same meaning as in Eq. (9). If the classifier predicts all of the objects perfectly, Q_S will be 1, because every $\hat{q}(\vec{x}) = 1$. The selection of the best classifier just comes down to selecting $\max(Q_S)$ over all possible classifiers S.

Boosting the performance by using $q(\vec{x})$ can be done by using it as a reject mechanism. By rejecting the objects with a low confidence, the performance increases. This is important, because many applications do not allow a wrong prediction. In these cases it is better to return the object to the operator for a second classification. In the experimental section an application is described in which the confidence was used as a mechanism.

A last possibility is to use the different $q(\vec{x})$ as input to train a new classifier, thus constructing, it is hoped, a more reliable classifier. We will not go into the details of such multistage classifiers; the interested reader is referred to [37].

B. CONFIDENCE ESTIMATORS

Because in real applications parameters such as distributions of the objects and the a priori class probabilities are unknown, there is a need for estimating the confidence values. In the previous section it was discussed how the different estimators can be compared, but it was not explained how such an estimation can be made. Two kinds of estimations are considered: the method used to calculate the estimate and the place in the network where the estimate is calculated.

A feedforward neural network maps the input space on the hidden layer(s) and then on the output layer. Thereby, in the input space as well as the hidden unit space or the output space $q(\vec{x})$ can be estimated by the methods to be described next. Consider the example of two overlapping classes that must be separated by using a quadratic discriminant function. A neural network consisting of two input units, two hidden units, and two output units was trained on the data set as depicted in Fig. 10. Figure 10 also shows the optimal Bayes decision function in the input space. However, if one would consider the hidden unit space, shown in Fig. 11 (left), the classes might be more easily separated and it may therefore be advantageous to estimate $q(\vec{x})$ in that part of the network. As a result the level of training (undertrained or overtrained) of the network determines the layer to estimate in. For sufficiently trained networks, it may be better to estimate $q(\vec{x})$ in layer other than the input space.

Second, there are different methods for estimating the confidence. Here four methods will be introduced that were used in experiments:

1. Network output
2. Nearest-neighbor method

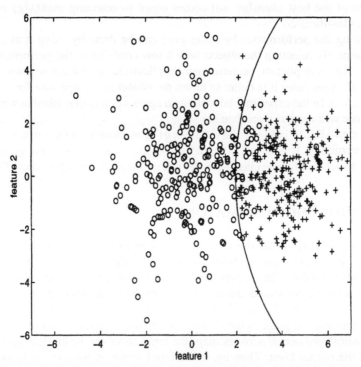

Figure 10   The data set used to train the neural network. The solid line shows the optimal Bayes decision function.

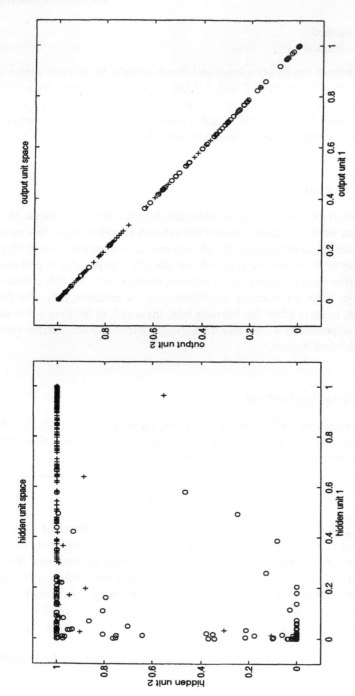

Figure 11 Here the mapping of the objects into the hidden unit and the output unit space is shown. The figure on the left shows how the objects are mapped into the hidden unit space. The figure on the right shows the mapping of the objects in the output unit space.

3. Parzen method
4. Logistic method

Each of the methods has its advantages and disadvantages. In the experiments we restricted ourselves to methods 2 and 4. Method 3 has been extensively tested [41], but appeared to be outperformed by the other methods. However, the Parzen method is suited to detecting outliers and is mentioned for the sake of completeness. Now the methods will be discussed in more detail.

Network Output

This method is the classical way to determine the reliability of a network. However, in general we do not know whether the network is well trained. This means that the a posteriori probabilities of the objects may not be estimated well. Moreover, neural network outputs are generally not directly interpretable as probabilities. This implies postprocessing of the network outputs such that they constitute probabilities or adapt the learning algorithm; see, for instance, [38]. The final thing we want to do is adapt the learning rule, inasmuch as we have given networks. In the experiments we did take the network output into account, because it is a well-established method.

Nearest-Neighbor Method

Given a certain space with a defined measure, for example, the Euclidean distance, the k-nearest-neighbor density estimator (k-NN) can be used to estimate the confidence of the object under consideration:

$$\hat{q}_{knn}(\vec{x}) = \frac{N_{S(\vec{x})=\hat{\omega}}}{k}, \tag{11}$$

where $N_{S(\vec{x}=\hat{\omega})}$ is the number of correctly classified objects among the k-nearest neighbors (that is, the number of objects among the k-nearest neighbors sharing the same label as the object under consideration). Moreover, the more objects "agree" about the label of $\vec{x}$ the more certain we are that the label assignment is correct. If one were to take a 10-NN approach and five neighbors point to class $\mathcal{A}$, whereas the remaining neighbors point to class $\mathcal{B}$, the confidence of the object $\vec{x}$ would be 0.5. A general rule of thumb is to use $k = \sqrt{N_{\mathcal{L}}}$, where $N_{\mathcal{L}}$ is the number of learning objects.

A disadvantage of this method is that it is computationally heavy for large data sets.

Parzen Method

In the Parzen method, first the density functions for the classes are estimated and those estimates are used to estimate $q(\vec{x})$. It is assumed that a fixed Gaussian kernel is used:

$$\hat{f}_\omega(\vec{x}) = \frac{1}{N_{\mathcal{L}_\omega}} \sum_{\vec{x}' \in \mathcal{L}_\omega} (2\pi h^2)^{-d/2} \exp\left(\frac{-D^2(\vec{x}, \vec{x}')}{2h_\omega^2}\right), \tag{12}$$

where $D(\vec{x}, \vec{x}')$ is the Euclidean distance between object $\vec{x}$ and an object $\vec{x}'$ from a subset $\mathcal{L}_\omega$, that is, the set of objects with the same label ω. The dimension of the space in which $q(\vec{x})$ is estimated is denoted as d. Each class has a single kernel $\hat{f}_\omega(\vec{x})$, of which the smoothing factor h_ω must be estimated. This parameter can be determined by using a maximum likelihood estimation over the learning set. Having found the densities for each class, $q(\vec{x})$ can be approximated by

$$\hat{q}_{\text{Parzen}}(\vec{x}) = \frac{P_{\hat{\omega}} \hat{f}_{\hat{\omega}}(\vec{x})}{\hat{f}(\vec{x})}, \tag{13}$$

where $\hat{f}(\vec{x})$ is the estimated joint density function $\hat{f}(\vec{x}) = \sum_\omega P_\omega \hat{f}_\omega(\vec{x})$. Experiments show that the Parzen estimator never outperforms any of the other methods [38, 41]. Therefore, the Parzen estimator was not used in the experiments to be presented in a later section.

Logistic Method

The logistic method [42] was chosen for its simplicity. It is fast because the parameters only need to be calculated once. The logistic method models the conditional class probabilities by using a sigmoid function. For a two-class problem, the probability that $\vec{x}$ belongs to the correct class is given by

$$\hat{q}_{\text{logistic}}(\vec{x}) = P\big(\mathcal{C}(\vec{x}, \omega) = 1 | \vec{x}\big) = \frac{1}{1 + \exp(\vec{\beta}\vec{x} + \beta_0)}, \tag{14}$$

assuming equal prior class probabilities. The parameters to be determined are $\vec{\beta}$ and β_0. The total number of parameters is given by the dimensionality of the space $\vec{\beta}$ plus a bias β_0. They can be estimated by using a learning set and an optimization technique like Newton's method. As stated earlier, Eq. (14) only holds for the two-class case; however, it can be extended to more classes quite easily. This is done by taking one class as a base class, called g, and estimating all of the parameters of the other classes with respect to that base class. Rewriting Eq. (14) for the base class approach results in

$$\hat{q}_{\text{logistic}}(\vec{x}) = \left\{ 1 + \sum_{i=1}^{N_g-1} \exp\left(-\vec{\alpha}_{gi}\vec{x}'\right) \right\}^{-1}, \tag{15}$$

where $\vec{x}' = (\vec{x}, 1)$, α_{gi} is the $(\vec{\beta}, \beta_0)$ for class i with respect to the base class g, and N_g denotes the number of classes present.

C. VALIDATION SETS

In the previous section, three estimation methods for $q(\vec{x})$ were introduced. Each of these estimates should be tested by using an independent test set (see Eq. (9)). Usually these sets are not available or are hard to derive. Moreover, in most practical situations one has only a single set from which a learning set and a test set must be drawn. A possible solution might be to also use the learning set for estimation, but this is an unhealthy situation. Both the classifier and the estimator were found by using the same set, which makes the estimator biased. To overcome this situation we have studied the possibility of generating an artificial validation set. Such a validation set has roughly the same characteristics as the learning set, but is distinctive enough to act as a test set. To create a validation set, the k-NN data generation method [43] was used. The learning set is used as a starting point for creating a new set. Around each object in the learning set, new objects are generated using Gaussian noise around the original object. The objects are generated in such a way that the local probability density is followed. This local probability density is estimated using the k-nearest neighbors around an original object. In the experiments k was chosen to be the dimensionality of the space $+2$. Figure 12 shows the effect of the k-NN data generation method using a learning set.

Note that a validation set will *not* be able to replace an independent test set entirely, but it is an acceptable alternative. Experiments show that the k-NN data generation method generates a validation set that is as reliable in selecting the same estimators and the network layer as an independent test set would be. In the application described below, both a validation set and a test set were used. Many experiments not reported here can be found in [41]. These experiments show the validity of the data generation method for badly trained neural networks.

D. EXPERIMENTS

To test the applicability of the confidence value estimation for classifier selection, several experiments were performed. Here two experiments are reported, one on artificial data showing the influence of the level of training of the classifier

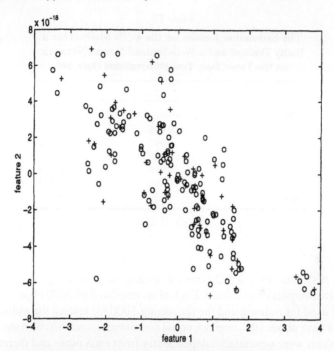

Figure 12   The effect of the k-NN data generation method. Here the validation set is denoted by o and the original set is denoted by +. The original set contained 50 objects, Gaussian distributed around (0, 0). The validation set was generated using five neighbors and consists of 150 objects.

on the place to estimate $q(\vec{x})$. The other experiment is concerned with using the confidence estimator as a reject mechanism. In this experiment real-world data, chromosome banding profiles, were used. Here the confidence was used to improve the performance of the classifier. The first experiment only uses the k-NN method and the network output for estimating the confidence, but estimates the confidence in different parts of the network. In the second experiment the logistic method is also used, and the confidence is used as a reject mechanism. Furthermore, in the real-life problem, the validity of the k-NN data generation method was tested.

Artificial Data

The experiments with an artificial data set were done to show that in some cases it is beneficial to estimate the confidence in a layer other than the input layer. Two data sets were generated: one two-class two-dimensional problem, and one four-class six-dimensional data set.

Table IV

The Estimation Results for the k-NN Method for a Badly Trained and a Well-Trained Neural Network on the Two-Class, Two-Dimensional Data Set

Estimator	J (well)	J (bad)
k-NN		
Input	0.093	0.093
Hidden	0.092	0.094
Output	0.080	0.093
Netout	0.080	0.209
J_{min}	0.080	0.080
Performance	90%	86%

On the first data set a 2-3-2 network architecture (two inputs, three hidden units, and two outputs) was trained. Each class consisted of 2000 objects, of which 1000 were used for training and the remaining 1000 for testing the estimator. The two classes have about 10% overlap, equal covariances, and different means. Note that the objects were generated independently from each other and therefore constitute a valid training set and a valid test set. The network was trained for 10 epochs, resulting in a badly trained network, and for 1000 epochs, resulting in a well-trained network. After the training was stopped, the test set was used to find the best layer in the network for estimating the confidence. In both experiments the k-NN method was used. Table IV shows the results for the two-class experiment.

The J for the different layers of the network where the estimator was used was determined using an independent test set. This test set was also used to calculate the network performance. The confidence itself was computed from the training set. Because the distribution of the objects is known, J_{min} can be estimated. The results of the k-NN estimator can be compared against this value. For the well-trained network this shows that the best layer to estimate $q(\vec{x})$ is the output space. Because the network is trained well, it best approximates the a posteriori probabilities in the output space. This is also shown by the *netout* values. These are the actual outputs of the network used as estimator. For a badly trained network the selection is unclear. None of the layers shows a dominance; it is unclear which layer the $q(\vec{x})$ can be best estimated. Using the network outputs in this case is certainly a bad decision. Because of the low level of training of the network, the a posteriori probabilities are not approximated very well.

The second experiment involved a 6-15-4 architecture. Again, the network was trained such that we obtained a well-trained and a badly trained network. Because

Table V

**The Estimation Results for the k-NN Method for a
Badly Trained and a Well-Trained Neural Network
on the Four-Class Six-Dimensional Data Set**

Estimator	J (well)	J (bad)
k-NN		
Input	0.170	0.146
Hidden	0.175	0.154
Output	0.171	0.149
Netout	0.173	0.210
J_{min}	0.149	0.129
Performance	73%	55%

of the higher dimension of the data, 2000 objects for training and 2000 objects for testing were used. Again the k-NN method was used in different layers of the network. Table V summarizes the results.

Because of the high dimensionality and number of classes, the optimal performance is much less than in the first experiment. More remarkable is the fact that, in contrast to the previous experiment, in the badly trained situation there is a clear preference for a layer (the input space). This is the consequence of the larger number of classes. In general, the J_{min} will increase for more than two classes, because in regions with overlapping classes, very bad classification yields lower values for J. However, both experiments do show that selecting a layer other than the input layer may be beneficial.

Chromosome Data

A normal human cell contains 46 chromosomes, which can be divided into 24 groups. There are 22 pairs of so-called autosomes and two sex chromosomes. The chromosomes have different features that can be used for classification like length, centromere position, and banding pattern. In this classification problem we only take the banding pattern into account. This banding pattern is sampled and then fed to a neural network for classification. Figure 13 shows a chromosome and its corresponding banding profile.

The sampling of a chromosome band resulted in 30 features (that is, 30 samplings per band), which are used for classification of a chromosome. Earlier studies indicate that this is a reasonable value to take [44]. Consequently, a neural network consisting of 30 input neurons and 24 output neurons (one for each class) was used. The number of hidden units, however, is still arbitrarily chosen and was

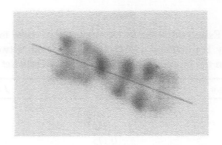

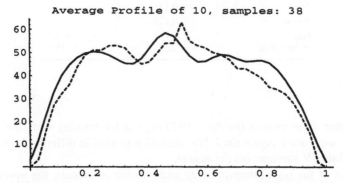

Figure 13 A chromosome and its corresponding profile. At top a gray-value image of a chromosome is shown, the profile on the bottom is derived by sampling the chromosome along the line drawn in the chromosome. Note that the banding profile (on the right dashed line) is obtained by averaging over 38 chromosome profiles of class 10. The solid line shows a single chromosome profile of class 10.

set to 100, a number derived from earlier experiments [44]. For training the network a total set of 32,000 training objects was used; the same number of objects was used for testing the network. Furthermore, each object was scaled between 0 and 1.

Network training was done for 200 epochs with momentum and adaptive learn rate. The momentum term was set to 0.7; the initial learn rate was set to 0.1. Each time the mean squared error of the network increased by 10%, the learn rate was halved. After training the network performance was 85% on the learning set and 83.5% on the test set (see also Table VI). Two estimators plus the output of the network were used for the estimation of the confidence values. Table VI, published earlier in [45], states the different values of J that were found for the different estimators. Furthermore, the k-NN and the logistic estimator were also applied in different parts of the network to estimate the confidence.

Table VI shows that the k-NN estimator in the output space has the best score over all of the different sets. The logistic estimator performs worse in the out-

Table VI

The J of the Estimators for Different Estimators and in Different Parts of the Network, Trained on the Chromosome Data Set

Used set	Learning set with l.o.o. est.[a]	Validation set	Test set
Estimator	J	J	J
k-NN			
Input	0.167	0.165	0.161
Hidden	0.119	0.119	0.119
Output	0.086	0.088	0.095
Logistic			
Input	0.140	0.141	0.141
Hidden	0.692	0.692	0.694
Output	0.147	0.150	0.158
Netout	0.482	0.479	0.474
Avg. SD (J)	0.001	0.001	0.001
Class perf.	85.0%	84.5%	83.5%

[a]l.o.o., leave-one-out estimation method.

Reprinted with permission from A. Hoekstra, S. A. Tholen, and R. P. W. Duin, "Estimating the reliability of neural network classifications," *Proceedings of the ICANN 96*, p. 57, 1996 (©1996 Spinger-Verlag).

put space than in the input space. Furthermore, the network's output is not very useful as an estimator for the confidence. This is due to the fact that the network has trained for only 200 epochs. The data generation method was also tested. The resulting validation set shows no advantage over using the learning set.

Now that we have the different estimators, these estimators can be used for rejecting objects. An obvious method is to first reject the objects with the lowest confidence. This way we can prevent accepting classifications with the risk of a high error. Considering Table VI it was expected that the k-NN estimator would have the best performance, which is indeed the case. In Fig. 14 the performance of the different estimators is depicted. Note that the lowest performance of the network is 83.5% when rejecting 0% of the objects. The performance of the network increases fast when rejecting objects. For a 90% performance only 13% of the objects must be rejected, that is, about 4,000 objects of the 32,000.

To summarize, the confidence values are useful for judging a classifier. By calculating the confidence levels for the objects in different parts of the classifier, an indication can be gained of the reliability of the classification made by the

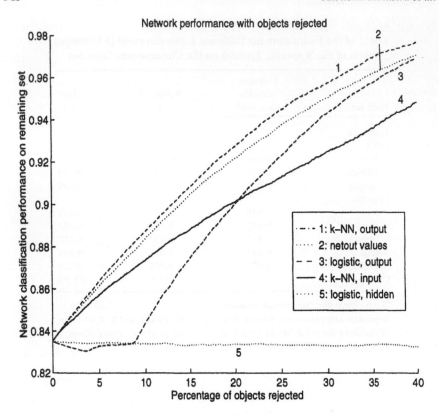

Figure 14 Network performance on the remaining test set as a function of rejected test objects, for several estimators.

network. Furthermore, in the real-life application, chromosome banding profile classification, it was shown that the confidence level can be used as a method for improving the classifier performance. By rejecting a small number of objects, those with the lowest confidence, the performance is increased significantly.

Although we have not shown any experiments on classifier selection, we do have a tool for judging the classifier. This confidence of the classifier can be used in various ways, as shown in the experiments. The next step is to train a classifier on a particular problem. This is quite hard, because we are interested in an optimal classifier, that is, one that is not overtrained. The next sections deal with this problem of classifier training.

V. CLASSIFIER NONLINEARITY

The previous sections explained how data can be analyzed and how trained classifiers can be selected for a particular problem. In this section we go into the details of classifier training. Moreover, the concept of nonlinearity in classifier training will be introduced. A strong point of neural classifiers is their ability to implement almost any classification function [46, 47]. However, this is also a weak point, because this means that one must be very careful not to select a classifier that implements a good function on the learning set but a bad one on the test set. Overtrained classifiers are expected not to generalize very well [48–50], which makes such a classifier useless for solving the classification problem [40, 51].

Overtraining can be studied by inspecting an estimate of the generalization. Whenever this estimate reaches a certain value, one might consider the classifier as well trained, and stop further training. Here the shape of the classification function implemented by the network is related to the overtraining behavior. This will be referred to as nonlinearity of the classifier. It is expected that overtrained classifiers show a larger nonlinearity than optimal ones. Moreover, the nonlinearity is also applicable to traditional classifiers (e.g., k-nearest-neighbor classifier), which makes it possible to judge neural networks versus traditional classifiers on given data. The nonlinearity measure presented in this section is closely related to the well-known complexity measures like the Vapnik–Chervonenkis (VC) [52, 53] dimension. This VC dimension gives a bound on the capacity of a classifier related to its architecture, for instance, the number of hidden neurons. The difference with the nonlinearity measure, however, is that the VC dimension is used without any knowledge about the data to be classified. Given a network, the VC dimension can be calculated and its maximum capacity is known. Here we are interested in the actual behavior of the classifier on the data.

In the next section the nonlinearity measure is introduced; this measure is quite computationally intensive, and therefore an estimation procedure is also presented. After that, a number of experiments will be studied for two-dimensional problems, as this enables us to illustrate the nonlinearities with the classification functions themselves and to show how this is related to the overtraining behavior of a neural classifier.

A. A NONLINEARITY MEASURE

As stated earlier, the classifier adapts itself to the data; therefore we relate the nonlinearity of a classifier to the data it has to classify. Consequently, nonlinearities that are not observed in the classification result are not interesting because these do not contribute. This can be the case for the behavior of the classifier in areas where no data are present or on a small scale between objects, but without influencing their classification.

Figure 15, derived from [54], shows a set of objects and two classifiers S_1 and S_2. The behavior of both classifiers is the same for objects in a remote area of the data space. In that case, the two classifiers are interchangeable—objects are classified the same for S_1 and S_2. Moreover, for remote objects it holds that a linear combination of objects (i.e., their feature vectors) sharing the same classification results in a linear combination of the outputs. That is, all interpolated objects have the same classification. This situation changes for objects located near the classifier. Consider again Fig. 15. Objects that lie between y_1 and y_2 have the same classification with respect to classifier S_1. However, objects that lie on a linear interpolation between y_1 and y_3 (or x_1 and x_2, depicted by the dotted lines) do not share the same classification. Here a fraction of the interpolated objects is assigned to a class different from that of y_1 (or y_3), depicted by the heavy dashed line in Fig. 15. In other words, here a nonlinearity of the classifier S_1 is observed. If one were to choose S_2, none of the nonlinearities observed with respect to the data and the classifier earlier would occur. Note that the relation of the classifier and the data is of particular importance. Suppose the objects $x_1, \ldots, x_3$ and

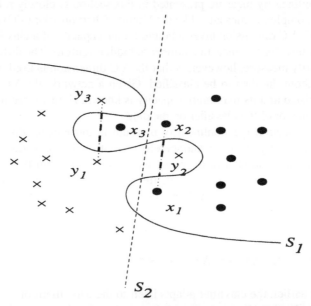

Figure 15 A highly nonlinear and a linear decision function on a set of objects. Reprinted with permission from A. Hoekstra and R. P. W. Duin, "On the nonlinearity of pattern classifiers," *Proceedings of the 13th ICPR, Vienna*, Vol. 3, 1996 (©1996 IEEE Comput. Soc.).

$y_1, \ldots, y_3$ are removed; then the nonlinearity of S_1 will not be observed, because all objects and their linear interpolations share the same classification.

These observations lead to the following definition of nonlinearity: The nonlinearity $\mathcal{N}$ of a classifier S with respect to a data set $\mathcal{L}$ is the probability that an arbitrary object, uniformly and linearly interpolated between two arbitrary objects in the data set with the same classification, does not share this classification. This definition of nonlinearity is independent of the true class labels of the objects, because only the classification made by the classifier is taken into account. Moreover, because of the independence of the true class labels, the nonlinearity is also independent of the classifier performance. However, it does depend on the data set used to train the classifier. Now the nonlinearity of a classifier is introduced more formally.

First we define the nonlinearity of a classifier S with respect to two objects x_k and x_l sharing the same classification, for example, x_1 and x_2 in Fig. 15. The following definition defines $n(\bar{x})$, the nonlinearity for two objects:

$$n(\bar{x}) = n((x_k, x_l)) = \frac{1}{\|x_k - x_l\|} \int_0^1 S_\Delta\big(\alpha x_k + (1 - \alpha)x_l, x_k\big)d\alpha, \qquad (16)$$

where $\bar{x} = (x_k, x_l)$ a pair of objects with the same classification. The term $1/\|x_k - x_l\|$ is used to normalize for the distance between two objects. Between the objects x_k and x_l, a linear interpolation is done by $\alpha x_k + (1 - \alpha)x_l$. Each of the objects in the interpolation is checked against the class of x_k using S_Δ:

$$S_\Delta(a, b) = \begin{cases} 0, & \text{if } S(a) \equiv S(b) \\ 1, & \text{otherwise} \end{cases}. \qquad (17)$$

Consequently, if all interpolated objects share the same classification, no nonlinearity is observed and therefore the nonlinearity will be zero. Any change in classification increases the nonlinearity, and the size of the increment is determined by the fraction of differently classified objects.

Now the nonlinearity of S with respect to a data set $\mathcal{L}$ can be defined by using the definition of $n(\bar{x})$:

$$\mathcal{N}(\mathcal{L}, S) = \frac{1}{\sum_{i=1}^M |\mathcal{L}^i \times \mathcal{L}^i|} \sum_{i=1}^M \sum_{\substack{\bar{x} \in \mathcal{L}^i \times \mathcal{L}^i \\ x_k \neq x_l}} n(\bar{x}), \qquad (18)$$

where $\mathcal{N}(\mathcal{L}, S)$ is the nonlinearity of a classifier with respect to a data set, and $\mathcal{L}^i$ is the set of objects sharing the same classification. This is needed because we interpolate between objects of the same assigned class label. The nonlinearity $\mathcal{N}(\mathcal{L}, S)$ is calculated by interpolation between all possible pairs of objects in the data set, provided that they have the same assigned class labels.

Depending on the required accuracy, the calculation of Eq. (16) and (18) requires a huge number of computations. This gets even worse when we calculate the nonlinearity at different stages of the training phase of the classifier. An algorithm was constructed that uses a Monte Carlo estimation to approximate $\mathcal{N}(\mathcal{L}, \mathcal{S})$:

1. Classify all objects according to the classifier $\mathcal{S}$.
2. Randomly draw n objects x_k from the data set $\mathcal{L}$.
3. Find for each x_k a corresponding x_l with the same classification label, that is, create an $\bar{x}$.
4. Randomly generate n α's, where $0 \leq \alpha \leq 1$ (for each pair $\bar{x}$ an α is drawn).
5. Compare the classification $\mathcal{S}(\alpha x_k + (1 - \alpha)x_l)$ with $\mathcal{S}(x_k)$, and count as nonlinearity if they are not classified in the same class. Do this for all pairs $\bar{x}$.
6. $\mathcal{N}(\mathcal{L}, \mathcal{S})$ is now determined by the number of nonlinearity counts divided by n.

B. EXPERIMENTS

To observe the nonlinearity behavior of classifiers and to relate that to their generalization behavior, several experiments were conducted. Moreover, one experiment shows the nonlinearity behavior of a traditional classifier. This classifier yields a stable nonlinearity and can therefore serve as a reference for the neural classifier in the experiment, because a neural classifier yields a nonstable nonlinearity. The data sets used were two-dimensional, to be able to visually inspect the behavior. The nonlinearity measure, however, is not restricted to these cases.

Nearest-Neighbor Classifier

In Fig. 16 the data set is depicted that was used to train a k-nearest-neighbor classifier. This data requires a high nonlinear decision function, but is perfectly separable. First the optimal k and its corresponding $\mathcal{N}$ were calculated. Second, the $\mathcal{N}$ for different k was determined.

The optimal k showed to be 1, which is not surprising. If k is large, meaning taking into account many neighbors, the separation between the two classes will not be observed. Figure 16 [54] shows the one nearest neighbor on the data set, its nonlinear nature clearly shown. The corresponding $\mathcal{N}$ was calculated and turned out to be 0.11, indicating a high nonlinearity.

In Fig. 17 [54] the results for the other experiment are shown. The nonlinearity of the nearest neighbor decreases when k becomes larger. This implies that the

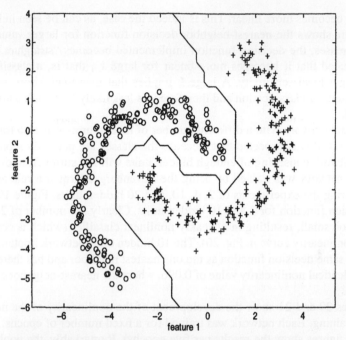

Figure 16 The data set with no overlap and requiring a highly nonlinear decision function. Also depicted is the decision function implemented by the 1 nearest-neighbor classifier, which is optimal in this case. Reprinted with permission from A. Hoekstra and R. P. W. Duin, "On the nonlinearity of pattern classifiers," *Proceedings of the 13th ICPR, Vienna*, Vol. 3, 1996 (©1996 IEEE Comput. Soc.).

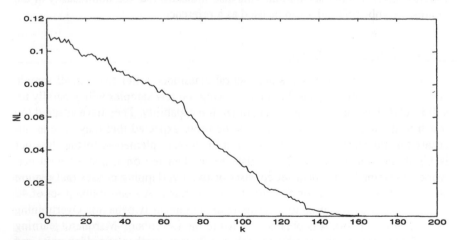

Figure 17 The nonlinearity behavior for the k nearest-neighbor classifier, for different k. Reprinted with permission from A. Hoekstra and R. P. W. Duin, "On the nonlinearity of pattern classifiers," *Proceedings of the 13th ICPR, Vienna*, Vol. 3, 1996 (©1996 IEEE Comput. Soc.).

classifier becomes more linear. This is indeed the case, as can be seen in Fig. 18. This figure shows the nearest-neighbor decision function for larger values of k. As k increases, the decision function implemented becomes "straighter." It can be concluded that it becomes more linear for large k , that is, a classifier that has a larger local sensitivity. A large k implies that many neighbors are taken into account for classification and therefore it is less likely that nonlinearities are observed.

A neural network with a different number of hidden units was also trained on this data set. It was expected that, because the classes are perfectly separable, a neural network consisting of enough hidden units will not suffer from overtraining. The network was trained by using the Levenberg–Marquardt rule and consisted during the experiments of 2, 4, 10, and 20 hidden units. Figure 19 shows the decision function for 2 and 10 hidden units. Clearly the number of 2 hidden units is too small, resulting in a weakly nonlinear classifier (which is confirmed by the nonlinearity curve in Fig. 20). The 10 hidden units network implements almost the same decision function as the one nearest neighbor and has therefore an almost identical nonlinearity value of 0.096, where the nearest-neighbor classifier had 0.11.

Figures 20 and 21 show the development of the nonlinearity of the networks during training. Each network was trained for a fixed number of epochs, namely 150 (the figures show the results per five epochs). Remarkably, the nonlinearity of the larger neural network starts high, and then stabilizes to a lower nonlinearity value. Probably the best network is already found in an early stage of the training. Inspection of the decision function at that early stage indeed shows that this function gives a better separation. This also indicates that the nonlinearity of the nearest-neighbor classifier can be used as a reference.

Neural Network Classifier

Like almost any other classifier, neural classifiers suffer from small sample size problems. Building the classifier by using too few samples will generally result in classifiers having a poor generalization capability. They have adapted too much to the noise in the data set. It is therefore expected that they have an increased nonlinearity, because the decision function implemented by the classifier is highly nonlinear. In Fig. 22 the data set is depicted on which a neural network was trained. This data set consists of two overlapping classes that require at least a quadratic decision function to be separated. A small training set of 40 samples per class was used to investigate the nonlinearity behavior. Overtraining in the neural network was obtained by using the Levenberg–Marquardt learning rule. This learning rule, combined with a sufficient number of hidden units and a small number of examples, leads relatively quickly to an overtrained network. The overtraining is desirable because the nonlinearity of the classifier during the

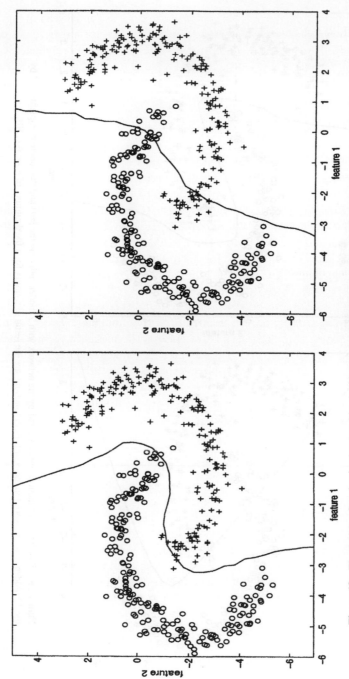

Figure 18 The decision function implemented by the 80 nearest-neighbor classifier (on the left) and the function implemented by the 140 nearest neighbor (on the right).

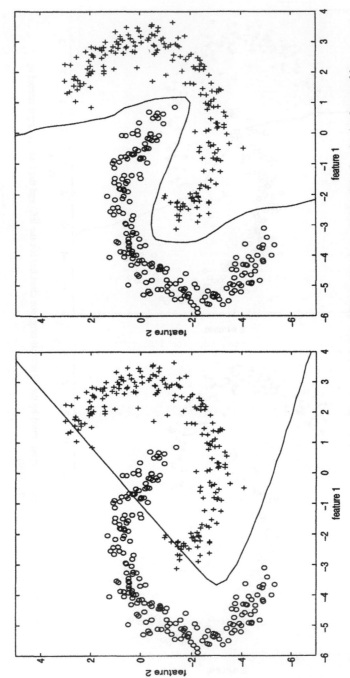

Figure 19 The decision functions implemented by the network with 2 hidden units (on the left) and the function implemented by the 10 hidden units network (on the right). Both functions are the result of training for a fixed number of epochs (150).

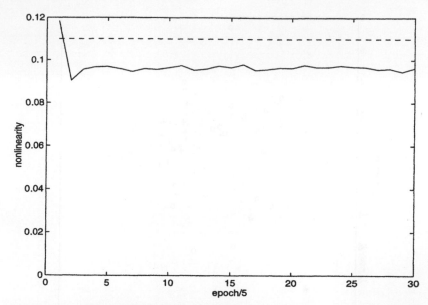

Figure 20 The nonlinearity development of the neural network with 10 hidden units. The dotted line shows the nonlinearity value for the 1 nearest-neighbor classifier. The nonlinearity quickly stabilizes to a high nonlinear value, indicating a highly nonlinear decision function.

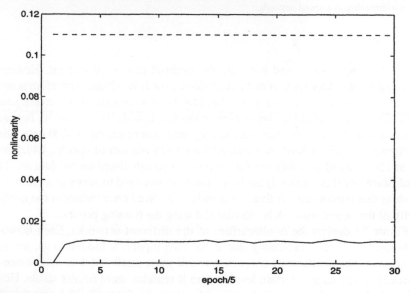

Figure 21 The nonlinearity development of the neural network with 2 hidden units. The dotted line shows the nonlinearity value for the 1 nearest-neighbor classifier. The nonlinearity quickly stabilizes to a low nonlinear value, indicating a more or less quadratic decision function.

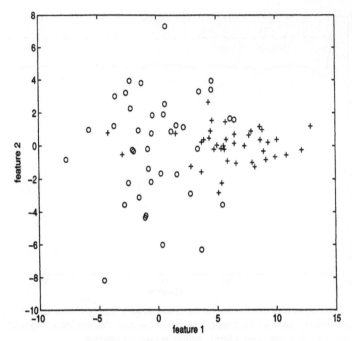

Figure 22 Two overlapping classes, requiring a quadratic decision function, but which can easily cause overtraining in a neural network.

whole learning process and not only the optimal case is of interest. However, the number of hidden units is difficult to determine beforehand. Therefore several neural networks with different sizes of hidden layer were trained and investigated. Six different sizes of hidden layer were inspected: 2, 4, 8, 10, 20, and 30. For each of these neural networks their nonlinearity was computed on 10,000 data pairs. Furthermore, each network was trained for a fixed number of epochs, which was set at 150. A quadratic decision function was also calculated on the data set. The nonlinearity of this (optimal) decision function was used to serve as a reference, because this nonlinearity is fixed. It is only calculated once, whereas the nonlinearity of the neural network is calculated during the training process.

Figure 23 depicts the nonlinearities of the different networks. Each network is denoted by 2-X-1, indicating that it has two inputs, X hidden units, are one output unit. The nonlinearity for each network starts small and then almost monotonically increases to a certain level, where it remains more or less stable. However, this does not occur in all situations, for instance, for the 2-20-1 network, the nonlinearity continues to increase and does not reach a stable point. When these curves are compared with the error curves for the networks (see Fig. 25), it turns

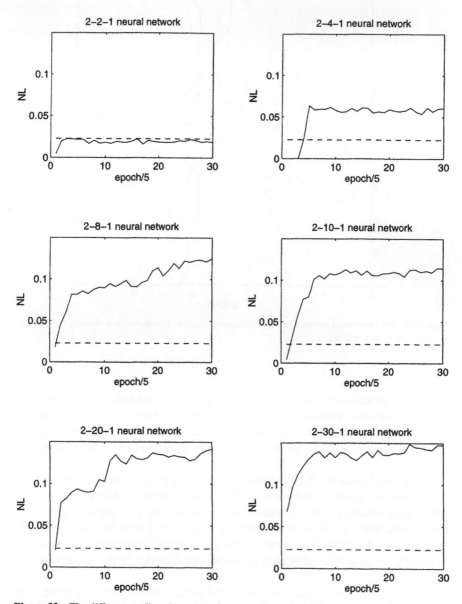

Figure 23 The different nonlinearity curves for networks with a different number of hidden units. The dashed line is the nonlinearity of the quadratic classifier, which is stable for each epoch.

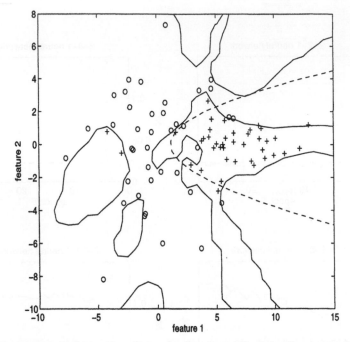

Figure 24 An overtrained network on the overlapping classes. The dashed line denotes the optimal, quadratic decision function.

out that the nonlinearity increases with increasing generalization error. Moreover if the test set error remains almost constant the nonlinearity also remains stable. Hence the nonlinearity is an indicator for the network's local sensitivity. A small local sensitivity results in a small training error, in general zero, and a large nonlinearity.

Figure 24 depicts the 2-20-1 network's decision function and the optimal decision function using a quadratic classifier. This network is clearly in a severely overtrained situation, which implies a high nonlinearity. Compared to the "optimal" nonlinearity, it is about 6 times higher. The network with 20 hidden units has far too much flexibility. For instance, the 2-2-1 neural network has just enough flexibility, because its nonlinearity is almost equal to that of the quadratic classifier.

In Fig. 25 the error curves for the 2-20-1 neural network are displayed. It is clear that the network reaches an overtrained situation because of the increasing test set error and zero training error. This behavior of the generalization curve is reflected in the nonlinearity curve. Up to epoch 50, $\mathcal{N}$ gradually increases just as the test set error; at about epoch 50 there is a large increase in nonlinearity and a

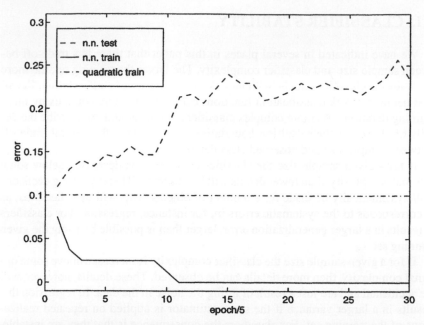

Figure 25 This figure shows the error curves for the 2-20-1 neural network and the quadratic classifier. For the neural network both the generalization error (dashed line) and the learning set error (solid line) are depicted.

relatively large increase in the test set error. The apparent error behaves the other way around—at epoch 50 it drops to a lower level, resulting in a test set error increase.

To conclude, training a neural network classifier results in a classifier that starts as a linear one and gradually increases to a highly nonlinear one. Experiments show that if the generalization error stabilizes, the nonlinearity also reaches a stable point. However, this behavior strongly depends on initial conditions, such as sample size, learning algorithm, and network size. The larger the neural network, the more flexibility it has and the higher its nonlinearity will be if no precautions are taken. However, because a traditional classifier yields a stable nonlinearity, it is possible to measure the performance of a neural network with respect to that classifier.

Another problem in classifier training is that due to initialization, and learning that the classifier might be unstable. That is, during training its decision boundary is frequently changing, such that no stable classification is obtained. The next section deals with this problem.

VI. CLASSIFIER STABILITY

We have indicated in several places in this paper that there is a trade-off between sample size and classifier complexity. The larger the training set, the more complex the classifiers can be without risking overtraining or noise fitting. Recall that neural network classification functions can be made more complex by more training iterations. As more complex classifiers are better able to describe the details of classes or their decision boundaries, we have here the natural trade-off between sample size and observed class detail.

If for a given sample size the classifier complexity is decreased below some optimal complexity, then fewer details will be observed. Thereby wrong decisions will systematically be made for a number of objects. This will be called *bias*, as it corresponds to the systematic errors in, for instance, regression. For classifiers it results in a larger generalization error, larger than is possible by using the given training set.

If for a given sample size the classifier complexity is increased above some optimal complexity, then more details can be observed. These details, however, will be accidental and are just a result of fitting the noise in the data. In regression this results in a larger variance if the same estimator is applied on repeated realizations of the training set. For classifiers the consequence is that they are instable, that is, one and the same test object has a large probability of being classified into a different class for small variations of the training set. This is the bias–variance dilemma [55, 56] encountered in choosing the complexity of the classifier.

The concept of classifier instability has been studied before by one of the authors [57]. It is defined here as the probability that an arbitrary object is changed in classification by some small disturbance of the classifier. This might be another initialization or the addition or deletion of a single training object. In the next section we will discuss a way to measure the instability using the training set, illustrated by some experiments. Thereafter we will go into the issue of finding good stabilizers and the consequence for the classification error.

A. An Estimation Procedure for Stability

As we are interested in investigating stabilizing techniques, we need to measure the stability (or the instability) of classifiers. In this section a possible estimating procedure will be discussed. This will be illustrated by the relation between the performance and the instability of some linear classifiers. Our procedure for the estimation of the instability of a classifier has the following steps:

1. Use the entire training set for computing the classifier S_0.
2. Compute a large set of classifiers S_i $(i = 1, 2, \ldots, n)$ using one and the same modified training procedure. Possibilities are:

- Delete one training sample and rotate over the entire set (leave-one-out procedure).
- Bootstrap the training set (that is, sample with withdrawal). Bootstrapped training sets are as large as the original set but may contain copies for some samples, whereas other samples are not represented.
- Use different initializations for the classifier optimization.

3. Compute the average different classification between S_0 and the classifiers S_i, averaged over the n classifiers S_i and the test set. For this test set the following might be used:

- the original training set
- a truly independent test set
- an artificially generated test set as discussed in Section IV.C

In the last step of this procedure we just count the number of different estimated classification labels. The true labels (if known) are not used. Thereby the size of the probability mass that is changed from classification is found. The classification error itself might be unaffected. The instability is a probability and thereby a number between 0 and 1. It may show a large variation from classifier to classifier. Therefore a large number of different classifiers (e.g., [24]) might be needed to get a reliable estimate. If the classifier training procedure is computationally heavy, like some neural network optimizers, the computation of the instability might become prohibitive.

An instability of zero points to an entirely stable classifier: no changes in the individual classification results whatsoever. Such a number can only be expected for very separable classes or for very bad classifiers that assign all samples to the same class. At the other end, an instability of 1 is only possible if all samples change classification, which is very improbable. As a result, for many situations the instability will clearly stay away from these two extreme values.

An example is presented in Fig. 26, originally published in [58]. It shows the instability based on 50 bootstrapped versions of a set of linear classifiers on the same 30-dimensional Gaussian problem as a function of the size of the training set. In the left graph of Fig. 26 the estimate is based on an independent test set, and for the right graph in Fig. 26 the training set itself is used. The absolute numbers differ, but the relative behavior over the classifiers is preserved. The classifiers used in this experiment are the Nearest Mean Classifier (NMC), the Pseudo Fisher Linear Discriminant (PFLD) (see [59]), the Small Sample Size Classifier (SSSC) (see [59]), a linear discriminant based on a Karhunen–Loève Feature Selection (KLLC), and a regularized version of the Fisher Linear Discriminant (RFLD) (see [60]).

The generalization error of this experiment is presented in Fig. 27. One can observe that the performance and stability of classifiers are related—more stable classifiers perform better. In general, the instability of a classifier depends on

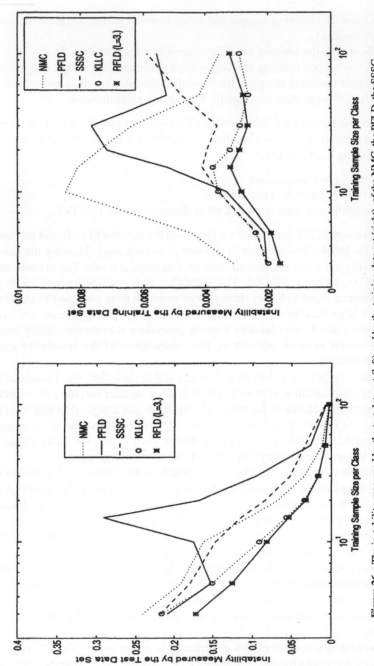

Figure 26 The instability measured by the test data set (left) and by the training data set (right), of the NMC, the PFLD, the SSSC, the KLLC, and the RFLD ($L = \lambda = 3$) for 30-dimensional Gaussian correlated data versus the training sample size.

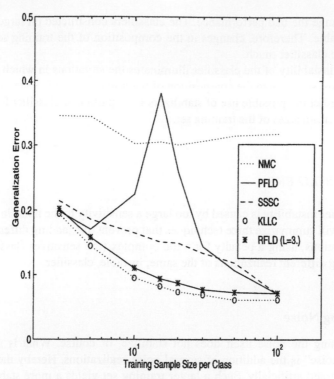

Figure 27 The generalization error of the NMC, the PFLD, the SSSC, the KLLC, and the RFLD ($\lambda = 3$) versus the training sample size for 30-dimensional Gaussian correlated data.

many factors, such as the complexity of the classifier, the distribution of data used to construct the classifier, and the sensitivity of the classifier to the size and the composition of the training data set. For different classifiers the instability shows a different behavior as a function of the training sample size. All classifiers are most unstable for small sizes of the training data set. After the number of training samples is increased above the critical value (the data dimensionality), the classifiers become more stable and their generalization error decreases. Only the Nearest Mean Classifier is an exception; it is almost insensitive to the number of training samples (see experiments in the following sections). In spite of becoming more stable with an increasing training set, its generalization error does not change much. The peaking of the Pseudo Fisher Linear Discriminant is discussed in [59].

The instability measured by the training data set (right figure of Fig. 26) increases for larger training sets, at least for the numbers studied here. Any classifier built on a very small training set is bad. So the changes in the training data set do not change the bad performance. The classifiers constructed on large sets are already stable. Therefore, changes in the composition of the training set do not change the classifier much.

As the instability of the classifier illuminates the situations in which the classifier is most sensitive to the composition of the training set, this instability could help to predict the possible use of stabilizers for a particular classifier for certain data and certain sizes of the training set.

B. STABILIZERS

Classifier instability is caused by too large a sensitivity to the noise in the data. Here we will summarize three techniques that prevent this: adding different noise generalizations, using a penalty for a too complex (too sensitive) classifier, and combining different realizations of the same, instable, classifier.

Adding Noise

Increasing the noise itself does not stabilize, of course. What is meant by "adding noise" is the addition of several noise realizations. Hereby the training set is enlarged artificially. Such a larger training set yields a more stable classifier. Sometimes it appears to be possible to add the noise in an analytic way. This holds for classifiers that are based on noise estimators. For instance, in the Fisher Linear Discriminant the covariance of the noise is estimated. This estimator $\hat{\mathcal{G}}$ can be made more robust by replacing it by

$$\hat{\mathcal{G}}_R = \hat{\mathcal{G}} + \lambda I, \tag{19}$$

in which I is the unity matrix and λ is some small constant (e.g., 0.1). In Figs. 26 and 27 a regularized version of the Fisher Linear Discriminant, RFLD, is used with $\lambda = 0.3$. In Figs. 28 and 29, the error and the instability of this classifier are shown as a function of λ.

These figures, borrowed from [57, 58], show that a large regularization parameter λ really stabilizes. They also show that for a large value of λ the classifier approaches the Nearest Mean Classifier (NMC), which is more stable, but performs worse for increasing sample sizes, as it is insensitive for covariances. Generally, this is the character of the technique of adding noise: it simplifies the structure of the problem.

This addition of noise is heavily used in neural network training procedures. In this area this concept is also used for adding noise to the weights or to the weight

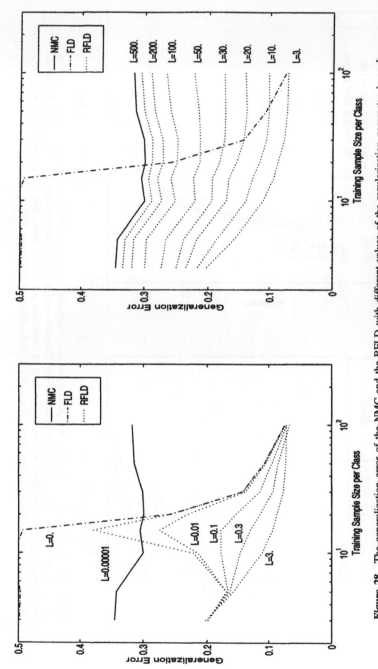

Figure 28 The generalization error of the NMC and the RFLD with different values of the regularization parameter $\lambda = L$ versus the training sample size for 30-dimensional Gaussian correlated data. Reprinted with permission from M. Skurichina and R. P. W. Duin, "Stabilizing classifiers for very small sample sizes," *Proceedings of the 13th ICPR, Vienna,* Vol. 2, 1996 (©1996 IEEE Comput Soc.).

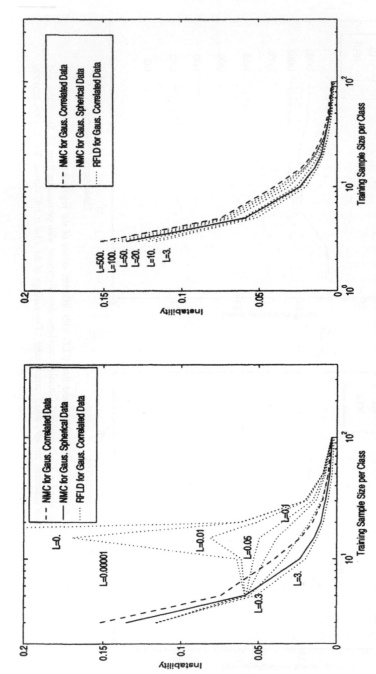

Figure 29 The instability of the RFLD with different values of the regularization parameter $\lambda = L$ for 30-dimensional Gaussian correlated data and the NMC instability for 30-dimensional Gaussian correlated and 30-dimensional Gaussian spherical data versus the training sample size. Reprinted with permission from M. Skurichina and R. P. W. Duin, "Stabilizing classifiers for very small sample sizes," *Proceedings of the 13th ICPR, Vienna,* Vol. 2, 1996 (©1996 IEEE Comput Soc.).

updates. The consequences of such procedures are hard to analyze mathematically. Both sides, the data as well as the classifier, are affected.

Weight Decay

Weight decay is a typical example of stabilizing by a simplification of the classification procedure. It is used in neural network training by penalizing large weights. As large weights correspond to large nonlinearities, they also correspond with complex and thereby noise-sensitive classifiers. An experimental analysis is computationally heavy, as both training and bootstrapping are very time consuming. The verification that weight decay stabilizes must therefore be skipped here.

An interesting observation on weight decay has been made by Raudys [61]. The use of a negative weight decay causes an "antiregularization," which might be helpful for finding better neural network classifiers (see also [62]). In our context this can be understood to mean that an increase in the instability might be useful for improving too stable classifiers like the Nearest Mean Classifier, as discussed in the next section.

Bagging

A third possible way of stabilizing might be to accept classifier instability, but to collect and combine a number of classifiers for the same problem in such a way that the combined result is better. A well-known technique is to combine neural networks derived from different initializations. Another, systematic approach has been proposed by Breiman [63], which is called bagging. It is based on bootstrapping and aggregating concepts.

In the case of linear classifiers, bagging can be implemented by averaging the parameters (coefficients) of the classifiers built on several bootstrap replicates. From each bootstrap replicate of the data set, a "bootstrap" version of the classifier is built. The average of these "bootstrap" versions gives the "bagged" classifier. Breiman has shown that bagging could reduce the error of linear regression and classification. It was noticed that bagging is useful for unstable procedures only. For stable ones it could even cause deterioration of the performance of the classifier. The performance of bagged classifiers was also investigated by Tibshirani [56], and Wolpert and Macready [64], who used the bias–variance decomposition to estimate the generalization error of the "bagged" classifiers.

An example is shown in Fig. 30 [57, 58]. Here the instability of the Nearest Mean Classifier is presented for the same Gaussian example as used in this chapter. This example shows that bagging might improve performance, but at the same time does not stabilize.

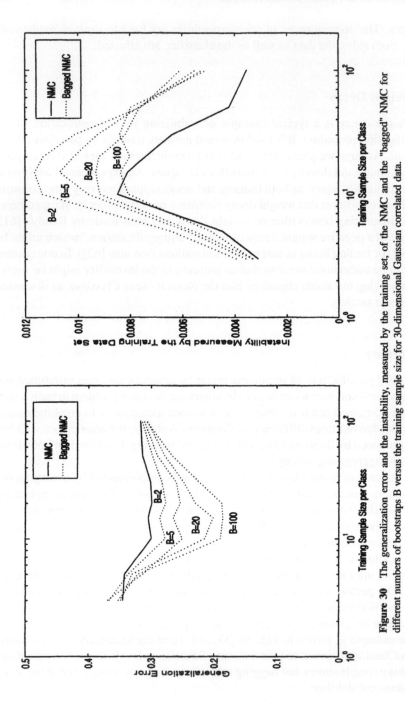

Figure 30 The generalization error and the instability, measured by the training set, of the NMC and the "bagged" NMC for different numbers of bootstraps B versus the training sample size for 30-dimensional Gaussian correlated data.

C. STABILITY EXPERIMENT

The stability of neural network classifiers depends on the architecture (the number of hidden units), the training algorithm, and the training set. An example is given in Figs. 31 and 32 for the instability caused by repeated initializations. The networks are trained on two different realizations of the same two-dimensional problem of spherical Gaussian distributed classes, with identical means but different variances. In the left figures the scatter plots of these two training sets are presented.

In the two right figures the instability as a function of the number of hidden units is shown. Levenberg–Marquardt optimization is used with a fixed number of 150 epochs. The label assignments for an independent test set are compared, yielding an estimate of the instability as discussed in Section VI.B. The instability curves for the two training sets are entirely different.

This section shows that classifier stability plays its role between bias and variance. As the above experiments illustrate, no fixed rules can be formulated for the architecture in relation to the size of the classification problem (numbers of features and samples). The use of some stabilizing technique, as discussed in this chapter or elsewhere, is thereby necessary in almost any case. This is due to the fact that neural networks have a large number of free parameters. A straightforward optimization yields unstable solutions in the case of limited data sizes.

Classifier stability has been studied in its relation to the bias and the variance of the resulting classification function. Very stable classifiers are biased and insensitive to class irregularities. They thereby tend to have a bad performance. Very unstable classifiers show large variances in the classification in which bad performances dominate. Somewhere in between, classifiers have sufficient sensitivity to follow data peculiarities without being too heavily affected by the noise. Each of the techniques we discussed here controls this stability in its own way. Adding noise in an artificial way and regularization by weight decay stabilize. Bagging might improve the performance, but it is certainly not a clear stabilizer. More research is needed to determine the conditions that can be expected from this method.

The way we measure the stability is very time consuming. For larger neural networks this will become impossible, certainly on a routine basis. Measuring the instability, however, might help us to understand why and the conditions under which certain techniques are useful and others are counter-productive.

Combining neural networks is a popular issue [37, 65, 66] and might certainly improve the performance. Bagging experiments presented here and elsewhere [58] show that this is not necessarily caused by stabilizing. This corresponds with the conclusions drawn by Raudys [61] and Hamamoto [62] that sometimes antiregularization might be useful in training neural networks. So sometimes neural network training procedures are too stable, are thereby insensitive to the data, and

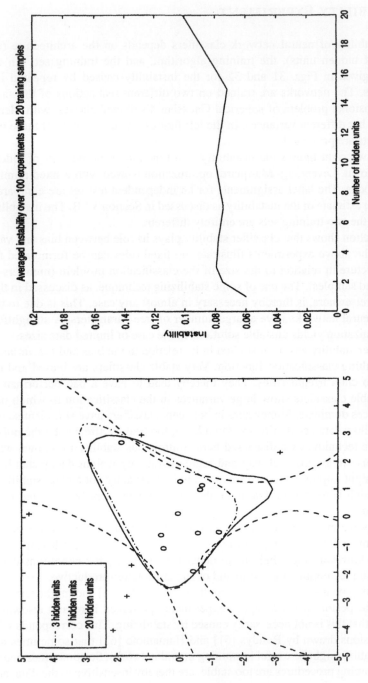

Figure 31 Instability as function of the number of hidden units (right) for a given training set (left). In the scatterplot some examples of neural network classification functions are given.

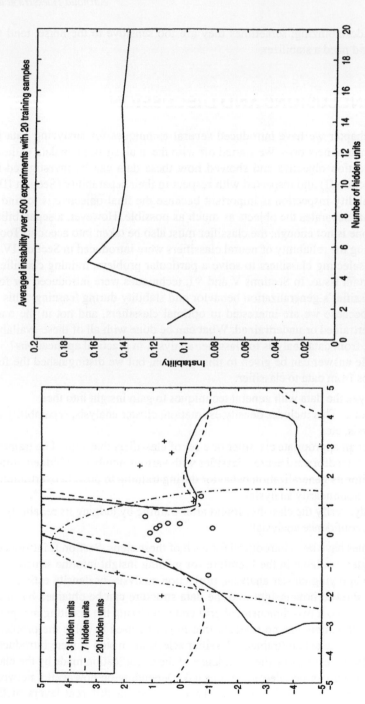

Figure 32 Instability as function of the number of hidden units (right) for a given training set (left). In the scatterplot some examples of neural network classification functions are given.

need some destabilizing; sometimes they are too sensitive to the noise, tend to overtrain, and need a stabilizer.

VII. CONCLUSIONS AND DISCUSSION

In this chapter we have introduced several techniques for analyzing data in relation to neural networks. We started off with the analysis of plain data without any classification objective and showed how these data can be investigated in general (Section II) and inspected with respect to their separability (Section III). This separability inspection is important because the final objective is to find a classifier that separates the objects as much as possible. However, a separability analysis alone is not enough; the classifier must also be taken into account. Tools for estimating the reliability of neural classifiers were introduced in Section IV.

Next to selecting classifiers to solve a particular problem, training classifiers is an important issue. In Sections V and VI, techniques were introduced for follow the classifier's generalization behavior and stability during learning. This is important because we are interested in optimal classifiers, and not in the ones that are overtrained or undertrained. What can be done with all of these available techniques, from data analysis to classifier analysis, in practical applications?

No single answer can be given to this question, but we distinguished the following steps from data to classifier:

1. Analyze the data with general techniques to gain insight into their structure. This includes density estimation, cluster analysis, separability analysis, etc.
2. Select an appropriate classifier or a set of classifiers that should be trained (e.g., a feedforward neural classifier with various numbers of hidden units).
3. Monitor its generalization behavior during training to prevent overtraining (e.g., nonlinearity analysis).
4. Finally, verify the classifier found after training by judging its reliability (e.g., confidence analysis).

Techniques have been introduced for each of these steps. Section II introduced the techniques available in the literature for gaining insight into the structure of the data by applying cluster analysis, projection analysis, or density estimation. Section III showed how insight into the data structure can be obtained by mapping the data onto a two-dimensional grid and visualizing the resulting mapping. In this way classifiers can be selected that might be used to solve the problem. Techniques for the actual (trained) classifier selection, in step 2, were introduced in Section IV. By estimating the confidence of the classification made by the classifier, a classifier can be selected or rejected. Depending on how well a network is trained, these confidence levels can be estimated for different layers of the network. Different methods for estimating the confidence levels were also introduced, next to the "classical" network output values. Step 4 is training a neural network classifier in such a way that the classification problem is solved in an optimal way. This can be done by monitoring the network's generalization capability and stability in relation to the data it has to classify. The nonlinearity measure can be inspected during training, in contrast to the VC dimension-related methods, which determine the generalization capability in advance. This nonlinearity measure is very useful because the tendency of a network to enter an overtrained situation can be seen almost immediately. The stability also must be monitored, because nonstable classifiers yield suboptimal solutions. Finally, the last step was introduced in Section IV, in which it was shown how reliability estimations can be performed.

In practical situations, however, one is not always interested in a general procedure of classifier selection and data analysis. The questions are more specific: "How many hidden layers should I select?" "How many hidden neurons do I need?" or "Which learning algorithm should I choose?" This paper has not dealt with this kind of questions in detail, although in the presented experiments the techniques have been applied to networks with various architectures. However, one must bear in mind that each of the presented techniques can be applied to answering particular questions. The authors' objective was to present a variety of techniques that can be applied in the various stages of analysis and training to solve a classification problem by using neural networks.

ACKNOWLEDGMENTS

This research was partially sponsored by the SION (Dutch Foundation for Computer Science Research), the NWO (Dutch Foundation for Scientific Research), and the SNN (Foundation for Neural Networks, Nijmegen). Servaes Tholen, Marina Skurichina, Jianchang Mao, and Anil Jain are gratefully acknowledged for their contribution to the research described.

REFERENCES

[1] E. Backer. *Computer Assisted Reasoning in Cluster Analysis*. Prentice-Hall, Englewood Cliffs, NJ, 1995.

[2] R. Beale and T. Jackson. *Neural Computing: An Introduction*. Hilger, Bristol, England, 1990.

[3] C. M. Bishop. *Neural Networks for Pattern Recognition*. Clarendon, Oxford, 1995.

[4] P. A. Devijver and J. Kittler. *Pattern Recognition: A Statistical Approach*. Prentice-Hall, London, 1982.

[5] M. R. Anderberg. *Cluster Analysis for Applications*. Academic Press, New York, 1973.

[6] K. Fukanaga. *Introduction to Statistical Pattern Recognition*. Academic Press, San Diego, CA, 1990.

[7] J. A. Hertz, A. S. Krogh, and R. G. Palmer. *Introduction to the theory of neural computation*. Sante Fe Institute Studies in the Sciences of Complexity. Addison-Wesley, Reading, MA, 1991.

[8] A. K. Jain and R. C. Dubes. *Algorithms for Clustering Data*. Prentice-Hall, Englewood Cliffs, NJ, 1988.

[9] B. Ripley. *Recognition and Neural Networks*. Cambridge Univ. Press, Cambridge, England, 1996.

[10] H. Ritter, K. Schulten, and T. Martinetz. *Neural Computation and Self-organizing Maps: An Introduction*. Addison-Wesley, Reading, MA, 1991.

[11] V. Vapnik. *Estimation of Dependencies Based on Empirical Data*. Springer-Verlag, Heidelberg, 1982.

[12] P. K. Simpson. *Artificial Neural Systems: Foundations, Paradigms, Applications, and Implementations*. Pergamon, Ehnsford, NY, 1990.

[13] J. A. Anderson and E. Rosenfeld. *Neurocomputing: A Collection of Classic Papers*. MIT Press, Cambridge, MA, 1987.

[14] J. A. Hartigan. *Clustering Algorithms*. Wiley, New York, 1975.

[15] T. Kohonen. *Self-Organization and Associative Memory*, 3rd ed. Springer-Verlag, Heidelberg, 1989.

[16] B. S. Duran and P. L. Odell. *Lecture Notes in Economics and Mathematical Systems—Econometrics—Cluster Analysis—A Survey*. Springer-Verlag, Berlin, 1974.

[17] T. Kohonen. The self-organizing map. *Proc. IEEE* 78:1464–1480, 1990.

[18] S. Grossberg. *Studies of Mind and Brain*. Reidel Press, Boston, 1982.

[19] S. Grossberg. *The Adaptive Brain I: Cognition, Learning, Reinforcement, and Rythm*. Elsevier/North-Holland, Amsterdam, 1986.

[20] S. Grossberg. *The Adaptive Brain II: Vision, Speech, Language and Motor Control*. Elsevier/North-Holland, Amsterdam, 1986.

[21] E. A. Oja. Simplified neuron model as a principal component analyzer. *J. Math. Biol.* 15:267–273, 1982.

[22] E. Oja. Neural networks, principal components, and subspaces. *Internat. J. Neural Syst.* 1:61–68, 1989.

[23] J. W. Sammon, Jr. A nonlinear mapping for data structure analysis. *IEEE Trans. Comput.*, C-18: 401–409, 1969.

[24] E. Parzen. On estimation of a probability density function and mode. *Ann. Math. Statist.* 33:1065–1076, 1962.

[25] D. Ackley, G. Hinton, and T. Sejnowski. A learning algorithm for Boltzmann machines. *Cognitive Sci.* 9:147–169, 1985.

[26] A. Barnas and A. La Vigna. Convergence of Kohonen's learning vector quantization. In *International Joint Conference on Neural Networks*, June 17–21, 1990, Vol. 3, pp. 21–26. IEEE Press, New York.

[27] E. Erwin, K. Obermayer, and K. Schulten. Self-organizing maps: ordering, convergence properties and energy functions. *Biol. Cybernet.* 6:47–55, 1992.

[28] H. Ritter and K. Schulten. On the stationary state of Kohonen's self-organizing sensory mapping. *Biol. Cybernet.* 54:99–106, 1986.

[29] H. Ritter and K. Schulten. Convergence properties of Kohonen's topology preserving maps: fluctuations, stability, and dimension selection. *Biol. Cybernet.* 60:59–71, 1988.

[30] H. Ritter and K. Schulten. Kohonen's self-organizing maps: exploring their computational capabilities. In *IEEE International Conference on Neural Networks*, Vol. 1. IEEE, New York, 1988.

[31] M. A. Kraaijveld, J. Mao, and A. K. Jain. A nonlinear projection method based on Kohonen's topology preserving maps. *IEEE Trans. Neural Networks* 6:548–559, 1995.

[32] G. Biswas, A. K. Jain, and R. C. Dubes. Evaluation of projection algorithms. *IEEE Trans. Pattern Anal. Machine Intelligence* 3:701–708, 1981.

[33] J. Mao and A. K. Jain. Artificial neural networks for feature extraction and multivariate data projection. *IEEE Trans. Neural Networks* 6:296–317, 1995.

[34] R. A. Fisher. The use of multiple measurements in taxonomic problems. *Ann. Eugenics* 7(Part 11):179–188, 1936.

[35] M. Anthony and B. S. Holden. On the power of linearly weighted neural networks. In *Proceedings of the ICANN'93* (S. Gielen and B. Kappen, Eds.), pp. 736–743. Springer-Verlag, Heidelberg, 1993.

[36] R. Battiti and A. M. Colla. Democracy in neural nets: voting schemes for classification. *Neural Networks* 7:691–707, 1994.

[37] M. Kittler, M. Hatef, and R. P. W. Duin. Combining classifiers. In *Proceedings of the 23th ICPR, Vienna*, Vol. 2, track B: Pattern Recognition and Signal Analysis, pp. 897–901. IEEE Comput. Soc., Los Alamitos, 1996.

[38] J. S. Denker and Y. Le Cun. Transforming neural-net output levels to probability distribution. In *Advances in Neural information Processing Systems* (R. P. Lippmann, J. E. Moody, and D. S. Touretzky, Eds.), Vol. 3, pp. 853–859. Morgan Kaufmann, San Mateo, CA, 1991.

[39] R. O. Duda and P. E. Hart. *Pattern Classification and Scene Analysis*. Wiley, New York, 1973.

[40] R. P. W. Duin. Superlearning capabilities of neural networks? In *Proceedings of the 8th Scandinavian Conference on Image Analysis*, May 25–28, 1993, pp. 547–554. Norwegian Society for Image Processing and Pattern Recognition.

[41] S. A. Tholen. Confidence values for neural network classifications. Master's Thesis, Delft University of Technology, Delft, The Netherlands, 1995.

[42] J. A. Anderson. *Handbook of Statistics*, Vol. 2, *Logistic Discrimination*, pp. 169–191. North-Holland, Amsterdam, 1982.

[43] R. P. W. Duin. Nearest neighbor interpolation for error estimation and classifier optimization. In *Proceedings of the 8th SCIA Tromsø*, 1993.

[44] J. D. J. Houtepen. Chromosome banding profiles: how many samples are necessary for a neural network classifier? Master's Thesis, Delft University of Technology, Delft, The Netherlands, 1994.

[45] A. Hoekstra, S. A. Tholen, and R. P. W. Duin. Estimating the reliability of neural network classifications. In *Proceedings of the ICANN 96*, Bochum, Germany, 1996, pp. 53–58.

[46] K.-I. Funahashi. On the approximate realization of continuous mappings by neural networks. *Neural Networks* 2:183–192, 1989.

[47] K. Hornik. Multilayer feedforward networks are universal approximators. *Neural Networks* 2:359–366, 1989.

[48] E. B. Baum and D. Haussler. What size net gives valid generalization? *Neural Comput.* 1:151–160, 1989.

[49] V. Roychowdhury, K.-Y. Siu, and A. Orlitsky, Eds. *Theoretical Advances in Neural Computation and Learning*. Kluwer Academic, Dordrecht, The Netherlands, 1994.

[50] D. H. Wolpert, Ed. *The Mathematics of Generalization. Proceedings of the SFI/CNLS Workshop on Formal Approaches to Supervised Learning*, November 1994.

[51] L. N. Kanal and P. R. Krishnaiah. *Handbook of Statistics 2: Classification Pattern Recognition and Reduction of Dimensionality*. North-Holland, Amsterdam, 1982.

[52] V. Vapnik. Principles of risk minimization for learning theory. In *Advances in Neural Information Processing Systems* (J. E. Moody, S. J. Hanson, and R. P. Lippmann, Eds.), Vol. 4, pp. 831–838. Morgan Kaufmann, San Mateo, CA, 1992.

[53] M. A. Kraaijveld and R. P. W. Duin. The effective capacity of multilayer feedforward network classifiers. In *Twelfth International Conference on Pattern Recognition*, pp. B–99–B–103, 1994.

[54] A. Hoekstra and R. P. W. Duin. On the nonlinearity of pattern classifiers. In *Proceedings of the 13th ICPR, Vienna*, Vol. 3, track D: Parallel and Connectionist Systems, pp. 271–275. IEEE Comput. Soc., Los Alamitos, CA, 1996.

[55] S. Geman, E. Bienenstock, and R. Doursat. Neural networks and the bias/variance dilemma. *Neural Comput.* 4:1–58, 1992.

[56] R. Tibshirani. Bias, variance and prediction error for classification rules. Technical Report, University of Toronto, Toronto, 1996.

[57] M. Skurichina and R. P. W. Duin. Stabilizing classifiers for very small sample sizes. In *Proceedings of the 13th ICPR, Vienna*, Vol. 2, track B: Pattern Recognition and Signal Analysis, pp. 891–896. IEEE Comput. Soc., Los Alamitos, CA, 1996.

[58] M. Skurichina and R. P. W. Duin. Bagging for linear classifiers. *Pattern Recognition.* To appear.

[59] R. P. W. Duin. Small sample size generalization. In *Proceedings of the 9th Scandinavian conference on Image Analysis*, June 6–9, 1995 (G. Borgerfors, Ed.), pp. 957–964.

[60] S. Raudys and M. Skurichina. Small sample properties of ridge estimate of covariance matrix in statistical and neural classification. In *New trends in Probability and Statistics*, Vol. 3, pp. 237–245, 1994. Tartu, Estonia.

[61] S. Raudys. A negative weight decay or anti-regularization. In *Proceedings of the ICANN 95, Paris*, 1995.

[62] Y. Hamamoto, Y. Mitani, H. Ishihara, T. Hase, and S. Tomita. Evaluation of an anti-regularization technique in neural networks. In *Proceedings of the 13th ICPR, Vienna*, Vol. 2, track B: Pattern Recognition and Signal Analysis, pp. 205–208. IEEE Comput. Soc. Los Alamitos, CA, 1996.

[63] L. Breimann. Bagging predictors. *Machine Learning* 24:123–140, 1996.

[64] D. H. Wolpert and W. G. Macready. An efficient method to estimate bagging's generalization error. Technical Report, Santa Fe Institute, Santa Fe, NM, 1996.

[65] G. Rogova. Combining the results of several neural network classifiers. *Neural Networks* 7:777–781, 1994.

[66] K. Tumer and J. Ghosh. Analysis of decision boundaries in linearly combined neural classifiers. *Pattern Recognition* 29:341–348, 1996.

[67] H. Demuth and M. Beale. *Neural Network Toolbox for Use with Matlab.* The Mathworks, 1993.

[68] R. P. W. Duin. *PRTOOLS a Matlab Toolbox for Pattern Recognition.* Pattern Recognition Group, Delft University of Technology, October 1995.

[69] A. Hoekstra, M. A. Kraaijveld, D. de Ridder, and W. F. Schmidt. *The Complete SPRLIB & ANNLIB.* Pattern Recognition Group, Faculty of Applied Physics, Delft University of Technology, 1996.

[70] T. Kohonen, J. Hynninen, J. Kangas, and J. Laaksonen. *SOMPAK: The Self-Organising Map Program Package*, version 3.1. Laboratory of Computer and Information Science, Helsinki University of Technology, Rakentajanaukio 2 C, SF-02150 Espoo, Finland. April 7, 1995.

Multimode Single-Neuron Arithmetics

Chang N. Zhang

Department of Computer Science
University of Regina
Regina, Saskatchewan S4S 0A2, Canada

Meng Wang

Department of Computer Science
University of Regina
Regina, Saskatchewan S4S 0A2, Canada

I. INTRODUCTION

Neurons, whether real or artificially modeled, are basic processing elements (PEs) of computational neural networks. Formalizing single-neuron computation has been inspired by two types of endeavors. For computer scientists, understanding the computation performed by real neurons is essential to the design of basic processing elements that equip new models of artificial neural networks (ANNs). In contrast, computational neuroscientists have been exploring the biophysical mechanisms that enable neurons to "compute," to support their computational explanation of brain functions. Computational ability and biophysical plausibility, respectively, are the two focuses of interest for researchers in these two different areas. New insights into either of these aspects would inevitably benefit both. In this chapter we shall alternatively take the standpoints of computational neuroscience and computer science. We choose to proceed this way because we believe that many fundamental problems in neuron modeling are, in fact, of the same importance to both disciplines.

The current generation of artificial neural networks makes use of highly simplified models of neurons, such as summation-and-firing models. The reason for the use of these simplified models is twofold. On one hand, many researchers believe that the complicated dynamic behavior and advanced functions of a neural network system are primarily the result of collective behaviors of all participating neurons, and are less relevant to the operational detail of each processing element [1]. Assuming this, simple neuron models, such as summation-and-firing

Implementation Techniques

models, are preferable to complicated neuron models because of their ease of implementation and understanding. On the other hand, there has been a lack of available models of single neurons that are both computationally powerful and biologically plausible as replacements of the current models. In fact, as a main source of novel neuron models, computational neuroscience is just at the initial stage of tackling the principles of single-neuron information processing [2].

Our present knowledge of the biophysical basis of single-neuron computation is largely based on the understanding of the functional structure of biological membranes [3]. In brief, membrane structures that separate the inner world of a single neuron from its environment form a leaky barrier for charged ions, resulting in a difference in electrical potentials across the cell membrane (membrane potentials). An important variable observable at the cellular level, membrane potential has been chosen as the basic variable describing the state of a single neuron in most modeling works. Neurophysiological studies at cellular and molecular levels have elucidated the fact that it is the opening and closing of ion channels provided by certain membrane proteins that are responsible for changes in membrane potentials [4]. In the investigation of how the opening and closing of ion channels change the membrane potentials, equivalent electrical circuits are a useful model. Figure 1b shows a typical equivalent circuit model of the membrane patch shown

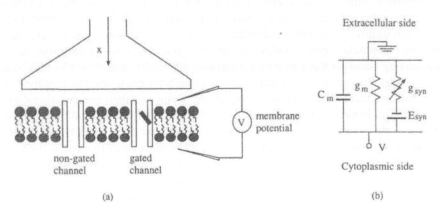

(a)   (b)

Figure 1 Single-neuron computation can be studied via equivalent circuit models. (a) Simplified model of a membrane patch subject to synaptic input. The nongated channel in the figure is an integrated representation of all nongated channels in this patch that are selectively permeable to various ion species; similarly, the gated channel on the right represents all chemical-gated channels in this patch whose opening/closing is controlled by the synaptic input x. (b) Equivalent circuit model for the membrane patch in (a). The nongated channels are modeled by the constant conductance g_m, and the gated channels are modeled by the E_{syn}–g_{syn} branch. The temporal property of the membrane potential is modeled by the capacitive branch C_m. Membrane potential is given by V measured in reference to the extracellular ground.

in Fig. 1a. In this electric model, membrane permeability of charged ions is modeled by lamped electric parameters (conductances). Consequently, the influence of a synaptic input signal x on the membrane potential V is studied in terms of how the variable input conductance g_{syn} determines the value of voltage V.

Mathematically, this equivalent circuit model defines the membrane potential V as a real function of the input conductance g_{syn}. Suppose that V is the membrane potential under observation and $\{g_1, g_2, \ldots, g_n\}$ is a set of input conductances. Then the task of single-neuron computation can be stated as a multivariate mapping $f : R^n \to R$ from the n-dimensional real space of input conductances to the one-dimensional real space of membrane potential. More generally, when n different spatial sites of a cell membrane are observed, n membrane potentials can be defined (Fig. 2). In this case, the mapping from input conductances to membrane potentials is $f : R^n \to R^n$. A central interest of single-neuron computation is to understand this mapping f for both its computational power and the supporting biophysical mechanisms.

During the last three decades, biophysical studies of membrane potential dynamics have led to several models of the mapping f [5–12]. From the viewpoint of computation, all of those models can be classified into two categories: arith-

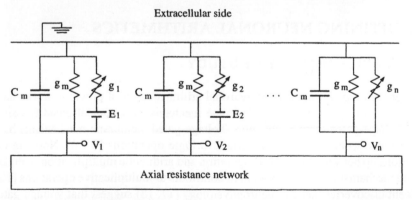

Figure 2 A typical equivalent circuit model for passive membranes. The entire surface of a cell membrane is considered as being paved by n membrane patches. For each of these patches a unique membrane potential V_i ($i = 1, 2, \ldots, n$) is measured. The difference between membrane potentials at different patches is caused by tangential membrane resistances, which are modeled by an axial resistance network. The resting property of the membrane is assumed to be the same throughout the membrane, and therefore the same g_m and C_m values are assigned to all patches. Each of the membrane patches is assumed to be subject to a synaptic input. Depending on the property of the synaptic input, the reversal potential of the synaptic potential can be negative (e.g., the E_1), positive (e.g., the E_2), or neutral (e.g., the missing E_n in series with g_n). (Throughout this chapter, the resting membrane potential is chosen to be zero, and all potential values are specified in reference to this convention.)

metical models and logic models. According to the arithmetical model, the mapping f can be described in terms of arithmetical operations, such as addition and subtraction [5, 12], multiplication [6, 7, 12], and division [5, 11, 12]. By combining these neuronally feasible operations, a single neuron can be regarded as a polynomial approximator [6, 7, 10, 13–15], a normalization functor [11], or a rational approximator [12]. In logic models, the mapping f from conductance space to membrane potential space is modeled as logic operations [10], such as AND-NOT [7], AND and OR [8], and XOR [8, 9]. All of these models represent a substantial challenge to the traditional view of the single neuron as a linear summing machine of input signals.

In this chapter we focus on arithmetical models. Because of the elementary importance of arithmetical operations in constructing any complicated mathematic operations, the single neuron's ability to perform arithmetical operations is a fundamental issue in understanding single-neuron computation. Questions related to this issue include: What is the biophysical basis of neuronal arithmetics? What kinds of arithmetical operation can a neuron perform? What are the potential and limitation of single-neuron arithmetics? Do neurons change their operational models under the control of certain input signals? How do neuronal arithmetical operations support higher level functions?

II. DEFINING NEURONAL ARITHMETICS

A. A Brief History of Study

For the biophysical basis of neuronal arithmetics, most previous works have relied on two types of gated membrane mechanisms: chemical-gated (passive) and voltage-gated (active) channels. Voltage-gated membrane mechanisms have been found to be especially important to logic operations [8–10]. Noticing the relationship between logic AND operation and arithmetic multiplication, voltage-gated mechanisms are also thought to contribute to multiplicative operations [16]. Recent discoveries made in neurophysiology [17, 18] suggest that voltage-gated mechanisms can, in fact, participate in all computations. They do so by converting computation results (the membrane potentials) into new operands (the conductances) and therefore play a role of integrating several intermediate computations (usually achieved in local dendritic structures) into more complicated outcomes [17].

In contrast, chemical-gated mechanisms (as depicted in Fig. 1) seem to contribute more directly to all types of arithmetic operations. Blomfield [5] studied three types of operations: addition, subtraction, and division, all supported by passive membrane properties. A notable passive membrane property, termed *shunting inhibition*, has been studied a great deal by many researchers, and has been found to contribute to multiplicative [6, 7, 16] and divisive [11] operations.

Almost all models of neuronal arithmetics studied so far have been built by following a "finite precision approximation" approach. In this approach, none of those model operations (say, multiplication) is precisely performed by a single neuron. Instead, all of them are approximations to the actual computation by the neuron. The idea is to set up a precision of approximation, and to determine the conditions under which the actual neuronal operation can be reduced to a model operation subject to the precision of approximation. Usually the actual operation is a composite operation, and the model operation is clean. The way the model operation is derived prescribes the restriction for the valid range of the model. For example, Torre and Poggio [6] derived their model of shunting multiplication by applying a Taylor expansion to the original function (a rational function). Accordingly, the result of [6] applies only to small conductance circumstances [16]. Furthermore, to give a clean multiplication, some additional procedures are required to remove the unwanted terms in the Taylor expansion [19]. To all researchers, addition and subtraction are merely the linear approximation to the actual membrane operation under the condition of small-input conductances [5].

This finite-precision approximation approach leads to a logical concern over the conditions under which an arithmetical model applies. Recently, the authors [12] have developed a phase space analysis on the arithmetic ability of passive membrane mechanisms. In that work, a rational function model is proposed to be the unified basis for the description of all four types of arithmetical operations $(+, -, \times, \div)$. The phase diagrams of all four arithmetical operations are determined in the space of input conductances, and serve as a quantitative measure for the potential and limitation of neuronal arithmetic operations. This result extends the previous works in several aspects. For example, subtraction is found to be an "observable" operation, not only for small input signals but also for large inputs; multiplication and division are found to have several possible realizations, not being restricted to the shunting inhibition.

B. POLARIZATION CONFIGURATION

In the equivalent circuit model shown in Fig. 1, the polarity of the battery E_{syn} is determined by the property of the synaptic connection: if the input is excitatory, then E_{syn} represents a positive potential with respect to the extracellular ground; if the input is inhibitory, then E_{syn} is negative. Neutral E_{syn} (that is, $E_{syn} = 0$) corresponds to a special inhibitory mechanism termed *shunting inhibition*.

In general, for two adjacent membrane patches, there are three types of configurations that are significant to computation (Fig. 3): (a) two isopolarized patches, that is, two patches with the same polarity of E_{syn}, such as the E_1 and E_2 in

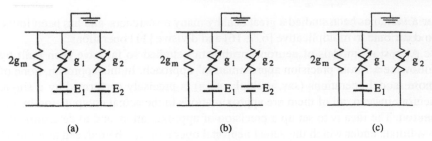

Figure 3 Equivalent circuit of two spatially adjacent patches. (a) Two isopolarized patches; (b) two heteropolarized patches; (c) a shunting patch and a polarized patch.

Fig. 3a; (b) two heteropolarized patches, that is, two patches with opposite polarity of E_{syn} (see Fig. 3b); and (c) a shunting (neutral) patch and a polarized patch (Fig. 3c). Notice that in these equivalent circuits shown in Fig. 3, the nongated conductances g_m of the two patches are assumed to be of the same value and are merged into a single conductance. Configurations that are not considered here are symmetrical to the listed configurations (e.g., two inhibitory patches are symmetrical to two excitatory patches) or computationally trivial (e.g., two shunting patches).

With the polarization configuration defined, various arithmetic operations can be termed accordingly. For example, the multiplication model studied in [6, 7, 16] can be referred to as the *shunting multiplication*, the divisive operations constructed by [11] as *shunting division*, and so on. Additions and subtractions studied by many researchers can be termed *isopolarized addition* and *heteropolarized subtraction*, respectively, or simply addition and subtraction, because the polarization configuration for these two linear operations is implied from the name of the operation.

C. COMPOSITE OPERATION AND CLEAN OPERATION

In a neuronal arithmetic computation, the operands are the input conductances and the result is the local membrane potential. The set of operators involved in a computation defines an *arithmetical mode*. The nature of a neuronal arithmetical mode is described by several specifications. First of all, we may distinguish between *clean* operations and *composite* operations. In a clean arithmetic operation, only one type of operator ($+$, $-$, $\times$, or $\div$) is involved (e.g., addition with several input conductances, yielding a membrane potential value). The clean operations considered here include the case in which an operand may be a variable or a variable multiplied with a constant (e.g., $ax_1 + x_2$, where a is a constant), and the case in which the result of the operation may contain an additive constant (e.g., $x_1 x_2 + b$ for constant b). In particular, group divisions are considered as a clean operation in which both the numerator p and the denominator q of a rational expression p/q are polynomials of several input conductances.

Composite operations are constructed by applying subsequent operations to the result of several clean operations (e.g., $x_1 x_2 + x_3/x_4$). Composite arithmetics are usually observed in the case of group operations where more than two input conductances are involved. Two famous examples of composite operation that have been considered by many researchers are:

$V = \sum_{i,j} A_j g_i g_j$: addition-after-multiplication/subtraction ($\Sigma \Pi$ operation),

$V = \left[\sum_{\{k\}} A_k g_k \right]\left[\sum_{\{j\}} B_j g_j \right]$: multiplication-after-addition/subtraction ($\Pi \Sigma$ operation).

Figure 4a shows a possible case of the $\Sigma \Pi$ operation. In that example, components of two input vectors are first multiplied by each other, and the products are then summed up (inner product of two vectors). An example of the $\Pi \Sigma$ operation is shown in Fig. 4b. In both figures, a total of eight input conductances is to be dealt with.

For the well-definedness of arithmetical operations, two values g_{min} and g_{max} are chosen as the lowest and highest values of the input conductances, respectively, and v_{min} and v_{max} are the lowest and highest values of local membrane potentials. For real neurons, $v_{min} = E_{IPSP} \approx -5$ mV and $v_{max} = E_{EPSP} \approx 65$ mV are usually assumed. For the conductances, a natural setting is $g_{min} = 0$, and g_{max} can be, say, 10^{-4} S. Following the finite-precision approximation approach, two

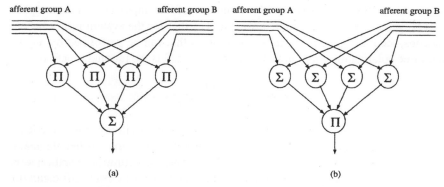

Figure 4   (a) Sigma-Pi operation. (b) Pi-Sigma operation.

types of measure are used to characterize a model, clean operation:

(1) For a given $\epsilon > 0$, the actual, composite operation $V = f(g_1, g_2, \ldots, g_n)$
    is said to be approximated by a clean operation $g_1 \circ g_2 \cdots \circ g_n$ in a
    subspace S of $R^n(g_1, g_2, \ldots, g_n)$, if for any $(g_1, g_2, \ldots, g_n) \in S$ we have
    $|f(g_1, g_2, \ldots, g_n) - g_1 \circ g_2 \cdots \circ g_n| < \epsilon$. S is referred to as the *domain
    range* of the operation $\circ$.
(2) Given a domain range S and $(g_1, g_2, \ldots, g_n) \in S$, the quantity $\eta =
    \max\{g_1 \circ g_2 \cdots \circ g_n\} - \min\{g_1 \circ g_2 \cdots \circ g_n\}$ is used to describe the
    dynamic range of the operation $\circ$.

D. DEVELOPEDNESS OF ARITHMETICAL MODES

The measures of domain range and dynamic range present quantitative criteria
for the biological plausibility of a model operation. Generally speaking, if a proposed model arithmetic can be implemented by a single neuron in very rare cases
(i.e., with small domain range), it can hardly be accepted as a reasonable model.
Formally, we can describe model operations in three categories: less developed,
developed, and well developed. An arithmetical mode is said to be developed if
it has a wide domain range (compared with g_m) in at least one input conductance
dimension; it is well developed if, in addition, the domain range S measures a
large portion of the input space $R^n(g_1, g_2, \ldots, g_n)$; and it is less developed if the
domain range is narrow in all dimensions.

III. PHASE SPACE OF NEURONAL ARITHMETICS

A. PROTOTYPES OF CLEAN ARITHMETICS

In this section we describe the structure of the input conductance space
$R^n(g_1, g_2, \ldots, g_n)$. It has been shown in [12] that for the system of n adjacent
patches, the most general composite operation that can be performed by any of
the three polarization configurations shown in Fig. 3 is the rational function

$$V = \frac{\sum_j^n E_j g_j}{n * g_m + \sum_j^n g_j} \, . \tag{1}$$

In this rational function, if we restrict ourselves to positive ohmic relations,
then all coefficients, with the possible exception of E_j, are positive constant.
It is obviously analytical everywhere in its domain of definition. Furthermore,
it is easy to verify that V is a monotonic increasing (or decreasing) function of
g_j, $j = 1, 2, \ldots$, if $E_j > 0$ (or $E_j < 0$). It also saturates itself for large-valued

input conductances because both the numerator and the denominator are of the same degree of g_j, $j = 1, \ldots, n$. In fact, we have

$$\min\{E_1, E_2, \ldots, E_n\} \leq V \leq \max\{E_1, E_2, \ldots, E_n\}. \tag{2}$$

An even looser estimator follows:

$$E_{\text{IPSP}} < V < E_{\text{EPSP}}. \tag{3}$$

In other words, the results of neuronal arithmetical operations are bounded at both the lower and upper ends.

Based on the general rational function (1), we construct the following prototypes of clean arithmetic operations subject to the criterion of developedness as defined in the last section:

1. *Summation and subtraction.* In these two clean operations, the rational function (1) is approximated by the linear arithmetic

$$V \approx \sum_{j}^{n} \left(\frac{E_j}{n g_{\text{m}}} \right) g_j, \tag{4}$$

where E_j $(j = 1, \ldots, n)$ are constant. In this linear arithmetic, summation takes place among the input conductances of isopolarized patches and subtraction among heteropolarized patches.

2. *Multiplication.* The composite operation (1) also has multiplicative approximations. In the case of $n = 2$, where (1) is reduced to $V = (E_1 g_1 + E_2 g_2)/(2 g_{\text{m}} + g_1 + g_2)$, we may construct an approximation of the form

$$V \approx \frac{E_2}{4 g_{\text{m}}^2} g_1 g_2. \tag{5}$$

3. *Division.* In (1), suppose that the index set $\{j\}$ is partitioned into two nonoverlapping subsets $\{k\}$ and $\{l\}$ such that

$$V = \frac{\sum_{k}^{K} E_k g_k + \sum_{l}^{L} E_l g_l}{n \times g_{\text{m}} + \sum_{k}^{K} g_k + \sum_{l}^{L} g_l}, \tag{6}$$

where $K + L = n$. A divisive approximation of (1) takes the form

$$V \approx \frac{\sum_{k}^{K} E_k g_k}{n \times g_{\text{m}} + \sum_{l}^{L} g_l}, \tag{7}$$

that is, the input conductances corresponding to the index set $\{l\}$ effectively divide the conductances in the subset $\{k\}$. For the case of $n = 2 (L = K = 1)$, the rational function $V = (E_1 g_1 + E_2 g_2)/(2 g_{\text{m}} + g_1 + g_2)$ is approximated by $E_2 g_2/(g_1 + 2 g_{\text{m}})$.

B. DOMAIN RANGE

For the case of $n = 2$, the domain range S of the linear arithmetics (4), (5), and (7) is described by certain inequalities about g_1 and g_2 which specify S as an area (finite or infinite) in the g_1–g_2 plane. (In all formulas below, $\epsilon > 0$ is assumed. For the derivation of these formulas, see [12].)

1. Linear Operations

Case I

$E_1 = E_2 \neq 0$ (isopolarized patches; additive operation):

$$0 < g_1 + g_2 < g_m \left[\epsilon + \sqrt{\epsilon(\epsilon + 4|E_1|)} \right] \Big/ |E_1|. \tag{8}$$

Case II

$E_1 > 0 > E_2$ (heteropolarized patches; subtractive operation. The case of $E_2 > 0 > E_1$ can be known by symmetry): when $g_2 \geq g_m[\epsilon + \sqrt{\epsilon(\epsilon + 4|E_2|)}\,]$ $/|E_2|$,

$$\sqrt{[g_2(|E_1| + |E_2|) - 2\epsilon g_m]^2 - 16\epsilon|E_1|g_m^2} - 2\epsilon g_m$$
$$< 2|E_1|g_1 + (|E_1| - |E_2|)g_2$$
$$< \sqrt{[g_2(|E_1| + |E_2|) + 2\epsilon g_m]^2 + 16\epsilon|E_1|g_m^2} + 2\epsilon g_m, \tag{9}$$

and when $g_2 < g_m[\epsilon + \sqrt{\epsilon(\epsilon + 4|E_2|)}\,]/|E_2|$,

$$0 < 2|E_1|g_1 < \sqrt{[g_2(|E_1| + |E_2|) + 2\epsilon g_m]^2 + 16\epsilon|E_1|g_m^2}$$
$$+ 2\epsilon g_m - (|E_1| - |E_2|)g_2. \tag{10}$$

It is seen from Fig. 5 that the domain ranges of the two types of linear operation possess different natures. In brief, the additive operation is performed when both g_1 and g_2 are small with respect to the g_m (refer to relation (8)). This observation is consistent with the general intuition that the linear approximation (4) is adequate for small signal situations. Nevertheless, as can be seen from Fig. 5b, the domain of subtractive operation is not described by small signals: its S occupies a band expanding over a wide range in both g_1 and g_2 dimensions. The slope of this band can be roughly described by the ratio $|E_2|/|E_1|$. For $E_1 = 65$ and $E_2 = -5$, this indicates that the input conductance of the inhibitory patch must be ~ 13 times higher than the input conductance of the excitatory patch to perform a subtractive operation.

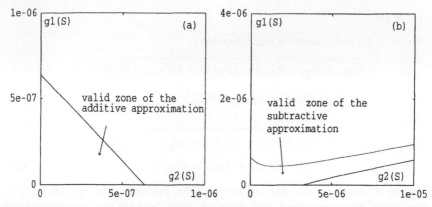

Figure 5 Domain range of linear approximation in the case of (a) $E_1 = E_2 = E_{EPSP}$ and (b) $E_1 = E_{EPSP}$ and $E_2 = I_{EPSP}$. Parameters for the curves: $E_{EPSP} = 65$, $E_{IPSP} = -5$, $g_m = 10^{-6}$, $\epsilon = 5$.

2. Multiplication

The domain range of (5) is determined for three cases:

Case I

$E_1 = E_2 \neq 0$ (isopolarized multiplication):

$$
\begin{aligned}
4g_m^2\big(|E_1| - \epsilon\big) &- |E_1|g_2\big(g_2 + 2g_m\big) \\
&+ \sqrt{[4g_m^2(|E_1| - \epsilon) + |E_1|g_2(g_2 + 2g_m)]^2 - 32E_1^2g_m^3g_2} \\
&< 2|E_1|g_1g_2 \\
&< 4g_m^2\big(|E_1| + \epsilon\big) - |E_1|g_2\big(g_2 + 2g_m\big) \\
&+ \sqrt{[4g_m^2(|E_1| + \epsilon) + |E_1|g_2(g_2 + 2g_m)]^2 - 32E_1^2g_m^3g_2}.
\end{aligned} \quad (11)
$$

Case II

$E_1 > 0 > E_2$ (heteropolarized multiplication):

$$
\begin{aligned}
4g_m^2\big(|E_1| - \epsilon\big) &- |E_2|g_2\big(g_2 + 2g_m\big) \\
&+ \sqrt{[4g_m^2(|E_2| - \epsilon) + |E_2|g_2(g_2 + 2g_m)]^2 - 32E_2^2g_m^3g_2} \\
&< 2|E_2|g_1g_2 \\
&< 4g_m^2\big(|E_1| + \epsilon\big) - |E_2|g_2\big(g_2 + 2g_m\big) \\
&+ \sqrt{[4g_m^2(|E_2| + \epsilon) + |E_2|g_2(g_2 + 2g_m)]^2 - 32E_2^2g_m^3g_2}.
\end{aligned} \quad (12)
$$

Case III

$E_1 = 0,\ E_2 \neq 0$ (shunting multiplication):

$$\sqrt{[g_2|E_2|(g_2 + 2g_m) - 4\epsilon g_m^2]^2 + 16(g_m g_2|E_2|)^2}$$
$$- \left[|g_2|E_2|(g_2 + 2g_m) + 4\epsilon g_m^2\right]$$
$$< 2|E_2|g_1 g_2$$
$$< \sqrt{[g_2|E_2|(g_2 + 2g_m) + 4\epsilon g_m^2]^2 + 16(g_m g_2|E_2|)^2}$$
$$- \left[|g_2|E_2|(g_2 + 2g_m) - 4\epsilon g_m^2\right]. \tag{13}$$

Figure 6 illustrates the domain range of the multiplicative operation (5) in isopolarized, heteropolarized, and shunting cases. In both the isopolarized and

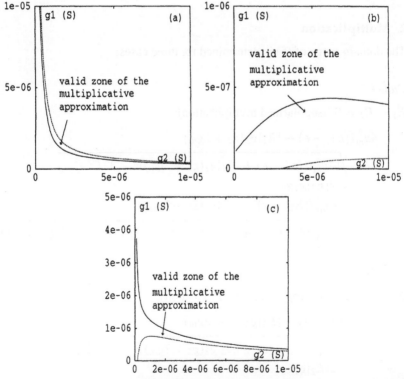

Figure 6 Domain range of multiplicative approximation in the case of (a) $E_1 = E_2 = E_{EPSP}$, (b) $E_1 = E_{EPSP}$ and $E_2 = E_{IPSP}$, and (c) $E_1 = 0$ and $E_2 = E_{EPSP}$. Parameters for the curves: $E_{EPSP} = 65$, $E_{IPSP} = -5$, $g_m = 10^{-6}$. For (a) and (c), $\epsilon = 5$. For (b), $\epsilon = 3$.

heteropolarized cases, S is a narrow band bounded by two curves (not strictly hyperbolic; see relations (11) and (12)). When one of the two patches is of the shunting type, the shunting conductance g_1 can vary over a wide range for small g_2, and this range becomes narrower as the shunted conductance increases (Fig. 6c).

3. Division

Case I

$E_1 = E_2 \neq 0$ (isopolarized division):

$$
\frac{-[\epsilon(g_2 + 4g_m) + 2g_m|E_1|] + \sqrt{[2g_m|E_1| - \epsilon g_2]^2 + 4|E_1|(|E_1| + \epsilon)g_2^2}}{2(|E_1| + \epsilon)}
$$
$$
< g_1
$$
$$
< \frac{\epsilon(g_2 + 4g_m) - 2g_m|E_1| + \sqrt{[\epsilon g_2 + 2g_m|E_1|]^2 + 4|E_1|(|E_1| - \epsilon)g_2^2}}{2(|E_1| - \epsilon)}.
$$
$$
\tag{14}
$$

Case II

$E_1 E_2 < 0$ (heteropolarized division):

$$
0 \le g_1 < \frac{\epsilon(g_2 + 4g_m) - 2g_m|E_1| + \sqrt{[\epsilon g_2 + 2g_m|E_1|]^2 - 4|E_2|(|E_1| - \epsilon)g_2^2}}{2(|E_1| - \epsilon)},
$$
$$
0 \le g_2 \le \frac{g_m|E_1|}{\sqrt{|E_2|(|E_1| - \epsilon)} - 0.5\epsilon}.
$$
$$
\tag{15}
$$

Case III

$E_1 = 0$ and $E_2 \neq 0$ (shunting division):

$$
g_1 > g_2\left[\sqrt{0.25 + |E_2|/\epsilon} - 0.5\right] - 2g_m.
\tag{16}
$$

The S of the isopolarized division is shown in Fig. 7a. As in the case of subtraction, the S is a band with a slope of almost 1. There are two possibilities with the case of $E_1 E_2 < 0$, that is $E_1 > 0 > E_2$ (Fig. 7b) and $E_1 < 0 < E_2$ (Fig. 7c). In both cases, the S stretches along the dimension of the inhibitory conductance. The S of the shunting division occupies one-half of the g_1–g_2 plane, indicating a very loose restriction to be met by the two participating conductances in performing a division.

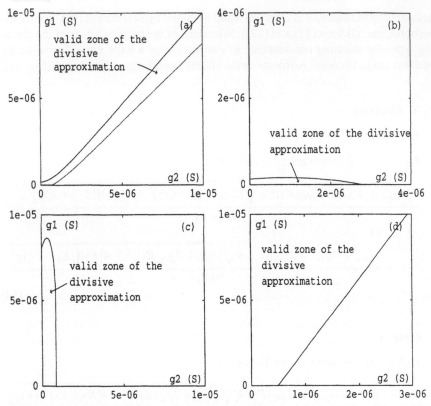

Figure 7 Domain ranges of divisive approximation. (a) When $E_1 = E_2 = E_{EPSP}$. (b) $E_1 = E_{EPSP}$ and $E_2 = E_{IPSP}$. (c) $E_1 = E_{IPSP}$ and $E_2 = E_{EPSP}$. (d) When $E_1 = 0$ and $E_2 = E_{EPSP}$. Parameters for all curves: $E_{EPSP} = 65$, $E_{IPSP} = -5$, $g_m = 10^{-6}$, $\epsilon = 5$.

C. Dynamic Range

Because of the monotonity of the rational function (1) and of its various approximations (4), (5), and (7), it suffices to determine the dynamic range of each prototype operation by looking at the function values on the boundaries of S. For the additive operation and the shunting divisive operation, it is readily known that $\eta = [\epsilon + \sqrt{\epsilon(\epsilon + 4|E_1|)}]/2$. With $\epsilon = 5$, it gives $\eta = 20.7$ (mV) for $E_1 = 65$ (EPSP) and $\eta = 8.1$ (mV) for $E_1 = -5$ (IPSP). Figure 8 illustrates the dynamic range of other prototype operations.

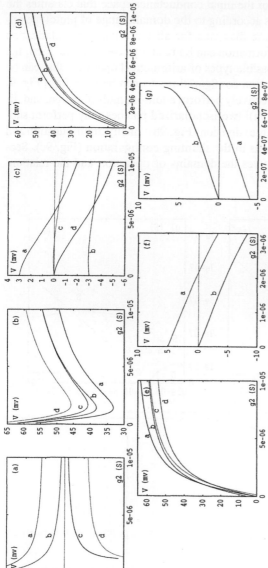

Figure 8 Dynamic ranges of the basic arithmetic modes shown as functions of g_2. (a) Subtractive mode with $E_1 = E_{IPSP}$ and $E_2 = E_{EPSP}$. Curves b and c: Upper and lower bounds of the subtractive approximation. Curves a and b: Original rational function (1) evaluated on the upper and lower boundaries of S, respectively (see Fig. 5b). (b–d) Multiplicative mode with (b) $E_1 = E_2 = E_{EPSP}$, (c) $E_1 = E_{EPSP}$, and $E_2 = E_{IPSP}$, and (d) $E_1 = 0$ and $E_2 = E_{EPSP}$. (b) Curves a and d: Lower and upper bounds of the multiplicative approximation. Curves b and c: Original rational function evaluated on the lower and upper boundaries of S, respectively (see Fig. 6a). (c) Curves c and d: Upper and lower bounds of the multiplicative approximation. Curves a and b: Original rational function on boundaries (Fig. 6b). (d) Curves a and d: Upper and lower bounds of the multiplicative approximation. Curves b and c: Original rational function on boundaries (Fig. 6c). (e–g) Divisive mode with (e) $E_1 = E_2 = E_{EPSP}$, (f) $E_1 = E_{EPSP}$ and $E_2 = E_{IPSP}$, and (g) $E_1 = E_{IPSP}$ and $E_2 = E_{EPSP}$. (e) Curves a and d: Upper and lower bounds of the divisive approximation. Curves b and c: Original rational function on boundaries (refer to Fig. 7a). (f) Curve b: Upper bound of the divisive approximation. Curve a: Original rational function on the upper boundary of S (Fig. 7b). (g) Curve b: Upper bound of the divisive approximation. Curve a: Original rational function on the upper boundary of S (Fig. 7c).

D. PHASE DIAGRAM

The phase diagram is a map of the input conductance space that classifies the subspaces of input conductances according to the domain range of prototype operations. Figure 9 gives the phase diagrams for all three types of polarization configurations. Two types of information can be read a phase diagram. First, the phase diagram prescribes the possible types of arithmetical operation that can be performed by a specific polarization configuration. As can be seen from Fig. 9, two isopolarized patches can effectively perform addition, multiplication, and division, but no subtraction (Fig. 9a); two isopolarized patches may perform subtraction, multiplication, and (a little) division (Fig. 9b); finally, multiplication and division are two typical operations in the shunting configuration (Fig. 9c). Secondly, the phase diagram also gives the domains of operation and the relation-

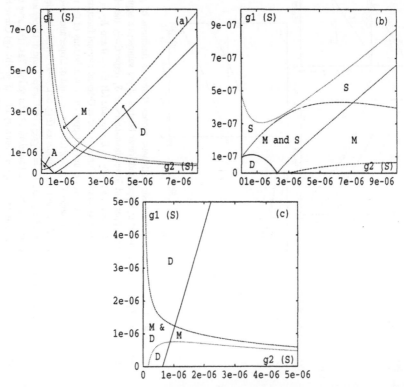

Figure 9   Phase diagram of (a) the system of two isopolarized patches, (b) the system of two heteropolarized patches, and (c) the system of a shunting patch and an excitatory patch. Add, additive phase; Sub, subtractive phase; Mul, multiplicative phase; Div, divisive phase.

ships between the domain of different operations. There are overlaps between some phases, indicating that for certain input values the arithmetic function of the system may be interpreted in different ways. The areas not marked with specific functions correspond to the general rational function (1).

IV. MULTIMODE NEURONAL ARITHMETIC UNIT

A. DEVELOPEDNESS OF ARITHMETIC OPERATIONS

Given a prototype of clean arithmetic operation, we can discuss its *developness* based on the phase diagram. This discussion defines the biological plausibility of that arithmetic operation in a specific polarization configuration. As shown in Fig. 9, a total of eight phases can be observed in the three possible polarization configurations. Their respective levels of developedness are described below and are summarized in Table I.

1. Subtraction

Subtraction can be observed only in heteropolarized patches, and is a developed mode because of its broad domain range in both the g_1 and g_2 dimensions (Fig. 9b). Moreover, its wide dynamic range (Fig. 8a) also suggests it to be a sig-

Table I
Developedness of Arithmetic Operations

Operation	Domain range in g_1	Domain range in g_2	Phase area	Developedness
+	Narrow	Narrow	Small	Less developed
−	Wide	Wide	Small	Developed
×(Isopolarized)	Wide	Wide	Small	Developed
×(Heteropolarized)	Narrow	Wide	Small	Developed
×(Shunting)	Wide	Wide	Small	Developed
÷(Isopolarized)	Wide	Wide	Small	Developed
÷(Heteropolarized, inhibitory/excitatory)	Narrow	Narrow	Small	Less developed
÷(Heteropolarized, excitatory/inhibitory)	Wide	Narrow	Small	Developed
÷(shunting)	Wide	Wide	Large	Well developed

nificant prototype operation in heteropolarized patches. However, it is not well developed because of its limited phase area.

According to Blomfield's work [5], the subtraction is plausible for small-input conductances. As an extension to this observation, it is evident from the phase diagram (Fig. 9b) that the subtraction operates not only for small values of input conductances but also for large values. In fact, the long, narrow band of the subtraction phase implies that it is the interrelation between the two input conductances, rather than the magnitude, that is critical to the formation of a subtractive operation.

2. Addition

A linear operation, addition (observable in isopolarized patches) is a less developed operation because of its narrow domain range in both dimensions (in comparison to g_m). This fact calls into question the validity of taking the summation-and-firing model as a widely observable operation, even though addition can be a fair prototype as long as the membrane input is sustained at a low level, as in the case of spontaneous presynaptic activities.

3. Multiplication

Multiplicative operation is found to be developed in all three configurations. The isopolarized and shunting multiplications possess a wide domain range in both the g_1 and g_2 dimensions (Fig. 9a and c), whereas the heteropolarized multiplication is widely defined only in the g_2 dimension. The dynamic range of the isopolarized and shunting multiplications is wide (Fig. 8b and d). In contrast, heteropolarized multiplication has a narrow dynamic range (Fig. 8c). Combining these, it can be implied that multiplication is a more widely observable operation in isopolarized and shunting configurations than in heteropolarized configurations.

4. Division

Division is also observed in all three configurations. As told by the small domain range (Fig. 7b), the heteropolarized division of the excitatory-divides-inhibitory type is a less developed mode. On the other hand, the division of the inhibitory-divides-excitatory type can be observed for a large range of inhibitory conductance values (Fig. 7c), suggesting it to be a developed operation (this is consistent with Blomfield's study [5]). This asymmetry results from the difference in the magnitude of E_{EPSP} and E_{IPSP}. The isopolarized division is a developed mode (Figs. 9a and 8e) and possesses a narrow-phase band similar to the case of subtraction. In all eight prototype clean operations, the shunting division is the only well-developed mode. This is evident from its broad domain range (Fig. 9c) and large phase area (a half phase plane). It also has a wide dynamic range, $\eta = [\epsilon + \sqrt{\epsilon(\epsilon + 4|E_1|)}]/2$, which is independent of the value of the two input conductances.

B. Multimode Arithmetic Unit

Most previous models can be regarded as "single-mode" models, in the sense that a single model neuron is usually equipped with a single type of composite or clean operation. Phase space representation provides a viewpoint for considering a single neuron as potentially capable of several arithmetical operations.

In a recent work of the authors [12], a concept of *multimode* single-neuron arithmetics is introduced. For a given polarization configuration, the developed and well-developed arithmetical operations correspond to possible operational modes in which the system may stay. If there is more than one developed or well-developed operation in the phase diagram of the given configuration, then that configuration is potentially capable of multimode arithmetical operations.

Thus, corresponding to the three polarization configurations in Fig. 3, one can define three types of two-input, multimode arithmetic units (AUs) (Fig. 10). In each type of AU, there is a set of internal arithmetic modes, in each of which the operation of the AU can be described by a clean, prototype operation. Computationally, we may consider these AUs as possessing a set of internal arithmetic instructions; the selection of these instructions is determined by the mode the AU is currently in. If the AU is in neither of these modes, then its operation is described by the general rational function (1).

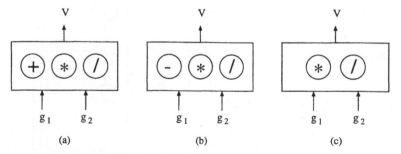

Figure 10 Three types of arithmetic units.

C. TRIGGERING AND TRANSITION
OF ARITHMETIC MODES

Triggering of clean arithmetic modes has been widely observed in neurophysiological experiments. As an example, we consider a normalization model for simple cells of primate visual cortex [11, 20]. In this model, the simple cell's response begins with a linear stage, which performs essentially a linear summation of input, followed by a normalization stage (Fig. 11). At the normalization stage, each cell's response is divided by a quantity proportional to the pooled activity of other cortical cells. This model can explain a variety of physiological phenomena [20, 21]. Recently the authors [12] considered an implementation of this model by using a group division of the form (7). In fact, if we interpret the group K in that formula as the input from the LGN and group L as the pooled cortical activity, then the normalization model is restated. A numerical simulation result is illustrated in Fig. 12.

This simulation introduces a general question about the conditions under which the input may trigger a specific arithmetic mode. In the case of $n = 2$, we have seen that as long as the value of the (g_1, g_2) pair falls into a specific phase in the phase plane, the corresponding arithmetical operation is performed. Functionally significant situations are those in which the input conductance pair (g_1, g_2) remains in a specific phase long enough for a sustained clean operation to be performed. Because in most practical systems, both g_1 and g_2 are time varying, we see that it is not the magnitude of a single-input conductance but the temporal pattern of several changing conductances that is relevant to the triggering of

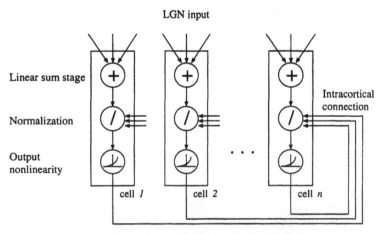

Figure 11   Summation and division by visual cortical neurons.

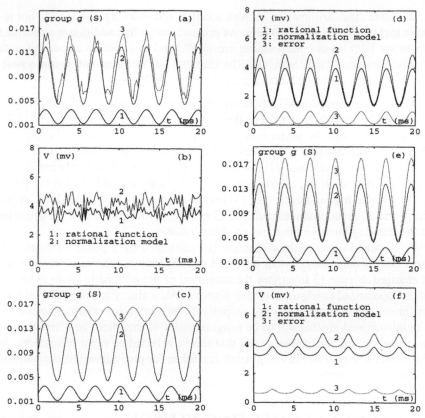

Figure 12   Simulation of the normalization model. A total of 400 patches were used, and the average LGN contribution to membrane potential is set to 20 mV. In (a), (c), and (e), a hypothetical sinusoidal temporal pattern of LGN activity $\sum_k g_k$ is shown as curve 1, the lower bound for intracortical activity level is shown as curve 2, and an admissible intracortical activity is shown as curve 3. Intracortical activity is determined in (a) by a white noise superposed with the lower bound, in (c) as an oppositely phased temporal pattern, and in (e) as an in-phase pattern. The corresponding original rational model and the normalization model are depicted on the right. For all curves, $\epsilon = 1$.

a specific arithmetic mode. From Fig. 9, we may distinguish the following two types of cases:

1. The persistent triggering of the isopolarized multiplication and division, of the heteropolarized subtraction, and of the shunting multiplication, demands highly ordered (g_1, g_2) activity patterns. Specifically, in-phase (g_1, g_2) temporal patterns may effectively trigger isopolarized division and heteropolarized subtraction, and oppositely phased (g_1, g_2) patterns may trigger a multiplication.

2. Some clean arithmetics, such as addition and shunting division, do not require highly ordered input patterns. As pointed out earlier, addition is performed whenever both input conductances are small, and is typically associated with spontaneous presynaptic activities. The shunting division does not require a well-organized input either, although a patterned input still triggers it.

For the three types of AUs shown in Fig. 10, the strategy of arithmetical operations can be summarized: (1) For the first type of AU, if the input level; is low, linear addition may be performed. If the input level is high and is highly synchronized, then division is performed. With high-level, oppositely phased input, multiplication is performed. (2) For the second type of AU, low-level input can effectively evoke division, subtraction, and multiplication, and high-level in-phase activity would trigger subtraction. (3) For the third type of AU, high-level, oppositely phased input produces multiplications, and sufficiently high-level activities in the shunting input terminal can produce divisions.

A sustained clean arithmetic mode is maintained by a particular input pattern. On the other hand, when the input pattern changes, the operational mode is changed. Figure 13 illustrates the transition of the arithmetic mode in an AU with isopolarized configuration. The neuronal AU's ability to change its internal arithmetic mode is an interesting property. In general, a necessary condition for a computational mechanism to be programmable is that there be a set of internal modes in the mechanism's state that can be selected by input instructions. In this sense, neuronal AU is a promising candidate for programmable, data-driven, arithmetic computation.

V. TOWARD A COMPUTING NEURON

So far we have investigated in detail the arithmetical power of single AUs. To summarize, the three types of AUs shown in Fig. 10 can effectively perform a set of prototypical arithmetical operations as specified by (4), (5), and (7), when the input values fall into those phase areas, and perform the general rational function (1) otherwise. Noticing that the rational function (1) is an approximation to a more general form of rational function model of neuronal spatial summation when the axial resistance network of Fig. 2 is short-circuited, these single AUs may represent local computations performed across a small piece of membrane patch. As shown in Fig. 14, for a typical cortical neuron with branching dendrites (Fig. 14a), we may approximate the local computation in each dendritic segment by an AU with multiple inputs. Because of the large value of axial resistances, all of the computational results of these AUs can be considered as making virtually no contribution to each other (Fig. 14b).

An integrated model of multimode single-neuron arithmetics is plausible by assembling these local computing AUs with certain active membrane mechanisms.

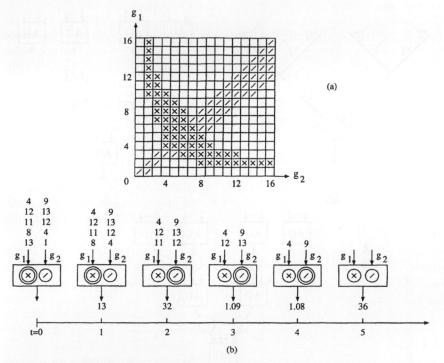

Figure 13 Transition between multiplicative and divisive modes. (a) A hypothetical "digitized" phase diagram of isopolarized configuration. The multiplicative phase is marked with × and divisive phase with /. (b) Operations performed by an AU of isopolarized type with two input terminals. The operator of the AU is chosen by the current operands. The currently active operator is indicated by a double circle.

Readers interested in the details of supporting biophysical mechanisms are referred to some recent neurophysiological experiments [18, 22, 23]. Some operational features of the integrated model of multimode single-neuron arithmetics are summarized as follows:

- A single neuron is modeled by a multilevel tree (Fig. 14c). Each node of the tree consists of an AU of multiple inputs; its output corresponds to the local computation result in a dendritic segment. The root node corresponds to the soma of the neuron, and the output of the root AU stands for the output of the integrated neuron. Synaptic inputs can be fed to leaf nodes as well as to any internal nodes. Each edge of the tree consists of a converter C, the function of which is a one-to-one mapping from voltage to conductance.

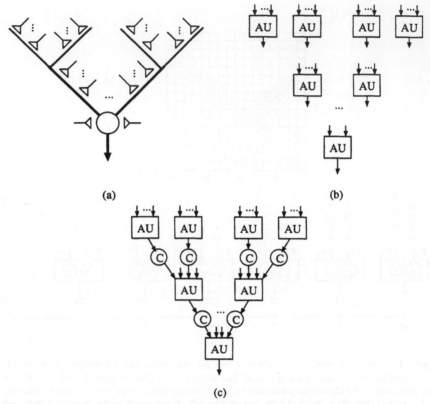

(a)   (b)

(c)

Figure 14   (a) A model dendrite with multiple synaptic inputs. (b) Local computation in each dendritic segment is approximated by an AU. The computations in different AUs are independent of each other. (c) Supported by active membrane mechanisms, local computation results can be integrated.

- For each leaf AU, rational arithmetic is performed on input conductances. The operands of an internal AU are either input conductances or the voltage-converted conductances produced by the afferent C. In particular, voltage-converted conductances can participate in both clean and composite operations.
- The cascaded operation may work either synchronously or asynchronously. For synchronous operations, all AUs are assumed to start a new operation at the same time, and to produce an arithmetic result in a unit time. The whole neuron thus works in a pipelining fashion.

VI. SUMMARY

Interest in modeling single-neuron computation has been constantly shaped by two types of considerations: computational ability and biophysical plausibility. In this chapter, we have carried out an introductory review of the potential and limitations of single-neuron arithmetics. Driven by suitably patterned input signals, passive membranes can effectively perform multimode arithmetic operations on the input conductances. Based on this observation, an abstract model of neuronal arithmetic unit is described. By taking active membrane mechanisms into account, an integrated neuron model can be constructed that may function as a programmable rational approximator.

REFERENCES

[1] J. J. Hopfield. Neural networks and physical systems with emergent collective computational abilities. *Proc. Nat. Acad. Sci. U.S.A.* 79:2554–2558, 1982.

[2] T. McKenna, J. Davis, and S. F. Zornetzer, Eds. *Single Neuron Computation*. Academic Press, Boston, 1992.

[3] A. Finkelstein and A. Mauro. Physical principles and formalisms of electrical excitability. In *Handbook of Physiology* (E. R. Kandel, Ed.), Vol. 1, Part 1, pp. 161–213. Am. Physiol. Soc., Bethesda, MD, 1977.

[4] E. R. Kandel, J. H. Schwartz, and T. M. Jessell, Eds. *Principles of Neural Science*, 3rd ed. Elsevier, New York, 1991.

[5] S. Blomfield. Arithmetical operations performed by nerve cells. *Brain Res.* 69:115–124, 1974.

[6] V. Torre and T. Poggio. A synaptic mechanism possibly underlying directional selectivity to motion. *Proc. Roy. Soc. London Ser. B* 202:409–416, 1978.

[7] C. Koch, T. Poggio, and V. Torre. Retinal ganglion cells: A functional interpretation of dendritic morphology. *Philos. Trans. Roy. Soc. London Ser. B* 298:227–264, 1982.

[8] G. M. Shepherd and R. K. Brayton. Logic operations are properties of computer-simulated interactions between excitable dendritic spines. *Neuroscience* 21:151–166, 1987.

[9] A. M. Zador, B. J. Claiborne, and T. J. Brown. Nonlinear pattern separation in single hippocampal neurons with active dendritic membrane. In *Advances in Neural Information Processing Systems* (J. Moody, S. Hanson, and R. Lippmann, Eds.), Vol. 4, pp. 51–58. Morgan Kaufmann, San Mateo, CA, 1992.

[10] B. W. Mel. Information processing in dendritic trees. *Neural Comput.* 6:1031–1085, 1994.

[11] M. Carandini and D. Heeger. Summation and division by neurons in primate visual cortex. *Science* 264:1333–1336, 1994.

[12] M. Wang and C. N. Zhang. Single neuron local rational arithmetic revealed in phase space of input conductances. *Biophys. J.* 71:2380–2393, 1996.

[13] T. Poggio and F. Girosi. Regularization algorithms for learning that are equivalent to multilayer networks. *Science* 247:978–982, 1990.

[14] R. Dubin and D. E. Rumelhart. Product units: A computationally powerful and biologically plausible extension to backpropagation networks. *Neural Comput.* 1:133–142, 1990.

[15] B. W. Mel and C. Koch. Sigma-pi learning: On radial basis functions and cortical associative learning. In *Advances in Neural Information Processing Systems* (D. S. Touretzky, Ed.), Vol. 2, pp. 474–481. Morgan Kaufmann, San Mateo, CA, 1990.

[16] C. Koch and T. Poggio. Multiplying with synapses and neurons. In *Single Neuron Computation* (T. McKenna, J. Davis, and S. F. Zornetzer, Eds.), pp. 315–345. Academic Press, Boston, 1992.

[17] M. Barinaga. Dendrites shed their dull image. *Science* 268:200–201, 1995.

[18] J. C. Magee and D. Johnston. Synaptic activation of voltage-gated channels in the dendrites of hippocampal pyramidal neurons. *Science* 268:301–304, 1995.

[19] T. Poggio and V. Torre. A theory of synaptic interactions. In *Theoretical Approaches in Neurobiology* (W. E. Reichardt and T. Poggio, Eds.), pp. 28–38. MIT Press, Cambridge, MA, 1981.

[20] D. Heeger. Normalization of cell responses in cat striate cortex. *Visual Neurosci.* 9:181–197, 1992.

[21] D. Heeger. Modeling single-cell direction selectivity with normalized, half-squared, linear operators. *J. Neurophysiol.* 70:1885–1898, 1993.

[22] W. A. Catterall. Structure and function of voltage-sensitive ion channels. *Science* 242:50–61, 1988.

[23] N. Spruston, Y. Schiller, G. Stuart, and B. Sakmann. Activity-dependent action potential invasion and calcium influx into hippocampal CA1 dendrites. *Science* 268:297–300, 1995.

Index

Printed and bound by CPI Group (UK) Ltd, Croydon, CR0 4YY

03/10/2024

01040428-0003